PART III   MATERIALS- AND OPERATIONS-CONTROL
                APPLICATIONS   159

Chapter 10   Order Filling   161
    10-1   An Inventory-Location Model   162
    10-2   Input Description   163
    10-3   The Order-Filling System   165
    10-4   Bin Location Analysis   178
    10-5   Management Implications   180

Chapter 11   Inventory Forecast and Control   185
    11-1   Creating an Updated Master Inventory File   186
    11-2   The Inventory Forecast and Order-Determination
           System   191
    11-3   Factor Buying   199
    11-4   Dangers Associated with a Computer Inventory
           Application   202
    11-5   Physical Inventory   204
    11-6   Management Implications   205

Chapter 12   Purchasing and Receiving   211
    12-1   Edit and Review by Purchasing Agents   212
    12-2   Purchase Order Input   214
    12-3   The Purchase Order System   214
    12-4   Input to Receiving   218
    12-5   The Receiving System   218
    12-6   Vendor Evaluation   222
    12-7   Management Implications   224

Chapter 13   Work-in-Process and Scheduling   229
    13-1   Input Data   230
    13-2   The Work-in-Process System   231
    13-3   Work-in-Process Reporting   242
    13-4   Management Implications   244

Chapter 14   Labor Distribution and Job Costing   249
    14-1   The Employee Time Card   249
    14-2   Preliminary Processing   251
    14-3   The Job Costing System   252
    14-4   The Labor Distribution Computer Application   258
    14-5   Management Implications   260

PART IV COMPREHENSIVE ACCOUNTING
         APPLICATIONS   263

Chapter 15   Fixed Assets and Depreciation   265
    15-1   Fixed Assets, Tax Write-Offs, and Depreciation   265
    15-2   Input Data   267
    15-3   The Fixed Assets and Depreciation System   267
    15-4   Management Implications   276

Chapter 16   The General Ledger   281
    16-1   Sources of Input to the General Ledger   282
    16-2   The General Ledger System   287
    16-3   The Company Chart of Accounts   294
    16-4   Management Implications   296

Chapter 17   Financial Statements   299
    17-1   Input to the Financial Reporting Computer
           Application   299
    17-2   The Financial System   300
    17-3   Management Implications   311

Chapter 18   Sales Analysis and Market Penetration   315
    18-1   Sales Analysis Input Requirements   316
    18-2   The Sales Analysis System   317
    18-3   Market Penetration   323
    18-4   The Market Penetration Computer Application   327
    18-5   Management Implications   329

Supplementary Readings   333

Index   339

BUSINESS COMPUTER SYSTEMS
AND APPLICATIONS

SECOND EDITION

BUSINESS COMPUTER SYSTEMS AND APPLICATIONS

Alan L. Eliason

Kent D. Kitts

SCIENCE RESEARCH ASSOCIATES, INC.
Chicago, Palo Alto, Toronto, Henley-on-Thames, Sydney, Paris

A Subsidiary of IBM

Acquisition Editors	Stephen Mitchell, Bob Safran
Project Editor	Gretchen Hargis
Designer	Carol Harris
Illustrators	Alex Teshin, Ted Hayashi
Compositor	Graphic Typesetting Service

Library of Congress Cataloging in Publication Data

Eliason, Alan L.
  Business computer systems and applications.

  Bibliography: p.
  Includes index.
    1. Business—Data processing. 2. Accounting—Data
processing. 1. Kitts, Kent D., joint author.
  II. Title.
  HF5548.2.E424   1978   658'05'4   78-18447
  ISBN 0-574-21215-9

We wish to acknowledge the following for permission to reprint or adapt material.

Reprinted by permission of International Business Machines Corporation. Figures 1–1, 1–2, 1–3, 1–4, 2–5, 5–7, 6–6, 10–10, 18–5, 18–9.

Courtesy of County of Clackamas, Oregon: Figures 4–7, 4–8, 4–9, 4–11, 4–12, 14–1.

Courtesy of Burke Concrete Accessories, Inc.: Figures 7–1, 7–7, 7–8, 7–9, 8–3, 8–4, 8–5, 9–1, 10–6, 11–2, 18–4.

Courtesy of Hudson House, Inc.: Figures 7–3, 9–4, 10–1, 10–5, 10–8, 10–9, 11–9, 12–1, 12–4, 12–7.

Courtesy of Bank Check Supply Co.: Figures 5–8, 6–3, 6–7.

Courtesy of Richardson, Richardson & Associates and Mr. Derald Johnson: Figures 6–2, 16–5, 16–7, 16–8, 16–9, 17–4.

Courtesy of Southern California First National Bank: Figures 17–1, 17–7.

Reprinted by permission of Capex Corporation: Figure 17–6.

Courtesy of F. W. Dodge Division, McGraw-Hill Information Systems Company: Figures 18–6, 18–8.

10 9 8 7 6 5 4 3

CONTENTS

To the Instructor   ix
To the Student   xiii

PART 1   INTRODUCTION   1

Chapter 1   Beginning Systems Concepts   3
   1-1   Business Computer Applications   4
   1-2   Computer Equipment   4
   1-3   Vendor-Supplied Software   9
   1-4   Systems Analysis   10
   1-5   The Role of Management in Systems Activity   13

Chapter 2   Components of a Business Computer System   17
   2-1   Stages in the Flow of Business Transactions   18
   2-2   Common Types of Computer Programs   20
   2-3   Systems Documentation   23
   2-4   Systems Flowcharting   26

Chapter 3   File Design   35
   3-1   A Computer File   35
   3-2   File Justification   38
   3-3   Reliability of Computer Files   40
   3-4   File Design   41
   3-5   File Creation and Verification   43
   3-6   File Updating   44
   3-7   Report Preparation   46

PART II   ACCOUNTING APPLICATIONS   51

Chapter 4   Payroll   53
    4-1   Preliminary Payroll Master File Update   54
    4-2   Input to the Payroll Application   58
    4-3   The Payroll System   59
    4-4   Periodic Reports   67
    4-5   Management Implications   71

Chapter 5   Accounts Payable   75
    5-1   Initial Input to the Payables System   76
    5-2   The Accounts Payable System   77
    5-3   Manual Processing of Invoice File Copies   87
    5-4   Management Implications   88

Chapter 6   Check Writing and Check Reconciliation   91
    6-1   The Check-Writing System   91
    6-2   The Check-Reconciliation System   98
    6-3   Check Design   100
    6-4   Manual Procedures in Check Processing   101
    6-5   Management Implications   103

Chapter 7   Invoicing   107
    7-1   The Computer-Prepared Invoice   107
    7-2   Inputs to the Stand-Alone Invoicing System   109
    7-3   The Stand-Alone Invoicing System   111
    7-4   Suspense Relief   120
    7-5   Price File Maintenance   122
    7-6   Invoicing after Computer Order Filling   122
    7-7   Management Implications   123

Chapter 8   Accounts Receivable   127
    8-1   Types of Accounts   127
    8-2   Open-Item Statement Input Description   129
    8-3   The Open-Item Accounts Receivable System   130
    8-4   Month-End Closing Problems   140
    8-5   Management Implications   141

Chapter 9   Cash Receipts   145
    9-1   Crediting Customer Accounts   146
    9-2   Inputs to the Cash Receipts System   147
    9-3   The Cash Receipts System   149
    9-4   Automatic Cash Application   152
    9-5   Cash Flow Prediction   154
    9-6   Management Implications   155

To the Instructor

Computer-based systems and business computer applications are becoming an integral part of daily business activities. Processing business data by computer has evolved from lower level accounting applications (for example, the company payroll) to applications for operations and to higher level applications that integrate both accounting and operations.

This text describes the most common business computer applications. Chapter materials have been organized so that students of business and of data processing will become aware of the process to be followed in designing computer systems, the characteristics and components of key business computer applications, and the interrelationships among computer applications.

For the most part, we have avoided discussing computer programming requirements for these applications. We believe it is more important for the student to know the inputs to a computer application, the main programs and files used in processing, the documents and reports resulting from processing, the special processing or maintenance requirements, and the managerial implications of each implemented application.

An exception to this approach occurs in Part III of the text where certain mathematical expressions are discussed in relation to the design of an inventory computer application. These expressions were added to help distinguish between two types of computer applications: those based on accounting principles and defined by programmed statements, and those dealing with uncertainty and requiring decision rules to estimate and project actual conditions.

Questions and exercises at the end of each chapter are intended to help students sharpen their comprehension of chapter materials and to provide experience in the actual design of a business computer application. Through studying these application materials and design exercises, students should come to understand and appreciate how computer processing relates to the inner workings of a business enterprise. This understanding is critical. In practice, successful systems design and implementation requires close cooperation between the manager and computer specialists.

This text is intended to be used as a basic text in business computer applications, as a supplementary text in a variety of courses, or in conjunction with systems analysis case materials. As a basic text, it has been successfully combined with programming language texts, or with a text that describes the technology of business computing, such as Marilyn Bohl's *Information Processing* (a Science Research Associates publication). When used as a supplemental text, it has proven especially useful in systems design coursework, as when students are required to select a particular application and to create COBOL programs based on application specifics. (When the text is used in this way, the entire book need not be read in sequence, although later chapters do require some knowledge of earlier ones.) Finally, when used in conjunction with case materials, *Case Study in Business Systems Design* and *Case Study II: Medco, Inc.* have each worked well. (Both cases are Science Research Associates publications.)

In this second edition, hundreds of changes have been made, although most are minor. We have attempted to improve the internal consistency of chapter materials. File names used in the flowchart illustrations, for instance, are more consistent with file names referred to in the chapter descriptions. We have corrected omissions and errors in chapter materials. We have reorganized Part II to improve the presentation of payables and receivables. We have altered the material on file design to add clarity to this important subject. Finally, although several people have requested that we incorporate on-line applications in the text, we decided not to do so. Such additions would have greatly increased the size (by as much as 50 percent) and scope of the text because on-line applications greatly differ in design from batch applications.

In preparing the first edition, we had difficulty developing a supplemental readings list, because the book was quite different from other text materials. Few materials that compared and contrasted computer applications could be found. Even though five years have elapsed between editions, an applications supplemental readings list remained difficult to prepare. The material crosses several business areas—accounting, operations, finance, and marketing—and integrates several traditional business functions. Computer applications are viewed as one way by which to achieve the integration of business activities.

We wish to express our appreciation to the many companies and individuals who have assisted in the preparation of the manuscript. Companies have generously given us permission to print computer-prepared forms as evidence of computer systems in use. Reviewers of the manuscript have given us helpful suggestions to better explain chapter materials.

Special appreciation is due to several individuals. We wish to thank the Science Research Associates staff, especially Steve Mitchell (computer science editor), Gretchen Hargis (project editor), and Gaye Talbot (manuscript typist). We also give special credit to our wives, Jane Eliason and Bonnie Kitts, for their patience, understanding, and cooperation again throughout the revision of this text.

To the Student

It is nearly impossible to find factual material that describes current business use of computers. Computer manufacturers or vendors often supply booklets that describe computer processing of specific business tasks; however, these booklets do not systematically tie together various types of processing. Thus, even though some excellent material on a particular computer application does exist, it does not help us understand how computer operations have altered and continue to alter basic administrative functions in a firm.

We wrote *Business Computer Systems and Applications* because we believe there is a need for students in business, data processing, or computer science—in school or out—to understand the important role of the computer in business. This text presents the 15 most common business computer applications and relates them to each other. We show how the computer can be used successfully in the processing of business transactions. After all, business computer applications can be viewed as a means of obtaining, improving, and using files of business information.

THE ORGANIZATION OF THE TEXT

The text has been divided into four parts. The first part deals with selected properties of systems design. Chapter 1 explains the purpose of a business computer application and clarifies the meaning of hardware and software to the application's designer. The work of the systems analyst and the role of management in systems activity are then described. Chapter 2 describes components of a business system, the computer programs common to business computer applications, and the flowchart notation used in illustrating the flow of a computer application. Because of the importance of the computer file in a business computer application, Chapter 3 looks at several features of file design.

The organization of the rest of the text follows a general framework from single-purpose to integrated business computer applications. Part II deals with six single-purpose accounting computer applications: payroll, accounts payable, check writing and reconciliation, invoicing, accounts receivable, and cash receipts. Each is designed to process a particular type of business transaction.

Part III builds on the basic principles of Part II and presents more complex systems. For example, a computer order-filling application integrates sales with production. An inventory control application ties demand for stock with additions to stock. A purchasing and receiving application serves as an interface between inventory control and company vendors. A work-in-process computer application ties product demand to production scheduling. And a labor distribution and costing computer application leads to the breakdown of operating costs, as costs directly relate to products manufactured.

Part IV considers more comprehensive, integrative computer applications. These include a fixed asset and depreciation application, preparation of the general ledger, and processing of financial statements. All three business computer applications are based on previously developed applications. The last chapter develops a further integrative application—sales analysis and market penetration. This application involves comparisons of actual sales data and correlation of external measurements to information stored in company files.

THE TEXT MATERIAL AND THE LEARNING PROCESS

The text material has been drawn from several years of industrial experience, coupled with theoretical concepts of systems design. Each of the 15 applications discussed either has been developed by one of the authors or results from close work with an implemented, successful design. Several companies have advised us on the content of the chapter materials and have supplied us with examples of actual reports and documents to use as illustrations. We have tended to avoid the use of fictitious illustrations. Instead, we show computer-prepared reports, as actually used in the business environment.

Please do not conclude from the text material that we are presenting the only way to design a given computer application, or even the one best way. We have described each application to help you understand computer systems and applications in general. We have therefore simplified many of the applications to render them more understandable.

You should not rely on this text as a single source of computer knowledge. We have assumed that readers will have had some basic training in computer programming and knowledge of computer hardware as well as of business accounting. If you are a data processing or computer science student with some business experience, you should have the necessary background. If you are a business administration student with some computer training, you should find the text of important value. If you are a business manager, a systems analyst, or a programmer/analyst, this text should be easily understood.

STUDY SUGGESTIONS

There are two ways you can use this text. First, you can study the entire book. While studying each application chapter, you should try to answer several broad questions.

1. What is the purpose of the computer application?
2. What are the major components of the application, and what function does each serve?
3. What steps are necessary to place the application on the computer?
4. What benefits does the firm receive from successful implementation of the application?
5. What might extended use of the application involve?

Some of the benefits of a computer application are obvious. For example, in a payroll application, an obvious benefit is the printing of a paycheck. However, other benefits can be associated with this application. To develop it, a comprehensive, current employee master file was prepared. The question then becomes: Can the master employee file be used for purposes other than printing employee paychecks? The answer is most certainly yes. Labor distribution studies and departmental labor costing are examples of extended use of the employee master file.

Second, you can use the text to refresh your memory about a specific computer application. You might, for example, refer to it if you are called upon to design a similar application in a company or in an advanced programming class. We hope and believe that *Business Computer Systems and*

Applications will become a permanent volume in your personal library and will serve your business career for many years.

You can help us realize this goal—for yourself and for the students who follow you. As your business career matures, you will discover that every business does things differently. You may also find a better method to accomplish an operating task by computer. If so, please share this knowledge with us, so we may pass along the improvements to subsequent students.

I

INTRODUCTION

To understand business computer systems and applications, one must study concepts common to computer systems, major components of the computer (apart from the hardware itself), and methods of depicting the structure and purpose of the applications. The first part of this text provides an overview of these fundamental considerations. As an overview, it does not thoroughly treat the computer equipment used in business systems, or features of computer file design. These are fields of study in themselves. In this part our attention is limited to the importance of processing business transactions, the procedures by which these transactions are processed by computer, and the role of the computer file in supporting processing. Our intent is to show how vital it is to provide a complete and accurate computer record of compliance to external and internal written agreements made by an organization.

1

BEGINNING SYSTEMS CONCEPTS

Many American and international organizations have come to depend on the computer to process data. They have committed millions of dollars to buy computer equipment and support expensive data processing personnel. Other organizations, however, have had little exposure to or experience with computer technology. For them, the possibilities of using computers to carry out data-intensive work processes (payroll, invoicing, accounts receivable, inventory, for example) appear unlimited. For both, the use of computers may eventually lead to the integration of many or all data-intensive activities.

Business computer systems do not develop quickly. An initial processing design usually needs several revisions. This seemingly never-ending process slowly reveals the procedures and documents an organization uses to conduct its business. Some procedures, such as those followed in the processing of payroll, can be easily identified; for example, hours worked are converted into wages paid. Some procedures may be informal and difficult to identify; there may be, for example, more than one method for determining when and in what quantity stock should be ordered.

Business computer systems are difficult to develop correctly. Problems of conversion continue to trouble persons involved with data processing. Conversion, as a concept, means changeover. It arises when computer-based business procedures replace manual ones or when methods of processing data by computer improve. Far too often managers know little or nothing about the design of an anticipated computer application and yet are asked to supervise its installation. The result is a poorly conceived, documented, and designed application that is expensive and does not meet the organization's processing requirements. The purpose of this text is not only to analyze the most common business computer applications and show the major processing steps and components of each, but also to show the managerial implications of these applications.

1-1   BUSINESS COMPUTER APPLICATIONS

What is a business computer application? Such an application involves the use of the computer to process a business transaction by following a consistent, formalized, programmed set of procedures. Most applications are single-purpose rather than integrated. That is, they process one type of business transaction, such as a customer invoice. An integrated computer application uses information produced by single-purpose processing to produce consolidated reports. In business the most common single-purpose computer application is payroll—processing payroll transactions and producing employee paychecks. Perhaps the most common integrated computer application is the preparation of the consolidated general ledger.

Business computer applications allow a user to obtain, improve, and use files of business information. This is a most important function of data processing, since files establish a necessary permanence within an organization. People come and go, but company files do not. Master computer files are created during the implementation of a business computer application. The master employee file, master customer file, and master parts file are but three examples. From these files, current and yearly summary reports can be prepared and presented to management. Separate analysis of file content is also possible, such as the analysis of the master customer file to determine profitable customers. This extension of data processing is believed crucial to modern business organizations in their attempt to refine management reporting systems.

1-2   COMPUTER EQUIPMENT

Computers have been available for use in business only about 25 years, but within this short time have evolved into an amazing variety of designs. Major technological breakthroughs (for example, the design and development of solid-state components) have occurred every few years. These breakthroughs continue to change the way in which the computer is viewed and used. Also, while the cost of computers once made them available only to large business firms, today's lower priced computers are accessible to most business firms.

Despite the constant development and change in computer equipment, computer use has remained fundamentally the same. Consider the procedure for preparing a computer to process a business payroll and put out employee paychecks. The information necessary to compute a payroll is much the same (hours worked, rate of pay, employee number); only the method of supplying this information to the computer has changed drastically. When payrolls were first placed on a computer, data needed to be encoded or made available in machine-readable form. A keypunch machine, similar to that shown in Figure 1-1, was used to encode payroll data. This machine produces a punched card, whose square holes are interpreted by the computer.

As the technology of computer processing changed, the method of acquiring data changed. An alternative to encoding payroll data used a magnetic tape "data entry terminal" similar to that shown in Figure 1-2. The terminal operates much like a keypunch machine, except that keyed data can be visually inspected and the data medium is magnetic tape rather than punched cards. Its secondary advantage is that the computer can read magnetic tape faster than it can read punched cards.

FIG. 1 - 1   Keypunch machine

FIG. 1-2 Data entry terminal

Technology continued to improve. Employees can now record hours worked on specially designed, optically readable payroll forms. The forms are then processed directly by the computer. That is, a keypunch or data entry terminal is not needed to translate data into machine-readable form. Instead, the optical forms are passed through an optical reader similar to the one in Figure 1-3.

Finally, it is now possible for employees to record hours worked directly, whenever they start or finish a day's work. A data collector terminal (Fig. 1-4) allows transmission of data directly to the central computer system. It permits computer records to reflect the most current activity of all employees, further reducing the time necessary to prepare an employee's paycheck.

But no matter how employee working hours are recorded—by keypunch machine, data entry terminal, optical reader, or data collection terminal—the actual accounting procedures for processing a payroll continue in almost exactly the same way. For example, taxes must be computed and deducted from gross pay. Social Security insurance must be deducted. If the employee

FIG. 1-3 Optical reader

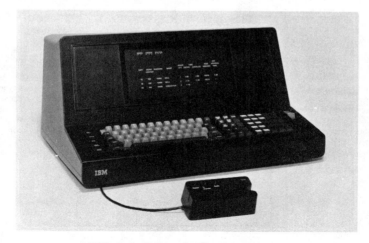

FIG. 1-4 Data collection terminal

is a union member, union dues must be deducted. In short, technological breakthroughs shorten processing time but do not change the procedures followed in processing. It is important to avoid confusing the electrical and mechanical components of a computer with the requirements of computer processing.

Figure 1-5 shows a computer system. The computer itself consists of three components contained in a central processing unit. The control unit integrates the operations of the entire computer system (inputs, processing, storage, and outputs) and coordinates processing called for by a submitted computer program. The arithmetic unit performs arithmetic calculations and makes logical comparisons. The internal or main storage contains all data being held for processing, data being processed, the results of processing (awaiting release as computer output), and program instructions. Input to the computer system can consist of punched cards (a variety of types exists), punched paper tape, magnetic tape, optical character read data, magnetic ink character recognition data, remote terminal transmission, and magnetic disk. External storage is possible through punched cards, magnetic tape, magnetic disk, magnetic drum, and data cells. Output is generally printed reports and documents but can also be external file storage or terminal display. Clearly, there are a number of alternatives available in a computer system.

In analyzing computer applications, this text avoids treating computer equipment associated with the various processing stages. It is assumed that no matter what equipment is used, the application can be made to function. For instance, the system flowcharts illustrated in this text indicate the use of

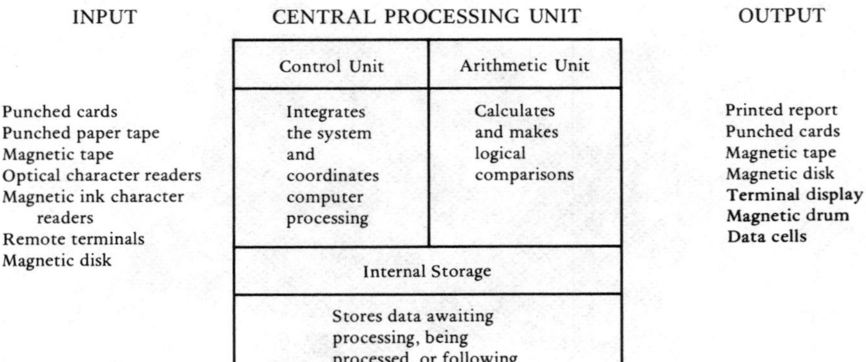

INPUT	CENTRAL PROCESSING UNIT		OUTPUT
	Control Unit	Arithmetic Unit	
Punched cards	Integrates	Calculates	Printed report
Punched paper tape	the system	and makes	Punched cards
Magnetic tape	and	logical	Magnetic tape
Optical character readers	coordinates	comparisons	Magnetic disk
Magnetic ink character	computer		Terminal display
readers	processing		Magnetic drum
Remote terminals			Data cells
Magnetic disk	Internal Storage		
	Stores data awaiting processing, being processed, or following processing and program instructions.		

FIG. 1-5   The computer system

magnetic disk storage files. Disk files, however, are not essential. The system could be made to function using magnetic tape or even a card computer and sorting machines.

1-3 VENDOR-SUPPLIED SOFTWARE

A computer does not run by itself. It is simply a machine composed of electronic and mechanical components. Before it can do anything other than draw electricity, it must be instructed (programmed) what to do and how. Some programs are supplied by the computer vendor. For example, vendors supply a number of programs to use in making computers operational. Other programs must be prepared by the organization's computer staff. *User-generated application programs* are instructions to process specific business computer applications. Taken collectively, all types of computer programs are commonly called "software," a term coined by the computer profession to distinguish computer programs from computer "hardware," or equipment. Sometimes software packages are provided as part of an initial lease or purchase agreement with a computer vendor. More commonly, software packages are separately priced, and the user pays for different types of software routines.

Four types of computer programs are normally classed as vendor-supplied software: program supervisors, compilers and assemblers, sort/merges, and utilities. Complex though it may be, the computer is completely helpless without these four types of supporting software. Even then the computer is of no practical value, for it needs application programs written by programmers for specific business jobs. Since it is possible to lease or purchase completed application programs, one might wonder why a company needs programmers. The answer is that this need arises from special data processing requirements, based on how a company decides to run its business operations. Application programs must be written specially to meet these processing requirements. Moreover, business firms require special interpretation of computer results in the form of report layouts, custom form printings, and report contents. Since each company is unique, its computer applications are unique.

Supervisors or Operating Systems

With the increase in size, complexity, and flexibility of computers, it has become necessary to devise controlling programs to instruct computers how to schedule processing and use the correct sequence and components for each processing task. These controlling programs are called *supervisors* or *operating systems*. For example, there may be more than one job being processed at one time by the computer. Multi-job processing also is controlled by supervisor programs. Or it may be necessary to switch from one type of processing operation to a substantially different one. Switching is controlled by supervisor programs.

Compilers and Assemblers

Besides the computer software supplied by the vendor, a company will want to develop its own programs for specific business computer applications. Since programmers do not develop program instructions in machine-readable format, computer programs called *compilers* are required. A compiler is a collection of computer programs used to convert programmer language instructions into machine-readable format. Programming languages such as FORTRAN or COBOL have been developed to assist in standardizing coded instructions, but these instructions are not machine-readable. A translation is necessary. This translation is accomplished by a compiler written to convert a specific programming language into a machine-readable language.

Sort/Merge

Several times throughout this book we refer to the sorting and merging of computer files of data. A sorting operation places computer records into a desired sequence (record 1, record 2, and so forth) for later stages of computer processing. Similarly, a merge operation places computer records from more than one file into one file in a desired sequence. Sort and merge programs are extremely complex to write and are frequently beyond the ability of the average programmer. For this reason, the computer vendor supplies sort/merge software.

Utilities

Utilities is a catchall term used to describe a number of computer programs supplied by the vendor for various routine processing tasks. One utility program leads the computer to empty, or "dump," its memory contents onto a printed sheet of paper. Another utility program instructs the computer to make a complete copy of a file of important records, so that the copy can be stored securely. Other utility programs perform similar housekeeping tasks. These programs eliminate the need to write a computer program each time a routine task arises.

1-4   SYSTEMS ANALYSIS

The systems analyst's job is to understand the unique aspects and operations of a company and then translate them into business computer applications. The analyst designs computer systems. Systems analysis, the discipline of the analyst, involves five phases that occur nearly every time a new application is developed or a major change is made in a previously developed application. The phases are

1. Investigate the existing operation.
2. Evaluate it to determine its best features and its obvious flaws.
3. Design a replacement that incorporates the best in the present operation but has fewer shortcomings.
4. Implement the new design.
5. Document and evaluate the implemented design to identify problems and to implement workable revisions.

Not all systems activity uses each of these phases in exactly this order. However, they are commonly experienced when new systems are developed. At each phase the analyst must view a system from a different perspective.

Investigation

Investigation of an existing system necessarily precedes development of a suitable replacement. It may seem superfluous to spend time and energy studying present methods of operation; one might expect them to be obvious. This is rarely the case. Companies are dynamic, growing entities that constantly change, usually becoming more complex. Methods of conducting business vary considerably with the passage of time and with changes in the firm's organizational structure. It is unlikely that a manager, preoccupied with daily problems and work to be completed, has—or is willing to take— the time necessary to review and revise written company procedures to match all recent business changes. Almost every corporation falls behind in documenting its internal functions.

Consider the organization chart for a company. It is rarely up-to-date. The company changes so rapidly that many entries on the chart are incorrect. Managers change jobs, and job titles change as a company is reorganized and jobs are reassigned. If the organization chart is incorrect, procedures written to depict company positions and operations are also likely to be incorrect, especially if the procedures are highly detailed. Therefore, reviewing actual operations is not time wasted.

Evaluation

Investigation and evaluation go hand-in-hand. Certainly, it is difficult to study an operation without forming some opinions about its advantages, faults, and limitations. It is important, however, not to confuse the facts about how a system operates with conjectures about how it might be improved. For a brief time during the beginning phases of investigation no opinions should be formed. This period of objectivity should be extended as long as possible, before personal bias begins to color investigation proceedings. Once enough information has been collected to provide a decent basis for evaluation, it is time to begin making judgments about the virtues and shortcomings of a present operation.

Criticizing an existing operation is quite different from designing an effective replacement that does not introduce further problems. For this reason new systems should not be designed in an informational vacuum. If a designed system is to avoid the flaws and obstacles encountered by present operations, then existing shortcomings must be clarified well in advance.

Design

Sometimes the objective of systems design is to improve operations without changing the existing method of operation. At other times the objective is to both improve and change the work process. When parts of the work process are to be automated, the systems analyst faces the design problem of how best to convert a manual operation to a computer method of processing data. Central to this problem is the determination of whether a computer operation will be an improvement over current operations.

There are three basic rules that have long been applied by systems analysts when deciding whether to use the computer in the processing of data.

1. If data are used once and then discarded, it is probably not necessary to use the computer in the processing of the data.
2. If data are used two or three times, justification for use of the computer is marginal.
3. If data are used more than three times or in more than three ways, it will probably be advantageous to involve the computer in processing.

This last rule underscores the value of the computer once the initial data have been obtained. It costs little more to produce several processing results using the same data than to produce one result. If, for instance, the computer is used to print paychecks, it can also be used to print a general ledger summary using the same data. The added cost of summarization is minimal, once the data necessary for the printing of checks have been acquired.

Design of a new computer system includes the programming of specific processing instructions, as well as devising the method by which the system should operate. Systems design and programming are the biggest expense in the development of a computer application. Some of the steps in design include the design of computer files, the preparation of computer input and report formats, the ordering of custom forms for application reports, and the identification of audit and control processing techniques. The next two chapters consider the main features of systems design.

Implementation

Implementation commonly involves long working days and attempts to cope with considerable worker stress. Existing files of data must be converted to new computer files with as few errors as possible. The old system must be operated in parallel with the new one until it proves itself, which often means a double work load for weeks or months. Expected, as well as unexpected, difficulties add up to extra time requirements and increased work stress. Only if potential problems are anticipated and time is allotted to them can there be the time to deal with inevitable and unforeseen complications. Planning for implementation is necessary to minimize human conflict.

Documentation and Evaluation

Documentation involves preparing a written record of what has been done. It helps to ensure that all aspects of a design have been completed. This reporting will eventually become obsolete, just as will other written material available at the start of the investigation. But it is still needed to explain the design of the computer application. Later, when an improvement is suggested, documentation will provide material to help in systems investigation.

One approach to evaluating a new system is the *procedures audit*. Here individuals outside the systems development and design group are asked to evaluate how well the new system meets its stated objectives. The virtue of this approach is that it utilizes individuals who need not defend the old or the new way of operating. The audit permits a comparison of old and new; the intended objectives of the new system can also be compared with the actual programming and conversion results. Outside groups of informed individuals quickly uncover flaws and weaknesses in the new system that are not apparent to those who have just completed implementation. If systems documentation is complete and clear, the audit can proceed quickly, at minimal expense.

1-5 THE ROLE OF MANAGEMENT IN SYSTEMS ACTIVITY

Thus far little attention has been given to the managerial role in the investigation, evaluation, design, implementation, documentation, and final review of a business computer application. And yet it is the manager, not the systems analyst, who is responsible for a system once it becomes operational. Transfer from the analyst to the manager can be extremely hazardous. To avoid problems, the managers must either be kept thoroughly informed of systems activity or be involved in the actual design and implementation of a new system. The second alternative is preferable, but neither is easy. Managers may be unfamiliar with what the computer can do. Without an appreciation for the strengths and weaknesses of computer technology, managers have difficulty being objective when asked to make decisions regarding the use of computer technology within their area of responsibility.

What are some solutions to this managerial dilemma? One is to acquaint managers with reading materials that cover business computer applications, such as the material presented in this text. Reading materials, however, are not enough. In a real situation, face-to-face confrontation between the analyst and the manager is necessary. Managers must not be afraid to probe and to ask questions, even simplistic ones. After all, managers must comprehend completely the overall scope of a proposed systems project, its design implications, and its eventual impact on the organization.

Managers should raise penetrating questions during the presentation of the analyst's system design proposal. They should not approve a proposal unless they understand specifics—both technical and behavioral. At the proposal stage, managers need to assess the objectivity with which the analyst reviewed the existing system, question the reasons for the proposed design, and ask for alternatives to it. During the review of the proposed design, the following must be carefully considered: the objectives to be satisfied by the new system; the procedures to be set up after conversion; the completeness of the new system; and the accuracy of the time and cost projections made by the analyst. Behavioral considerations are also important. These include the impact of the new system on present employees and the steps required to minimize human resistance before and after conversion. These issues are difficult to confront, and yet the initial proposal stage in systems development is where arduous debate should take place. Real and potential problems must be considered so that the analyst, the manager, and those affected by the proposed computer system avoid unnecessary misunderstandings.

For managers affected greatly by systems change, study and debate may not be enough. Short courses sponsored by computer vendors, courses by university staff, workshops within the company, or short-term systems analysis assignments may be required for managers to become fully acquainted with business computer systems. A company-sponsored workshop allows managers with previous exposure to computer systems to share their experiences with those soon to have similar experiences. Workshop content should be designed to familiarize managers with the lessons learned by other managers so that they will come to understand what it means to be objective and decisive in matters concerning systems change. Short-term systems assignments also aid the manager. These assignments need not be full time, nor need they cover all phases of systems analysis. They should include some exposure to both hardware and software, and some design activity such as flowcharting and file design.

The computer is in business to stay. Managers must acquaint themselves with computer systems and technology or face the consequences of becoming dated. Computer applications designed for business have and will continue to have a profound influence on the administration of a business and the processing of important business transactions. Today a manager must understand and be able to adjust to the increasing use of computer-based applications.

REVIEW OF IMPORTANT IDEAS

A business computer application is a means of obtaining, improving, and using files of business information. This is by no means a small task, as files establish a necessary permanence within a firm. The typical firm is growing, sometimes at a compound rate in excess of 15 percent. Business computer systems must be developed to add order and stability to the firm. A firm's growth may necessitate conversion to them because of increased volume and diversity.

Hardware and software are common terms in computer technology. Hardware is the mechanical equipment of the computer system. Software (supervisors, compilers and assemblers, sort/merge, and utilities) converts the hardware to machine-usable status. They permit user-generated application programs to be written and establish control over processing.

The work of the systems analyst and the role of the manager in systems activity pose an interesting interpersonal dilemma. The analyst is responsible for the investigation, evaluation, design, implementation, documentation, and final review of a business computer system. The manager is responsible for actual use of the system after its release by the analyst. Managers may experience a serious gap in awareness and understanding, especially if systems development has been treated lightly. To avoid this potential problem, managers must develop a systems orientation—through education, debate, and/or experience—compatible with the systems for which they are responsible. Otherwise, managers may be unable to alter their behavior to best suit the interests of the organization.

REVIEW QUESTIONS

1. What is a business computer application?

2. Explain the difference between a single-purpose computer application and an integrated computer application.

3. What basic purposes are served by the development of business computer applications?

4. Technological breakthroughs leading to more advanced and sophisticated computer hardware have shortened machine processing times, but not the procedures. Explain the implications of this statement in terms of the study of business computer applications.

5. What is the difference between hardware and software?

6. What are the four types of computer programs supplied by computer vendors? What function does each type serve?

7. What are the five phases of system analysis?

8. Why is it important to separate the investigation phase of systems analysis from the evaluation phase?

9. What are the basic rules for deciding whether to place a manual processing operation on the computer?

10. What is a procedures audit?

11. At what phase in systems analysis should a manager be especially critical? What types of questions should be asked during this period?

EXERCISES

1. Why has management been less than totally receptive to the design and installation of business computer systems? Give several reasons.

2. Explain why the job of the systems analyst is considered by many to be very difficult.

3. The creation of business computer systems involves three interconnected subsystems: a computer subsystem, an analysis (development and conversion) subsystem, and a management-control subsystem. Give several reasons why business firms have difficulty coordinating the activities of these three subsystems.

2

COMPONENTS OF A BUSINESS COMPUTER SYSTEM

Business computer systems are large and complex. They are difficult to design and almost as difficult to comprehend once they have been designed. Systems analysts use several methods of reporting to enable observers to understand business computer systems. *Procedures manuals* provide instructions for uniformity in the preparation of systems manuals, systems flowcharts, program flowcharts, and other documentation. The importance of uniformity cannot be overemphasized, since many people may be involved in the development of a system before it is operational. The most common types of documentation are:

- *Systems documentation* provides a complete technical and descriptive set of materials to accompany a system. Programs, file formats, input and output specifications, error routines, and processing audits are spelled out in this type of documentation.

- *Systems flowcharts* use symbols to depict the highlights of a proposed or designed system. They are used by analysts to visually represent the concepts of a business system.

- *Program documentation* provides materials that describe computer program specifications within a system. These specifications include program block diagrams, numbering assignments, program listings, identification of variables, and computer operator instructions.

- *Program flowcharts* (the familiar block diagrams) show the logical sequence of all decisions, data movement, calculations, and linkages. They present visually the steps that must be followed in fulfilling the objectives of a program.

Understanding a business computer system depends, in part, on thorough knowledge of terms and concepts used in reporting systems activity. Thus a portion of this chapter is devoted to a review of common terms in documentation. Another portion reviews systems flowcharts and flowchart notation. Both of these review sections aid in following the flowcharts for each computer application later in the text. However, before entering into this review, you need to understand the stages of a business system and the major types of computer programs common to business data processing. With this additional framework, the components of a business computer system, expressed in systems notation, should become clear.

2-1 STAGES IN THE FLOW OF BUSINESS TRANSACTIONS

A business system consists of a series of procedures for creating or updating business files, for producing official business documents, and for providing a written record and summary of processing. Business documents serve several purposes:

1. They record the terms and conditions of an initial agreement between two parties.
2. They record compliance by the first party with the terms and conditions of the agreement.
3. They record compliance by the second party to the agreement.
4. They reconcile the fact that compliance is satisfied.
5. They summarize the number of agreements made, first party compliance, second party compliance, and reconciliation by both parties.
6. They project or estimate the expected number of agreements, first and second party compliance, and reconciliation, based on historical data contained in outstanding, or pending, business files.

Figure 2-1 illustrates the four stages of a business system; each stage results in a business document. At the first stage, the initial transaction agreement, two parties reach an agreement and record its terms and conditions on a document. Examples of this stage would be an employee accepting employment at a stated rate of pay or a customer placing an order for stock at a specified price. At the second stage, first party compliance, one

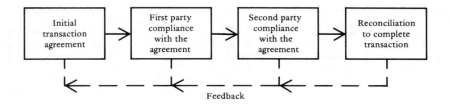

FIG. 2-1   Four stages of a business system

party complies with the terms and conditions of the initial agreement. The employee works the agreed number of hours; the company fills and ships ordered stock to the customer. At the third stage, second party compliance, the second party to the agreement responds to compliance by the first party. The employer pays the employee according to the rate of payment stated in the initial agreement; the customer pays for merchandise received. Next, it is necessary to reconcile first and second party compliance. The employee must be able to cash the check received as payment; the employer must determine that the check was cashed by the employee. Similarly, payment sent for merchandise received must be reconciled to indicate that the company did indeed receive the payment.

The feedback loop shown in the diagram means that information from a previous stage is required to complete reconciliation. For instance, the number of checks outstanding must be matched by the number of checks written. Reconciliation is accomplished through use of pending files. Once checks are processed by a bank and returned to the company, they are matched against the outstanding check file, and cancelled checks are separated from pending checks.

The documents that result from the four stages of a business system support and summarize the activity completed at each stage. For example, a bank statement is a listing of individual transactions; it also summarizes the entire list of transactions. The packing slip, which is sent with orders filled from stock, documents first party compliance. An outstanding invoice list or register documents transactions in which first party compliance has been satisfied, but second party compliance is pending. An accounts receivable register is similar to an invoice register. It summarizes the total number of invoices pending, by customer. This is in contrast to the accounts payable register, which summarizes pending bills, by vendor.

Figure 2-2 shows the flow of documents required in the processing of a typical customer order.

1. The customer order—an offer to buy—is most often accepted by the salesperson and approved by a business office manager. When it can

Stages of a Business System	Common Documents

1. Initial transaction agreement
2. First party compliance
3. Second party compliance
4. Reconciliation to complete
    transaction
	Customer order
	Packing slip, bill of lading, invoice, billing statement
	Voucher-check, receiving slip
	Cancelled check (second party reconciliation), paid invoice
	    (first party reconciliation)

FIG. 2-2   Documents common to a customer order cycle

be verified that the customer's reputation and credit rating is satisfactory, stock release documents can be written.

2. First party compliance is accomplished by shipment of the filled order to the customer. At least two documents accompany the shipment. The shipping papers—the packing slip and the bill of lading—tell the customer the products shipped and the freight charges. The customer invoice is sent separately. It informs the customer that merchandise has been shipped and that appropriate payment is expected. If the customer does not pay the invoice, a billing statement is sent. This statement summarizes all outstanding invoices to the customer for merchandise received.

3. Two main documents accompany second party compliance by the customer. A receiving slip is prepared by the customer to match materials shipped and received against the initial order for merchandise. A voucher-check is prepared once received goods are found acceptable. The voucher-check is the authorization to pay outstanding invoices.

4. Reconciliation is accomplished by receipt of the voucher-check, which is matched against an outstanding invoice to indicate a paid invoice. The cancelled check received by the customer documents receipt and acceptance of payment.

As this example shows, common business documents allow business transactions—in this case, a customer order—to be processed in an orderly fashion.

2-2   COMMON TYPES OF COMPUTER PROGRAMS

The design of computer programs for a business system follows the four stages of a business system. Figure 2-3 illustrates the five computer programs most used in business computer applications. These programs are the:

1. edit program
2. update program
3. register program
4. action-document program
5. summary program

While these programs serve a wide variety of purposes, they still resemble each other in at least general function. The following discussion of these programs should help you in understanding a business system and the flowcharts and concepts used in describing computer applications.

The Edit Program

Nearly every good computer application begins with an edit program—particularly if new data are being introduced into the application. The edit program tests for all detectable errors in the input data. Testing is done in

FIG. 2-3 Five common types of computer programs

two ways. First, transactions to be processed are totaled by the computer and compared to a manually prepared batch control. Second, each data element or field of information is tested to determine whether character codes are in error or quantities seem unreasonable. The edit program also creates a computer file that is used for further processing. This file, the *transaction file,* is usually stored on a reel of magnetic tape or on cylinders of magnetic disk.

The importance of testing for errors is often underemphasized. If errors are not discovered and corrected when data are first introduced into a computer application, they may damage existing computer files; upset audit controls; enrage customers, vendors, and employees; and generally cast doubt on the accuracy of the entire computer operation. Therefore, prior to further processing of business transactions, the edit program should detect and identify all possible incorrect data.

The Update Program

The update program compares edited input transactions to a reference or master file. (This procedure further validates the accuracy of data passed by the edit program.) *Reference files* contain records that correspond to input transactions being processed, such as standard cost data. Data are usually transferred from the reference file to the transaction file created by the edit program. At other times, input data are simply matched against data stored in the reference file. If a match is made, it helps verify the accuracy of input data. *Master files* contain current, historical, and other accumulated totals, as well as reference file detail. Master files are updated during processing by adding current data to historical file totals. Thus the update program enlarges the content of the transaction file prepared by the edit program and alters the contents of a master file. Reference file contents are not altered during processing; rather, data are only transferred from the file.

If more than one master or reference file must be consulted, there may be several update programs in one computer application. Finally, if errors are discovered, they are either separated from a transaction file or flagged for special handling at a later point in processing.

The Register Program

The register program provides a complete, printed record of all transactions that enter the computer application. The printed register enables processing control clerks to look over the actions of the computer. It is also a legal document suitable for long-term storage; company auditors use this document along with batch control slips to verify the accuracy and completeness of processing. The register is also frequently used in determining the best way to modify subsequent steps in processing. If errors are found in this report, the transaction file should be corrected immediately.

The Action-Document Program

Almost every computer application is designed to produce a printed business document as an end result. The action-document program prints this document, which is usually intended for external use. (That is, the documents will be used by people outside the computer or accounting departments.) Action documents include paychecks, invoices, billing statements, and picking labels.

The Summary Program

Finally, each business computer application normally includes a summary program which produces a summary report. This report reduces the details of all transactions into consolidated totals. The totals are then passed to a higher accounting document such as the general ledger. The creation and retention of these totals provides the basis for integrated accounting computer applications.

Figure 2-4 illustrates how the five computer programs work together to complete a single stage of a business system. In this example, the accounts payable computer application represents vendor invoices awaiting payment on second party compliance. As illustrated, keyed vendor invoices are inputted to the *edit program* and examined for error. A listing of input detail in error is produced together with a transaction file. The *update program* processes input transactions from this file against a vendor reference file, thus checking the correctness of the vendor number and leading to the printing of a missing vendor listing and an approved invoice file—the file from which vendors will be paid. The *register program* lists the transactions being paid by this particular computer processing run. Actually, not all invoices are paid from the approved invoice file at one time. A company may choose to delay a bill, make partial payment, or pay the bill in full. (Chapter 5, which deals with accounts payable, discusses the splitting of the invoice file.) Figure 2-4 indicates that all approved invoice detail will be paid. The *action-document program* then produces vendor voucher-checks. The vendor reference file is used again to add vendor names and addresses to the checks. Finally, the *summary program* produces a report used in posting vendor invoice payment totals to the general ledger.

2-3   SYSTEMS DOCUMENTATION

The discussion of the four stages of a business system and the five common types of computer programs has introduced some terms and expressions that may not be familiar to the beginning reader of computer applications materials. The purpose of this section is to help answer some of the questions prompted by an inadequate understanding of systems terminology.

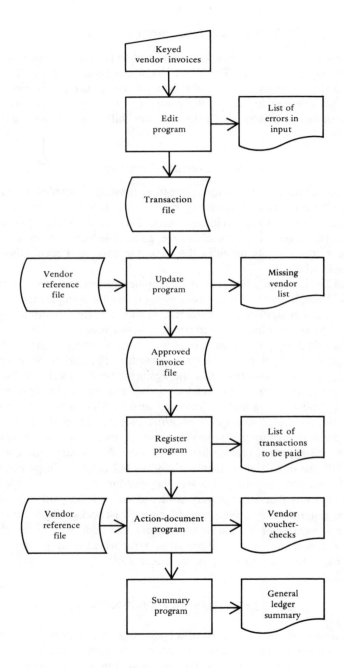

FIG. 2-4 The five common types of computer programs as used in an accounts payable computer application

Systems documentation clarifies concepts and terms used in systems activities. Instructions for documentation and clarification of terms are found in standard procedures manuals and guides. These materials are then used in preparing systems proposals, systems documentation, and program documentation.

Systems Proposals

Systems proposals provide a brief, nontechnical description of what a system will accomplish. They are written to explain the purpose of the system; provide a systems flowchart of the proposed system; describe the reports to be produced, the input requirements, and the computer files needed in processing; and, most importantly, provide cost/time estimates. Three such cost/time estimates are usually prepared: one for systems investigation and evaluation; one for systems design, computer programming, and program implementation; and one for computer processing requirements.

Systems Documentation

Systems documentation provides a detailed description of what a system will accomplish. It consists of a statement of purpose, the systems flowchart, and an overview of the computer programs designed for the system. The systems design generally includes a technical description of the report layouts, input forms, data entry instructions, computer file layouts and identification, and file coding structures.

- *Report layout* involves designing the report formats which are to follow a computer application. The reports are printed either on computer stock paper or on special made-to-order forms.

- *Input layout* involves designing input formats. Where input consists of punched cards, single- and multiple-card format sheets are used. Where input consists of computer terminal entry, the terminal screen must be formatted to handle input.

- *Data entry instructions* are prepared for every type of input required by the system.

- *File layout and identification* are required for every file used in a system. These documents contain the system name, the file name and number, and the name and description of each data element internal to a file.

- *File coding* structures are explanations of each data element in the file codes.

Besides systems description and design characteristics, systems documentation contains working procedures for operating and controlling a computer application. These procedures include:

- *User procedures* are instructions for submitting data to the application and for requesting processing by a computer operation.

- *Operating procedures* clarify the steps necessary in processing, so that a computer operator can follow them in running an application.

- *Production control procedures* specify the job stream necessary to properly schedule the application. The job stream listing identifies each computer program by name and number. It also contains the computer files required to complete a processing operation. Because several programs may be used for several jobs, each one appears on the appropriate job stream.

- *Audit trails* allow an external audit of a computer application. They provide the ability to trace documents through a system in order to validate the accuracy of the data processed by the computer.

- *Batch control* compares manually prepared accumulated totals from batches of data submitted to processing to totals calculated by the computer application.

Program Documentation

Program documentation is a function of individual computer program design and implementation. It includes block diagrams, program number assignments, the program listing, error diagnostic routines, computer run times, variables identification, and program revision instructions. This type of precise documentation permits tracing through a developed computer program to comprehend the logic of the symbolic coding.

2-4 SYSTEMS FLOWCHARTING

Systems flowcharts are an essential part of good systems documentation. Because of the extensive use of flowcharts in this text, this section reviews the purposes served by a flowchart and the meaning of the symbols used throughout the text.

A flowchart is exactly what the name implies. It is a chart of the flow of information or procedures throughout a business system. Since this text deals with business computer applications, the flowcharts illustrated are concerned with the flow of information through a computer application. As such, the flowcharts will not cover subjects such as report distribution or mail handling techniques, because these operations are external to computer processing. Rather, the flowcharts presented identify major stages of computer processing.

The systems flowchart can be used in a variety of ways:

1. As a vehicle for communication and comprehension between people. Through it systems designers can discuss the relative virtues of alternative solutions for a system, without becoming enmeshed in excessive technical details.

2. As a device for solving or evolving complex systems. At first glance, a large system may seem beyond comprehension or solution. However, if the analyst solves one problem or area of design and prepares a concise statement of the operation, using standard symbols, he or she can then proceed to the next point or operation and thus work through the entire system. Slowly, one point at a time, the complex system will evolve into a comprehensible picture that the mind can assimilate at one time.

3. As a record of thoughts and discussions for later review. It should be possible to return to a flowchart after several days or weeks and still recover almost all of the original thinking that went into its development.

4. As a working document that outlines the relationship between a computer program and the results expected of the program. From flowcharts, program specifications and block diagrams may be developed. In this sense, flowcharts serve as the main framework on which the analyst and programmers build a complete computer system.

Clearly, a great deal is expected of simple flowchart diagrams. In this text, a systems flowchart is provided for each business application discussed. The contents of each chapter are clarified by studying the flowcharted examples. First, however, it is necessary to agree on the symbols used and their meaning.

The flowchart symbols used in this text are standard in the computer industry. They have been obtained from the IBM template, Form GX20-8020-1 (Fig. 2-5). The symbols on this template are much like those found on other brands of templates. Moreover, they are used in a manner that is consistent and in agreement with most published standards, and contrary to none of the known standards. For purposes of clarity and simplicity, the number of symbols used has been limited to six. These six adequately describe all the possible actions to be taken in the systems described in this book. The six symbols are the manual input symbol, the document symbol, the on-line computer storage symbol, the computer process symbol, the

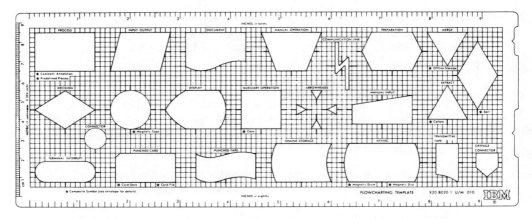

FIG. 2-5   IBM template (form GX20-8020-1)

manual operation symbol, and the off-line storage symbol. Each symbol is illustrated and described to aid in understanding how they are used in subsequent flowcharts.

The Manual Input Symbol

In most computer systems, the original input is first encoded on keypunch machines or on data entry terminals. The manual input symbol is used to indicate the input of data to processing, regardless of method selected.

The Document Symbol

This symbol serves three functions. First, it symbolizes the presence of original documents, such as invoices from vendors, time cards from employees, and cancelled checks from the bank. Second, it represents the printed output of the computer, such as paychecks, customer statements, or aged trial balances. Printed output also consists of edit reports, update reports, register listings, action documents, and summary reports. Third, it indicates the existence of batch control. As stated earlier, it is customary to batch documents before routing them to the computer. The batch should be accompanied by a batch control total. In the case of payroll, the batch control is total employee hours worked. In the case of receipts, the batch control is the dollar amount received from customers. These control totals are needed to verify the accuracy of data fed into the computer and stored in transaction files.

The On-line Computer Storage Symbol

Storage of data on computer files can take many forms, such as magnetic tape, magnetic disk, or magnetic drum. In this text, the on-line file storage symbol is used to depict a computer file. However, it is important to remember that the particular file (for example, tape, disk, or drum) would be determined by the storage devices available on the computer used.

The Computer Process Symbol

The rectangle is used to symbolize each computer program. A program is a complete computer operation with specified input data and output in the form of printed reports or output files.

Separate computational steps are usually not considered as individual programs. For example, in the case of payroll, calculation of federal and state taxes is normally accomplished by the same program. Separate symbols are not required to distinguish these steps. They are included within the program that computes net pay. In the same way, rewinding reels of magnetic tape is not considered a separate computer program—it is normally included in the last part of another program.

However, the payroll operation involves more than one operation. Thus more than one symbol is used. For example, printing paychecks is a separate operation from summarizing the results for the general ledger, although the same files may be used. Moreover, each program is associated with certain input and output files.

Finally, on occasion computer files must be sorted or merged. The process of arranging file records in a different sequence is accomplished by a sort or merge package. Generally, a sort and merge package is supplied by the computer vendor. Hence, it might be considered a special type of computer program.

The Manual Operation Symbol

There are always activities associated with the computer that do not affect its operation. Examples of these activities are bursting or detaching paychecks, stuffing them into envelopes, and mailing them to employees. Much of this activity is disregarded in this text, since it is not important to an understanding of the computer system. However, it is desirable to know when manual activities can aid the computer operation. Therefore, on occasion, the manual symbol is used to indicate an auxiliary activity.

The Off-line Storage Symbol

This symbol is used when it is necessary to document the storage of data external to the computer operations. Backup magnetic tapes, filed copies of invoices, and other filed documents are examples of off-line storage. Like the manual operations, off-line storage does not directly affect computer operations.

The Flowchart Layout

Just as there are standards for the use of flowcharting symbols, so must there be common agreement on the layout of the systems flowchart. The closer standards are adhered to, the more information the flowchart will convey. The following guidelines are offered in designing a flowchart.

1. Each complete flowchart should be simple enough to be placed on one page.
2. Detail sheets should be attached to enlarge on special features or complex stages, if elaboration is necessary.
3. The main flow of the system should move from the top of the page to the bottom. Arrows should be used to point out subsequent stages of

operation. (Broken arrows are sometimes used to delineate secondary flow such as batch control tests.)

4. The on-line computer storage files used by a program should be placed on the left side of the program symbol.
5. Documents produced by the program should be placed to the right of program symbols.
6. The titles of a symbol should be written inside the symbol, unless there is not enough space for an adequate description.

Figure 2-6 illustrates these guidelines. The flowchart shows the application of cash receipts to the customer's accounts receivable file, followed by the preparation of new statements. Although this illustration does not rep-

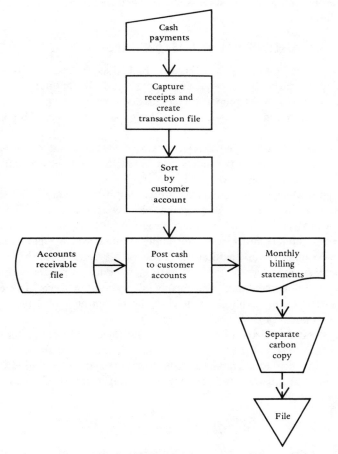

FIG. 2-6   The layout of a flowchart: cash receipts posting and customer statement preparation

resent a complete receivables system, it does show how the flowcharting standards are used. This flowchart may be described as follows:

1. Keyed input representing customer payments is submitted to the computer. The first computer program uses the input data to create a transaction file. This file can be indicated by the computer storage symbol. However, it is usually not shown, since its existence is obvious and the symbol would only clutter the chart.
2. A sort program is used to arrange the cash payment records in their proper sequence.
3. Customer payments are combined with the accounts receivable file, and statements are printed showing the balance on account.
4. Carbon copies of the statements are filed in customer folders for later reference.

REVIEW OF IMPORTANT IDEAS

Business computer systems are large, complex sequences of different processes that are difficult to design and comprehend. To facilitate understanding, the systems analyst prepares systems documentation and designs flowcharts that summarize the logic and the design specifications of a completed system.

Four business stages characterize business systems and the use of the computer in a business: a two-party agreement, first and second party compliance, and reconciliation of parties.

Five types of computer programs are common to a business system: the edit program, the file update program, the register program, the action-document program, and the summary program. These not only process and control data entered into a computer application, but also yield satisfactory business documents and facilitate an audit of all transactions processed.

To further support computer processing, systems proposals and systems and program documentation accompany all systems activity. These documents clarify the procedures followed in the design and implementation of computer applications.

The systems flowchart allows overall visual review of a computer system. It should be brief—not more than one page in length—and should be consistent with documentation standards. Six flowchart symbols are used throughout this book to illustrate the primary processing features of business computer applications.

REVIEW QUESTIONS

1. Differentiate among a systems proposal, systems documentation, and program documentation.

2.   What four stages are required to complete a business transaction?

3.   What is meant by the term *feedback* in a business system?

4.   Briefly describe each of the five types of computer programs most common to business computer applications.

5.   What are the three cost/time estimates in a systems proposal? What purpose does each estimate serve?

6.   What are the main types of technical procedures that accompany systems documentation? Why is each type necessary?

7.   What objectives are served by systems flowcharts?

8.   What is the major difference between a computer sort operation and a computer program?

9.   Explain the ways in which the document symbol is used in a systems flowchart.

EXERCISES

1.   Using the standard symbols shown in this chapter, develop a systems flowchart that illustrates your method of paying monthly bills by check. Then make another flowchart showing your method of balancing your checkbook. (In each flowchart, use the manual file symbol to illustrate any files being maintained.)

2.   Using the flowcharts you prepared in the first exercise, explain the following:

   a.   the use of feedback in processing

   b.   the type of file (reference or master) maintained in processing

   c.   the audit trail preserved in processing

   d.   the types of computer programs that would be required in place of manual processing operations (Refer to the common types of computer programs in preparing your answer.)

3

FILE DESIGN

A business computer operation was earlier defined as a means of obtaining, improving, and using files of business information. Computer files house or store related sets of business records. If these files of records are accurate, complete, and easily accessible, the desired goals of a computer application will almost certainly be realized. Because the computer file is dominant in computer business applications, it is appropriate to consider the following questions:

1. What is a computer file?
2. How is its existence justified?
3. How is its reliability determined and maintained?
4. How is a computer file designed?
5. How is it created?
6. How is it brought up-to-date?
7. How is it used in report preparation?

3-1   A COMPUTER FILE

Most newcomers to data processing are confused by the concept of a computer file. Many find it difficult to grasp how such files can be organized and used. And yet files are an essential part of everyday life. For instance, a household budget (a summary file) typically contains the following information: what was purchased, where the purchase was made, the amount paid, and the date of payment. In other words, the household budget is a file that consists of a related set of records. Each record consists of a single purchase entry. In a similar manner, a computer file contains related sets of records. Each record in an accounts payable file might describe a single purchase entry.

Another file most people maintain is the one contained in a checkbook— the check register. Whenever a check is written, it is necessary to record the pertinent facts about the check. These facts include whom it was written to; the amount and date of the transaction; and sometimes the purpose of the check, such as paying the balance due on an account. The same pertinent facts will be found in a computer file of check payments. One record exists for every written check.

Obviously, computer files are different from a household budget or a check register. They differ in the form of storage used, in size, in the means of modification and retrieval, and in the necessity for brevity. Computer files are composed of either decks of punched cards, magnetic tape reels, magnetic disk packs, magnetic drums, or data cells. *Punched cards* contain small holes, which the computer is able to detect and translate into characters of information. *Magnetic tape reels* are similar to tape recorders, but they store bits of information rather than bars of recorded music. *Magnetic disk files* store bits of information in a manner similar to the storage of recorded music on a phonograph record. Just as a phonograph needle can be raised and shifted to another position on the record, so can the read and write heads of a magnetic disk drive be shifted to a particular collection of data.

The computer file is much larger than a personal file. Even though one punched card holds a small amount of data (80 to 90 characters), boxes of punched cards collectively represent thousands of characters. A reel of magnetic tape can store far more data. An inch of tape typically stores either 800 or 1,600 characters. A single reel of tape can store up to 25 million characters. A large disk pack can store as many as 100 million characters. However, the main advantage of a disk is flexibility. Data can be accessed directly from a disk. As such, a disk file features "direct" retrieval of information, which eliminates the need to undergo a sequential search (see Fig. 3-1).

The fact that a computer file can be read or modified without human intervention is another distinction between computer and manual record-keeping procedures. Comparing a manual to a computer-printed check register, a person immediately realizes that the computer file is more formal, or rigid, in design. Each record for each check must be of a specified length and in a specific area of a file. The computer program must be able to determine exactly where a record of information can be found. A computer cannot

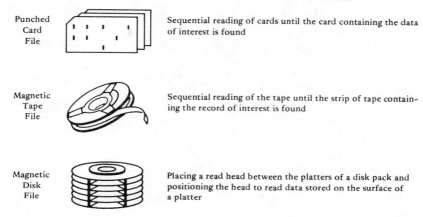

FIG. 3-1 Computer file comparisons

grope around as we can, to find information that is not in its proper place. The computer requires an exact location for data being recorded or stored.

Another difference between manual and computer files is the presence of codes and controlling numbers for retrieving data from computer files. If we have a dispute with the power company about an electric bill and need to collect all the utilities checks we have sent during the past year, we are able to do so even though we did not always spell the name of the company the same way on each check. Computer programs normally do not have the flexibility to match similar, but not exactly the same, names. What is customary, therefore, is the use of *account numbers* to group transactions, or, in this case, checks written to a customer. The computer is able to determine the dollar amount of checks written to the power company by accumulating the amounts paid to the company's assigned customer account number.

The computer file also contains *record codes* to distinguish various types of transactions (Fig. 3-2). If, for example, as a result of our conversation with the power company, a credit is issued, we, as individuals, could note this on the face of the next bill to be paid. The computer, however, must use a distinctive record code to signal that a transaction be treated as a credit rather than as a payment to the customer account.

The last distinction between computer and personal file records is that computer records must be as compact as possible. A computer is expensive to own and to operate. A major part of this cost is the retention and processing of computer files. Unlike manual files, material printed by computers is apt to be terse and impersonal.

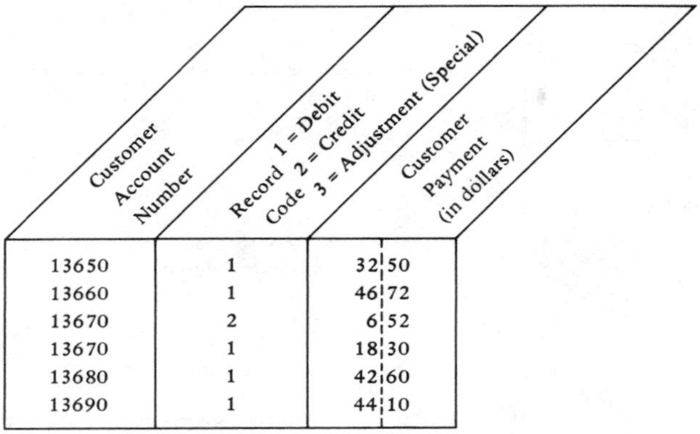

FIG. 3-2   A record code

3-2 FILE JUSTIFICATION

How much will it cost to obtain and retain the information in a computer file? What is the value of each data element to the computer application? The answers to these two questions determine what information will be included in a computer file. For example, one might believe that an employee's address is a vital piece of information to include in a file for a payroll application. After all, the need may arise to mail a check to an employee, rather than to pass it to her or him during office hours. But how valuable or vital is the address to payroll operations? How much will it cost to maintain the accuracy of the address once it is placed in the file? Employee address records are probably correct only when the employee first accepts employment and when the employee decides to leave the firm. (When an employee leaves a job, the payroll department must verify the employee's home address in order to mail final tax records.) Employees may move several times while working at the firm. Thus the company must take definite steps to periodically check and perhaps update each address. Updating the address portion of the payroll file, therefore, becomes expensive.

Will the cost of maintaining data be worth the additional expense? In some cases it will, because use of the data offsets the investment required for storage and periodic updating. In other cases, use of the data is so minimal that the cost of maintaining it is disproportionate. This implies, however, that cost analysis must be applied to all items of data or data elements proposed for a computer file. If the costs of storing or retaining the data and the costs of acquiring and inserting up-to-date corrections are both measured against the value, or utility, of the data element, a surprisingly large number of elements will prove to be unprofitable—not worth the costs incurred in retaining them.

File retention must also be assigned a dollar value when determining whether or not to include a data element in a computer file. Suppose the maximum size for an employee address is 75 characters, including embedded, or blank, spaces between city and state; all other information required for one record in the payroll file totals 150 characters. It is clear that the addition of address characters will increase the overall size of the payroll file by 50 percent. This percentage can be converted into dollar costs. For instance, the cost of storing information will increase by 50 percent or more, since an additional computer storage unit may be required to store the additional data. If the smaller file fits on one disk pack, for example, and the additional address data create an overflow to another pack, storage costs will double. An additional disk drive may be required to allow both segments of the file to be used by the computer at the same time. All this greatly increases the cost of the payroll computer application.

As a final consideration, an enlarged file requires greater computer central memory or core storage, since larger employee records must be read into the central memory of the computer. With larger records, more central storage is required and it is even possible that a larger memory may be needed, or the blocking factor might be reduced. (The blocking factor refers to the process of grouping records together to take advantage of minimal file storage and movement of data into central memory.) This aspect further increases the cost of processing the payroll application.

Although somewhat exaggerated, this payroll example points out what can happen when data elements of minimal value are included in a computer file. Computer files are frequently larger than they should be and contain material that cannot be justified. A definite need thus exists to evaluate both the cost and the value of each data element proposed for a computer file.

Unlike employee addresses, many data elements can be obtained with little effort. An example is the current date. This information is normally obtained from the computer operating system and its accuracy should be absolute. Since Julian dates consist of two digits for the year followed by three digits for the number of the day within the year, the field required for a current date is five digits, or three bytes. (A storage *byte* can contain one alphabetic character or two digits, such as those that compose the Julian date.) Clearly, including the Julian date adds a negligible cost to the expense of the file. Of course, the data element has relatively little value. It is used to document the date when a record is added to or removed from a file. Thus it is well that the cost of acquisition and retention is small.

Most data elements suggested for a computer file range in cost between the extremes represented by the payroll address and the Julian date. A good way to establish file contents is to list all possible data elements, enumerate all possible uses for each, and project the anticipated cost of acquiring and maintaining each element. From these projections, an evaluation of cost versus usefulness can be made.

3-3   RELIABILITY OF COMPUTER FILES

One frequently overlooked problem in acquiring file data is the reliability of input information. Incoming data and its source must be appraised to determine whether manually prepared input records are likely to be both complete and accurate. Computer systems require individuals to prepare input record forms and to detail necessary information for the computer application. Some applications pose considerable problems in obtaining complete and accurate information. For example, a problem may occur when individuals are required to submit data for a purpose in which they have no strong interest. As a result, they may fail to accurately prepare the required input. This situation recently occurred in a sophisticated legal reporting application. The system was intended to monitor the status of legal cases handled by an attorney's staff. Legal experts were required to complete special forms for input to the computer system. The forms were not part of their traditional work and were designed for ease of data entry, rather than for ease of preparation by the legal staff. The staff resisted completing the forms since they could not correlate them with the important parts of their jobs. Consequently, the forms were carelessly prepared, if at all, and the computer records were found to be worthless. This type of problem occurs all too often.

Some employees purposely alter input data, especially if they are concerned about how a computer application might affect their jobs. For example, hourly employees such as mechanics are often expected to record how they spend their time while at work. Daily time cards have provisions for recording what job was worked on, how long it took to complete the job, and how much time was not spent working on a specific project or order. A data input problem occurs when employees assume that idle-time entries will be used against them. To cover the fact that they are occasionally idle, employees adjust productive work entries to match the total hours shown on the time card. If no idle times are recorded, the accuracy of data input becomes very suspect. This makes any breakdown of hours to jobs relatively worthless. Once again, in order for input data to be usable, it must be both complete and accurate.

To be usable, input data must also be timely. Data processing staff specify cutoff times—deadlines for the submission of data—for most computer applications. For example, customer payment information and information on customer charges must be submitted to data processing no later than the twenty-fifth of the month. This deadline allows time to prepare and mail customer statements by the first of the following month. If input data are delayed, the statements must either be prepared using incomplete data or be delayed until the necessary customer information arrives. Use of incomplete data leads to both customer complaints and payment mistakes. A delay in processing results in delayed mailing of statements to customers, which in turn delays customer payments. In either case, a company may ultimately have to secure a short-term, high interest loan to meet its financial obligations. In short, the timeliness of input data is extremely important. It often determines the success of a computer application.

The question of file reliability must be carefully considered during the initial design stages of a computer application. Input data that can be acquired without imposing additional work on personnel are more apt to be reliable. Timeliness of data is another important planning consideration. Finally, the best way to guarantee input reliability is to devise external controls, which exist apart from the computer application, to verify both accuracy and completeness. For instance, one common control for inventory is total parts on hand. This can be expressed as follows: total parts on hand is equal to the beginning on-hand total plus additional receiving or returns less sales to customers.

New on hand = old on hand + receipts − sales

Each of these expressions can be controlled externally.

3-4   FILE DESIGN

The data in the computer record may be arranged in a variety of ways once data elements have been selected for a computer file. Several years ago, when manual processing of punched cards was an important part of data processing, arrangement of data in a record was determined mainly by the way in which punched cards were processed by hand through mechanical equipment. This feature limited the variety of choice for the order and location of data in a file. The arrangement of fields of data became very important in file design. The term *field* was used to signify the exact storage location for a data element within a computer record. Each field location held exactly the same type of data within each record of a computer file. Figure 3-3 displays this important data hierarchy. Several fields are within one record, and several records are within a computer file. Thus a computer file may contain many thousands of records, all stored on a reel of magnetic tape or on several cylinders of a disk pack. For each record, fields are known and used for a specific purpose. The process of record design therefore consists

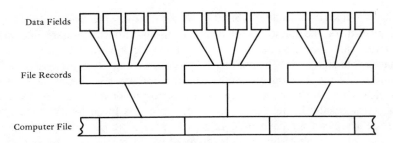

FIG. 3-3   Data hierarchy in a computer file

of selecting the fields for a computer record and arranging them in the best sequence.

Since most data processing now uses magnetic tape or disk storage, field locations are not determined by mechanical sort routines, as was the case with manual processing of punched cards. The file itself can consist of fixed- or variable-length records and can be rearranged by using a computer sort routine. The principles of file design, however, have not significantly changed. The following four operations continue to be of major importance:

1. data extraction
2. data field arrangement
3. common characteristic arrangement
4. sort-key selection

Data Extraction

Data extraction begins with studying the data entry operation and the original input document. The data entry operation can be made substantially easier if the input records are designed to fit the extraction of data from the input document. Occasionally, the input document itself is revised to simplify the extraction process. However, it is more important to design the document so that the individual charged with its completion will be able to use it, than to design the document to fit data entry activity. The general rule is to design the input record to permit extraction of data once the input document is designed.

Data Field Arrangement

Data field arrangement does influence computer file design. Fields in records are commonly arranged in the same order as they are extracted from the input document unless there are compelling reasons to rearrange them. This standard practice helps reduce confusion when attempting to review the contents of a computer file. If the sequence of data input differs from that of computer records, it is difficult to compare the two to resolve discrepancies. Standard location of fields also eases the programming burden.

Common Characteristic Arrangement

Information within a computer file may be arranged by common characteristics. For example, one design practice is to arrange current dollar information in one section of a file. Year-to-date information (the accumulated totals of current information since the beginning of the fiscal year) is stored in another section. Name and address information is held in still another section. Arranging by common characteristic makes it easier to obtain a dump listing (that is, a listing of the data stored within a section of the file maintained by the computer).

Sort Keys

Sort keys are fields that are frequently used in sequencing the records of a file. For instance, a customer's request for the purchase of an inventoried part may require a sort of the inventory file by part number. It may also be necessary to sort the inventory file by warehouse location number, as in an order filling computer application. Customer, employee, vendor, product, location, and numerous other record codes function as sort keys—they are used to arrange the ordering of a file. The reason for grouping them in a common location is to reduce confusion when planning sort processing procedures.

3-5 FILE CREATION AND VERIFICATION

Considerable time is spent in the design and programming of a new computer system. However, as a general observation, an inadequate amount of both time and effort is spent in creating and verifying new computer files. Although file reliability and validity are important features of a business computer system, they may be slighted since file creation is one of the last steps in implementing a new system and there may be pressure to complete the system by a certain deadline and within specified cost projections. Shortcuts may be taken in creating and verifying the file to make up for earlier delays and cost overruns. Once the new system is in operation, the cost of shortcuts becomes apparent and returns to haunt the programming staff. It is far better to take an adequate amount of time to develop and test a new computer file and to correct mistakes immediately.

File creation generally consists of combining existing computer files with manual files for a new computer application. During this process, all possible balance totals should be computed and tested. For example, dollar fields, hours, quantities on hand, and number of orders processed can be totaled. These balance totals can then be compared with balance totals computed from the newly created computer file. This method is far more reliable than proofreading computer print listings, since mistakes can be visually overlooked. Even so, proofreading is the common way to validate the bulk of data in a new computer file. Proofreading names and addresses is a dull and error-prone process, but it is the best method known. As another alternative, when the system becomes semioperational, individual users of the system should be asked to review the printed results for errors. Users are often happy to respond when they find an error.

Another common practice is to operate a new computer system in parallel with its predecessor so that any tendency of the new system to deviate from the expected can be detected. For example, a computer payroll application will often be operated in parallel with the old system for several pay periods. If there are errors in the file or other parts of the system, parallel operations should uncover them. However, to ensure accurate test results, a typical period must be selected. In the case of payroll, it is possible to perform a parallel operation early in the year and miss programming or file design errors. Several payroll processing steps, such as Social Security insurance limit testing (the determination of whether an employee has paid the maximum required for Social Security), occur later in the year. Therefore, Social Security insurance limit testing cannot be adequately done until the last few months of a calendar year.

Once a new computer file is considered valid, a complete listing of its contents should be printed to help answer questions if they arise. For payroll, the payroll register provides a useful reference to the initial contents of the file.

3-6 FILE UPDATING

A newly created computer file is an active, usable source of information. However, for it to continue to be of value, it must be updated and cleared of input error. Two major types of input are used to update a file. Each type must be processed by the computer in a different way.

Change or Addition Record

The first type of input is the change or addition record. Every computer file must accept some change of its contents. For example, a payroll file will be changed and updated whenever information for a new employee is available.

The name and address of an employee might also need to be altered. Even dollar fields are occasionally changed. In other words, this type of file update adds to file contents, alters contents, and/or adjusts for errors.

File update for changes or additions cannot be easily controlled. When changes are not limited to dollar fields, external balance control totals cannot be computed. It is also possible during file update to submit input errors that cannot be detected by the computer program. For example, it is impossible for the computer to detect the correct spelling of a customer's name. For this reason, alphabetic or alphanumeric changes should be made with caution and should be completed before the file is used for actual processing. A comprehensive listing of all changes should be printed and reviewed. Any errors that are found should be corrected immediately and rechecked by a separate listing. Fortunately, the volume of change and addition records is typically small, allowing entries to be thoroughly checked.

Transaction Record

The second type of input to a computer application is the transaction record. Transaction records do not alter the fundamental information stored in master computer files. Instead, they update or add to variable fields only. For instance, if an employee's pay rate is changed, this change is made with a change record, not with a transaction record. Transaction records alter the current and year-to-date dollar fields on the master payroll file. An error in a transaction record can be identified and corrected using external balance controls.

Transaction records constitute high volume movement through data entry and into the computer. Because of such traffic considerations, it is necessary to design input documents, input record layouts, and computer files that minimize the amount of data to be extracted. For every keyed stroke saved, substantial savings are made in data acquisition costs. Transaction records should also be carefully examined and designed to allow extraction of data with a minimum of data entry. As an illustration, consider the following example. Imagine a group of people paid an hourly wage. A normal data processing procedure might be to key the hours worked as recorded on time cards for each employee. However, if all employees work the same number of hours, a control or lead record can be used to state the number of hours for them all. Then, if an employee worked the normal number of hours, it would be necessary to key hours worked. Instead, the computer would assign normal hours to the employee from the normal hour standard recorded on the lead record. If an employee worked a nonnormal number of hours, this exception condition would be keyed. In either case, the edit program could be used to distinguish between normal and exceptional occurrences. This use of the edit program would reduce the data entry work load and, at the same time, increase the reliability of data input.

Another illustration of reducing the data entry work load can be observed in processing accounts payable. Normally, every vendor invoice has a prompt-payment discount. Data entry staff usually key this discount when extracting data from the invoice. However, if the discount percentage remains constant for a vendor, it should be stored in the vendor master file so that the actual discount can be computed by the computer. The rule for reducing the data entry work load is as follows: *Key only exceptions to standard conditions, using a computer master file to store the standard and the computer to distinguish between the exception and the standard.*

3-7 REPORT PREPARATION

The major investment in a business computer system and the most important system components are the computer files. However, the dominant reason for creating the system lies in the documents, statements, and reports prepared from the files. Payroll checks, receivables statements, aged trial balances, and sales analysis reports are but a few illustrations of why computer systems are developed.

Most reports can be produced directly from a computer file if the sequence of the file is suitable for producing a printed report. When this is not the case, files are sorted to sequence them in a desired order. In other words, the sequence within a file determines the sequence of a printed report. However, the content of a file determines what sequencing procedures are permitted. To see how file content is made available for the printing of a report in a computer application, consider the following illustrations. In a payroll application, employee numbers are initially validated by an employee master file. Following this procedure (see Figure 3-4), computed

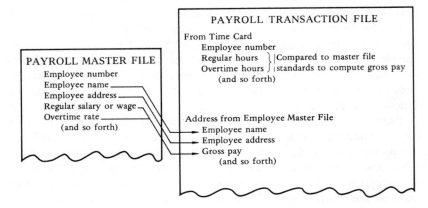

FIG. 3-4 Combination of files within a system—an abbreviated payroll transaction file

payroll detail, gross pay, net pay, and so forth are combined with data from the employee master file to extend the payroll transaction file. This combined file, sequenced alphabetically, is then used to prepare written checks and the check register. As a second illustration, consider an order-filling application. Customer order records are validated by the customer master file. When customer numbers match, records for name and address (as well as shipping address) are transferred from the customer file to the transaction file, which now includes customer data and current order information. Printed reports are prepared for this combined file, permitting the computer to process one file instead of several.

Combination of files within a system is one aspect of report preparation. Another is the actual process of printing reports. Report files most often contain a massive number of records. The files for a monthly customer statement report, for example, may contain thousands of records and require several reels of magnetic tape. The printing of statements may take hours or even days. Should anything go wrong with the computer or the print program, the entire printing may have to be repeated, causing delay, to say nothing of the expense. To avoid rerun possibilities, print programs should contain a restart capability.

Restart is the ability to begin printing with a statement specified when the program is started. Suppose that during a monthly customer billing statement, a large volume print operation, problems are experienced halfway through the print run. A restart capability makes it possible to stop the program, correct the error, and then restart the program. Thus actual printing of statements begins where the error occurred. If, in addition to printing customer statements, summary totals are also being printed and a summary file is being prepared (for example, a summary total for every 500 customers), restart would not suppress the reprinting of the totals. A second printing of the summary totals ensures that the error was corrected when the printing of customer statements resumed. The restart technique therefore minimizes the loss in time and the investment in printing due to a malfunction of any part of the print operation. At the same time, if a running summary is maintained, it ensures that the recovery procedures do not introduce additional errors into the system or the files that support the system.

REVIEW OF IMPORTANT IDEAS

In this chapter we have considered the need to justify the inclusion of data elements in a file, ways to ensure the accuracy of the contents of a file, and the use of a computer file in a business computer application. In principle, the file is the most important component of a computer system. Without a complete and accurate file, the objectives of a computer application are difficult, if not impossible, to achieve.

A computer file is similar to personal files such as the records we maintain to note the checks written on our bank account. File storage, the size of the file, file modification, file codes, and the compact nature of computer files differentiate computer files from personal files.

Because of the high cost of retaining data in a file, every data element selected for a file must be carefully reviewed. The cost of obtaining and retaining file data must be measured by their value to the application now and in the future. Data elements that can be obtained reliably at an acceptable cost and that have a high value should be included in a file. Elements that cannot be obtained reliably or whose value is questionable should not be included.

During the initial planning stages of file design, the methods of acquiring data should be carefully considered. If the acquisition of data inconveniences the people who are responsible for supplying it, data input to a computer system may well be sporadic and unreliable. Acquisition of data for computer files should parallel the normal work activities of those supplying it— even if input documents are less convenient for the data entry department than they would be if an input-oriented document were required.

Files should be designed for ease of extracting data from input documents by data entry. Whenever possible, files should either retain the same sequence of data fields found on input documents or group similar fields for ease of file content identification.

One of the most neglected aspects of the design of a computer application is the creation and verification of initial computer files. Data input testing and parallel operations should be encouraged during the early stages of the implementation of a system to ensure that pertinent, error-free data are included in a file and that file totals balance with external, manually prepared control totals.

Files are updated by two types of input records: the adjustment or change record and the transaction record. The first type typically alters the constant or master portion of the file and must be carefully checked for error. The second type is the more common of the two. It serves to change variable fields within a file and is therefore easier to control.

While the file may be the most important component of a computer system, the reason for file development is to produce documents and reports. Reports are easily prepared from a well-designed file, even though some sequencing of the file may be necessary for proper formatting of the report. While some detail in a file used for preparing a report may be needed for additional processing, it is unlikely that all detail must be saved.

Many reports printed by the computer require several hours to process. A restart option should be incorporated into the print program, so that if processing experiences problems, the program can resume printing where the error occurred. This saves many hours of computer time and reduces the cost of custom forms required for a computer application.

Data processing is an active and growing component of most business operations. The computer files prepared today may have profound uses in later computer applications, if sufficient care in their design allows for flexibility. One cannot assume that the possible uses for a file are known at the time of initial creation. Rather, one must plan so that the file can be used for a variety of purposes in the future. The longer a file and a computer application can be used by a company, the greater its return on capital invested to develop the application.

REVIEW QUESTIONS

1. What is a computer file, and how does it differ from a personal file?

2. How are records grouped in a computer file?

3. What is a record code, and how is it used?

4. Why must the cost of acquiring and maintaining data elements in a file be closely evaluated?

5. For what reasons is file reliability a major issue in the design of computer files?

6. What data hierarchy is followed in the design of a computer file?

7. How should a newly created computer file be verified?

8. What are the major types of input to a file? How does each type alter file content?

9. What rule should be followed in order to reduce the data entry work load?

10. What is meant by the phrase *restart capability*?

EXERCISES

1. Identify the fields contained in each record of your personal check register. Then answer the following:

   a. How are records grouped in the file?
   b. How does a new check entry alter file content?

    c.   What would have to be added to the file to enable a month-end summary of expenditures by major expense category?

    d.   What detail would be keyed from the check in the creation of a computer file record?

2.   Why do files establish a necessary permanence in a business organization? What would occur if all business files in an organization were destroyed?

II

ACCOUNTING APPLICATIONS

Many companies are introduced to the computer and to data processing through single-purpose accounting computer applications. The conversion from manual to computer methods of operation entails systematically analyzing input and output processes; structuring file contents and layouts; and developing computer programs to process data, update files, and prepare action documents and managerial reports. Large savings in clerical labor are likely to result from successful implementation of the applications discussed in this part of the text. However, they may serve other perhaps more important purposes: creating master and summary files of data, providing accurate and timely computer printed accounting documents, and acquainting members of an organization with the results of computer processing.

4

PAYROLL

Payroll is one of the oldest and most common business computer applications. A decade or two ago, company payrolls were frequently computed using punched card calculators. The payroll was then printed by tabulating machines. This primitive computing system introduced data processing to many organizations. In fact, mechanical calculators and early mechanical treatments of payroll may have had as much to do with the emerging usage of the computer in business as did innovations such as magnetic tape, disk files, and other features of computer technology. It may be that if automatic payroll computation and printing had not become valued business procedures, the computer would have been little understood and not much in demand, no matter how adept it was at processing data.

In spite of the modern high-speed computer, the processing of payroll remains fundamentally the same as in the past. Preparing a payroll requires collecting employee work hours, converting hours to gross earnings, and computing deductions and net pay. Of course, there are usually other activities to be performed as by-products of payroll operations. These include accumulating summary data for general ledger reports, printing quarterly and year-end reporting statements, and making labor distribution and job costing or job performance measurements and reporting them. (The last subject is covered in Chapter 14.) In addition to accounting activities, a payroll system commonly performs activities that might be viewed as personnel operations: sick leave and vacation time accrual and usage, time-in-labor-grade accrual, and home address maintenance. While these activities enlarge the size of computer records retained for the payroll operation, they do not significantly increase the complexity of managing the overall application.

The payroll computer application is one of several business systems that can be processed using a combination current and year-to-date master computer file. This file consists of records for the current reporting period and for yearly reporting. Combining both types of records into one master file reduces the operating complexity and the manual bookkeeping necessary to maintain the file. A combination file is particularly advantageous when use of the application is infrequent, as is the case with payroll. Such a file introduces some additional programming complexity and requires more computer processing time, but maintaining one file rather than two offsets this added difficulty.

The master file used in payroll processing also contains permanent and current data. Each type requires different computer processing, including the sequencing of file updating. The permanent portion of the file must be updated before current transactions are entered into the system, since information such as employee's rate of pay, accumulated vacation, and Social Security withholding is used to transform gross into net pay. Moreover, changes made to the master portion are complex and require careful visual editing, whereas current transactions entered from time cards can be edited quite well by programmed edit tests. Therefore, prior to the actual processing of a payroll, a preliminary master file update must usually be completed.

4-1 PRELIMINARY PAYROLL MASTER FILE UPDATE

Before time cards are submitted at the end of a pay period, the accounting or payroll office obtains data on new employees and on recent changes to existing employees. Typical types of data include correct spelling of name, Social Security number, number of tax exemptions (on occasion, a separate number for state and federal), marital status, pay scale, overtime rate (if distinctive), rates for sick leave and vacation accrual, department employed by, and an employee number.

An employee number is used by companies to control payroll processing. Two alternative employee numbering schemes are common for sequencing a payroll file. These are the Social Security number and an alphabetically sequenced employee number. The Social Security number satisfies most payroll processing requirements in that the number is unique, not too long, is known by an employee, and must be retained anyway for quarterly reports. The one disadvantage is that the Social Security listing does not sequence employees alphabetically. Consequently, many firms use an alphabetically sequenced employee numbering system to produce an alphabetic listing of names.

To simplify the assignment of an employee number to an employee, there are listings that show the average distribution of last names over a range of numbers. These listings allow numbers to be selected for new employees so that they fit into an alphabetized sequential file. Unfortunately, listings do not always work. For example, when a female employee marries during the fiscal year, either her payroll records must be shifted to a number that properly sequences her new name, or the file is in error for the remainder of the year. On occasion, all numbers for a region of a file are allocated. If a number is then required from the filled area, the file becomes out of sequence or requires an extensive adjustment.

New employee information is submitted to data entry on a *payroll change input form*. (Typical input forms are shown in Fig. 4-1.) These custom-printed input sheets contain space for all vital data to be entered into the system. To minimize errors in transcribing, it is desirable to use the same form (or a similar one) for existing employees as well as for new employees. Scribbled notes on memo pads or odd pieces of paper are apt to do more harm than good when updating employee records. After data entry has been completed, the input form is stamped to show the date data were submitted to computer processing. If an error is discovered during the next payroll period, the input document can be checked to assist in correcting the error.

Figure 4-2 flowcharts the preliminary master file update procedure. Keyed employee additions and changes update the most recent version of the payroll master file. In this instance, the most recent version means either the file resulting from the last processing of payroll or the last update of the master file—since the file can be updated more than once between weekly or bi-weekly payroll runs. In any event, the final version of the updated master file, which results from this preliminary activity, serves as an input to the actual processing of payroll.

The flowcharted system shows that the input master file and output master file are the same. The production of a new file can be accomplished in one of two ways. In one, the input change file can be sorted into the same sequence as that of the master file. The two files—input change and master—can then be merged to form a new output file. The other way is to randomly update the master file with the input change transactions. The resulting file is then copied onto an available disk pack. In either case, copies of the master file should be retained before and after updating. Then, if an error is found, it can be corrected and updating can be repeated.

Figure 4-3 illustrates a change report for a new employee. The change report is produced on ordinary stock computer paper, since it is a working document of temporary value. The report format indicates every change in the records of an existing employee. If an employee is new, employee master file records are printed. It is convenient to have the change report printed in the same sequence as the input documents, since the report can then be

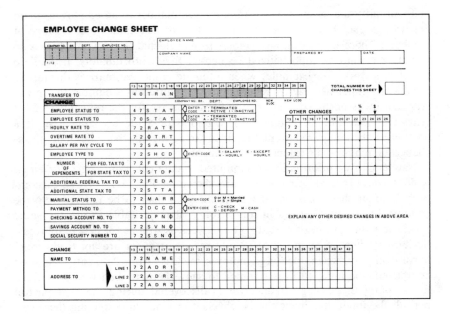

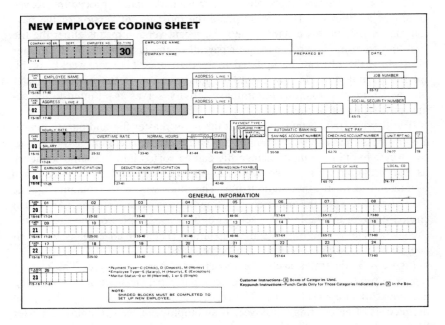

Fig. 4-1 Payroll change input forms

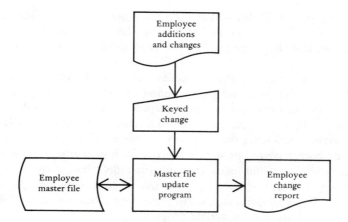

FIG. 4-2   Preliminary master payroll file update flowcharts

12/23/		N E W E M P L O Y E E R E P O R T			PAGE 37
E M P L O Y E E N A M E		PAYROLL CODES DEPT–EMP.#–DIST BEGIN	TAX INFORMATION EXM SIAC SOC SEC #	WAGES RATE REG. AMT	
JOHN Q. MC GILLICUDDY		91 90350 22 11/29/ 1224 S. W. JEFFERSON STREET	03 7401 540–34–1353 APARTMENT NO. 1239	1.3571 1234.55 SAINT AUGUSTINE, FLORIDA	

FIG. 4-3   Employee change report

edited manually without searching for the corresponding payroll change input sheet. This procedure offers the strongest reason for updating the master payroll file on a random basis, rather than sorting the input before updating.

Other employee change information is also printed on the employee change report. When new employees are placed in the file, an appropriate phrase such as "new employee" is prominently printed. When employee records are deleted from the file, these transactions are labeled "deleted." However, when an employee is terminated, the year-to-date and other master file information for the employee is usually left in the file at least until the end of the fiscal year, since periodic reports require the appearance of terminated employee records to reflect the entire year-to-date payroll balance. Therefore there is usually some provision for a termination code to indicate that an employee is no longer active. This code triggers the message "terminated," which appears alongside a terminated employee's records. On the other hand, it is often desirable to suppress the appearance of a terminated employee's records on reports produced during each payroll run. Some payroll groups prefer reports that show only employees who are active during the pay period. If this is the case, a separate code is provided and the message "suppressed" is printed to indicate that an employee's records are on file, but that the employee has not been active during the current pay period.

Often it is necessary to alter the dollar totals kept for an employee in the payroll master file. For example, an employee may have dropped from a union, but this fact may not have been recorded in the file when the employee's first paycheck was printed. Hence the standard union dues would have been charged. Following the discovery of this error, a special paycheck is prepared between payroll periods to account for improperly paid union dues. The corresponding dollar totals are altered to reflect the corrected paycheck. The employee's year-to-date records also require correction, based on this adjustment to the employee's check. All these steps should be accomplished by the preliminary master file update program.

4-2   INPUT TO THE PAYROLL APPLICATION

After changes to the payroll master file, the actual payroll run begins. *Time records* (prepared by hourly employees) are submitted to data entry. Records are usually some form of time card that has been completed by the employee and initialed by the employee's supervisor. Figure 4-4 illustrates a typical time card. Hours worked may be recorded as regular or overtime. The employee also records his or her name, employee number, date, equipment

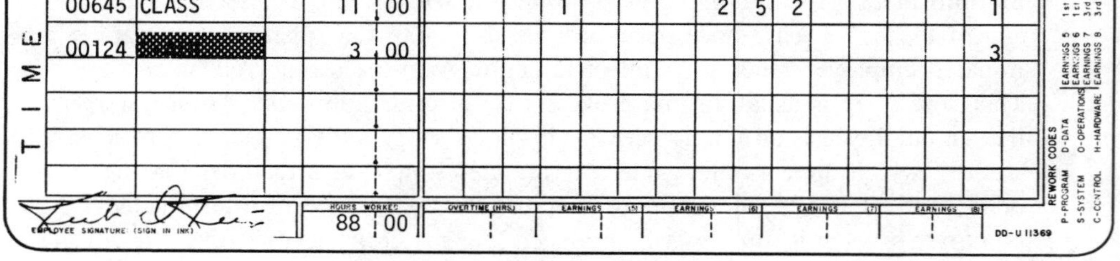

FIG. 4-4   Employee time card

used, project number, and any additional remarks. The form may also provide space for a supervisor's signature. Although payroll requires only the employee number and the hours worked, other computer applications for job costing and equipment utilization require additional data contained on the time card. Thus the time card serves more than one purpose for business computer systems.

If an employee is paid on the basis of a regular salary, no time card or other document is submitted to payroll for determination of hours worked. Rather, the employee master file contains salary information, and a salary or wage code is used to compute gross pay—except when salary must be adjusted to compensate for an unusual situation, such as sick leave or vacation. In this case, a salary adjustment document is required as input to processing.

Ideally, information on employee hours is batch controlled. For hourly employees, the normal control procedure is to total regular and overtime hours. This total is used to verify that the computer receives actual time card hourly figures. For salaried employees, the normal control procedure totals only the number of extra, or overtime, hours to be paid. Usually, no other control total is needed, since salaried employees will be paid according to the computer pay schedule, unless an employee's records contain a termination code. For salaried employees who receive variable pay such as commissions or expense account reimbursement, the normal control procedure is to prepare a batch slip showing the total of these variable payments.

Batch control information is keyed to a *lead record* (the first record in a batched set of records prepared for payroll input). This lead record usually contains information to appear on paychecks, such as the branch office submitting the employee time cards. Lead record information is used by the computer to check the accuracy and completeness of the batch of payroll records. Following the lead record, employee records are entered as input to processing. These records may be of variable length. One record might contain the employee's identification number and hourly pay information. Another record might consist of the employee's identification number, hourly pay information, and hourly sick time used.

4-3   THE PAYROLL SYSTEM

Figure 4-5 shows the processing of payroll. Inputs to the system consist of keyed data from time cards, batch control information, and the employee master file, updated by the preliminary master payroll file update. Outputs from the system include a completed employee master file, updated by time card information, and the following reports and documents:

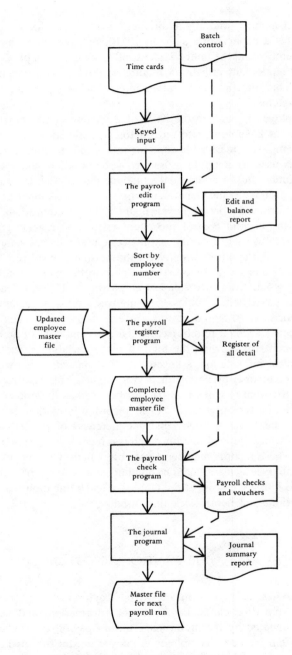

FIG. 4-5 Payroll processing flowchart

1. edit and balance
2. the payroll register
3. payroll checks and vouchers
4. the payroll journal

All reports carry forward the batch control total from the input lead record. Batch control balances are made for each of the four programs to allow a clear audit of the various processing stages.

Figure 4-6 shows possible contents of the payroll master file and input from time cards. The master file stores not only basic employee data (for example, name, address, and phone number), but also salary, wage, tax, and other current pay period detail—as well as running accumulations or year-to-date (YTD) fields since year-to-date figures are used to prepare quarterly and year-end reports. Whereas the contents of the payroll master file are extensive, detail from employee time cards is minimal. This information is used to update current and year-to-date fields within the master file. The remaining fields are updated by the preliminary master file update.

The Payroll Edit Program

The computer program that accepts time card input data is the *payroll edit program*. The first function of this program is to detect errors in the input data (for example, an invalid employee number, excessive hours worked, or an hourly employee showing no regular hours worked). If an error is detected, it is immediately printed to permit correction. If accumulated totals from individual records do not balance control totals contained on the lead record, the difference is also printed. Processing is discontinued at this point so that errors can be corrected. Once this is done, the edit is rerun to produce an error-free input file. Figure 4-7 shows an edit report produced by the payroll edit program.

Note that in the illustration regular hours worked, overtime hours worked, sick leave hours used, and vacation time hours used are summed to arrive at employee total hours. In addition, the column lead control is used to accumulate hours worked and hours of sick leave and vacation time. This accumulation is used in the balancing of control totals. Finally, the department number is entered alongside each employee entry. This information is recorded on the lead record, for placement alongside each employee input record contained in a batch.

The input file produced by the payroll edit program is recorded on magnetic tape or disk. Each employee record in the file contains data from employee time cards, plus information common to all employees extracted from the lead record.

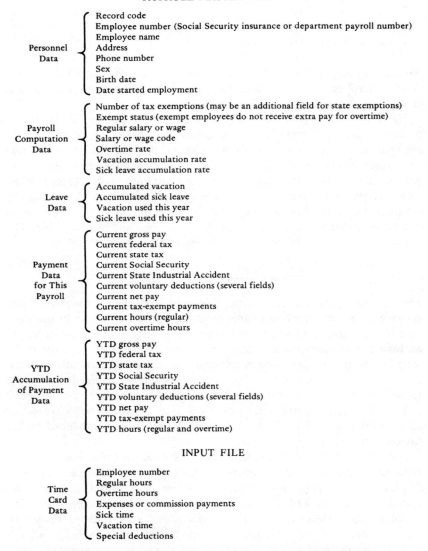

PAYROLL MASTER FILE

Personnel Data
- Record code
- Employee number (Social Security insurance or department payroll number)
- Employee name
- Address
- Phone number
- Sex
- Birth date
- Date started employment

Payroll Computation Data
- Number of tax exemptions (may be an additional field for state exemptions)
- Exempt status (exempt employees do not receive extra pay for overtime)
- Regular salary or wage
- Salary or wage code
- Overtime rate
- Vacation accumulation rate
- Sick leave accumulation rate

Leave Data
- Accumulated vacation
- Accumulated sick leave
- Vacation used this year
- Sick leave used this year

Payment Data for This Payroll
- Current gross pay
- Current federal tax
- Current state tax
- Current Social Security
- Current State Industrial Accident
- Current voluntary deductions (several fields)
- Current net pay
- Current tax-exempt payments
- Current hours (regular)
- Current overtime hours

YTD Accumulation of Payment Data
- YTD gross pay
- YTD federal tax
- YTD state tax
- YTD Social Security
- YTD State Industrial Accident
- YTD voluntary deductions (several fields)
- YTD net pay
- YTD tax-exempt payments
- YTD hours (regular and overtime)

INPUT FILE

Time Card Data
- Employee number
- Regular hours
- Overtime hours
- Expenses or commission payments
- Sick time
- Vacation time
- Special deductions

FIG. 4-6 Payroll master file and time card information

The Payroll Register Program

The payroll detail is next posted against the employee master file, which has already been updated by the preliminary master payroll file update. The term *posting* means using a master file to modify or to improve the contents

```
PAYROLL  EDIT                    DECEMBER  31,  19XX

DEPARTMENT    EMPNO                 HOURS    TOTAL    CONTROL

10212        83166
             REGULAR  HOURS         40                  40
             OVERTIME  HOURS                             0
             SICK  LEAVE  HRS.                           0
             VACATION  HRS.                              0
                EMPLOYEE  TOTAL              40          40

10212        90335
             REGULAR  HRS.          40                  80
             OVERTIME  HRS.         10                  10
             SICK  LEAVE  HRS.                           0
             VACATION  HRS.                              0
                EMPLOYEE  TOTAL              50          90

10212        75232
             REGULAR  HRS.          20                 110
             OVERTIME  HRS.                            10
             SICK  LEAVE  HRS.      20                  20
             VACATION  TIME                              0
                EMPLOYEE  TOTAL              40         140
```

FIG. 4-7 Payroll edit report

of a transaction file. (Posting is an old accounting term that describes the process of entering a detail figure in an accounting ledger; it implies verifying the correctness of the entry, as well as modifying the ledger.) For this application, posting is accomplished by the *payroll register program*. The file produced by this program is a combination of new payroll detail and employee master file stored data.

The register program is designed to serve four basic purposes.

1. Each new input record is checked for correctness. For example, some salaried employees are exempt from overtime pay. (They do not receive extra payment for working overtime as it is assumed that their normal salary is adequate to compensate for any overtime.) If overtime hours are submitted for an exempt employee, the detail is in error and a message to that effect is printed on the employee register. Other error messages include too much vacation time (more than an employee has earned), no time card for an active employee, and inaccurate special deductions such as for union dues. These errors cannot be detected by the payroll edit program since it does not reference the master file.

2. The program converts hourly information to gross pay, totals gross pay for an employee; and computes net pay after subtracting for taxes,

Social Security insurance, and voluntary deductions. Sometimes net pay becomes negative—another error condition. An alternative to printing this error is to reduce federal and state tax deductions or other deductions until net pay is exactly zero.

3. Having computed current payment information, the program computes year-to-date figures for an employee. The employee payroll master file contains year-to-date totals through the last payroll processing. New year-to-date figures are the sum of the old year-to-date and the current figures. Year-to-date figures are also used to determine whether an employee has paid enough Social Security withholding tax. Once the payment limit is reached, the deduction is discontinued.

4. Batch control totals of hours worked are balanced once more. This check establishes that input detail was processed completely and accurately.

The completed employee master file resulting from the register program contains information extracted from time cards, current payroll information computed in processing, and year-to-date payroll information updated in processing. In other words, it contains detail for printing payroll checks. From this file, the *payroll register* is printed. As shown by Figure 4-8, the register (quarterly register illustrated) is a printed record of detail in the completed employee master file. It includes the employee's department, employee number, name, job status, marital status, and gross and taxable in-

```
           YEAR-TO-DATE AND QUARTER EARNINGS      QUARTER ENDING JUNE 30, 19XX

DEPT LINE EMPNO EMPLOYEE NAME              STATUS    SOC SEC NO  MAR STATUS    SEX
    LAST GROSS  LAST FICA  THIS GROSS  THIS FICA     TAXABLE     NON TAX  QTR RENT  QUARTER GROSS

059 10510 80285                           PERM                  MARRIED    MALE
    2,184.00    113.58     4,368.00    227.16        4,368.00      .00       .00      2,184.00

030 10305 80594                           PERM                  SINGLE     MALE
    2,757.20    143.83     5,409.20    281.29        5,409.20      .00       .00      2,652.00

190 10103 80595                           PERM                  SINGLE     MALE
    1,710.00     88.92     3,420.00    177.84        3,420.00      .00       .00      1,710.00

060 10302 80765                           TERM                  MARRIED    MALE
      995.06     51.74       995.06     51.74          995.06      .00       .00          .00

190 10531 80815                           PERM                  MARRIED    MALE
    2,051.52    106.67     4,146.85    215.62        4,146.85      .00       .00      2,095.33

029 10999 80818                           TEMP                  MARRIED    MALE
    1,361.14     70.78     2,777.94    144.45        2,777.94      .00       .00      1,416.80

010 10417 81008                           PROB                  MARRIED    MALE
        .00       .00       258.75     13.46          258.75      .00       .00        258.75

059 10999 81033                           TEMP                  SINGLE     FEMALE
      703.00     36.55     1,484.29     77.18        1,484.29      .00       .00        781.29
```

FIG. 4-8 Payroll register

come. A register report produced during each regular processing run is similar to the quarterly register, but it contains a printed record of all the detail in the master file. Other typical detail (not shown in Figure 4-8) might be values used for tax purposes (such as the number of exemptions), hours worked during the period, and itemized deductions from gross pay. The payroll register becomes the legal document for the pay period, suitable for storage and review. It is a register of all activities since the printing of the last register during the previous payroll operation. Thus a continuing set of registers provides a complete documentation of changes in payroll during the year.

The Payroll Check Program

Since the file produced by the payroll register program contains detail for printing payroll checks, no computation is necessary by the payroll check program. However, the check program should accumulate hours worked and employee payments to balance back to the register program. The results of this balance should be printed on the last check form at the end of the printing operation. This check is overprinted with the word "void," so that no attempt will be made to cash it.

Figure 4-9 illustrates a typical payroll check and payroll voucher. (Checks are normally accompanied by a voucher, or statement, which records the time card information used to compute gross pay and the explanation for deductions from gross pay.) The sequential printing of checks is regulated by the sequencing of records in the master employee file. Checks are printed either by employee number or by employee last name within a department or branch.

When employee Social Security numbers are used to sequence a master employee file, alphabetic file sequencing becomes difficult. In this case, it is necessary to append to every employee record in the file a small field containing enough letters from an employee's last name to allow sequencing. The appended field is then sorted to provide alphabetic listings. Even then, a basic processing problem exists. Payroll details (from the edit program) do not contain the appended field data, nor can these data be added to the detail until employee records are posted to the employee master file. This means that the payroll register program must be split into two parts: one to update the master file with payroll details and another to print from the file after a sort to alphabetize employee records. This also means that the file to retain for the next payroll period is the one produced during update; the file to retain for preparing the payroll register and payroll checks is the one produced after the sort operation. The latter file is discarded after the payroll has been balanced and approved.

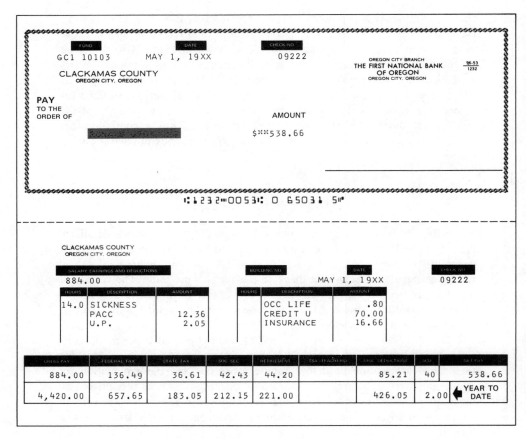

FIG. 4-9 Payroll check

The Payroll Journal Program

A *journal* report is used to supply current and year-to-date entries to the general ledger, which is the final consolidated accounting document. This ledger describes the overall financial status of a company. Journal reports, therefore, record total funds expended by source and by disposition. For example, total dollars for overtime and total dollars for sick leave are summarized by separate accounts on the general ledger. Similarly, total Social Security insurance deductions, union dues, and federal withholding taxes make up other accounts. Figure 4-10 illustrates a format followed in printing the payroll journal. Itemized by department or district (or some other breakdown), this report accumulates and totals—by general ledger code—wage payments or salaries, retirement deductions, Social Security insurance withholdings, federal and state tax withholdings, and so forth.

```
              PAYROLL  JOURNAL-BUDGET  REPORT
              DISTRICT  OR  DEPT,      JUNE  12,  19XX      PAGE  1

   GENERAL          DOLLAR
 LEDGER CODE        AMOUNT      DESCRIPTION

     110          3,201.85     SALARY

     121          3,000.00     SALARY

     210            685.50     SPECIAL  TESTING  WAGES

     610          1,250.00     REGULAR  PAY

    8511            325.00     RETIREMENT  DEDUCTIONS

    8512            733.25     SOCIAL  SECURITY  DEDUCTIONS

    8514          1,251.60     FEDERAL  WITHHOLDING  TAX

    8516            600.00     STATE  WITHHOLDING  TAX
```

FIG. 4-10 Payroll journal

4-4 PERIODIC REPORTS

Government regulations require quarterly reports on payroll activity. The 941-quarterly report of Social Security insurance withholdings (see Fig. 4-11) is prepared directly from the employee master file, using the last payroll file for the quarter as input. There are two ways (see Fig. 4-12) to accumulate quarter-to-date information. Alternative A requires that gross income for the quarter and year-to-date be added to Social Security insurance funds withheld during the quarter. After the printing of the 941-quarterly report, the quarter-to-date special fields must be reset to zero to begin the next quarter. Alternative B uses the payroll file from the preceding quarter as an additional input to the program. In alternative B of Figure 4-12, quarter-to-date figures are the difference between the two sets of year-to-date records.

At the end of each year, an additional report is required by federal and state governments. The W-2 withholding form must be prepared for every active employee. These forms are simple listings of gross taxable pay and the amounts withheld for state tax, federal tax, and FICA. This report is the prime justification for including an employee's address in the employee master file. Figure 4-13 illustrates the standard W-2 tax withholding form. Figure 4-14 flowcharts the processing required in preparing W-2 statements. As shown by this flowchart, once W-2 forms are printed, master records in the employee file are reset to zero. Terminated employees are then deleted

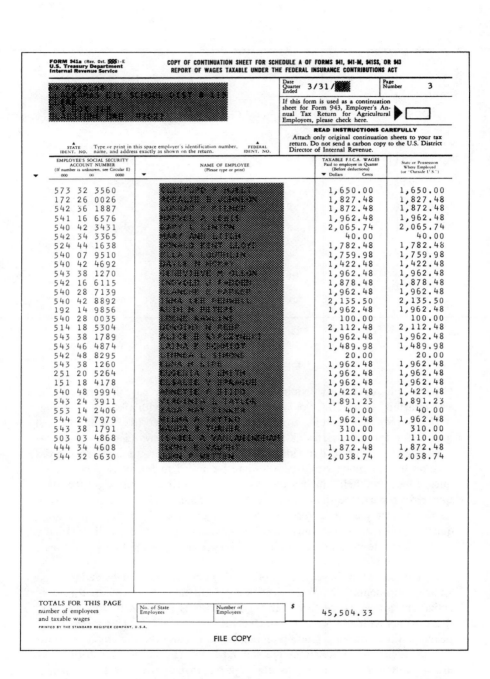

FORM 941a (Rev. Oct. 00005)-E
U.S. Treasury Department
Internal Revenue Service

COPY OF CONTINUATION SHEET FOR SCHEDULE A OF FORMS 941, 941-M, 941SS, OR 943
REPORT OF WAGES TAXABLE UNDER THE FEDERAL INSURANCE CONTRIBUTIONS ACT

Date Quarter Ended 3/31/XXXX

Page Number 3

If this form is used as a continuation sheet for Form 943, Employer's Annual Tax Return for Agricultural Employees, please check here.

READ INSTRUCTIONS CAREFULLY
Attach only original continuation sheets to your tax return. Do not send a carbon copy to the U.S. District Director of Internal Revenue.

STATE
IDENT. NO.   Type or print in this space employer's identification number,
name, and address exactly as shown on the return.   FEDERAL IDENT. NO.

EMPLOYEE'S SOCIAL SECURITY ACCOUNT NUMBER (If number is unknown, see Circular E) 000 00 0000	NAME OF EMPLOYEE (Please type or print)	TAXABLE F.I.C.A. WAGES Paid to employee in Quarter (Before deductions) Dollars Cents	State or Possession Where Employed (or "Outside U.S.")
573 32 3560		1,650.00	1,650.00
172 26 0026		1,827.48	1,827.48
542 36 1887		1,872.48	1,872.48
541 16 6576		1,962.48	1,962.48
540 42 3431		2,065.74	2,065.74
542 34 3365		40.00	40.00
524 44 1638		1,782.48	1,782.48
540 07 9510		1,759.98	1,759.98
540 42 4692		1,422.48	1,422.48
543 38 1270		1,962.48	1,962.48
542 16 6115		1,878.48	1,878.48
540 28 7139		1,962.48	1,962.48
540 42 8892		2,135.50	2,135.50
192 14 9856		1,962.48	1,962.48
540 28 0035		100.00	100.00
514 18 5304		2,112.48	2,112.48
543 38 1789		1,962.48	1,962.48
543 46 4874		1,489.98	1,489.98
542 48 8295		20.00	20.00
543 38 1260		1,962.48	1,962.48
251 20 5264		1,962.48	1,962.48
151 18 4178		1,962.48	1,962.48
540 48 9994		1,422.48	1,422.48
543 24 3911		1,891.23	1,891.23
553 14 2406		40.00	40.00
544 24 7979		1,962.48	1,962.48
543 38 1791		310.00	310.00
503 03 4868		110.00	110.00
444 34 4608		1,872.48	1,872.48
544 32 6630		2,038.74	2,038.74

TOTALS FOR THIS PAGE
number of employees
and taxable wages

No. of State Employees	Number of Employees	$ 45,504.33	

PRINTED BY THE STANDARD REGISTER COMPANY, U.S.A.

FILE COPY

FIG. 4-11 941-quarterly report

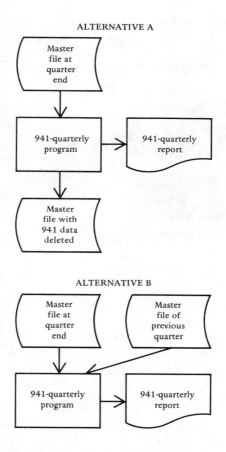

FIG. 4-12 Payroll periodic report flowchart

from the file. One possible exception to resetting year-to-date figures to zero is voluntary deductions, such as the United Fund. These deductions may require pay to be withheld for a specified period of time or up to a specified limit. As such, voluntary deductions may continue from one year to another, and the amount deducted must be retained.

As a final consideration, there is occasional demand for the preparation of an annual payroll recap showing final year-to-date figures. Since the last payroll register provides this information, the additional report has questionable value. Some payroll groups are accustomed to using separate employee ledgers during the year to show the detail of payroll information for every pay period to date. This is a carry-over from the days when payroll was

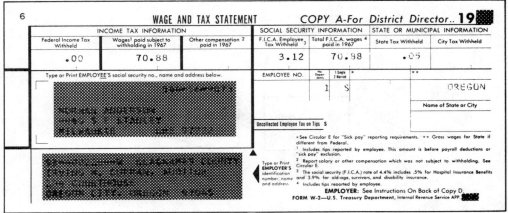

FIG. 4-13 W-2 tax withholding form

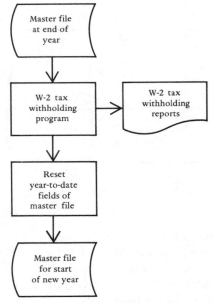

FIG. 4-14 Year-end processing flowchart

prepared on posting machines. These ledgers can be prepared by creating a computer file for every pay period. However, most companies find that once payroll staff overcome their initial insecurity about using computer systems, they no longer require ledgers for every employee and pay period.

4-5 MANAGEMENT IMPLICATIONS

No computer system does things in exactly the same way as its manual predecessor. Not only the results differ but also the methods of supplying data and the operating procedures. This is true of payroll and of every other system discussed in this text.

The most important objective of a computer payroll operation is faster processing of payroll checks. The benefits derived from faster processing can be surprising. One company was able to process checks several days earlier by using a computer. This capability was kept confidential and later proved to be an effective bargaining tool in annual union contract negotiations: When the company offered to distribute payroll checks earlier than specified in previous contracts, this believed concession greatly advanced the contract talks. Had this concession not been possible, more expensive concessions might have been necessary.

Another effect that can be expected from a computer payroll system is the reduction in labor (though small) and in the delay normal to preparing payroll reports. As we have seen, the average company must prepare a series of reports detailing payroll activities. These include reports for state and federal governments and for managers interested in wage and salary distributions. Most payroll reports can be prepared by the computer, saving days or weeks in the process. However, this improvement is not obtained without cost. The penalty is greater rigidity in payroll procedures. For instance, payroll deductions must be of a specified format and correctly coded, stored, and maintained if they are to function properly in the computer system. These restrictions can exasperate payroll personnel.

Management concern about payroll security increases when payroll is converted to the computer. Payroll detail—salary, benefits, and so forth—is considered very sensitive information by most companies. Employees are regularly instructed not to discuss their salary level with others, since disappointment and frustration can result when employees compare paychecks. Fortunately, the problem of security after conversion to a computer method of processing payroll is not serious. Data processing staff must be relatively discrete if they are to retain their jobs. Data entry staff are so busy encoding data that they seldom retain knowledge of what they process. In much the same way, a computer operator will be able to identify a processing error, but will generally not recall the meaning of the sentence containing the error. In sum, company experience with computer payroll systems has shown that (1) most employees already know as much about payroll detail as they want to know; (2) leakage of sensitive information from data processing is minimal in most installations; and (3) the initial concern for security is unwarranted.

The most important implication of a computer-operated payroll system is its impact on company employees. Since payroll is commonly the first application converted to the computer, every employee becomes part of the processing changeover. The quality of the computer-prepared payroll, especially the professional appearance of printed payroll checks, strongly affects employee appraisal of the computer system. If the payroll system functions well, systems implemented later are more likely to win employee acceptance and support. If the payroll system experiences difficulty (with million dollar payroll checks, for instance, and entire payroll runs called back for reprinting), the problem of employee acceptance becomes substantial. Subsequent computer systems will encounter opposition, even when they are well designed and implemented.

REVIEW OF IMPORTANT IDEAS

Payroll is one of the oldest and most common business computer systems. Many companies who use computers for a variety of purposes were introduced to data processing by this application.

Payroll can be prepared with a single master file, as opposed to several specialized reference files. The single-file approach may require somewhat more computer time, but payroll is an infrequent operation and any addition of time is small. The master file must be updated before time card information is entered into the computer. New employees should be added to the file, as well as corrections to the records of existing employees.

Time card information should be batched and controlled. Control totals are used to balance keyed detail from time cards. This balancing helps detect and reduce errors. The edit program should exhaustively check for other types of errors.

The other primary data processing programs are the payroll register program, which posts input detail to the master payroll file, and the payroll check program, which prints employee paychecks. Both programs require custom printed forms, since printed outputs are legal and permanent documents. After their preparation, a summary or journal report is printed for general ledger accounts.

Periodic reports are prepared for government regulating agencies. The two major examples are the 941-quarterly report, required by the Social Security Administration, and the W-2 withholding statement, used by employees in preparing their federal and state income tax forms. Other reports for internal accounting purposes are printed on a quarterly or an annual basis.

Management is concerned with payroll security and the quality of the designed and implemented computer payroll system. However, the real danger with payroll is that it exposes all employees in a company to the computer, in many cases for the first time. Even small design errors prompt employee questioning of the computer's ability to process data accurately. This questioning has led to poor and slow utilization of expensive computer facilities by many companies.

REVIEW QUESTIONS

1. What advantage is there in using a combination current and year-to-date employee master file in the processing of payroll detail?

2. What is accomplished by the preliminary master file update computer program?

3. What information is recorded on the employee change report? How is this information used?

4. What function is served by the lead record, which is placed in front of a batched set of payroll input records?

5. When an error is discovered by the payroll edit program and then corrected, why must the payroll detail be checked again by the edit program? What might occur if this practice were not followed by a firm?

6. What purposes are served by the payroll register program?

7. Should the employee master file be sequenced by employee number or by Social Security insurance number? What factors would determine your choice?

8. What are two ways to prepare quarter-to-date master payroll information as used to report 941 Social Security insurance withholdings?

EXERCISES

1. Flowchart a payroll computer application in which the current and year-to-date files are maintained separately. Explain the purpose served by each program shown on the flowchart.

2. Using Figures 4-1 through 4-3 as guides, design an employee change report. Show what information needs to be printed for new employees, deleted employee records, and employees who decide to terminate.

3. Flowchart how processing of payroll would work when the payroll register program is split into two parts: one to update the employee master file and another to print from a sort to alphabetize employee records.

4. Several banks advertise that they will process an entire company payroll provided that all employees open accounts at the bank. For a firm, what are the advantages and disadvantages of this banking service?

5

ACCOUNTS PAYABLE

The purpose of an accounts payable computer system is to pay for merchandise or services received from vendors. Most services and supplies are purchased "on account," rather than by cash payment at the time of purchase. Therefore a number of unpaid invoices accrue to a vendor. An accounts payable system is the logical opposite of an accounts receivable system—the company in this case is the customer rather than the supplier or vendor.

Prompt payment of outstanding invoices can be very important to the vendor, since money is needed to satisfy the vendor's creditors. To encourage prompt payment, most commercial vendors allow their customers cash discounts for paying a bill or invoice within a specified time. A *cash discount* is usually 2 percent of the total bill, although it can be much more. Vendors frequently exclude freight charges from their discounting procedures, since they must pay the full freight amount. Some vendors also attempt to collect interest for late payment as another method of forcing prompt payment. This practice is usually not very successful; customers either will not pay the interest charges or will take their business elsewhere.

At first glance, it might appear wise to pay every invoice promptly in order to obtain a vendor discount, thereby reducing the cost of the purchased merchandise. Most of the time this is what happens. Not every bill, however, should be paid as soon as possible, nor should every discount be taken. Companies profit through full utilization of capital. Every dollar available for immediate use improves return on investment. The longer a payment is delayed, the longer that amount of money is available for other purposes.

Since an unpaid bill does not normally draw interest, the delay in paying a bill can be viewed as an interest-free, short-term loan from the vendor. While this view has some obvious risks (a 2 percent discount for payment within 10 days yields approximately 36 percent annual interest), the practice of delay is quite common.

A main objective in the management of accounts payable is to determine when to pay as well as what amount to pay. When to pay is based partly on the invoice due date, which is determined by the recorded date of the invoice and the stated discount policy (usually printed on the face of the invoice). The computed discount is used to determine not only the net amount to be paid but also whether it is worth paying the invoice on time. Another objective is to provide management with a way of allocating available cash. (Cash flow considerations are discussed in the management implications section of this chapter.) A third objective of the overall system is discussed in Chapter 6: the ability of a firm to reconcile its cancelled payment checks. Cancelled checks, returned from a bank, are proof of payment. A final objective of the payables system is to allow evaluation of company vendors, which aids in selecting the best sources for goods and services.

5-1   INITIAL INPUT TO THE PAYABLES SYSTEM

The initial input to accounts payable are batches of invoices supplied by accounting. Before explaining how initial input is received, it is necessary to review the documents that accompany the purchase of material from a vendor. First, a written *purchase order* is usually sent from the customer to the vendor. When goods are shipped, a *packing slip* and a *bill of lading* are included. The packing slip shows the quantity shipped, but usually does not have the dollar charges recorded on it. The bill of lading only shows the freight charges. Dollar charges are submitted by the vendor to the customer on an *invoice,* which is mailed to the customer after the goods are shipped. Finally, at the end of the month, the vendor may prepare *a billing statement* for each customer, showing unpaid invoices.

Vendors most often consider the invoice their legal request for payment. This document usually has the terms of purchase (for example, 2 percent, net 30) printed on its face. In some cases, the vendor requests payment on receipt of goods, based on the date printed on the packing slip. In other cases, the vendor asks for payment on the basis of the date recorded on a monthly billing statement.

There are a large number of vendor invoices to process in the payables system. Moreover, every vendor has a personal idea of what constitutes an ideal invoice form. As a result, payables forms vary considerably in size, layout, information content, and readability. It is difficult for data entry personnel to search for desired information on widely varying forms and also attempt to key input records at a reasonable speed. Therefore a common practice is to extract by hand vital data from the invoice, before it is submitted to data entry, and to record this information on a standardized *detail slip*. This detail slip is then stapled to the invoice it represents, and both documents are sent to data entry.

It is also desirable to compare charges on the vendor invoice to those on the company purchase order, on the receiving report, or on a return-for-credit slip. A purchase order shows what goods were ordered from a vendor and the actual or estimated charges for these goods. The receiving report then shows what goods were actually received by a business. Finally, a return-for-credit slip indicates what quantity of goods were sent back to the vendor. This comparison between vendor invoice charges and purchasing and receiving information can be done automatically, as described in Chapter 12, or the charges can be manually verified. In the latter case, someone must be responsible for checking and initialing the detail slip to show approval.

Figure 5-1 shows that the detail slip requires information not found on the vendor invoice, such as vendor identification number and the date payment is due. This information must be provided by the payables clerk, who must also calculate the discount. When the batch of invoices is finally packaged and sent to data entry, the detail slips should be completed and ready for immediate input to processing.

When vendor invoices are batched, the payables clerk should prepare a batch control slip by adding the net amount due from every invoice. The adding machine tape is later used for comparing computer totals to input totals. If there are errors in addition or in the input of payables detail, this slip helps locate them.

The batch control slip normally is processed as a control record. It records the batch number, the branch office that sent the batch to central accounting (if there are several branches), and the batch control slip total. This record is the first in the set prepared for the batch of invoices. It will be followed by input records for each invoice in the batch. In addition, special input records may be prepared for changes of vendor name and address or to set up records for new vendors. Usually, these are prepared at a different time to avoid confusing data entry personnel.

5-2   THE ACCOUNTS PAYABLE SYSTEM

Figures 5-2 and 5-3 illustrate the processing stages of the accounts payable system. Figure 5-2 flowcharts the stages in preparing the accumulated pending invoice file. Vendor invoices are processed daily or every other day,

```
BRANCH OFFICE _____      DATA ENTRY
                                 STAMP
BATCH NUMBER   _____

VENDOR NUMBER _____

INVOICE NUMBER _____

INVOICE DATE   _____

DUE DATE       _____

OVERRIDE CODE  _____

DOCUMENT CODE _____
```

```
G.L. ACCOUNT NUMBER _____    $AMOUNT _____

G.L. ACCOUNT NUMBER _____    $AMOUNT _____

G.L. ACCOUNT NUMBER _____    $AMOUNT _____

G.L. ACCOUNT NUMBER _____    $AMOUNT _____
```

```
APPROVED FOR                     INVOICE TOTAL_____
PAYMENT BY:
                                 DISCOUNT     _____

                                 NET $AMOUNT  _____
```

FIG. 5-1 Accounts payable detail slip

enlarging the pending invoice file. Figure 5-3 flowcharts the stages in producing voucher-checks, which are payable to vendors. This second processing arrangement, distinct from daily processing, is run weekly or biweekly.

Inputs to daily processing of vendor invoices consist of accounts payable detail slips, batch control records, and vendor change records. File input includes the *vendor master file* and the *pending invoice file,* produced by the last daily processing run. Both of these files are updated during daily processing of invoices. In addition to these two updated files, the following reports are produced:

1. edit report
2. vendor update report
3. payables merge report

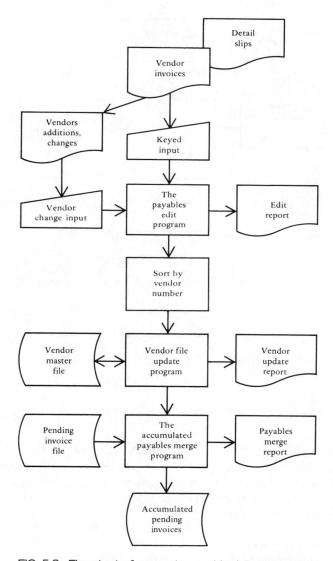

FIG. 5-2 Flowchart of accounts payable daily processing

After the payables merge report is produced, the application is stopped to await new invoice detail to enlarge the pending invoice file. Or, processing advances to the next processing operation—the production of voucher-checks for vendors. This second operation requires cutoff date information

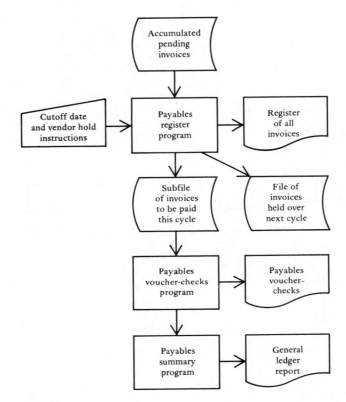

FIG. 5-3 Flowchart of accounts payable check processing

and vendor hold instructions in addition to the accumulated pending invoice file. *Cutoff date instructions* specify which pending invoices should be made due and payable. *Vendor hold instructions* are entered into processing in order to defer payment to vendors. The printed reports and documents produced by this operation are:

1. payables register
2. payables voucher-checks
3. general ledger report

Figure 5-4 shows the typical contents of the accumulated pending invoice file. Most of the detail to the payables system must be keyed, verified, and edited. For this reason, the actual writing of voucher-checks is kept separate from careful machine and visual edit of the pending invoice file. The vendor master file adds vendor number, name and address, and discount percentage

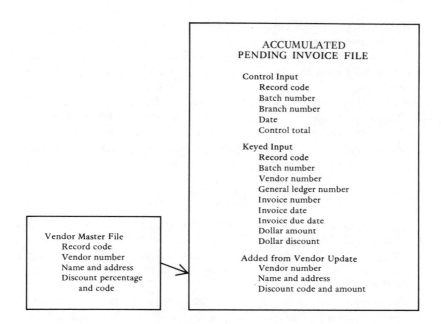

FIG. 5-4 Typical file contents of accumulated pending invoices

to the invoice input file. Lastly, a special field (not shown) must be added to the file if vendor hold instructions are used.

The Payables Edit Program

Every well-designed business computer application has an edit program as its first step or early in the sequence of computer operations. An initial edit of keyed payables input serves three basic functions in an accounts payable system:

1. It balances the detail dollar figures to batch control totals (if totals do not match, an error message is printed).
2. It examines the input stream of data for other detectable errors—invalidity, improper kinds of data in improper fields, missing information, excessive discounts, and wrong due dates, for example.
3. It converts the keyed input into the first of a series of ordered and accurate computer files.

If the edit program is not too large and complex, it may be able also to edit changes in vendor names and addresses. Vendor change instructions are read into the computer along with the invoice detail. However, if the edit program is large, vendor corrections and additions will have to be edited by a separate program.

The edit program produces a computer file, which is stored on magnetic tape or disk. This file contains batch numbers and branch office numbers obtained from the batch control lead record and copied onto every detail record for every invoice in a batch. As shown in Figure 5-5, because of this distribution of batch and branch numbers, it is possible to identify the source of detail submitted to the computer. Each detail record will also contain a code indicating what the original document was: credit memo, regular charge, or account adjustment. This code assists in editing the payables file.

The Vendor File Update Program

Next, the file of transactions produced by the edit program is sorted by vendor number. If changes to the vendor file are included in processing, the sort program should place them in front of the invoice records. This permits the updating of vendor records before the vendor file is used to validate the transaction detail.

After vendor changes and additions have been made, the invoice detail is processed. Processing consists of testing the validity of the vendor numbers. That is, each transaction record must match an active vendor on the vendor master file. If an unknown vendor number occurs, an error message is printed. Incorrect vendor numbers must be corrected by a new vendor record or by changing the invalid vendor number in the transaction record.

Other information may also be obtained from the vendor file. As indicated, the allowable vendor discount is usually computed by hand before the invoice is sent to data entry. However, if the vendor consistently offers a standard discount, as most of them do, it may be possible to extract this information from the vendor master file, rather than computing it manually and entering it each time an invoice is processed. If information is extracted,

				ACCOUNTS PAYABLE INPUT EDIT REPORT JANUARY 19, 19XX			BRANCH 082 BATCH 1142 PAGE 1
VENDOR NUMBER	RECORD CODE	INVOICE NUMBER	G.L. ACCOUNT NUMBER	$AMOUNT /ACCOUNT	$TOTAL INVOICE	ERROR MESSAGE	
112	1	621-35G	351	200.00			
			357	75.00			
			507	12.75	287.75	NO DISCOUNT	
17095	1	XYZ - 23.4	425	1,350.00		DUE DATE	
			507	175.50	1,525.50		
BATCH TOTAL		CONTROL = 1,823.25			1,813.25	BALANCE ERROR	

FIG. 5-5 Payables edit report

discounting is automatic, except in those cases where there is a special reason to compute the discount by hand. This will not only reduce the data entry load, but also eliminate mistakes in discount calculations—where errors are difficult to detect.

As shown in Figure 5-6, the vendor update report indicates changes or additions to the vendor master file. Any errors detected are also shown. The report also prints the total dollar payables due (not shown), as a means of balancing the file of transactions to the accumulated total of all batch control slips in the original input data.

The Accumulated Payables Merge

By now the payables transaction file should be in good condition. The majority of errors should have been detected and corrected, or plans should have been made for offsetting the erroneous entries. After the file is merged with other pending vendor invoices, the accumulated file is set aside for the next collection of invoices, or until the second half of the payables system: the preparation of vendor payment checks. The merge program should accumulate and print the total of pending invoices and record any adjustments (the records entered into the system to compensate for earlier mistakes). The total shown on the payables merge report should then balance to external audit controls.

The portion of the payables system described so far can be updated frequently, and it should be. Payment checks are usually prepared on a regular basis, but not oftener than once a week or twice a month. However, if the preliminary part of the system is updated whenever there are adequate batches of invoices, there will be no last-minute bottleneck of error corrections to delay the second part of the system. In short, the edit, update, and merge programs are run in series almost daily, while the rest of the system runs every week or two.

```
          ABC CORPORATION
          VENDOR UPDATE REPORT
          MARCH 1, 19XX

 NUMBER   VENDOR NAME            STREET ADDRESS        CITY,STATE                  DATE        AMOUNT

   112    BANK OF HONG KONG      52 FIFTH AVE          PORTLAND, OREGON 97201   720331      5,000.00
   107    BEEHIVE OFFICE SUPPLY  104 WEST 300 SOUTH    SLC, UTAH 84112          720331          9.92
   110    COMMERCIAL SECURITY BANK 82 WEST BROADWAY    SLC, UTAH 84102          720331      1,000.00
   109    CONTINENTAL FOODS      3302 SOUTH 400 WEST   SLC, UTAH 84182          720331         82.00
   108    FIRST SECURITY BANK    10 SOUTH MAIN         SLC, UTAH 84111          720331      1,789.44
     0    INTERMTN APPLIANCE SUPPLY P.O BOX 1406       SLC, UTAH 84001               0
   104    MOUTAIN BELL TELEPHONE 45 WEST 200 SOUTH     BOUNTIFUL, UTAH 84110    720331         68.54
   102    RASMUSSEN DISTRIBUTING CO 2315 KIESEL ST.    OGDEN, UTAH 84401        720331         81.30
     0    SCHREYER.S INC.        28 WEST FIRST SOUTH   SLC, UTAH 84111               0
     0    TURF EQUIPMENT CO.     P.O. BOX 2188         SLC, UTAH 84001               0
   111    UNITED CALIFORNIA BANK 7869 LA HABRA DR.     LONG BEACH, CAL. 98401   720331      2,450.50
     2
```

FIG. 5-6 Vendor update report

Besides printing the total of pending invoices, the merge program should compute and print the amount of cash needed to pay pending invoices. *Computed totals should be provided for more than one payment cycle.* For example, the payables merge report should show how much cash it will take to pay outstanding invoices when checks are prepared on the fifth of the month, the amount needed to pay invoices due by the twenty-fifth, and the amount needed to pay by the fifth of the next month. In addition to computed cash totals, the report should show the cash discount obtained if payments are made on time. This information can be used by the payables staff to establish the best use of company cash resources.

The Payables Register

When approval is given to prepare vendor checks, the payables system must be told how many invoices to pay. This is accomplished by specifying a *cutoff date.* In the transaction records, the due dates range from past due to sometime far in the future. Information on available cash aids in deciding on the cutoff date to use. A cutoff date therefore determines which invoices will be paid and which will be held for payment at another time.

Sometimes it is necessary to defer payments to certain vendors. For example, vendors may owe the company money and be asked to pay their bills first. Or, material supplied may be defective and payment may be withheld while a settlement is negotiated. In any event, provisions should be made to stop payment to specific vendors. These *vendor hold instructions,* together with the payment cutoff data, are submitted to processing by the payables staff.

Besides selecting the invoices to be paid, the payables register program should list all invoices in the pending file and indicate whether they are to be paid at this time or held over. Figure 5-7, an accounts payable register listing, shows that those invoices to be paid are flagged, usually by an asterisk printed in an obvious place. If payment to a vendor is purposely delayed, this fact should also be flagged. Finally, the total amount due and the total being paid should be computed and printed for each vendor.

Some companies allow an override to the due date cutoff provision, so that even though a due date will not occur for some time, the invoice can be paid. This is true whether there is a discount to be taken or not. Some common examples of this type of payment are lease charges for autos and legal fees. The inclusion of an override code at the time the invoice is keyed will cause it to be paid during the next check cycle, regardless of the due date.

Since the register program selects invoices to be paid during a check-writing cycle, the input file of pending transactions is split into two output

```
DATE  8/12/--                        ACCOUNTS PAYABLE TRIAL BALANCE                         PAGE  2
                                            AUGUST 12, 19--

VENDOR          VENDOR NAME                    INVOICE                                        DIST
NUMBER                                  NUMBER      DATE      DUE DATE    GROSS      DISC      AMOUNT

10001-0         ABBOTT HARDWARE         165431    6/10/--    --/07/20     50.00      1.50     48.50*
10001-0         ABBOTT HARDWARE         175342    6/14/--    --/08/01     75.00       .75     74.25

                VENDOR TOTAL                                             125.00      2.25     122.75

20302-0         BAKER BUILDING CO       005613    6/10/--    --/07/15    100.00      1.00     99.00*
20302-0         BAKER BUILDING CO       007400    6/20/--    --/07/22     75.00      1.50     73.50*

                VENDOR TOTAL                                             175.00      2.50     172.50

20612-1         CARPENTERS INC          526134    6/15/--    --/07/25     75.00      1.50     73.50*

                VENDOR TOTAL                                              75.00      1.50     73.50

20752-3         CAYLITE HEAT CO         111246    5/20/--    --/06/20     75.50      1.51     73.99*
20752-3         CAYLITE HEAT CO         111251    6/03/--    --/07/03     19.00       .00     19.00*

                VENDOR TOTAL                                              94.50      1.51     92.99

20962-9         ELECTRIC SUPPLY         006668    6/10/--    --/07/10    175.00      3.50     171.50*

                VENDOR TOTAL                                             175.00      3.50     171.50

40816-9         KILLGAARD PARTS         100322    6/25/--    --/07/25   2,000.00    40.00    1,960.00*

                VENDOR TOTAL                                           2,000.00    40.00    1,960.00

50406-0         LARSON BUILDERS         636366    6/10/--    --/12/15    100.00      2.00     98.00
50406-0         LARSON BUILDERS         636380    6/10/--    --/12/15    100.00      2.00     98.00

                VENDOR TOTAL                                             200.00      4.00     196.00


                GRAND TOTAL                                           6,764.50   137.76    6,626.74
```

FIG. 5-7 Accounts payable register listing

files. These are an updated pending file, which contains invoices held over for later payment, and a file of transactions to be paid this cycle. The dollar amount for each file should be accumulated and balanced with established audit controls.

Payables Voucher-Checks

The subfile of invoices to be paid, together with the vendor master file, is used to prepare checks for the vendors. The voucher portion of the printed check should list all invoices being paid by the check and the amount for each invoice after the discount. This information aids the vendor in reconciling the check with receivable records. Usually, the vendor is fairly lenient about allowing discounts, so long as errors or delays are not too great. However, if the vendor cannot determine how the final payment figure was computed, the entire discount may be rejected and full payment demanded.

Check design and printing are discussed further in the next chapter. The process of reconciling cancelled checks is also covered there. A voucher-check is shown in Figure 5-8. The amount paid has the support of considerable detail. The vendor should be able to reconcile his or her accounts with the detail printed on this voucher.

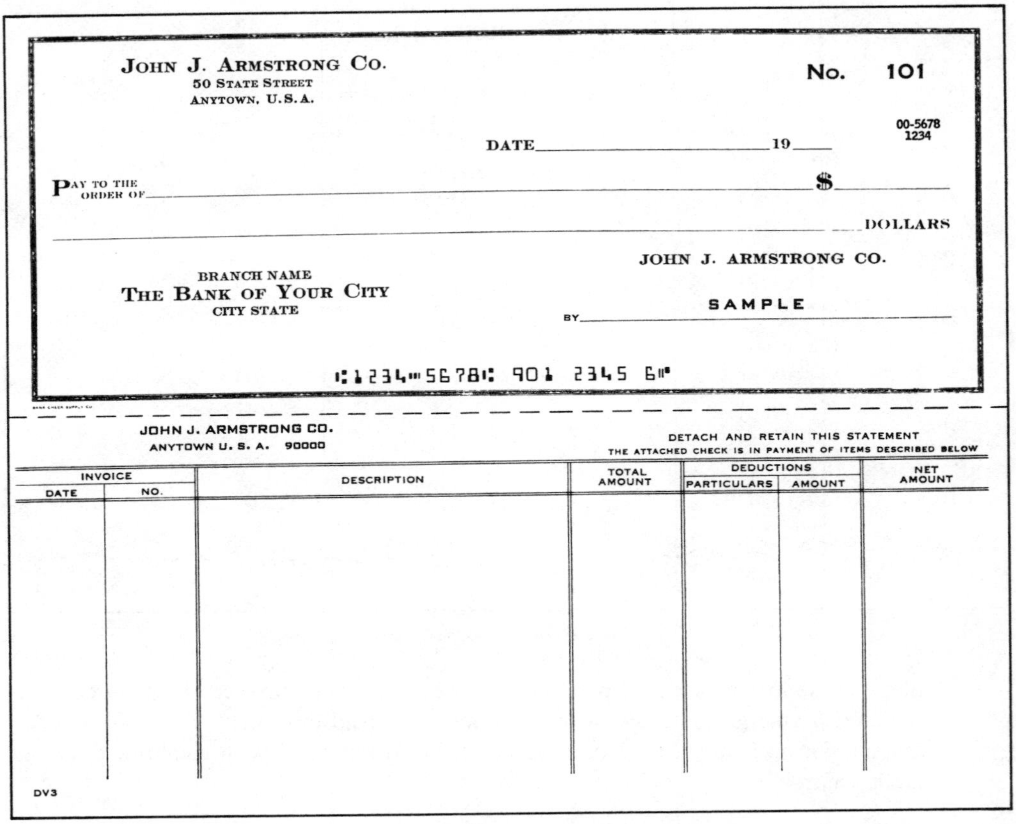
JOHN J. ARMSTRONG CO.
50 STATE STREET
ANYTOWN, U.S.A.

No. 101

00-5678
1234

DATE ______ 19___

PAY TO THE ORDER OF ______ $ ______

______ DOLLARS

JOHN J. ARMSTRONG CO.

BRANCH NAME
THE BANK OF YOUR CITY
CITY STATE

SAMPLE
BY ______

⑆1234⑈5678⑆ 901 2345 6⑈

JOHN J. ARMSTRONG CO.
ANYTOWN U. S. A. 90000

DETACH AND RETAIN THIS STATEMENT
THE ATTACHED CHECK IS IN PAYMENT OF ITEMS DESCRIBED BELOW

INVOICE		DESCRIPTION	TOTAL AMOUNT	DEDUCTIONS		NET AMOUNT
DATE	NO.			PARTICULARS	AMOUNT	

DV3

FIG. 5-8 Accounts payable voucher-check

Other Payables Reports

It is possible and often desirable to summarize all payment information on a form suitable for posting to the general ledger. The original input documents that were keyed and edited contain line numbers from the company chart of accounts (the set of account numbers that are used to classify financial data by department of function within a business). The freight portion of an invoice, for example, may be posted to one account number, and the merchandise portion to another. The chart of accounts numbers make it possible to print a summary report showing the total amounts to be posted to all ledger accounts. It may also be possible to determine the correct general ledger account number by another characteristic, such as the vendor number. For instance, typewriter repair services would always use the same general ledger account number. In this case, the keying of the ledger account number can be avoided, thereby reducing the work load and the chance for error.

Payables information has other possible uses, such as evaluating vendors. Information used in evaluation includes the average delay from ordering until delivery; the frequency of ordering (useful for deciding to order in bulk); the average and total value of orders placed with a vendor; and the discounts allowed. It is easier for a company to deal with a vendor if it can be pointed out that the vendor's dealings with the company are worth many thousands of dollars. This knowledge may enable a business to obtain unusually good discounts or payment terms.

5-3 MANUAL PROCESSING OF INVOICE FILE COPIES

To best support the computer processing of payables, it is necessary to have a systematic approach to handling vendor invoices. As started earlier, invoices should be attached to payables detail slips, which show the essential information to be entered as input. The batch number should also be recorded on this slip, so that any data in the payables file can be traced to the invoice or vice versa. The flowchart in Figure 5-9 illustrates how vendor invoices can be processed manually after data have been recorded on detail slips.

When the payables staff are through with the invoices, the invoices are placed in labeled file folders, one folder per vendor. If there is no folder, data processing should be informed about a new vendor. A label for the folder can then be typed. This procedure ensures that the vendor file is as up-to-date as possible. If the address on the invoice does not match the label on the file folder, data processing should be notified of the change in vendor

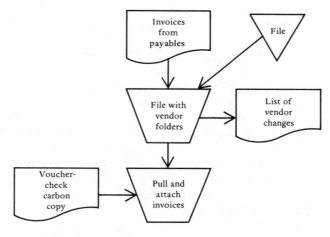

FIG. 5-9 Manual filing procedure for vendor invoices

address. Again, a new file label should be prepared. The invoices are then placed in this file folder, by invoice number sequence, for easy access.

When the vendor voucher-checks are printed, the detail on the voucher portion is used to locate the invoices in the folders and to verify the information printed by the computer. This ensures that the right vendor is being paid the right amount for the right merchandise. The invoices that appear on the voucher should then be selected from the folder and stapled to a carbon copy of it. This places in one group all material relevant to the paying of the vendor, so that later inquiries and audits can be handled quickly. Stapled forms are filed in the back of the vendor folder.

5-4 MANAGEMENT IMPLICATIONS

The accounts payable system is one place where a company can manage its cash flow, since the system entails reports on how much money is due vendors, when it is due, and the discounts to be saved by prompt payment. Other factors to consider are what money is available and what will it cost to borrow more. It is also possible to predict the amount of cash to be received from company customers through the accounts receivable system (see Chapter 8). If this prediction is as good as the computation of how much is needed to pay vendors, the accounting staff can estimate both the supply of and the demand for capital.

An important managerial function is to weigh the cost of obtaining capital against the advantages of paying most or all of the pending payables invoices. Most companies have lines of credit that they use to obtain short-term loans. However, short-term credit is expensive, and it may be better to delay paying some vendor invoices, even if this delay means a loss of discounts. The accounts payable system, in other words, provides the senior accounting staff with the information they need to decide how invoices are to be paid.

Much of the effort to manage or to modify the supply of or the demand for capital is complicated by company policies relating to payables. One of these is to kite payments to vendors—to mail them before money has been deposited to cover the checks. It is assumed that funds will be available before the vendors deposit the checks and they clear the banks. Sometimes, checks are held a day or two to ensure that funds will be available; this delay may lead to a dispute between the buyer and seller over the allowance for prompt payment discounts. Some invoices may be withheld from payment until satisfactory resolution of a dispute over the quality or the quantity of goods shipped and received. Finally, some invoices may be paid ahead of schedule, while others are held back.

All of these activities complicate the average computer payables operation, making it difficult to prepare an accurate projected cash requirements report. The payables staff often discover that they have more difficulty reconciling the results of their activity with the computer than they do convincing the vendor that their actions were necessary. This causes considerable communications problems between the payables staff and data processing personnel. These problems are often unresolved unless the overall payables operation is reviewed and revised to meet the needs of both parties.

As this chapter has shown, the design of a basic payables system is not difficult. However, the design of a truly responsive system is another matter. The system must be flexible enough to serve the needs of the payables staff. It must also be able to control expenditures for outstanding payables. For most companies, flexibility and control evolve as the first payables system becomes obsolete or cumbersome and more mature methods of managing are developed. In all probability, a payables system will be substantially revised or completely replaced as systems analysts and accountants develop better methods of processing payables.

REVIEW OF IMPORTANT IDEAS

The accounts payable system is designed to pay vendor invoices at the most appropriate time. This time is determined by the invoice due date; the amount of discount allowed by the vendor; and the availability of cash, either actual or anticipated, to cover the cost of the accounts payable.

Vendor invoices are batched and submitted to the computer every day, even though voucher-checks are prepared only every week or two. By scheduling the work load on a daily basis, a careful edit of input data is permitted and bottlenecks are avoided.

Vendor voucher-checks are prepared by the payables system, which indicates the invoices to be paid. Vendor discounts are calculated by the computer and serve as one criterion of whether to pay an outstanding invoice.

A carbon copy of the voucher-check is compared to the manual folder file of vendor invoices to ensure that the correct vendor is paid for received merchandise. Invoices should be stapled to the carbon to provide a permanent record of payment.

Senior accounting staff are able to use cash requirement information provided by daily processing of invoices to determine which vendor invoices to pay and whether short-term loans offer a cash advantage. Availability of cash is used to establish the cutoff date for splitting the payables pending file.

REVIEW QUESTIONS

1. Why is it not a wise company practice to pay every outstanding invoice when it is first received?

2. Describe the purchase order, the packing slip, the bill of lading, the invoice, the billing statement, and the voucher-check. Which of these documents accompany first party compliance to a purchase transaction, and which accompanies second party compliance?

3. How does a company determine whether it is being billed correctly for received merchandise or being billed incorrectly for merchandise that was not ordered, ordered but not received, or received but returned?

4. What three main functions are served by the edit program in the accounts payable computer application?

5. What must be done if an incorrect vendor number is found during processing?

6. Why should computed totals for more than one payment period be printed on the payables merge report?

7. Prior to the printing of voucher-checks, the pending file of invoice transactions is split into two parts. Why is this done?

8. What information is printed on the voucher portion of a voucher-check? How is this information used by the company? By the vendor?

9. Why is flexibility important in the design of the accounts payable computer application?

EXERCISES

1. The payables system described in this chapter does not include one very desirable feature: the ability to automatically pay recurring billings such as auto leases or property mortgages. How would you modify the payables system to support this feature?

2. Compare and contrast the accounts payable system with the payroll computer application. In what ways are the two applications similar? In what ways do they differ?

3. Even though a vendor voucher-check has been printed, a company might decide to hold back the cash payment to a vendor. How might this situation be handled by the accounts payable system? Would your solution work if the business decided to tear up the check? If not, what solution would?

6

CHECK WRITING
AND
CHECK
RECONCILIATION

Several computer applications produce bank checks as a major product during processing. Among such systems discussed in this text are payroll, accounts payable, and fixed assets. The payment of commissions and expenses to members of the sales force also requires check writing. Profit sharing in a company suggests yet another possible need for check writing.

Because of these many possibilities, standard techniques are usually developed for check-writing systems and programs. If possible, a standard check-writing application should be integrated with a standard check-reconciliation application. The former application produces a check; the latter is used to reconcile that the check has been properly cancelled. Standardized applications reduce the possibility for confusion and error. To further prevent confusion and error, standards should also be adopted for the design of the check and its accompanying voucher. Finally, manual processing of the checks, the voucher, and the carbon copies of each should also be standard procedures.

This chapter describes standard computer procedures for check-writing and check-reconciliation systems. Standards for manual processing of check materials are also discussed. Finally, the chapter reviews some of the considerations of check design.

6-1   THE CHECK-WRITING SYSTEM

Figure 6-1 shows a flowchart for the check-writing computer application. As shown, several processing stages are required besides the production of

91

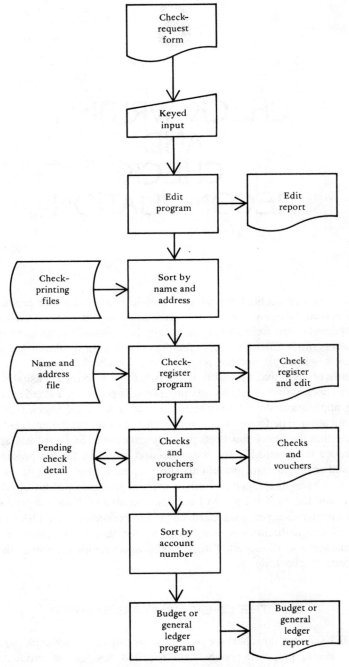

FIG. 6-1 Check-writing system flowchart

check and voucher documents. Inputs to the system (other than keyed *check-request forms*) consist of:

- *check-printing files,* if checks are printed directly from a preprocessed file
- *name and address master files,* which are used to validate the account number for which the check is written
- *a pending check-detail file,* which stores written checks that have not yet been returned by a bank

Outputs from the system (other than check and voucher documents) include the *check-detail file,* which is used in check reconciliation, and three reports:

1. edit report
2. check register and edit
3. budget or general ledger summary

Check-Request Input and the Edit Program

Besides the previously mentioned payroll, accounts payable, sales force, and profit-sharing checks, checks are occasionally needed for travel expenses, sudden cash needs, cash dividends, and miscellaneous expenses. At times, checks are prepared in advance. For example, an employee may be paid a termination check, even though regular payroll processing is not due for a week or more. An employee may also receive a manually prepared check when there is a need for confidence, such as the payment of an executive bonus. A vendor may require a cash payment upon delivery of goods. Lastly, cash is needed to cover expenditures too small to warrant the preparation of a purchase order. For example, an employee may need to obtain a dozen tablets of computer coding paper for a total cost of ten dollars. If the cost of preparing a purchase order is also ten dollars, the net cost of the minor purchase would be twenty dollars, with half the cost administrative. Special checking accounts solve these problems. These accounts are called *imprest, revolving,* or *petty-cash* accounts. In many cases, they are manually operated and controlled, and the checks are manually prepared.

Most companies write more checks manually than they like to. One reason for this is that most computer check-writing systems are involved and take too long to produce a single check. The system described in this chapter is both fast and simple. It can be used as often as needed to prepare various types of checks. The major advantage of a computer check-writing system is that it makes check reconciliation and cash control simpler. Otherwise, check detail must be prepared manually and then transformed into machine-readable input to provide the necessary check-detail files for check reconciliation. This is a waste of both employee time and company resources.

The customary input for small-value checks to a computer check-writing system is the *check requisition.* Figure 6-2 illustrates this form. The indi-

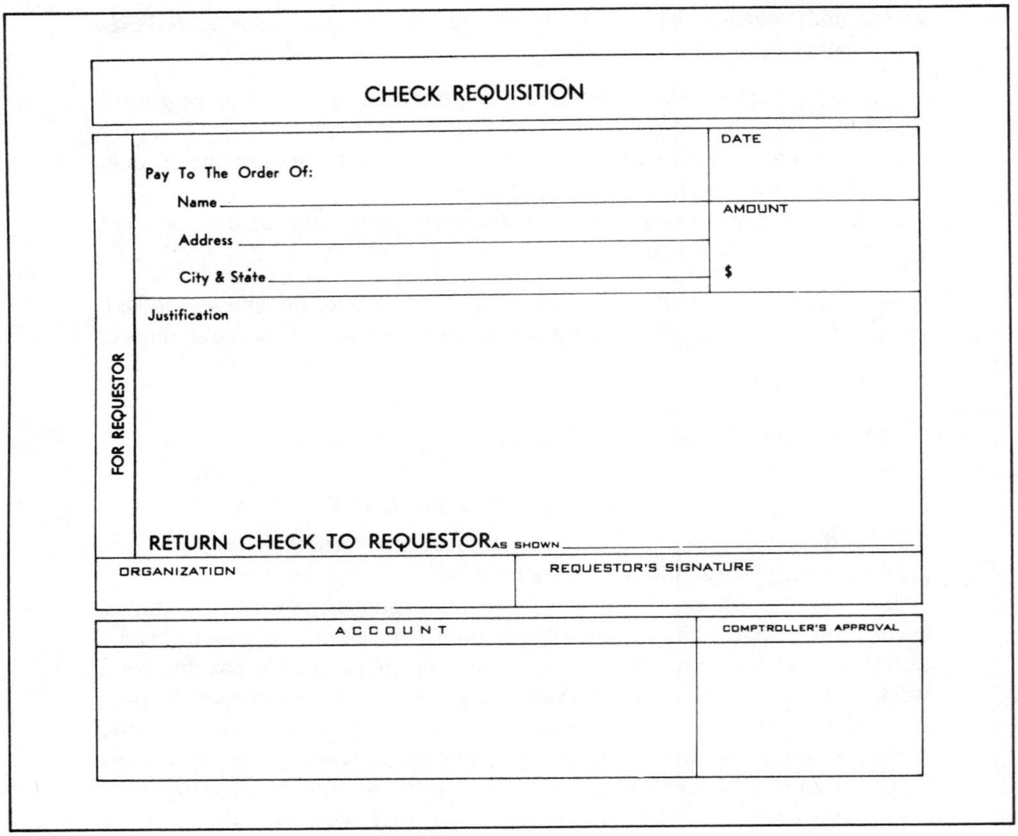
CHECK REQUISITION

FOR REQUESTOR

Pay To The Order Of:

Name

Address

City & State

DATE

AMOUNT

$

Justification

RETURN CHECK TO REQUESTOR AS SHOWN

ORGANIZATION

REQUESTOR'S SIGNATURE

ACCOUNT

COMPTROLLER'S APPROVAL

FIG. 6-2 Check requisition

vidual requesting a check notes the payee, the amount of the check, the reasons for the expenditure, and the budget line number or account number to be charged. The request is signed by an officer who has authority to disburse requested funds.

The check-request document is keyed and verified before input is submitted to the computer. Much of the information appearing on the request (such as the reason for expenditure) is so unique that there is no good way for the computer to use an existing file to establish the validity of the input. Consequently, a double-checking technique of verifying must be used.

It is also possible to use the edit program to apply limited computer edit procedures to the input data. For example, an imprest checking account should have a specified maximum limit, such as fifty dollars, for any expenditure. The presence of a check for more than this limit can then be detected. It is also possible to test for the absence of data and to make sure that no letters appear in the fields reserved for numbers. The report produced by the edit program also provides a batch control total. After this report has been reviewed and approved, processing can go on to the next stage, the preparation of the check register.

The Check Register and the Voucher-Check Program

After the edit program, detail records must be sorted by vendor number, customer number, or some other control. This sort allows a corresponding master file to be used as a source of additional information or as a reference. It is unlikely that different types of account detail, such as payroll data and payables data, will be mixed for the same check-writing operation.

A suggested processing practice is to prepare the check register before actual printing of voucher-checks, unless previous comprehensive testing has been done. In spite of the controls used in preparing the check-request form (verifying keyed materials and editing input detail), an invalid control number will sometimes appear. The check register is printed first because it is easier to locate and correct errors before checks are printed than to do so when expensive voucher-check blanks are used.

An invalid control number is discovered when the corresponding number does not appear in the payroll, the accounts payable, or some other master file. Since there is no matching number, the check-register program prints a message indicating the error condition. This allows the error to be corrected before processing continues. At times, a correction can be made directly to alter the contents of check-writing detail. This permits the immediate running of the voucher-check program.

Figure 6-3 shows a typical check register. The information normally printed on the register includes the name of the person or company receiving the check, the control or account number, the amount of the check, and the general ledger number. The reason for disbursement may also be given. The check register, in other words, provides a complete listing of all the information contained in the check-detail file. After processing, this register is frequently filed as a legal record of company expenditures.

After errors have been corrected and the register approved, voucher-checks are printed. Information that appears on the register also appears on the voucher portion of the check (see Fig. 6-4). The check itself records the payee, the control number, the dollar amount, and the date of the check. (It is suggested that the computer be used to print the check number. The reason for this suggestion is discussed later in this chapter.)

Check-printer alignment is usually a problem in the running of the voucher-check program. Check alignment refers to the process of inserting continuous check blanks into the computer printer. Form designers have attempted to make this process easier by printing alignment markings

			CHECK REG	3/31/	1
0809	10200	3460			100.00
0809			CHECK TOTAL		100.00
0808	20700	3461			9,711.09
0808	20800	3461			9,576.00
0808	21000	3461			2,000.00
0808	11500	3461			484.47
0808	61600	3461			107.00
0808			CHECK TOTAL		21,878.56
0810	61000	3462			41.62
0810			CHECK TOTAL		41.62
0810	60200	3463			10.00
0810			CHECK TOTAL		10.00
0810	60228	3464			39.00
0810			CHECK TOTAL		39.00
0810	61100	3465			6.70
0810			CHECK TOTAL		6.70
0810	60200	3466			29.93
0810			CHECK TOTAL		29.93
0810	60200	3467			6.90
0810			CHECK TOTAL		6.90

FIG. 6-3 Check register

alongside the blank forms to serve as guides in the setup of the computer printer. However, these alignment marks do not entirely solve the problem. Frequently, the computer operator does not understand how to use alignment marks correctly, and may insert forms into the computer the wrong way.

Because of these possibilities, the first few checks printed by the computer are often printed slightly off registration. To get around this problem, a setup routine should be incorporated into the voucher-check computer program. This routine allows computer operators to print one or more voided checks, while examining and adjusting printer alignment to the custom check blanks. Once satisfied, the operator informs the computer that the process of alignment has been completed. At this point, actual printing of voucher-checks begins.

Voided checks are also required at the end of check printing. To maintain control in processing, it is necessary to print the dollar amount for which checks were written. The word *void* is clearly printed on the face of any blank check or on the face of any check that shows this total dollar amount. In all cases, voided checks are torn and destroyed.

It is very dangerous to use checks that are presigned or can in any way be considered negotiable. There are too many ways in which a presigned check

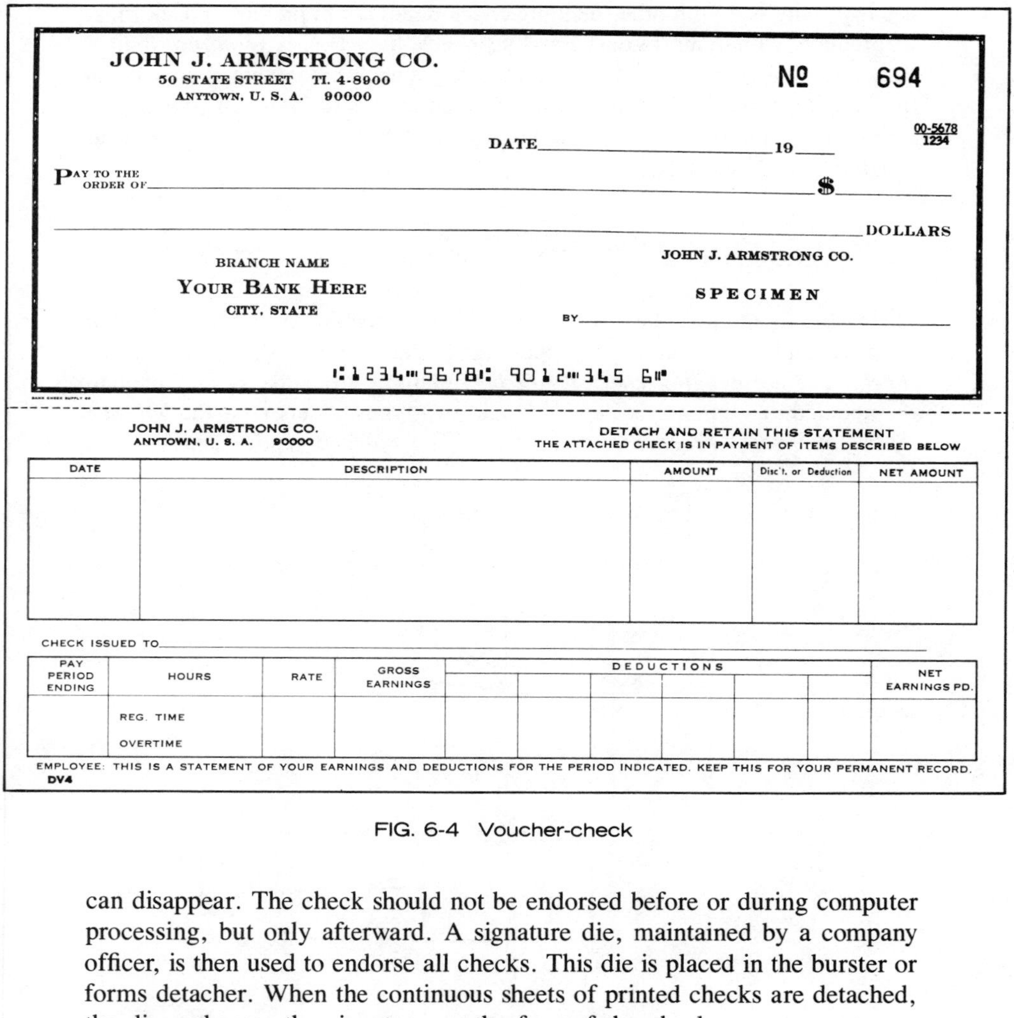

JOHN J. ARMSTRONG CO.
50 STATE STREET   TI. 4-8900
ANYTOWN. U. S. A.   90000

N⁰   694

00-5678
1234

DATE_____ 19____

PAY TO THE
ORDER OF_____   **$**_____

_____**DOLLARS**

BRANCH NAME
YOUR BANK HERE
CITY, STATE

JOHN J. ARMSTRONG CO.

SPECIMEN

BY_____

⑆1234⑈5678⑆ 9012⑈345 6⑈

JOHN J. ARMSTRONG CO.
ANYTOWN, U. S. A.   90000

DETACH AND RETAIN THIS STATEMENT
THE ATTACHED CHECK IS IN PAYMENT OF ITEMS DESCRIBED BELOW

DATE	DESCRIPTION	AMOUNT	Disc't. or Deduction	NET AMOUNT

CHECK ISSUED TO_____

PAY PERIOD ENDING	HOURS	RATE	GROSS EARNINGS	DEDUCTIONS				NET EARNINGS PD.
	REG. TIME							
	OVERTIME							

EMPLOYEE: THIS IS A STATEMENT OF YOUR EARNINGS AND DEDUCTIONS FOR THE PERIOD INDICATED. KEEP THIS FOR YOUR PERMANENT RECORD.
DV4

FIG. 6-4   Voucher-check

can disappear. The check should not be endorsed before or during computer processing, but only afterward. A signature die, maintained by a company officer, is then used to endorse all checks. This die is placed in the burster or forms detacher. When the continuous sheets of printed checks are detached, the die embosses the signature on the face of the check.

Summary Reports and the Pending Check-Detail File

After voucher-check printing, the check-detail file can be used directly to prepare a summary report for posting expenditures to either company budgets or general ledger accounts. It may be necessary to sort the file by account number sequence before a printed summary can be produced. In any event, the file of check detail should be retained for use in reconciling cancelled checks received from the bank. In completing this step, check detail is usually combined with other pending check detail (from previous check runs) to produce a final, up-to-date pending check file. This is more convenient than retaining individual files, one for every check-processing run made in the past few weeks. When the check-reconciliation system is run, this aggregate pending file is used to match newly cancelled checks for all past runs at one time.

6-2   THE CHECK-RECONCILIATION SYSTEM

Figure 6-5 illustrates the check-reconciliation system, a rather short and simple computer application. Inputs to the system consist of keyed *cancelled checks* and the *pending check-detail file*. Outputs from the system include the updated pending check-detail file and two types of reports—the *balance report* and *check-reconciliation reports*. The balance report establishes a

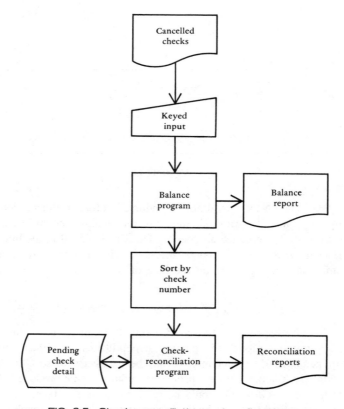

FIG. 6-5   Check-reconciliation system flowchart

batch control for the input detail. Check-reconciliation reports identify the checks deleted from the pending check-detail file.

As shown by the flowchart, cancelled checks returned from the bank are entered as initial input. These checks are accompanied by a bank-prepared check register which generally lists and totals checks cancelled by each page of the register. The bank will also batch cancelled checks by page number, making check reconciliation easier. These steps permit checks to be keyed by page while the check number and amount are extracted from each check. A page total is also prepared. The balance program is then able to compare check totals against page totals and establish a batch control early in the system. If there are errors or balancing problems, they are corrected before processing is permitted to continue.

Once the balance report is approved, the resulting detail file is sorted by check number to follow the same sequence as the pending check-detail file. These two files are then matched to allow check-reconciliation reports (see Fig. 6-6) to be printed. The program also updates the pending check-detail file by removing cancelled checks from it. However, if the amount of the cancelled check does not agree with the amount stored in the corresponding pending record, this discrepancy is clearly stated on the reconciliation reports. If the cancelled check contains an account number not in the pending file, this is also stated. Both of these cases may indicate fraud, but are more often legitimate mistakes. Nevertheless, they should be reviewed to determine the reason for the discrepancy.

DATE 8/12/--　　　　　　　　　　　CASHED CHECK REGISTER　　　　　　　　　　　PAGE 1
　　　　　　　　　　　　　　　　　　　　　AUGUST 12, 19--

CHECK NO	VENDOR NUMBER	VENDOR/ASSIGNEE NAME	CHECK DATE	CHECK AMOUNT
333	11581-0	ABBOTT HARDWARE	8/15/--	122.75
334	22116-0	BAKER BUILDING CO	8/15/--	172.50
335	22116-3	FUND LOAN ASSOC	8/15/--	92.99
336	22116-9	FINANCE MONIES	8/15/--	171.50
338	43821	FLOOR COVER CO	8/15/--	1,975.00
NUMBER OF CHECKS RECONCILED			5	2,534.74
NUMBER OF CHECKS CASHED			5	2,534.74

DATE 8/12/--　　　　　　　　　　　OUTSTANDING CHECK LISTING　　　　　　　　　　PAGE 1
　　　　　　　　　　　　　　　　　　　　　AUGUST 12, 19--

CHECK NO	VENDOR NUMBER	VENDOR/ASSIGNEE NAME	CHECK DATE	AMOUNT OUTSTANDING
337	36114	PEOPLES MARKET	8/15/--	166.35
339	33002	JOHN LOAN CO	8/15/--	142.15
340	36410	EQUITY INS	8/15/--	99.16
341	17832	PEOPLES INS	8/15/--	453.20
342	14560	PROPERTY FUNDING	8/15/--	985.67
GRAND TOTAL		NUMBER OF CHECKS	5	1,846.53

FIG. 6-6　Check-reconciliation reports

There are several ways to prepare check-reconciliation reports. One is to show only checks that have been cancelled and returned. Another method (shown in Fig. 6-6) is to list both checks that have been cancelled and those that remain in the pending file. However, such a complete register of pending and recently cancelled checks is often too massive to be useful.

6-3 CHECK DESIGN

There are many ways to design checks. Figure 6-4 illustrated one example. Other examples are shown in Figure 6-7. One unfortunate aspect of check design is that most decisions concerning their appearance and contents are made before a computer system is contemplated. This is troublesome in that check design greatly affects the efficiency of computer check preparation and handling and the overall processing of the reconciliation system.

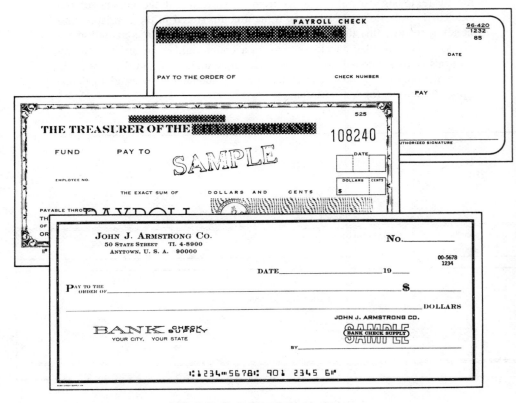

FIG. 6-7 Samples of check designs

One important design factor is the printing of the check number. This number must be unique to each check. It serves as the means of tracing the document through the payee, to the payee's bank, to the company's bank, and finally back to the company as a cancelled check. The check number is also used to reconcile the original printing of the voucher-check to a company account. It is therefore of primary importance. A common practice is to preprint the check number—to have the check supplier place the number on the check. The number is large and distinctive in color, so that it cannot easily be altered.

Unfortunately, preprinted checks in the computer system cause more problems than they solve. Great care must be used in the setup of a computer printer so that a check is correctly printed. The check number must be stored in the pending check records if a computer file is used to reconcile cancelled checks. If something misfunctions during check printing and it becomes necessary to begin again, the stored number will no longer agree with the preprinted check numbers. Previously printed checks must be destroyed and processing started with checks bearing different starting numbers. The computer program that assigns the number to records must also be rerun to keep numbers in agreement.

Since there are always one or two checks wasted at the beginning of check printing and another check or two destroyed at the end of printing, sequential check numbers will be lost, even if nothing misfunctions during the check-printing operation. Hence it is not possible to account for every number in a check series when the numbers are preprinted. Moreover, the security reasons for preprinting are compromised, since some checks must by necessity be wasted.

Another alternative is to use the computer to print the check number together with other information printed on the check. If something misfunctions with check printing, errors can be corrected and the program restarted. Other computer records need not be altered, and time is not wasted. In addition, this system provides more security since computer printing is indelible, and every consecutive check number can be accounted for. If any checks are damaged during initial printer setup or during the check-printing run, they should be taken directly to a company officer for proper destruction.

6-4 MANUAL PROCEDURES IN CHECK PROCESSING

A check-processing computer system, while simplifying check writing and reconciliation, does not remove all of the clerical burden. For example, a carbon copy of the check-voucher is often prepared and filed with the original source documents. In the case of payroll, the carbon may be stapled to the employee's time card to show that payment has been made. The same approach is used for payables—the carbon and the vendor invoices are stapled as proof of payment. When this technique is used, cancelled checks returned from the bank can be left in order, along with the accompanying bank statement. This preserves an audit trail of the current balance of the account. The following sequence of events is usually followed in the manual processing of computer-printed checks.

1. The original and the carbon copies of the voucher-checks are separated. Usually, a special type of machine called a deleaver accomplishes this. Both stacks of documents are separated into individual sets of voucher-checks by a second type of machine, called a burster. The forms are then forwarded to a control clerk for review.

2. The clerk staples the carbon copy of the voucher-check to the original source document. If an error is detected, the clerk can immediately prepare a special check and void the computer-prepared check. A corresponding journal entry is also necessary to adjust company ledgers.

3. The clerk locates and extracts multiple-page vouchers. That is, it is possible that more than one voucher-check will be required for a given payment. This is particularly true for an accounts payable vendor check. There may be several purchases from one vendor, resulting in a number of invoices to be paid. If this detail is too much to print on a single voucher, the corresponding check is voided by the computer and the invoice detail continued on the next voucher. This necessitates the removal of the voided check from the material sent to the vendor. It should be stapled to the check carbon along with the invoices being paid. To assist in multiple-page voucher removal, some check-writing systems print a list of all multi-page vouchers either as a separate report or as part of the check register. This list aids in locating and extracting voided check blanks.

4. The checks are endorsed. After voucher-checks have been compared to the original source documents, they are passed through a check-signing machine if the burster is not used to hold the signature die. The die is then locked away to prevent unauthorized use.

5. The checks are stuffed into envelopes and mailed. This process requires some forethought, since voucher-checks can be printed in three ways: the check beside the voucher, the check following the voucher, and the voucher following the check. Side-by-side printing is often recommended because the computer can print both documents at the same time. However, side-by-side design does not save any appreciable

time, as the forms are difficult to work with. More important, mailing equipment is designed to fold and stuff documents into window envelopes, so that name and address information will show. The machines fold the documents horizontally, as we do when folding a business letter for an envelope. This means that voucher-checks printed side-by-side cannot be passed through stuffing machines. The voucher preceding the check can be passed through folding and stuffing equipment, but the voucher portion will be placed against the envelope window, instead of the name and address. The best arrangement—the check printed first and the voucher second—does process properly through mailing equipment. This method usually requires modification of the check-writing system to place check-summary records in front of corresponding detail records in the check-printing file. Fortunately, there is ample opportunity to prepare this summary record as a by-product of the check-register program. A brief sorting program immediately following the register program will place summary information with name and address information in front of corresponding voucher detail. The check can then be printed first and the voucher second, allowing easy insertion into envelopes.

6-5 MANAGEMENT IMPLICATIONS

Very little in the check-writing and reconciliation systems need concern management. It is one of the most clerical and least impressive of all computer systems. Fortunately, it is also one of the least expensive to develop and to operate.

The computer-printed check exposes the computer operation to outsiders—company employees and vendors. As mentioned in the chapter on payroll, the appearance of check forms is important because it can add to the prestige of the company and to the acceptance of computer operations.

Many organizations use punched-card forms as computer checks. This practice dates back to attempts to reprocess a check through old-style card-reading equipment. These systems were not very successful when they were in vogue a decade ago. There is even less justification for their use today because banks use magnetic ink character recognition (MICR) encoding on the face of the check to record pertinent data. Banks are also willing to supply a reel of computer tape representing checks deposited against a company account. They will even assume the burden of check reconciliation if the company supplies data to the bank. In these circumstances, there is little merit in trying to reprocess punched cards through an expensive computer system, delaying other applications while card reading is underway.

REVIEW OF IMPORTANT IDEAS

Check-printing systems should be standardized as much as possible to reduce processing errors and to increase processing efficiency. With standard procedures, it is possible to combine all checking accounts into one, transferring funds from other accounts to cover the expenditure. A free-form voucher and a common check can then be used for a variety of purposes.

The check-writing system processes summary files from other computer applications or check requests for special purposes. An edit should be made of new data, and a complete register of all checks to be printed should be prepared. Checks should be supported by a general ledger summary report showing how funds for checks were obtained.

The file of detail records used to print checks is saved for reconciling cancelled checks after their return from the bank. The reconciliation report lists checks returned and reconciled and may also list outstanding pending checks.

There are several factors to consider in designing checks for a computer system. Among these are the problems with prenumbered checks and the location of the printed voucher with respect to the check. Most checks have an accompanying carbon copy to facilitate manual processing required for invoices or other documents paid by check.

REVIEW QUESTIONS

1. Under what circumstances are checks prepared manually, when the majority of checks released by a company are computer printed?

2. What is meant by the term *check reconciliation*?

3. Why is the check register printed in advance of voucher-checks in a check-writing computer application?

4. Why are checks not endorsed before they are printed by computer?

5. What occurs in the check-reconciliation system when a check is not cashed? What provisions should be made to handle situations such as this?

6. Should preprinted checks be used in the writing of voucher-checks, or should the computer be used to assign check numbers? Cite the advantages of each method.

EXERCISES

1. In spite of criticisms of prenumbered checks, such as we discussed in this chapter, some companies have their checks numbered when originally prepared by a forms printer. These checks are consecutively numbered before they are used by the computer. Describe how you would modify the check-writing and reconciliation systems to accommodate prenumbered checks.

2. Government checks (for example, GI Bill payments and tax refunds) are commonly printed on punched cards. The holes punched in them correspond to the dollar amount, account numbers, reference numbers, and so forth. When a card-check is returned to a federal agency, it is processed in the same way as a normal punched card. Name a virtue of and a drawback to this use of punched cards. What changes, if any, must be made in the reconciliation system to utilize card-checks?

3. A firm decides to print its stockholder dividend checks by computer rather than by hand. Two types of stockholder name and address records must be processed: personally managed accounts (the check is mailed to the stockholder's home address) and stockholder accounts maintained by major brokerage firms (the check is mailed to the brokerage firm).

   Flowchart a dividend-check-writing computer system that permits all stockholder records to be processed and dividend checks to be printed. Explain the purpose of each computer program depicted by the flowchart.

4. A business permits its employees to apply for a payroll advance when special circumstances arise. When the application is approved, a check is written in advance of the normal payroll. Explain how the payroll computer application must be designed to handle payment-in-advance situations.

5. At times, a vendor requests down payment on merchandise before shipment (and the mailing of a vendor invoice). Explain how the accounts payable system must be designed to handle a payment-in-advance situation.

7

INVOICING

For large organizations, customer orders are often taken and packed and shipped from several locations. In a decentralized environment, a centralized order-filling system may not be feasible; however, a centralized billing or invoicing system will be. But, whether an organization is centralized or decentralized, customer, product, and sales analysis are becoming fundamental to profitable business enterprise. Managers need to know which customers are profitable, which products to carry in inventory, and what sales to anticipate. Accordingly, even in a highly decentralized organization, a centralized billing system serves a necessary purpose in addition to preparing the invoice for the customer. It maintains a file of customer purchases that can be analyzed to identify customer, product, and sales patterns.

This chapter discusses first the stand-alone method of invoicing and then an invoicing system tied to computer order filling. Two other subjects important to invoicing are also covered: the method of maintaining a suspense relief file and the characteristics of price file maintenance.

7-1 THE COMPUTER-PREPARED INVOICE

The invoice is the one document that commercial customers require in making their cash payments. It informs the customer of the individual line-item charges for merchandise received and shows the terms of payment, product adjustments, and customer credits. These conditions separate the invoice from the three other documents that accompany shipped merchandise: the packing slip, the bill of lading, and the monthly billing statement. (The packing slip is sent with the shipment of merchandise to acknowledge the actual items shipped. The bill of lading is also sent to indicate freight or transportation charges. The monthly billing statement is a summary of outstanding invoices itemized by invoice number and total charges per invoice. This document is mailed to the customer if the customer has not paid an outstanding invoice.)

Figure 7-1 illustrates a typical customer invoice. It is a neat, readable record of compliance to a sales agreement. It shows quantity ordered, quantity shipped, item codes, description of the items ordered, unit price, and net and total amount of the invoice. Space is provided to record the customer purchase order number. This number permits the customer to match the invoice to a copy of the original purchase order and thus reconcile the information recorded on the invoice. Similarly, the customer uses the printed invoice number to allow cash payments to be matched against outstanding invoices.

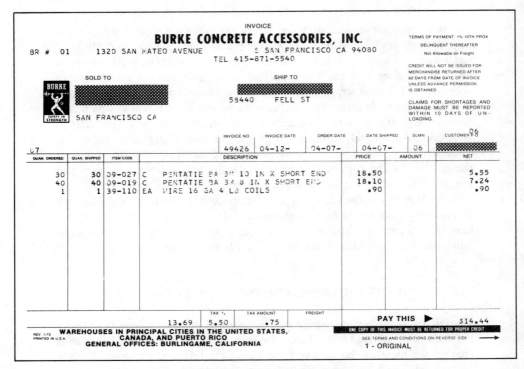

FIG. 7-1 Customer invoice

The ability to match different types of business documents quickly is a basic reason for using the computer to prepare invoices. Another reason is to permit standard costs, part numbers, units of measure, and part descriptions to be readily obtained and printed on invoices. Both of these functions cause considerable dollar savings because of reduced clerical search and computation times—in addition to the savings in time required to type the invoices. The information captured by the computer during the processing of invoices is also vital to the preparation of monthly billing statements. Additional clerical time is saved by this activity. Finally, a computer system of invoicing makes possible customer, product, and sales analysis. Before the computer, these tasks were seldom attempted because of the large amounts of clerical time required.

7-2 INPUTS TO THE STAND-ALONE INVOICING SYSTEM

There are three main inputs to the stand-alone invoicing system:

1. revised customer order
2. credit memo or request
3. customer change slip

Revised Customer Order

The primary input is a revised customer order. Since the order shows what quantities were desired, it must be modified to show what quantities were shipped and what freight charges were incurred. Two documents lead to revisions in the customer order. A packing slip, sent with the goods shipped, shows which products and quantities were in stock. These must be compared against the products and quantities ordered. A bill of lading is also sent to the customer to show freight charges. These charges must be added to the revised customer order. Figure 7-2 shows a typical bill of lading. A packing slip is similar in design to the customer invoice, but does not contain invoice charges.

The revised customer order is prepared in stages. First, by the person taking the customer order. Second, by the warehouse crew filling the order. Third, by shipping personnel reviewing whether the order is complete. After final preparation of the revised customer order, a copy is forwarded to data entry.

If warehouses or branch sales offices are located some distance from the computer installation, revised customer orders are batched and mailed for invoice processing. A batch control total specifying the quantity of items shipped is prepared for batched documents. This total can be easily checked

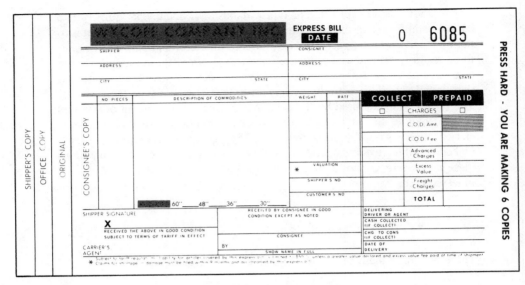

FIG. 7-2 Bill of lading

by the computer edit program. It can also be retained by decentralized office groups, which otherwise might question the validity of the computer invoicing system.

Credit Memo or Request

The credit memo or request is the second major input to the invoicing system. Occasionally, there is a disparity between what the warehouse records as merchandise shipped to the customer and what the customer reports as received. Moreover, supplies shipped to customers are frequently returned for credit. Both of these adjustments can be handled with a credit memo. Figure 7-3 shows that a credit memo provides a dollar credit for the customer. This credit is later used to adjust sales analysis data by invoice number, customer number, and item code. Requests for credit can be submitted with regular customer invoicing documents, but most often they are batched separately to reduce confusion in handling and processing.

Customer Change Slip

The customer change slip is the third input to the invoicing system. Customer change—addition, deletion, or correction—is made to the customer master file before invoice posting. In contrast to payroll, where a preliminary master file update was permitted, an invoicing system updates cus-

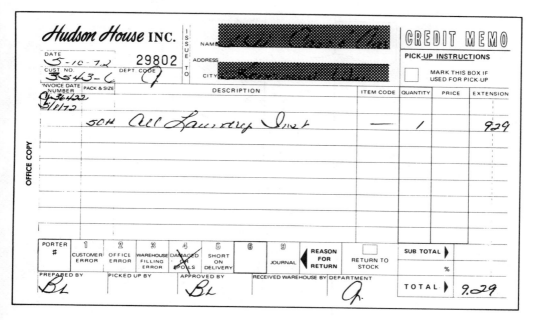

FIG. 7-3 Credit memo

tomer records as part of the main processing. This method of updating complicates the computer program that validates customer data, but it has certain virtues. For payroll, it was assumed that information to update employee records is available before actual payroll processing begins. This assumption is valid in that most employees will have worked for some time before receiving their first payroll check. However, customer change notification occurs when customer orders are received. Since current customer data must be used immediately, it is necessary to process customer change data with details from the customer order. As a final consideration, the customer order contains revised customer data. Hence, by initially underscoring new customers or customer changes, the data entry staff is able to key customer changes immediately.

7-3 THE STAND-ALONE INVOICING SYSTEM

Figure 7-4 illustrates the systems flowchart for production of customer invoices. Inputs to the system consist of keyed data from revised customer orders, requests for credit, and customer change slips. Three main files are also inputs to the system:

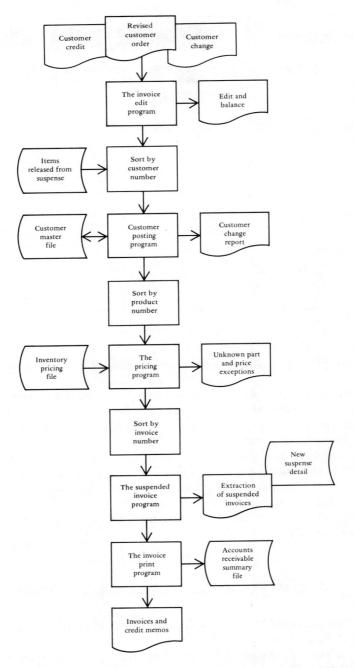

FIG. 7-4 Invoicing flowchart (without prior computer order filling)

- The *items-released-from-suspense file* inputs data for corrected orders initially found to be in error.
- The *customer master file* contains an up-to-date listing of all customers for whom orders are filled.
- The *inventory pricing file* represents an accurate accounting of the price for all merchandise in stock.

Outputs from the system consist of updated or created files, summary reports, and printed invoices. During processing, the customer master file is updated by customer change inputs. Two files are created by processing. The *new suspense detail file* stores data for orders found to be in error. The *accounts receivable summary file* retains data for preparing customer monthly billing statements. The following reports and printed material are also produced during processing:

1. edit and balance report
2. customer change report
3. unknown part and price exception report
4. extraction of suspended invoices
5. invoices and credit memos

Figure 7-5 shows typical contents of the approved invoice file created during the preparation of invoices. Figure 7-6 shows the summary detail retained for preparing monthly billing statements. The major portion of the approved invoice file is supplied by the revised customer order. The keyed customer number and the part number are used to locate supporting detail from the customer and price files, respectively. After the customer invoice is printed, only invoice identification information and the total amount due for each invoice are retained for the accounts receivable summary file. All other invoice detail is removed from the file.

The Invoice Edit Program

Keyed input read by the computer creates a file of invoice details that require editing. Two types of information are extracted from each customer order:

- *Header information* records at least the record code, customer order number, customer number, salesperson number, and batch number. (The record code distinguishes between types of records such as invoices and credit memos.) The header record might also include the extended (prebilled) invoice total, and special shipping instructions.
- *Trailing information* contains one keyed entry for each order line completed on the customer order. Each entry includes the quantity of parts

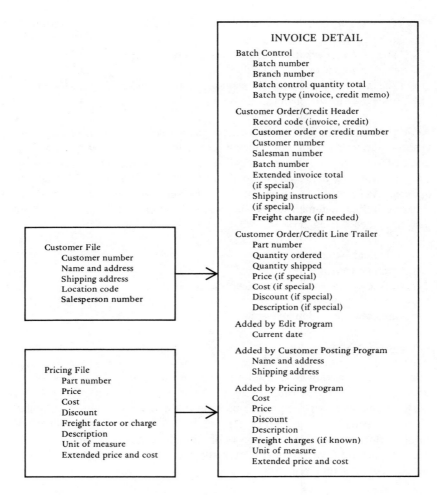

FIG. 7-5 Typical contents of approved invoice detail

shipped, the part number, and sometimes the quantity ordered by the customer. Optional data include special price, cost, discount, or descriptive information.

The fields that require encoding—record code, document number, customer number, salesperson number, batch number, quantity shipped, and part number—can be machine edited for input errors. Record codes are tested to see whether they fall within a certain range. Like document numbers, customer order numbers allow missing or duplicate numbers to be detected. The customer number and the salesperson number (in most cases)

ACCOUNTS RECEIVABLE SUMMARY DETAIL

Identification
Information

Customer number
Record code
Invoice or credit number
Invoice or credit date
Branch office number
Salesperson number

Total invoice or credit charge/adjustment

FIG. 7-6   Accounts receivable summary detail for preparing monthly customer billing statements

can be validated by the customer master file. The batch number should match the number appearing on the batch control record. The quantity shipped total for all customer orders must balance the total punched in the batch control. Finally, the part number is validated by the pricing file.

All other keyed entries are very difficult to edit. A shipping date cannot be verified other than proving it is later than the date of processing. The quantity ordered is not testable, except that it should be greater than or equal to the quantity shipped. Special prices or discounts cannot be verified. It is possible only to screen them to detect unusual differences. Other narrative or descriptive information cannot be tested since it may take several forms. Thus nonstandard input entries are both time-consuming to key and difficult to verify. They should be minimized, although they probably cannot be eliminated altogether.

The edit program produces a file of invoice detail on a fast access storage device. One record exists in this file for every order line from the customer order. Each record contains *specific* information for an order line and includes the part number and the quantity shipped. It also contains information *common* to the entire customer order copied from the header detail, such as customer number and customer order number. Finally, each record contains information *common* to all customer orders copied from the batch controls, such as branch office information and batch number.

Another input that requires edit is the customer change information that adds, deletes, or alters a customer's name and address. If designated in a distinctive way, this information can be extracted directly from the customer order. However, it should not be keyed at the time customer order detail is encoded. It is more efficient to process customer changes after order detail. Customer changes are then submitted as a group to the edit program rather than mixed with customer order information, which is subject to batch controls.

The edit report reflects all details entered as input and prints any diagnostics or error messages. Two types of error conditions occur. Some errors are of an advisory nature, or warnings. Examples of this type include "batch control imbalance" or "excessive quantities shipped." The second type of error is clearly unacceptable, or fatal. Errors such as "missing customer numbers or part numbers" require correction and resubmission of data to the computer. The difficulty with a fatal error is that it is nearly impossible to separate good data from data in error. If a part number is missing, it is impossible to backtrack to determine which records have been processed for a particular customer order. It is necessary, therefore, to correct the errors appearing on the edit report and to resubmit the entire batch for editing. However, if a second edit is required, printing of all detail information is unnecessary. Printed data (Fig. 7-7) are limited to batch control totals and any further diagnostic messages. The initial invoice edit report is enough to support the content of the invoice detail file.

The Customer Posting Program

The customer posting program follows the completed edit of invoice detail. This program serves two purposes: to update the customer file as a result of customer change input and to verify the customer numbers on customer order header records. Changes or additions to the customer master file precede header record verification. This update can be completed randomly if the customer master file is stored on disk. It is essential that the customer master file contains the most recent version of customer data, since data extracted from the file are used in printing customer invoices. If customer changes are not processed before customer number verification, orders will be suspended without good reason.

Figure 7-8 illustrates the customer change report printed from the customer posting program. This report lists all changes made in the customer

```
BRANCH 11    BATCH 13                              EDIT REPORT

 DATE          ----TAX----          DOCUMENT              UNIT DISC QTY    ITEM   UNIT    EXT
SHIPPED  SLSMN  CD  AMOUNT  FREIGHT    TOTAL     USED CV   COST  %  SHIPPED  CODE  PRICE  AMOUNT INVOICE CUST
04-11-   AC 99                                                                                  94476 00010
                                                                22  21-110
                                                                22  21-115
  INVOICE TOTALS                                                 44
04-11-   BB 04                                                                                  94474 14725
                                                               100  14-300
  INVOICE TOTALS                                               100
04-09-   BC 04                                                                                  94479 17200
                                                                 1  48-105
  INVOICE TOTALS                                                 1
04-10-   DU 05                                                                                  94466 17500
                                                                55  47-420
  INVOICE TOTALS                                                55                              50000 00005
                                                                24  26-205
  INVOICE TOTALS                                                24
04-11-   BB 02                                                                                  94478 18975
                                                                 2  39-112
                                                                 4  56-115
  INVOICE TOTALS                                                 6
04-11-   BB 04                                                                                  94473 20675
                                                               900  09-027
                                                               500  09-229
                                                               250  09-019
  INVOICE TOTALS                                             1,650
04-11-   DP 05                                                                                  94480 22842
                                                             1,000  09-013
                                                               200  09-019
  INVOICE TOTALS        BATCH CONTROL      3,135             1,200
  BATCH TOTAL          ::DIFFERENCE           55             3,080
```

FIG. 7-7 Invoice edit report

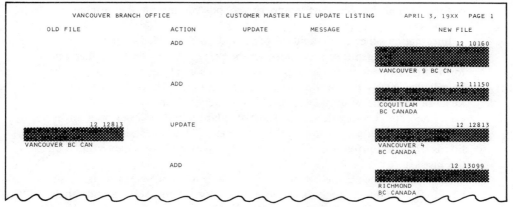

FIG. 7-8 Customer change report

master file. It is reviewed visually with considerable care. Since there is no adequate method for testing the validity of customer changes by the computer, a visual review is the only way to identify questionable alterations to the customer master file.

Once the customer file is updated, invoice header records are posted. The customer number appearing in each header record is verified by the customer master file, and name and address are extracted and included with header record detail. Other information can also be extracted, depending on the contents and the size limitations imposed on the customer master file. For instance, if one salesperson is responsible for a customer, the salesperson number need not be keyed but can be retained and extracted from the customer file. If sales are reviewed on the basis of geographical location, location codes can also be retained in the customer file.

If the customer number in the header record does not correspond to an active customer, it is necessary to suspend the invoice. A *suspense flag* or code is inserted in the header record to allow all records for the invoice to be sidetracked later to a suspended order file. If header records are stored in a file different from the line item records, it is possible to locate all records that accompany the suspended invoice. If both records are in one file but not grouped by document number, it is necessary to sort the file in order to locate line item records for suspension.

The Pricing Program

The pricing program updates line item records by inserting standard price and cost data by part or product number. Before updating begins, however, it is necessary to verify the part number. This procedure is known as *part number testing*. In testing, the invoice file is sorted by part number sequence. Then, invoice part numbers are posted against the pricing file numbers.

Information other than standard price and cost is added to the line item records. A unit of measure is added, if the price is based on more than one form of measurement. For example, liquids are sold by the gallon and by the barrel; dry goods by the dozen, hundred, or thousand, or by the pound, sack, or ton. These units of measure are entered in the invoice record for each line item. There will also be some standard narrative description of the part number such as "sack of portland cement." Such descriptive information is transferred from the pricing file to the invoice file and then printed on the invoice.

In some instances, special numbers in the pricing file need to be transferred. For instance, ledger account numbers for freight, service and repair, and stock replenishment charges are needed for entry on the invoice. These are set up as dummy part numbers and segregated when sales analysis reports are prepared. Another exception occurs when salespersons enter special prices on the customer order. They might do this when they encounter highly competitive situations and find it necessary to reduce prices below the standard in the pricing file. If a special price is entered on the customer order, it is extracted by data entry and allowed to override the standard price. However, all price exceptions should be tested to determine whether the discounted price results in low gross profit, high discount, or low override price. These price overrides are printed on the *price exception report* (see Fig. 7-9). This report indicates which override prices were low and which led to low gross profit. (The data in Fig. 7-9 are not factual and are intended only to illustrate the use of the form.)

During the posting of line item records, some will be found to be unacceptable (for example, a part number may not be contained in the pricing file for a specified branch office). Unacceptable records are suspended and

580120	BRANCH 04			DAILY SELLING PRICE EXCEPTION REPORT				APRIL 3, 19XX	PAGE 2
INV	CUST.	SLS	INVOICE DATE	ITEM CODE	ITEM DESCRIPTION	QUANTITY	UNIT PR	DISC	OVERRIDE PRICE	ERROR MESSAGE
56139	11110	47	04-03-	25-901	36 IN FLAT STAKES	136		.20	.99	HIGH-DISCOUNT
										LOW OVERRIDE PRICE
56139	11110	47	04-03-	25-901	30 IN FLAT STAKES	24		.20	.75	HIGH-DISCOUNT
										LOW OVERRIDE PRICE
55321	27290	43	04-03-	48-125	N1825 SPRAY BAR EXT	6	1.26	.10	1.26	LOW GROSS PROFIT
56112	17675	45	04-03-	53-320	FIBRE EXPN JOINT 3/8 X 4 IN	500	9.40	.27	9.40	LOW OVERRIDE PRICE
56112	17675	45	04-03-	53-430	FIBRE EXPN JOINT 1/2 X 4 IN	500	11.15	.27	11.15	LOW OVERRIDE PRICE
55966	26315	47	04-03-	53-430	FIBRE EXPN JOINT 1/2 X 4 IN	2,000	11.15	.35	11.15	HIGH-DISCOUNT
										LOW OVERRIDE PRICE
55930	37750	44	04-03-	53-675	CURB + GUTTER 3/8 IN COUNTY NO 1	575	.69		.38	LOW OVERRIDE PRICE
55930	37750	44	04-03-	53-676	CURB + GUTTER 3/8 IN COUNTY NO 2	150	.79		.43	LOW OVERRIDE PRICE
										LOW GROSS PROFIT
55930	37750	44	04-03-	53-677	CURB + GUTTER 3/8 IN NO 13	325	.69		.38	LOW OVERRIDE PRICE
56077	16940	43	04-03-	55-163	JOINT SEALANT PRC 5000 5 GAL	5	24.08		21.06	LOW OVERRIDE PRICE
										LOW GROSS PROFIT

FIG. 7-9 Price exception report

flagged, just as records were suspended for invalid customer numbers. Separation of suspended records from valid records, however, is more complex in the pricing program than in the customer posting program. An invalid part number suspends only one line item record. All other line item records and the header record for this customer order must also be suspended, since one invalid part number makes it impossible to print the invoice. It becomes necessary to sort the invoice file to locate all records for one customer invoice. If the header record is in a separate file, it is possible to insert the suspension flag in the header record immediately. This approach has considerable merit and is the primary reason for placing header records and order line records in separate files.

The Suspended Invoice Program

The suspended invoices report lists all suspended invoice records that have been flagged by the customer posting and the pricing programs, together with the reason for suspension. A new suspense detail file is separated from acceptable invoice detail. In other words, the invoice detail is split into two parts. Flagged detail, or detail in error, is placed in the new suspense detail file. Valid or approved detail is retained in the other file, which is now ready for invoice and credit memo printing.

The Invoice and Credit Memo Print Program

All data necessary to print invoices are now contained in the approved invoice file (or files if header records are kept separate). Customer posting has added customer name and address and other essential information associated with the customer to the invoice detail. Part numbers have been used to obtain price, cost, unit of measure, part description, and other pertinent information. Printing the invoice can begin immediately, provided the file is sequenced in proper order—but once again this is not likely to be the case. One common sequence for printing invoices is by customer order number within each branch office. If revised customer order documents are preprinted and prenumbered, this number is the logical one to use as the invoice number, since it ties directly to the original customer order document used between the sales force and warehouse, the sales force and customer, and the warehouse and customer. This number simplifies combining copies of the customer order and the invoice, but it makes it difficult to group a customer's invoices for mailing in one envelope.

An alternative to sorting and printing invoices by customer order sequence is to sort and print them by customer number sequence. This method groups all invoices for one customer, making them easier to insert in a customer envelope. If customer orders are filed by customer number in customer folders for later follow-up, the invoice file should be sorted by customer number within branch office number before invoice printing begins.

Invoice printing is primarily a printer-bound program. The computer may print invoices for just a few minutes if the invoice file is small, or for several hours. In the latter case, a restart feature (see Chapter 3) should be incorporated in the invoice print program. The reprinting of balance controls is necessary even if a restart feature is part of the invoice print program. For example, the total quantity shipped for every branch office is printed, although invoices have already been prepared. The purpose of printing balance control totals is to verify that no records were inadvertently overlooked during an additional pass through the invoice file. Since the accounts receivable summary file is one output of the invoice program, it should be reproduced when restart is necessary. This ensures that no unexpected errors are introduced as a result of error correction and restart procedures.

As a final caution concerning protection of balance controls, the original customer order inputs are used to prepare a batch control total. This total is a tally of quantities shipped for all bills contained in the batch. The edit program recapitulates this total and allows differences to be reconciled. The customer posting and the pricing programs are also balanced against the total quantity shipped, at least the gross total by branch office. When suspended documents are separated from the main invoice file, a control total is printed for the suspended orders. Finally, the invoice print program produces a batch control total for all approved invoices.

This procedure makes it possible to reconcile all control totals and to establish that no records have been added or dropped from any of the files. This is an audit trail that is approved by company auditors. The trail becomes slightly complex because of items released from the suspense file, which makes it necessary to account for the quantity held in suspense at the time the invoice system was started for the day (see section 7-4).

Accounts Receivable Summary Detail

The file produced by the invoice print program is the *accounts receivable summary detail*. (The contents of the file are shown in Fig. 7-6). This computer file is retained for monthly processing of customer billing statements. These monthly statements do not contain all the detail printed on the invoice. Rather, they are summary statements sent to the customer as charges if payment does not follow from the invoice.

7-4 SUSPENSE RELIEF

Invoices containing invalid customer or part numbers are suspended by the customer posting and pricing programs, instead of being dropped from the invoice file. This procedure ensures that all original input records will eventually be processed to completion. The new suspense detail file, produced by the suspended invoice program, is combined with prior suspense files to create an updated suspense file. From this file, the *suspense report* is prepared.

It is necessary to correct the error that resulted in suspension and then process corrected records through the invoicing system again. Error identification is made possible by the suspense report, which serves as a worksheet to locate and correct errors in the invoice records. Corrections are then keyed and processed against the suspense file.

The flowchart for the suspense relief program is shown in Figure 7-10. The inputs to this program are the updated suspense file and keyed corrections. Outputs from the program are two computer files. The *items released from suspense file* contains documents that have been corrected and thereby

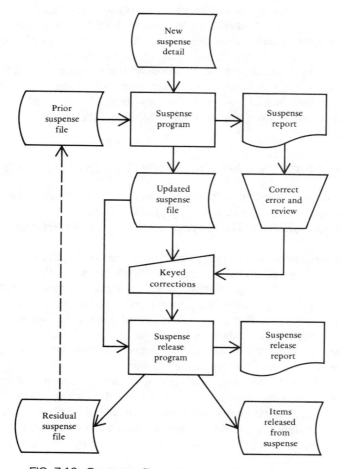

FIG. 7-10 Suspense file update and release flowchart

relieved or removed from the updated suspense file. The *residual suspense file* contains the documents not selected for correction and thus still suspended. The suspense release report that accompanies this program lists the documents removed from suspense and reestablishes balance control totals. Items released from suspense are recycled as a special batch of data and inserted into the invoicing system after the edit and balance program.

7-5   PRICE FILE MAINTENANCE

Price file maintenance entails an update of the price file. The price file update should be separate from the processing of invoices. This is advisable for several reasons. When prices require change, either the selling price or the cost of obtaining stock items or both may necessitate change. Prices may change for one branch sales office or for all offices. They may change by a fixed amount or may be raised or lowered by a certain percentage for the entire price file. Finally, if the price file is also the inventory file, as is the case with an order-filling application, the total on-hand value of stock changes as prices are altered. All these possibilities require study if the price maintenance program is to be designed correctly. Moreover, because of the various possibilities, all price changes should be reviewed before the price file is used, since any error directly affects the accuracy of invoice processing.

7-6   INVOICING AFTER COMPUTER ORDER FILLING

The use of the computer in filling customer orders is discussed in Chapter 10. This section deals with invoicing procedures that follow the computer order-filling application. The flowchart for this system is diagrammed in Figure 7-11.

The three inputs to this system are the *customer order file,* which is used to prepare computer-printed order picking labels, packing slips, and bills of lading; *special billing information,* which is keyed as input; and the *customer master file.* Special billing information includes such items as special freight charges and dollar credits. It is passed against the customer master file to verify customer numbers and to obtain customer names and addresses. The customer order file is allowed to bypass this program since customer posting is accomplished in preparing the file.

As in the stand-alone invoicing system, invoicing computer order filling produces an accounts receivable summary file and computes internal control totals that balance external control totals. In this system, the problem of maintaining balance is simplified since invoices are not suspended. All data found to be in error have been previously suspended by the order-filling application.

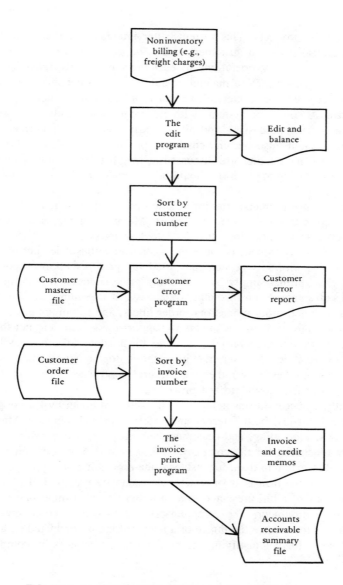

FIG. 7-11 Invoices and credit memos after order filling

7-7 MANAGEMENT IMPLICATIONS

Managerial implications of invoicing lie, in part, with the finished product—the neat, accurate, printed customer invoice. The more important benefits that result from an invoicing system, however, stem from its components and by-products. This system better integrates marketing and operations because it uses a customer master file and a master price file. Merchandise shipped by operations to customers is directly related to orders taken by marketing. With manual operations, it can become extremely difficult to correct simple clerical mistakes and customer order-shipment imbalances. A computer system, with its programmed audit trail, uncovers mistakes during processing and allows early and accurate corrections. An invoicing system also permits customer, product, and sales analyses to be conducted. These topics are discussed at length in following chapters. For now, the invoicing application should be remembered as the beginning stage of analysis.

The most useful managerial information provided by a stand-alone invoicing system is the price exception report. Members of the sales force often make excessive concessions that lead to low gross profits or even losses. These can be controlled, because the system identifies sales personnel who are reducing profits. One company used the price exception report to increase gross profits simply by controlling price concession patterns.

A disadvantage of an invoicing system is that it requires standardization. Sales personnel, order processors, order fillers, and shipping personnel must supply standard written documents to support the system and not their particular operation. Generally, those who must adapt to a new system are likely to resist it. However, the justification for standardization is that it establishes one best way rather than several good ways. Fewer mistakes in billing result from standardized procedure.

Finally, a successful invoicing system is brought about by the cooperation of several parties, both internal and external to the company. Marketing, operations, accounting, and customers help ensure that the invoicing system is fully functional for the company. This system is more difficult to implement and to maintain than, for instance, the processing of payroll. Moreover, the image of the firm is at stake when invoices are prepared. The form and the accuracy of a bill presented to a customer are most important in today's business environment. The computer-printed invoice, if consistently accurate, serves to enhance the image of a firm. Billing is conducted on a professional basis, further justifying the preparation of invoices by computer.

REVIEW OF IMPORTANT IDEAS

Invoices are valuable documents. They are used to establish the nature of a debt between a company and its customers. The invoice (as opposed to the customer order, packing slip, or bill of lading) serves as the legitimate billing document. Computer-printed invoices are more efficient to prepare than manually prepared invoices and save clerical time. The creation of master files for the invoicing application permit a company to conduct customer, product, and sales analyses—activities seldom attempted manually.

The initial input document to the invoicing system is the revised customer order. It details merchandise shipped and the customer to be billed. Other inputs include requests for credit and changes in customer name and address. These changes are extracted from the customer order and verified by the edit program.

The invoice detail file created by the edit program is verified first by the customer master file and then by the pricing file. Information from these files is combined with keyed information extracted from the revised customer order. The resulting file is used to print customer invoices.

The invoice print program is generally printer-bound for an extended period of time. A restart programming feature is incorporated into this program in case the computer suffers a mechanical failure. The invoice print program also creates a file of summary data which is retained for accounts receivable processing.

If errors are detected during the preparation of invoice data, the entire set of records for a particular bill of lading may be suspended. Newly suspended records are combined with other records awaiting error correction. When errors are resolved, computer records are corrected and released from the suspense file. They are then entered into the invoicing system. Thus the suspense file ensures that invoice records are properly controlled and that records within the system are not lost.

To further ensure that all documents are processed completely, external controls are maintained by a tally of the quantity shipped. These controls can be used even though documents are shuttled in and out of the suspense file. For the entire application, controls for input data must balance those for output data.

The customer name and address file is updated as an integral part of invoicing. Customer change data are available at the last minute, and changes are made immediately. Price changes can be made in advance and with caution, since any change in the pricing structure directly alters company profitability.

If the invoicing system follows computer order filling, the process of invoicing is simplified. File input not only exists, but also is thoroughly edited. The printing of invoices can thus begin immediately. The only complication would be due to the introduction of additional data resulting from dollar charges or credits that do not flow through the order-filling system.

REVIEW QUESTIONS

1. Why does a firm prepare an invoice rather than use the packing slip or the monthly billing statement to request payment?

2. What fields of input data entered into the invoicing computer application can be machine edited? What batch control is maintained by this application?

3. What purposes does a credit memo serve in the processing of customer invoices? The customer change slip?

4. What procedure is followed if a customer number recorded in the invoice header record does not correspond to an active customer in the customer master file? How does this procedure differ from that used when a part number does not correspond to an active part in the inventory pricing file?

5. What information is transferred from the inventory pricing file to line item invoice records?

6. In those instances where a member of the sales force is permitted to grant price concessions, what special processing requirements are added to the invoice application?

7. What main advantage is there in using the same number for both the customer order and the customer invoice? What main disadvantage? How would one determine which procedure would be better to use?

8. Why is a restart feature often incorporated in the invoice print program?

9. What basic information is provided to management as a result of the computer invoice system? Of what importance is this information?

EXERCISES

1. Design typical header and detail input records, keeping the number of characters to a minimum and yet not excluding valuable input data.

2. A customer complains that a computer-prepared invoice is incorrect. Outline the procedure to follow in deciding whether the customer's complaint is valid.

3. Compare and contrast the processing of customer invoices with the processing of vendor invoices discussed in Chapter 5. What are the similarities? What are the main differences?

8

ACCOUNTS RECEIVABLE

There are three types of accounts receivable systems:

- *balance only*
- *balance forward*
- *open item*

Each refers to a different method of retaining and reporting the amount of money a customer owes a firm. In each case, the term *accounts receivable* means the process of obtaining information about what the customer owes and what amount has been paid. This information is used to prepare up-to-date customer statements (for example, monthly statements) and supporting collection reports. The usual collection report is called the *aging schedule* or the *aged trial balance*. It identifies customers who are behind in their payments.

8-1 TYPES OF ACCOUNTS

Balance Only

Most receivables systems we as individuals encounter are balance-only accounts. Credit card and department store accounts are almost always this type. The customer statement shows the amount due for purchases made during the month and the amount due from previous months. Any past-due amount usually carries with it an interest charge. This is rather meager bill-ing statement information, but the billing company usually includes carbon copies of purchase slips to support current monthly charges. Past-due charges are not supported, nor are they aged or broken down by the number of months they have existed. This accounts receivable system is the least informative, as well as the least expensive to prepare with a computer. It requires small, simple computer files and brief customer statements.

Balance Forward

The balance-forward system provides considerably more detail both on the customer statement (for example, more information about current charges) and on the past-due customer charges, thereby increasing the complexity of the computer file and of the system itself. Each invoice or purchase is listed by a separate line showing the invoice number, the date of purchase, and the dollar amount of the purchase. Normally, the customer must compare the original customer invoice with the detail listed on the customer statement. This is the only way to be sure that billing is correct.

The balance-forward system is used by industries that serve commercial customers rather than private individuals and that expect customers to pay their total bill each month. As a result, the detail for each month is not retained for reprinting during the following month. Only the balance due is retained: hence the name balance forward or balance carry forward. If the customer fails to pay the total bill before the next printing of customer statements, the unpaid balance is printed as a separate amount, generally with an interest charge, as in the case of balance only. However, rather than just a single past-due amount, the unpaid balance is segregated by age: 30 days past due, 60 days past due, and 90 days and over past due. This aging procedure may not have any great effect on the customer—if the customer is simply not paying bills, a large past-due balance is not threatening. How-ever, the age and size of the past-due balance is important for collection activity. Accounts that are excessively past due are given greater attention. Follow-up telephone calls or legal action is initiated to collect the unpaid balance. Alternately, the customer with excessively past-due balances may be put on a cash-only basis until all debts are paid.

Open Item

The most complex receivables system is the open-item system. In this case, purchase details are printed not only for current monthly purchases, but also for any invoice that has not been paid in full. If an invoice shows an unpaid balance, it will be printed on the statement. If payments or credits partially reduce the balance of the outstanding invoice, the net amount to be paid will be printed. The end result of an open-item system is a complete accounting of customer activity for all invoices that are either unpaid or being contested.

An additional feature of the open-item system is that the customer can, and usually does, select the invoices to be paid when a cash payment is submitted. If a customer desires to protest a charge, this may be stipulated at the time of payment. The invoice in question then remains in the receivables file. Sometimes, a customer orders material and later returns it for credit. If the monthly statement is printed before a credit memo is processed, the invoice charge appears. The customer disregards this charge, knowing it will be accounted for by the next statement.

Unlike the balance-only and balance-forward systems, the open-item system probably does not specify service or interest charges for late payments or past-due invoices. Instead, discounting of the invoice is allowed to encourage prompt payment. That is, invoices for material purchased during the past month will appear first on a monthly statement. If the customer pays the current invoice before a specified closing deadline (generally the tenth of the month), the amount due for the invoice is reduced, in most cases, by 1 or 2 percent. If the invoice is not paid before the closing deadline, no discount is allowed and the balance is due in full.

It is possible to use an open-item receivables system and yet process payments *made on account;* that is, payments that do not designate which invoices are to be paid. This procedure is called *automatic cash application.* It provides a collections department with a great deal of flexibility. (The application of cash payments can be accomplished with a minimal amount of human effort. Moreover, the collections department retains the option of specifying exactly how customer payments should be applied to outstanding invoices.)

8-2 OPEN-ITEM STATEMENT INPUT DESCRIPTION

The computer application described in this chapter is an open-item accounts receivable system. The other two systems for processing accounts receivable are simpler versions of this system. Figure 8-1, the accounts receivable flow-chart, shows that three files of data are used as input to the open-item receivables system:

1. invoice summary detail
2. cash receipts file
3. accounts receivable master file

The first, the *invoice summary detail,* is produced by the invoice system described in the previous chapter. This file contains one record for every invoice (or credit memo). Each record provides the appropriate record code, customer number, invoice number, date of invoice, and amount due. (The record code distinguishes between types of records. For instance, a credit memo will be applied against a specific invoice number, but it will also be given a separate document number, which is stored and printed from the file.) Since invoices may be prepared daily, while receivables are often processed monthly, several invoice files may be used as input to processing. These files should be combined during the month, thereby removing this merge operation before month-end receivables processing begins.

The second input file, the *cash receipts file,* is produced by the cash receipts application, which is discussed in the next chapter. This file contains payments received from customers. Each record in the file identifies an invoice for which payment has been made. The record detail includes the invoice number, customer number, date of payment, and the amount of cash applied to an outstanding invoice. Cash receipts are also processed several times during the month. Hence several input files are often required in an initial accounts receivable sort.

The third input file, the *accounts receivable master file,* contains the accumulated unpaid invoices from the previous processing of the receivables system. It is the end product of the receivables processing and contains the status of every aged, unpaid invoice.

8-3 THE OPEN-ITEM ACCOUNTS RECEIVABLE SYSTEM

Figure 8-1 shows that after input of the three major files, other input to the open-item receivables system consists of three types. *Inquiry request* instructions are used to call customer accounts of interest. Details for requested customer records are printed on the inquiry report. *Adjustment details* alter customer accounts after accounting visually reviews the inquiry report. A typical adjustment results from account balance negotiations with a customer. Lastly, the *customer master file* is required during processing to add customer name and address information to the printed monthly statement. The coded customer number is used to reference customer records in this file.

Outputs resulting from the accounts receivable system consist of printed reports, since special files are not created by this computer system. The reports or printed materials produced are:

1. the inquiry report
2. the deleted invoice report
3. monthly statements
4. the aging schedule

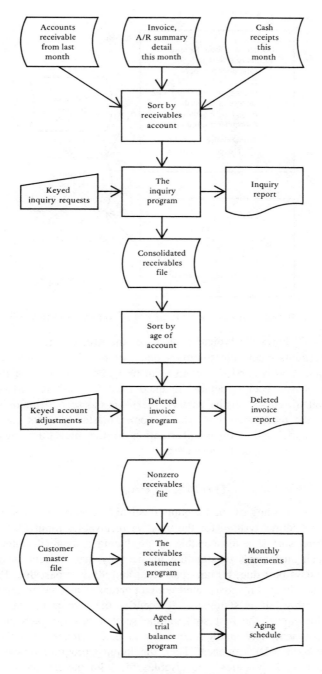

FIG. 8-1 Accounts receivable flowchart

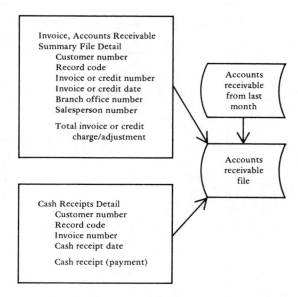

FIG. 8-2 Typical contents of the accounts receivable file

Figure 8-2 shows the typical contents of the accounts receivable file. As shown, accounts receivable summary detail prepared by the invoicing computer application is carried over to form part of the contents of the receivables file. Cash receipts detail—retained from the cash receipts computer application (discussed in the next chapter)—is the second major source of detail for the receivables file. The customer master file (not shown) adds customer name and address information to the file, allowing monthly statements to be mailed to customers.

The Inquiry Program

Successful processing of the accounts receivable system depends in part on the sort procedures written for the massive receivables input files. The end result of the sort is a file capable of producing a detailed statement that groups each customer's outstanding invoices by age: current invoices, invoices 30 days past due, 60 days past due, and 90 days past due. Payments, credits, and adjustments associated with a particular invoice are also printed on the monthly billing statement, adjacent to the invoice number.

After file input, the first sort routine sequences—for each customer—invoice, payment, and credit records by invoice number, with the invoice located first in each sequence. Then the inquiry program processes these sorted records. It prepares a receivables file with the invoice date copied from the lead invoice record onto all trailing records—payments and credits—pertaining to that invoice. The created file, although not in order for producing monthly billing statements, allows a later sort to be performed, since each record in the file now contains the originating invoice number and invoice date.

With the receivables file arranged in this order, it is possible to partially process the file. For instance, an invoice can be deleted from the receivables file if it nets to zero (that is, if the sum of debits and credits becomes zero). When this occurs, all records relating to the invoice should be removed from the accounts receivable file. Although the purpose of the inquiry program is not to remove invoices from the file, it does flag records to be deleted. The inquiry program also calculates the balance due for each invoice and adds this information to the record.

The inquiry program produces a very worthwhile report called the *inquiry report*. At the time monthly processing begins, accounting may want to know the status of specific customer accounts. For example, account balances may be in the process of negotiation, or it may be necessary to correct errors that appear on specific records. For these and other reasons, inquiry request instructions are prepared to allow accounting personnel to investigate certain customer accounts. The inquiry report (Fig. 8-3) is the printed output resulting from the use of keyed inquiry instructions. All detail for a customer's account is printed. This information is used to determine whether adjustments should be made prior to the printing of customer statements.

The inquiry report can be used to provide other information of considerable value. It offers the first opportunity to obtain a complete balance of the

AR0120	BRANCH	08			SELECTED CUSTOMER ACTIVITY					APRIL 4, 19XX PAGE 05
CUST	INVOICE	INVOICE DATE	REC. TYPE	TAX	TOTAL COST	BATCH	SLSMN	DEBIT/ CREDIT	BALANCE	CUSTOMER TOTAL
30400	17553	04-04-	S	0.87	11.00	58	04	18.32		
									18.32	18.32
41450	17207	04-04-	S	49.44	718.40	57	99	1,038.27		
									1,038.27	
	17333	04-04-	S	1.52	21.12	58	99	31.90		
									31.90	
	17436	04-04-	S	1.35	12.60	57	99	28.35		
									28.35	
	17490	04-04-	S	0.99	13.04	57	99	20.74		
									20.74	
	17491	04-04-	S	5.94	84.00	57	99	124.74		
									124.74	
	17526	04-04-	S	0.34	4.66	57	99	7.09		
									7.09	
	17539	04-04-	S	1.25	18.00	57	99	26.27		
									26.27	
	17555	04-04-	S	1.28	11.40	58	99	26.93		
									26.93	
	17581	04-04-	S	1.11	15.52	58	99	23.31		
									23.31	1,327.60
87515	17488	04-04-	S	2.60	21.28	58	03	54.60		
									54.60	54.60
97110	17518	04-04-	S	2.36	27.50	57	03	49.61		
									49.61	49.61
97540	17545	04-04-	S	0.97	11.00	58	99	20.37		
									20.37	20.37

FIG. 8-3 Inquiry report

entire receivables file—the sum of all transactions during the month. If manually prepared batch totals are correct and are properly maintained, the total value of the receivables file should equal the sum of these individual batch totals. If not, as is usually the case, errors must be located immediately. Almost without exception, failure to balance the receivables file is a result of errors in the manually prepared batch control totals. Any discrepancies must be reconciled before further processing.

It is possible to obtain still other information from the inquiry report. Since customers may compute discounts differently from the way the collection department computes them, discount calculations may differ by a few cents. If these differences are not resolved, invoices showing a balance-due of one to ten cents will appear on billing statements month after month. It is also possible for a payment or credit to slightly exceed the amount due shown on the invoice. This, too, will cause the invoice to reappear on the statement. Small shortages or excesses such as these should be printed on the inquiry report. They can then be deleted automatically through use of cutoff instructions.

However, before a cutoff point is established, it is necessary to know the effect of deleting small account balances. That is, unless a cutoff point is tested, the accounting department will not know in advance what effect it will have on the receivables balance. Actual testing is accomplished by the inquiry program as it creates the balance-due records. On completion of the program, a printout of the total loss to receivables is recorded if all transactions with balances less than the cutoff point are deleted. It is prudent to print the resulting loss for several limits such as fifty cents, one dollar, and two dollars. This information is used by accounting to select the best cutoff point for deleting small invoice records from the file. The final cutoff is then used as an input to the next program—the deleted invoice program.

The Deleted Invoice Program

There is considerable manual work that the accounting department needs to complete before the deleted invoice program can begin. For example, small balance-due cutoff totals must be reviewed to determine whether automatic deletion is necessary. The total receivables balance must be compared against manually prepared batch controls and any differences reconciled. If customer accounts were detailed by the inquiry program, these must be reviewed. Finally, any adjustments to customer accounts must be completed.

While manual work is underway, the computer is used again to sort the receivables file. During this sort, the file is sequenced for printing monthly billing statements. This sequencing requires that customer records be aged so that the oldest invoice is printed first on the statement, then the next invoice, and so forth until the most recent invoice is printed. Alongside each invoice are accompanying payments and credits. The ordering within each group of records for one invoice is sorted so that the balance-due record created by the inquiry program is the first of each group of records pertaining to an invoice. The invoice record should come next, followed by other records that accompany the invoice. Hopefully, accounting will have completed their manual review of the inquiry report by the time the entire sort is completed; otherwise the next step in processing will be delayed.

If accounting decides to use a cutoff figure of, for example, one dollar to delete small balance-due amounts from the receivables file, this information is entered via a keyed cutoff instruction at the start of the deleted invoice program run. Current invoices must not be compared to the cutoff, since a customer could escape paying for merchandise that originally cost less than one dollar. If any adjustments are in order for customer accounts, these are inserted next as special processing instructions. Customer adjustments are then entered in the same order as the sorted receivables file—aged by invoice date within each customer account.

Actual processing by the deleted invoice program begins with the balance-due records. Since these records are the first encountered for each invoice, they are used to determine whether all subsequent records for an invoice should be deleted. After this procedure, the balance-due records are dropped from the file, since they are of no further use and could become a source of confusion later on. The second stage of processing is to match cash receipts to unpaid invoices. During either of these stages, if the balance due for an invoice becomes zero, the invoice and its associated records are deleted from the receivables file. Therefore, the output from this step in processing consists only of unpaid invoices whose balances exceed the cutoff point, together with associated partial offsetting payments—credit memos and adjustments for a particular invoice.

As one might imagine, it is necessary to maintain a listing of all records dropped from the receivables file. The *deleted invoice report* meets this need. Any invoice deleted from the file is printed on this report, along with associated records removed at the same time. This listing becomes extremely long, since cash receipt records must delete the majority of outstanding receivables for the file to be stable in size. However, the deleted invoice report is invaluable as an audit trail of receivables activity.

The deleted invoice program serves other purposes. For example, it determines whether a customer needs to be sent a *multi-page receivables statement*. Some customers require a mass of printed detail on their monthly statement. In fact, the detail may exceed one page and overflow to a second statement form. Since it is advantageous to use automatic equipment to fold and stuff statements into envelopes after computer processing, multi-page statements should be segregated from normal, single-page statements. The computer counts the number of lines to be printed for each customer—one line for each receivables record—and determines whether a customer requires a multi-page statement. When more than one page is required, the customer number is printed to facilitate the segregation of multi-page statements. Then folding and stuffing can proceed without interruption.

As a final use of the deleted invoice program, control totals are accumulated for the output file created by the program. This is especially important if adjustments and balance-due cutoffs alter the balance calculated by the inquiry program. The new balance control total created at this point in processing indicates the amount of unpaid invoices and should match printed statement totals calculated by the next program—the accounts receivable statement program.

The Accounts Receivable Statement Program

Several hours or even days have generally passed from the start of receivables processing to the start of the accounts receivable statement program. Preliminary activity was necessary to ensure that input to the statement program is as accurate and complete as possible and that as much unnecessary detail as possible is eliminated.

The statement program is usually one of the longest running programs in a computer library, requiring several hours or even more than one eight-hour shift to complete. The length of the run is one reason why all control balances must be correct. It is too costly to locate and correct errors appearing on monthly printed statements. Because processing is lengthy, it is imperative that the program contain restart provisions.

In most instances, accounts receivable statements are printed in batch lots. If the receivables system serves several branch sales offices, the statements for one office will be printed following the batch control for that office. Then, the next branch office statements are printed, and so forth. For each batch, a separate control total is accumulated and printed. During restart, batch control totals should be produced a second time, even though the printing of statements is suppressed. Only then can the two runs be compared to determine whether something unexpected has occurred during the error correction.

If restart is used, it should also create new output files rather than attempt to pick up where the last run was aborted. For example, during printing, a special output file is prepared of invoice details for all customers who are considered collection accounts. These accounts require special handling in that their statements are not mailed with other customer statements. Instead, details for collection accounts are segregated during the running of the statement program. Statements are then printed separately from this special file. During restart, the creation of this special file should begin again. This procedure ensures that no unexpected problems occur.

The accounts receivable statement is the major reason for the entire accounts receivable system, as well as part of the reason for other systems such as the invoicing and the cash receipts systems. Consequently, the accounts receivable program should be carefully designed and form-fitted by the forms supplier. Care should be used in formatting receivables data to the printed statement.

Figure 8-4 illustrates one possible format. Note that it represents a balance-forward monthly statement. It shows the customer name and address, the customer account number, and the sales branch that services the customer's account. The body of the form provides room for the invoice number and date and the original amount due. If there are subsequent charges or credits, they appear directly beneath the invoice, showing (by document number) their effect on the invoice balance. The final net balance is printed so that the customer knows the amount to be paid. There is also some explanation for each document printed, with a legend to allow deciphering of the code. It is important to make the statement as readable as

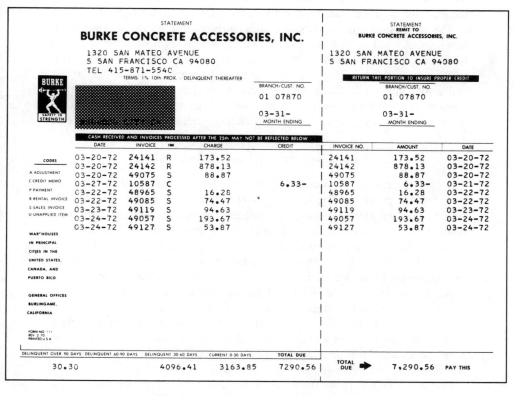

FIG. 8-4 Accounts receivable statement

possible since it is a request to the customer for payment. If the customer does not understand the details of the statement or becomes confused for lack of explanatory detail, the statement has not served its basic purpose.

The open-item monthly billing statement, as well as the balance-forward statement, has provisions for printing an aging of the balance due. The totals of current invoices, those 30 days past due, and so on are printed on the statement. This breakdown shows the customer the age of the account and serves as a reminder if he or she has become lax in meeting outstanding payments.

Another important part of the statement is the *remittance stub*. Some companies provide the customer with an extra copy of the statement in place of the stub, to use in indicating how payment is to be applied. A more common approach is to attach a remittance stub to the right side of the statement. This stub contains the customer number, the outstanding invoice numbers, and the balance due on each invoice. In preparing a payment, the customer tears off the stub, marks those invoices to be paid, and returns the stub with payment. Since the payment is returned along with the customer number, the payment can be directly applied to the proper account.

The remittance stub is preferred to a carbon copy of the statement for several reasons. It is less expensive to buy a custom form with the stub than to provide a carbon. Carbon copies are also messy to process, handle, and stuff into envelopes. They are often smudged on arrival at the customer's office and make a bad impression. Finally, the full copy of the statement contains more information than is necessary to post cash payment detail to outstanding invoices. This feature will be made clear in the next chapter.

The Aged Trial Balance Program

The last program in an accounts receivable processing system is the aged trial balance program. The term *aged trial balance* is an old phrase referring to precomputer procedures for accounts receivable. Before data were retained in computer files, records could be misplaced or could be in error. As a result, it was necessary to prepare a trial balance—the first attempt to balance the manual files—as early in a month-end operation as possible, so that errors might be detected, the cause determined, and the file corrected. Since computers have been utilized for receivables processing, errors that occur now are generally limited to external control totals—the computer is less likely to lose records. The resolution of the first balance is also completed much earlier than was the case with a manual trial balance. However, although an anachronism, "aged trial balance" still is used to designate the last accounts receivable report.

Perhaps a better, more fitting term for this final report would be "the aging schedule" or "the customer receivables report." This is certainly what the report really is. Figure 8-5 shows that the aged trial balance report summarizes the detail found on receivables statements. Most aged trial balance reports are nothing more than a reproduction of the last printed line of the receivables statements—the line that shows the amount currently due, 30 days past due, and so forth.

If just the last line of data (the aging summary totals) from the receivables statement is printed on the aged trial balance report, then this report serves as a recap of all receivables statements. However, other information can be provided by the computer program to enhance the value of this report for management. As one example, the program is often used to detect accounts that deserve special attention. These accounts are flagged by the printing of a special message, so that the collections department is immediately able to identify delinquent accounts. A common rule for separating delinquent from nondelinquent accounts is that any account whose past-due balance exceeds current sales is to be flagged for scrutiny by the collections department. Another common rule is to identify all accounts which are more than 90 days past due and above a specified dollar limit such as $500 or $1,000.

The aged trial balance program can also be used in evaluating the performance of the collections department(s). This is especially necessary when money is collected at separate branch offices. Offices that do not pursue delinquent customer accounts do not make as great a contribution to profit as offices that do. The percentage of receivables past due is a telling piece of information for branch office collections personnel. It is used as one criterion for evaluating collections performance.

BRANCH 01 SAN FRANCISCO BRANCH	ACCOUNTS RECEIVABLE AGING SCHEDULE		APR 31, 19XX	PAGE 2
CUSTOMER	TOTAL	CURRENT DUE	31-60 PAST	61-90 PAST	OVER 90
23970	417.92	417.92			
24100	74.38	72.27	2.11		
27415	91.77		91.77		
27758	162.75		162.75		
28000	13.64			11.10	2.54
28300	38.40	38.40			
28860	191.57	191.57			
29350	110.10		110.10		
29525	25.31	2.73		22.58	
32005	1,378.57	958.15	420.42		
35725	245.14	149.63	95.51		
36349	4.62	2.31	2.31		
36560	218.26	299.45	81.19-		
37050	110.63	110.63			
37150	81.90			81.90	
37310	204.14	204.14			
37600	360.91	338.58	22.33		
38200	230.34	230.34			
38805	612.04	595.57	16.47		
38900	23.63	23.63			
40830	687.62	665.07	22.55		
40900	741.02	741.02			
41930	18.89	17.85	31.50		30.46-
42185	245.41	245.41			
45020	42.00	42.00			
44260	652.72	546.09	24.08		82.55
45595	52.11	52.11			
46430	315.80	236.52			79.28
46800	23.70-	10.08			33.78-
47300	53.84	53.84			
48324	21.00				21.00

FIG. 8-5 Aged trial balance report

As a final consideration, the aged trial balance program uses the output file from the accounts receivable statement program—the final accounts receivable file. This entire file must be saved at the close of processing to be reused the following month as initial input to the system. The system continues from month to month and provides a running serial of aged customer accounts.

8-4   MONTH-END CLOSING PROBLEMS

The accounts receivable system is not very complex, nor difficult to understand or operate. The major procedural difficulty lies in the timing of inputs to the system and the results produced by the system. It is important to present receivables statements to the customer as close to the first of each month as possible, since the first statement the customer receives is the one most likely to be paid. Statements arriving late may not be paid at all, especially if the customer runs short of available cash. At the same time, the longer a company has to wait for payment from its customers, the more pressing will be its need to obtain funds to cover its own obligations. Ideally, therefore, statements should be mailed a day or two before the first of each month so that customers receive and pay them promptly.

Unfortunately, there is one situation that conflicts with the timely production of receivables statements. Sales personnel and others want to include as many outstanding invoices on the statement as possible so that the customer is billed in full—especially if salespersons, branch offices, or the billing division of a company is rated on its monthly sales activity. That is, sales activity is often measured by the volume of receivables at the time of closing the receivables file. For affected parties, there is considerable pressure to delay closing the file to permit last minute invoices to be included in processing.

To avoid the internal conflict between those involved with the processing of accounts receivable and those affected by it, month-end closing dates are generally set well in advance. Even such dates, however, are more often avoided than observed. For instance, if the final batch of invoices is due in a central location by the twenty-fifth of each month, invoices are apt to be mailed on that date, arriving a day or two later. This ensures that all possible invoices will appear on the monthly billing statements. But it also causes the entire receivables statement run to be delayed, with the resulting loss in customer payment revenue.

This internal quandary is much like Hobson's choice—there is no good alternative. On the one hand, it is necessary to make the system run as smoothly as possible, limiting the time between closing the file and printing customer statements to an absolute minimum. On the other hand, it is necessary to make the statement run of highest priority, especially if it has been delayed by balancing or adjustments. The only logical position, one followed by many firms, is to enforce the closing deadline rigidly, so that millions of dollars in receivables are not delayed for a few late arriving invoices.

To shorten the time of processing, the system may be partially run twice a month. During slack time at or around mid-month, the accounts receivable system can be processed up to the running of the statement program. This split-run operation serves two purposes: it reduces the size of the input files to the receivables system by deleting all invoices that have been paid, and it allows the deleted invoice detail to be printed—a lengthy print operation. Since the majority of cash payments are received during the first two weeks of the month, processing at mid-month substantially reduces the size of the outstanding invoice file. Since every deleted invoice is also printed, the print run that precedes the statement run is considerably shortened at month-end when actual statements are printed. Although a split-run operation requires more computer time, it reduces the work load at month-end, when human and computer time are at a premium.

8-5 MANAGEMENT IMPLICATIONS

In recent years, considerable emphasis has been placed on the management of company assets to increase profits and return on investment. Capital investment analysis has become increasingly important as a means of attaining satisfactory returns. Decisions to build or to expand factories or to select new sites for plants or sales outlets are based on the expected return of profits from a capital investment. Inventory is also managed with techniques that attempt to minimize the requirement for capital investment. In spite of all this emphasis on protecting company capital investment, the authors have observed little application of investment analysis to the most important resource of all—the investment tied to past-due invoices stored in the receivables file.

One company, for example, is known to have annual gross sales in excess of $200 million, with high enough profits to enable it to purchase other firms at a rapid rate. Yet it manages its receivables so poorly that the average invoice is 60 days past due before being paid. The company must wait two months, on the average, before receiving payment for purchased merchandise. For an item purchased in May, the company prints billing statements for May, June, and July before receiving payment in August. The customer has use of the merchandise for three months, while the company is deprived of any return on its investment.

The maximum receivables turnover for a company such as this is limited to, at most, four times a year, which is hardly often enough to cover normal business expenses. To obtain the necessary gross margin to support continued sales and this expensive receivables process, the company must charge excessive markups on its merchandise. The fact that the company's position in the market is strong of and by itself does not justify this pricing behavior. It imposes a penalty on customers who pay their bills on time. Moreover, since higher prices are passed to the consumer, it affects the customer's cost of living.

Better management of the receivables operation by this company would not only improve company profits and return on investment, thus supporting future expansion plans, but also reduce prices to customers, offsetting other inflationary pressures. The moral of this illustration is very simple: Overdue receivables profit no one—not the seller, not the buyer, and certainly not the consumer. The longer receivables are uncollected, the longer funds are withheld from the marketplace and the higher the cost of receivables becomes. Furthermore, extended receivables commonly result in a higher rate of returned merchandise and default in payment. For this reason, outstanding receivables are frequently discounted when evaluating the net worth of a company. To financial analysts, a high percentage of long-standing receivables must be considered uncollectable. This loss is passed to the customer in the form of higher costs or reduced service.

The case for sound management of accounts receivable is clear. What is less clear is how to design a highly functional system. With a computer application, it is possible to evaluate the percentage of receivables past due and to translate this into performance figures for evaluating collection practices. Even then, it is necessary to continue by analysis to evaluate existing collection and credit practices and to suggest improved alternatives.

With foresight, a computer receivables system can be designed to support a program of receivables analysis. Because of its ability to deal repeatedly with minute detail and to summarize computations, the computer can be used to evaluate each customer in the receivables file. This evaluation can then be used to set or to alter credit limits and to offer discounts to individual customers. Practices such as these improve the management of receivables—a primary company asset.

REVIEW OF IMPORTANT IDEAS

There are three types of receivables systems: balance only, balance forward, and open item. The system described at length in this chapter is an open-item system. This system retains records for every invoice and for every payment, adjustment, or credit associated with the original invoice, until the entire collection of records nets to zero.

All records associated with an invoice contain the invoice number and date so that they can be aged. This practice permits monthly billing statements to be printed showing the oldest invoice first. The statement also summarizes the balance currently due, 30 days past due, 60 days past due, and 90 or more days past due. Company policy generally permits a customer discount if payment for current charges is made by a specified deadline. The exact provisions for the discount are printed on the statement.

The monthly statement program is one of the longest running in the computer library. It is necessary to incorporate a restart feature in the program so that if mechanical problems develop, it is possible to correct the problem and start the program where the problem occurred.

The aged trial balance, or customer receivables report, is a very useful document for managing the receivables operation, provided that certain features are added to the trial balance program. One feature is to compute the accounts whose past-due balances are excessive. Another is to review the performance of collection departments by comparing the trends associated with past-due listings.

Most problems associated with the receivables system result from conflicting interests between the people responsible for operating the system and those directly affected by outstanding invoices included in the system. There is a need to include as much last minute detail as possible and also to place statements in the hands of customers as early in the month as possible. This conflict can be minimized but not completely resolved by reducing the size of the receivables files that support the system. Split-run processing allows time-consuming file processing activities to be completed during the month, rather than processing all files at month-end.

REVIEW QUESTIONS

1. Explain the differences among the following accounts receivable systems: balance only, balance forward, and open item.

2. What file detail is supplied to the accounts receivable computer application from the invoice computer application?

3. In what order are records filed as a result of the first sort routine in an accounts receivable computer application? As a result of the second sort routine? Why are these different file sequences required?

4. What information is shown on the inquiry report? Why and for whom is it printed?

5. What purposes are served by the deleted invoice computer program?

6. Why is a remittance stub attached to an accounts receivable statement? Why is the stub preferred to a carbon copy of the statement?

7. Of what importance is the aged trial balance report to management?

8. What company benefits can be realized by good management of an accounts receivable system?

EXERCISES

1. Flowchart a balance-only accounts receivable system. Compare this flowchart to the open-item flowchart and explain any differences in processing.

2. A firm determines that by eliminating from the receivables file all invoices that have outstanding balances within certain ranges, the total balance due from customers will be reduced as follows:

Range	Reduction
$.01 to $ .50	$18
$.51 to $ .75	$35
$.76 to $1.00	$60

What criteria should be developed by the firm to decide which cutoff point to use?

3. Design an open-item receivables statement. Show how this statement differs from a balance-forward statement, as illustrated in this chapter.

9

CASH RECEIPTS

Invoices and billing statements are prepared by a company and sent to customers in order to transmit current and past-due charges for merchandise shipped. *Cash receipts,* the reverse condition, are payments by customers to acknowledge receipt of merchandise and acceptance of stated terms of payment. As with customer invoices, cash receipts must be processed to update customer accounts. In this instance, however, accounts must be credited to record payments rather than debited to list customer charges for merchandise.

The accounting department of an organization processes incoming cash receipts on a continuous basis much as it posts customer charges. Since some customers decide what to pay on the basis of their receivables statements, the volume of receipts is generally heavier the first few days after monthly billing statements are issued. In spite of this one payment characteristic, the actual cash receipts pattern is difficult to predict. Many companies pay directly from the invoice. Others purchase merchandise on a cash-only basis. Still others do not pay all or even part of their bills, losing discounts and placing their credit rating in jeopardy. The flow of receipts, while heavier after delivery of monthly statements, continues unevenly throughout the month. Consequently, the management of cash flow within the organization requires careful attention. Herein lies the value of an integrated accounts receivable and cash receipts computer system. Incoming cash receipts can be matched against outstanding receivables in order to determine the availability of cash for accounts payable. The benefits of being able to predict the availability of cash will be made clear in this chapter. For now it is important to understand the cash receipts system and how the different types of receivables statements affect the way in which receipts are credited to customer accounts.

9-1 CREDITING CUSTOMER ACCOUNTS

Just as there are three major types of accounts receivable statements—balance only, balance forward, and open item—there are three general rules by which cash receipts are credited to customer accounts:

1. If payment follows from a balance-only statement, it is credited first to the past-due amount, and the remainder is applied to current charges.

2. If payment follows from a balance-forward statement, which details current invoices and shows the total past due, it is credited first to the past-due amount and second to remove the greatest number of invoices from current charges.

3. If payment follows from an open-item statement, it is applied to the oldest invoice, the next oldest, and so forth, until the payment is exhausted or all outstanding invoices have been paid.

On the open-item statement, the customer is given the opportunity to specify which invoices he or she wishes to pay. In practice, a customer may be forced to delay payment of an invoice until cash payment is received from the customer's customers. This frequently happens in the construction industry, where a contractor will defer payment of an invoice until payment is received from the buyer or the bank. A customer may choose not to pay an invoice if merchandise is to be returned. This action permits an invoice to be removed from a customer's account by a credit memo. Finally, a customer may withhold payment because he or she disagrees with the charges and is negotiating a settlement. Because of these and other reasons, open-item statements are paid according to the instructions of the customer rather than using the general rule of paying the oldest invoice first.

Open-item receivables statements sent to a customer contain a remittance advice or stub. The customer indicates on the stub how payment is to be applied to the accounts receivable balance. The stub accompanies the cash payment (that is, a bank check drawn on the customer's account). This information is used by the computer to apply the payment to an outstanding receivables balance. Before this can take place, however, the remittance stub must be reviewed by accounting. Since it is customary to allow discounts for payments made within a designated time, the customer deducts the discount when making payment. This deduction must be reviewed, since it is quite possible that the customer discounted incorrectly. Cash payment review is also necessary if a customer submits payment without indicating how it should be applied. Accounting must then contact the customer to obtain these directions, or the computer must be programmed to apply cash directly.

Since the most complex method of processing cash receipts follows from the use of open-item accounts receivable statements, this chapter describes the open-item receipts system in detail. The other systems, balance only and balance forward, are simpler versions of the open-item system. The second purpose of this chapter is to describe a method by which the computer is used to apply cash directly to a customer's receivables balance. The latter description assumes that the customer has not specified how payment is to be applied to the receivables account.

9-2 INPUTS TO THE CASH RECEIPTS SYSTEM

Because most companies emphasize cash flow, cash payments are delivered to the bank as quickly as possible. A predictable cash flow plays a major role in the short-range plans of many corporations. When a bank deposit is made, a deposit slip is prepared showing the customer's check number, account number, and the amount of the check. This slip is reviewed by bank personnel to verify each check for deposit. However, this control is fragile and represents one of the areas most vulnerable to embezzling. Shortages in cash, for instance, can be hidden by excessive discounting of customer invoices. Suppose a customer payment of $4,000 is received, half of which is applied to past-due invoices and half to current invoices. If the company allows a 1 percent discount for prompt payment, the customer receives a $20 credit, adding up to a total payment of $4,020. However, the deposit slip records the check for only $4,000.

If the full amount of money received is not deposited or is mysteriously withdrawn, the shortage can be covered by excessive discounting of customer accounts. To prevent this possibility, two actions are normally taken. First, the bank deposit slip records the amount of discount allowed and the exact amount of each check for bank verification. The deposit slip then becomes the basis for preparing the batch control slip for the cash receipts computer application. Second, cash payments are deposited in a closed account and withdrawn only by a designated company officer, such as the controller. The closed account should not be used for payables or revolving charges and definitely not for petty cash. The account is only for the deposit and withdrawal of cash receipts.

The main input to the cash receipt system is keyed remittance stubs. Figure 9-1 illustrates a typical remittance stub. It shows how a customer might note which invoices are to be paid by check. The items to be paid in full are crossed out, and amounts are indicated for those to be partially paid. Since the check amount and the total amount applied to the rece:vables file may differ because of discounts, the discount figure (not shown) is also printed on the stub for audit review. Moreover, the stub is prepared so that data entry personnel can extract the invoice number and payment amount for each invoice affected by a payment. The stub also contains the customer account number, which is keyed as an input to processing.

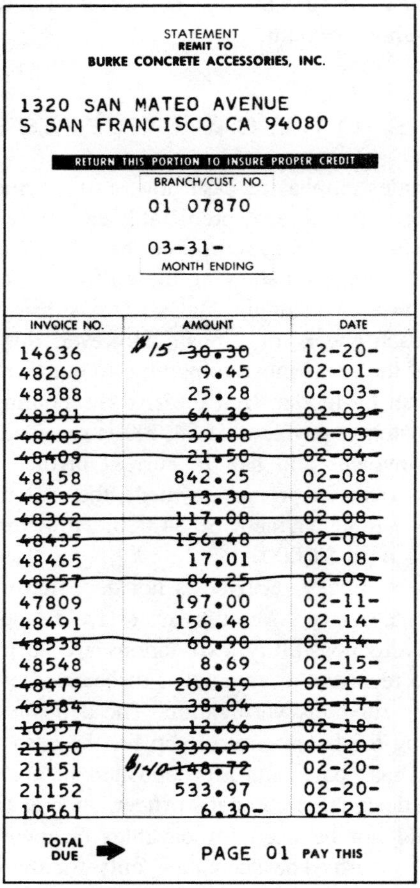

STATEMENT
REMIT TO
BURKE CONCRETE ACCESSORIES, INC.

1320 SAN MATEO AVENUE
S SAN FRANCISCO CA 94080

RETURN THIS PORTION TO INSURE PROPER CREDIT

BRANCH/CUST. NO.

01 07870

03-31-
MONTH ENDING

INVOICE NO.	AMOUNT	DATE
14636	$15 30.30	12-20-
48260	9.45	02-01-
48388	25.28	02-03-
48391	64.36	02-03-
48405	39.88	02-03-
48409	21.50	02-04-
48158	842.25	02-08-
48332	13.30	02-08-
48362	117.08	02-08-
48435	156.48	02-08-
48465	17.01	02-08-
48257	84.25	02-09-
47809	197.00	02-11-
48491	156.48	02-14-
48538	60.90	02-14-
48548	8.69	02-15-
48479	260.19	02-17-
48584	38.04	02-17-
10557	12.66	02-18-
21150	339.29	02-20-
21151	$1/10 148.72	02-20-
21152	533.97	02-20-
10561	6.30-	02-21-

TOTAL DUE ➡   PAGE 01 PAY THIS

FIG. 9-1   Remittance stub

9-3 THE CASH RECEIPTS SYSTEM

Figure 9-2 flowcharts the cash receipts system, the main purpose of which is to produce the cash receipts register and create the accounts receivable summary file. Only one file supports the processing of cash receipts detail. This is the *customer name and address file,* used to identify unknown customers.

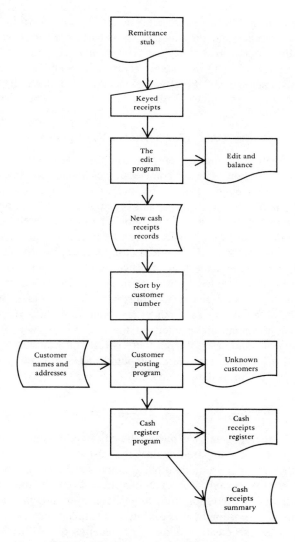

FIG. 9-2 Cash receipts flowchart

(The appearance of unknown customers in processing often results from incorrect entry of customer account numbers.) A *cash receipts summary file* is produced by processing. As discussed in the last chapter, this file is a main input to accounts receivable processing. Other outputs are:

1. edit report and balance
2. unknown customer report

The contents of a typical cash receipts detail file was shown in Figure 8-2. The customer number and the invoice number are used to match the cash receipts payment detail to the original invoice number stored in the receivables file. The record code indicates whether the receipt is a payment or a credit to a customer account. Finally, the cash receipt date can be matched to the invoice date to determine whether a discount should be allowed.

The Cash Receipts Edit Program

As shown in Figure 9-2, the first program for the cash receipts system is, as usual, the edit program. The program examines input data and creates the initial cash receipts detail. Data entry prepares an input record for each invoice being paid. Because the amount of input data is minimal—invoice number, customer number, and dollar amount (approximately 12 digits to key and 5 to duplicate)—cash receipts can be processed quickly. The batch control then contains the total amount of cash to be applied to the receivables file, a batch number, and the branch office number (if applicable).

Any adjustments processed by the system are specified by a record code to distinguish them from cash receipts. Adjustments include bad debt write-offs and write-offs of small invoice balances resulting from faulty discount calculations. All adjustments are printed on the edit report, which provides a detailed listing of input, even though there is little information to print. Following this listing, batch totals are computed and compared, and any variance is flagged for immediate correction.

The Customer Posting Program

After the cash receipts detail has passed the edit requirements, it is sorted by customer number and compared against the customer master file. Although every customer number from remittance stubs should be valid, this is not always the case. A customer account may have been discontinued, or the number reassigned. Keyed input may be in error, even though input has been visually verified. Accordingly, it is essential to validate the customer number immediately after the creation of the cash receipts detail file. In this way, errors can be resolved while original documents are accessible.

The Cash Register Program

The final processing program produces the cash receipts register (see Fig. 9-3). Besides containing information needed by the bank (such as the checking account number, the company name, and deposit date), the register details the customer account number, the check number, and the amount for each check in the deposit. Total cash receipts reflect the total of all deposited checks. The amount of discount allowed each customer also may appear. The sum of the deposits (plus the discounts) is computed and used as a batch control to validate the accuracy of data entry.

It may seem wasteful to indicate the customer account number on the cash receipts register, since the remittance stub already contains this information. However, if a customer questions whether a payment was processed, it becomes necessary to trace the check number. This is accomplished by matching the customer number to the check number, as recorded on the cash receipts register.

Cash receipts detail stored in the cash receipts file lacks the date of the original invoice, which is essential to producing an aged accounts receivable statement. Because of this, the cash receipts file must be sorted by invoice number within each customer number. This sequence can also be used for

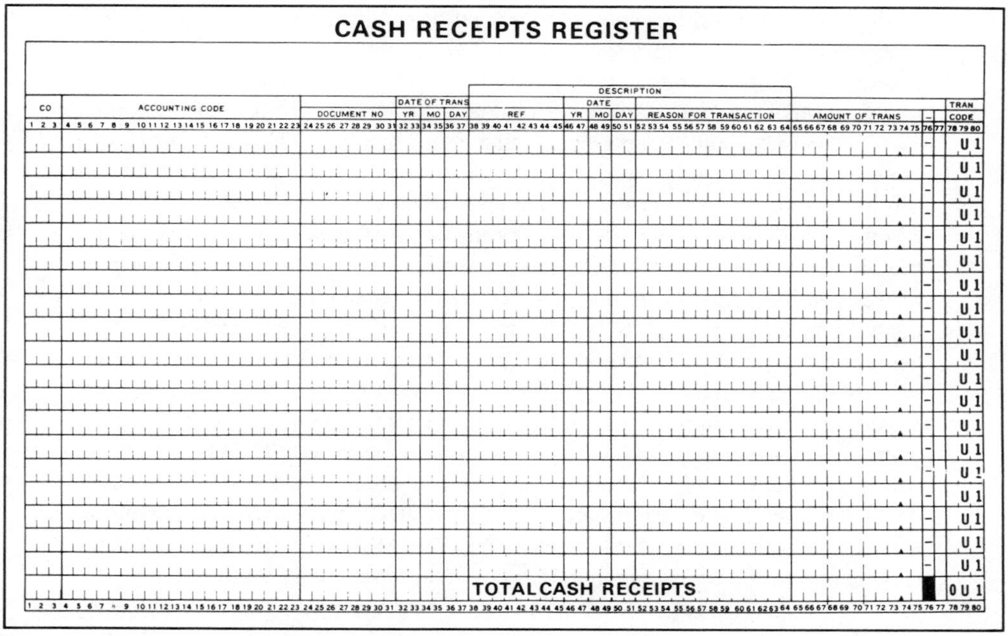

FIG. 9-3 Cash receipts register

customer number editing, and so one sort may serve for both customer editing and updating the accounts receivable master file. Finally, this sequence is used to create the cash receipts summary file. However, the accounts receivable file must also be sorted by invoice number within customer number. Only after both files are in the same order is it possible to combine them, copying the invoice date from the receivables record to the cash receipts record. This procedure reduces data entry time since the invoice date is not punched. More importantly, it reduces error in that if the date were entered as input, it would at times be incorrect. By using the date stored in the receivables file, all records for an invoice can be combined until the invoice is paid in full.

9-4 AUTOMATIC CASH APPLICATION

The system described thus far requires customers to indicate which invoices they intend to pay with their payment. However, if individual invoices or purchases are consolidated into one receivables total, the computer can apply payment first to the past-due or prior month balance and then to the current month balance. Most credit card accounts use this procedure. The customer cannot specify how a payment should be applied. Allocation of cash to each invoice, therefore, is not necessary.

The open-item receivables statement can be retained even when automatic cash application procedures are used. This complicates the design of the accounts receivable computer application but it has considerable merit for many companies. For example, a customer submits a check and does not specify how it should be applied to outstanding invoices. This is a *payment-on-account*. Or, the total of all payments posted to a single invoice is slightly different from the amount due. Since an invoice cannot be deleted from the receivables file until it nets to zero, the invoice may appear on the statement month after month. Such imbalances confuse the detail printed on the monthly billing statement and complicate the managing of customer accounts. In both cases, it is helpful to apply cash payments automatically, using the computer to determine how uncommitted money should be applied to customer accounts.

Automatic cash application requires an interesting modification to the accounts receivable application. In particular, a *cash application program* needs to be added as an essential step in processing. A sort program precedes the cash application program. This sort places payments-on-account in front of committed payments for each customer. Payment-on-account detail, or uncommitted cash, is accumulated and held temporarily while the receivables file is processed. Since both the receivables file and the cash receipts file are sequenced by invoice number within customer number, posting of uncommitted cash is processed by lowest invoice number first. That is, if a net balance remains for the lowest invoice number following a committed payment, uncommitted cash is applied in an attempt to reduce the invoice to zero. In the reverse situation, if a committed payment exceeds the amount due, excess cash can be added to the total of payment-on-account detail. This cash can then be applied to the next lowest invoice number in a customer's account. If an amount of uncommitted cash remains after a customer's invoices have been processed, it is inserted into the updated receivables file as an unapplied cash record and used during the next processing of the accounts receivable system.

This procedure is obviously not perfect. It pays the invoice with the lowest invoice number first rather than paying the oldest invoice first—as desired by the general rule for processing. While the oldest invoice may well have the lowest number, this is not always the case. Another problem is that when a surplus of cash is uncovered, it is immediately applied to the next invoice in a customer's file rather than to the oldest invoice. This again may not clear the oldest invoice from the file. These problems can be circumvented by making uncommitted cash processing a two-stage operation. The first stage simply discovers uncommitted cash. The receivables file is then sorted by age. The second stage applies uncommitted cash to the oldest invoice. Even then, however, one problem remains. The customer may not agree with the manner in which cash was applied or not understand how an account balance was derived.

When cash is being automatically applied to a customer's account, the net effect on a customer's balance can be printed. Figure 9-4 illustrates such an application of cash. Many collection departments rely heavily on the *cash application report* to assist in follow-up on customer payments and late or delinquent accounts. For instance, in industries where customer credit is questionable, it is common to place customers on a cash-only basis if a statement is not paid by the fifteenth of the month. The cash application report is very useful for this purpose. However, if cash receipts are combined with accounts receivable frequently, an entire listing of all customer accounts may contain too much detail or exist in too many versions. In this case, it is desirable to print the details of a customer's account on an inquiry basis. This means that if details for an account are required, only that account (unless others are also requested) is printed. All other accounts are omitted from the cash application report.

The updated accounts receivable file produced following customer instructions on payment-on-account procedures contains the original receivables data and the cash receipts detail. The enlarged file should be set aside and used for the next running of the accounts receivable system. Even though a customer account nets to zero, the cash receipts detail is saved.

```
 UPDATE AUDIT                    ACCTS RECEIVABLE    DATE 05/17/    PAGE 22

 CUST  NAME                      ADDRESS                    ORDER    TYPE    DEBIT       CREDIT
 7833  ▓▓▓▓▓▓▓▓▓▓▓▓▓▓▓▓▓▓       30TH AND OCEAN BEACH       G99999    6                   584.38
 7833  ▓▓▓▓▓▓▓▓▓▓▓▓▓▓▓▓▓▓       30TH AND OCEAN BEACH       G99999    6                  4019.79
 7833  ▓▓▓▓▓▓▓▓▓▓▓▓▓▓▓▓▓▓       30TH AND OCEAN BEACH       G99999    1                  5917.27
 7856  ▓▓▓▓▓▓▓▓▓▓▓▓▓▓▓▓▓▓       620 NE HALSEY              G99999    6
 7856  ▓▓▓▓▓▓▓▓▓▓▓▓▓▓▓▓▓▓       620 NE HALSEY              G99999    6                     9.22
 7856  ▓▓▓▓▓▓▓▓▓▓▓▓▓▓▓▓▓▓       620 NE HALSEY              G99999    6                     9.22
 7856  ▓▓▓▓▓▓▓▓▓▓▓▓▓▓▓▓▓▓       620 NE HALSEY              G99999    7      10.89
 7856  ▓▓▓▓▓▓▓▓▓▓▓▓▓▓▓▓▓▓       620 NE HALSEY              G99999    6                    64.95
 7856  ▓▓▓▓▓▓▓▓▓▓▓▓▓▓▓▓▓▓       620 NE HALSEY              G99999    6                    58.60
 7856  ▓▓▓▓▓▓▓▓▓▓▓▓▓▓▓▓▓▓       620 NE HALSEY              G99999    1                    69.61
 7861  ▓▓▓▓▓▓▓▓▓▓▓▓▓▓▓▓▓▓                                  G99999    6                   128.96
 7861  ▓▓▓▓▓▓▓▓▓▓▓▓▓▓▓▓▓▓                                  G99999    8       2.73
 7861  ▓▓▓▓▓▓▓▓▓▓▓▓▓▓▓▓▓▓                                  G99999    6                  1720.36
 7861  ▓▓▓▓▓▓▓▓▓▓▓▓▓▓▓▓▓▓                                  G99999    7      14.23
 7861  ▓▓▓▓▓▓▓▓▓▓▓▓▓▓▓▓▓▓                                  G99999    1                   139.21
 7873  ▓▓▓▓▓▓▓▓▓▓▓▓▓▓▓▓▓▓       10TH AND COURT             G99999    6
 7873  ▓▓▓▓▓▓▓▓▓▓▓▓▓▓▓▓▓▓       10TH AND COURT             G99999    6                    43.55
 7873  ▓▓▓▓▓▓▓▓▓▓▓▓▓▓▓▓▓▓       10TH AND COURT             G99999    7      29.50
 7873  ▓▓▓▓▓▓▓▓▓▓▓▓▓▓▓▓▓▓       10TH AND COURT             G99999    6                    22.95
 7873  ▓▓▓▓▓▓▓▓▓▓▓▓▓▓▓▓▓▓       10TH AND COURT             G99999    6                    45.52
 7873  ▓▓▓▓▓▓▓▓▓▓▓▓▓▓▓▓▓▓       10TH AND COURT             G99999    6                    60.02
 7873  ▓▓▓▓▓▓▓▓▓▓▓▓▓▓▓▓▓▓       10TH AND COURT             G99999    6                    57.90
 7873  ▓▓▓▓▓▓▓▓▓▓▓▓▓▓▓▓▓▓       10TH AND COURT             G99999    6                    87.72
 7873  ▓▓▓▓▓▓▓▓▓▓▓▓▓▓▓▓▓▓       10TH AND COURT             G99999    6                    19.50
 7873  ▓▓▓▓▓▓▓▓▓▓▓▓▓▓▓▓▓▓       10TH AND COURT             G99999    6                    10.66
 7873  ▓▓▓▓▓▓▓▓▓▓▓▓▓▓▓▓▓▓       10TH AND COURT             G99999    1                    19.50
 7901  ▓▓▓▓▓▓▓▓▓▓▓▓▓▓▓▓▓▓       PO BOX 1020                G99999    6
```

FIG. 9-4   Cash application report

9-5   CASH FLOW PREDICTION

One of the most difficult tasks in accounting, particularly in accounts receivable, is to predict accurately how much and when customer payments will be collected. The average company does not maintain more than minimal cash reserves, since cash (even in a savings account) is nearly always less productive than investments in inventory, production facilities, and the like; and yet there are monthly expenses to be met such as payroll, travel, production, and bills due company vendors. In order to meet the demand for cash, a company must be supported by cash reserves, by borrowing, or by collecting cash from customers. One problem is that several days are generally needed for a company to obtain a loan, even when it has an established line of credit. Consequently, it is necessary to be able to predict almost on a daily basis what cash receipts can be expected. If receipts to receivables can be predicted, loans to offset lack of cash may be obtained only as needed.

The key to cash flow prediction is the ability to model or predict the way in which customers pay their bills, based on past receipts history. Often referred to as *simulation,* the computer model must reflect seasonal variations as well as variations during the average month. Most industries experience some fluctuation in sales during a year, and this fluctuation affects the status of accounts receivable. The amount of cash payment due when statements are printed also affects the potential cash flow during the month to follow. This is particularly true of current balances; the past-due balance is less predictable. In short, it is both possible and necessary to model the flow of cash receipts based on past receipts history. As a word of caution, however, the model must be subject to extensive testing before any funds are staked on its reliability. It may be better to use no model at all than to rely on a misleading predictive model.

9-6 MANAGEMENT IMPLICATIONS

Cash receipts systems have received considerable attention in recent years. More aggressive banks, for instance, are promoting "lock-box" or "payment drop" systems, where the customer mails a remittance directly to the nearest branch of the bank and the bank immediately credits the payment to the seller's account. A more extreme case is where companies kite their checks—mailing payments on their own bills before their customers have made payments. Another alternative is to mortgage expected receipts to obtain even faster use of anticipated receivables.

These business practices are ways to gain faster use of customer cash receipts. Each has its advantages and disadvantages. Use of the computer, however, offers a more advanced approach. Computer programs are written to predict available cash receipts. One method used in prediction is to analyze customers' payment habits. This method requires current information concerning cash receipts and demand for cash. Normally, there is some delay between acquisition of cash—the deposit into company accounts—and its being recorded as input to the cash receipts system. This delay occurs partly because the cash receipts system is normally a low-priority computer operation compared to payroll and invoicing and partly because manual activity must precede the submission of cash receipts data. For example, cash remittance stubs must be manually reviewed and altered before they are ready; discounts must be allowed, or disallowed and adjusted; and control totals must be manually computed. All this takes considerable time. If, in addition, receipts are collected at several locations, incoming data must be transmitted from the branch to the computer location, resulting in further manual delay in data acquisition. To be highly supportive, a computer receipts system must be given higher priority than it usually is, particularly in highly leveraged companies, where the timeliness of cash acquisition is nearly as important as the actual volume of business.

REVIEW OF IMPORTANT IDEAS

The way in which customers pay their bills depends on the type of monthly billing statement they receive. In the cash receipts system for the open-item statement, cash payments are processed in accord with instructions submitted by the customer with the cash payment.

Most cash receipts systems expect the customer to return a remittance stub noting how payment is to be applied. This stub, together with the customer's payment, is used to input data to the cash receipts system. The process of supplying correct computer input is complicated by discounts, since there may be different interpretations of the discount a customer is entitled to. Each remittance stub must be manually checked so that receipts can be properly applied. This checking must take place prior to data entry.

Cash payments on account can be applied by the computer automatically. The procedure for processing uncommitted cash payments is not always ideal, in that either the oldest invoice is not removed from a customer's account, as would be desired, or the customer is confused about how uncommitted cash is applied. The cash application report is used in determining the account status of customers, when and if customers require classification of their cash payment obligations.

If customer payment habits can be reasonably predicted, it is possible to model cash received throughout a month. Simulation, or predictive modeling, generally requires a reordering of priorities, but an accurate simulation is of immense value in the planning of the cash flow in a company.

REVIEW QUESTIONS

1. Just as there are three types of accounts receivable systems, so there are three methods by which cash payments are credited to customer accounts. Explain what these methods are.

2. Why is a closed bank account recommended for deposits of cash payments by customers?

3. What is the keyed input to the cash receipts computer application? How does this input differ from that discussed in Chapters 4 through 6?

4. What types of adjustments must be made to the cash receipts system?

5. Why must the customer number on the remittance stub be verified during processing? What would happen if this step were omitted in processing?

6. Why must new cash receipts file detail be sorted prior to the printing of the cash application report?

7. What happens to customer records when cash receipts file detail is combined with accounts receivable detail? Why is cash receipts detail saved?

8. Explain what is meant by automatic cash application.

EXERCISES

1. Some sales agreements include special payment provisions such as full payment within 90 days and one-third of the outstanding balance due every 30 days. No discount is allowed nor is any service charge assessed during the 90-day period. How would cash payments be processed under this type of sales agreement?

2. As the financial manager for a company, you are approached by a banking representative who tries to convince you that your company should develop a lock-box system. (In a lock-box system, customers are asked to mail their payments to a local post office box maintained by the bank, which deposits the payments and sends the company a record of the transactions.) What difficulties might you anticipate from such a system? What would determine whether a lock-box system would be of value to your firm?

3. Develop a conceptual framework (a systems flowchart) integrating the six computer applications discussed thus far. Within the framework show the effect of each computer application on the cash resources of a firm. Also identify and illustrate the use of short-term loans to adjust the level of cash resources. (*Note:* The framework should be limited to a one-page systems flow. Use one symbol to indicate the effect of customer invoices, another to show the effect of cash receipts, and so forth.)

4. Design a revised accounts receivable application to illustrate automatic cash application. Show what, if any, changes need to be made to the accounts receivable file—before and after the deletion of invoices that net to zero.

III

MATERIALS- AND OPERATIONS-CONTROL APPLICATIONS

The uncertainty under which firms operate necessitates scientific treatment of such materials-related business transactions as processing customer orders, stocking and restocking inventory, scheduling orders for manufacture, analyzing and costing work projects, and analyzing labor-hours expended. Computer processing of such activities can greatly benefit company efficiency. Decision rules can be programmed to process the routine transactions and to anticipate normal operating conditions. However, flexibility must be built into the design so that alternative plans can be enacted if unexpected situations occur.

10

ORDER FILLING

This chapter describes how a computer order-filling system (or order-entry system) provides fast response to customers' requests for merchandise. The typical order-filling system serves three primary functions.

1. It provides order-filling information used by warehouse crews to pick stock from inventory to be shipped to customers.

2. It updates computer inventory records based upon incoming stock to inventory and filled order shipments to customers.

3. It retains summary data for accounting and invoicing computer applications as well as for predicting future inventory requirements.

Other activities, combined with these three, make the order-filling system one of the more valuable as well as one of the more complex business computer applications.

Since an order-filling system is designed to serve more than one processing function, it must be highly efficient to work successfully. For example, the goal of fast response to customer orders creates considerable pressure to meet daily deadlines for production of printed documents, particularly *picking labels* (labels used for locating stock in a warehouse) and *packing slips* (slips used to ship stock to customers). Warehouse crews must complete shipments of orders by five o'clock on the day received. This crew deadline, combined with the latest possible computer start-time (set late to process as

161

many orders as possible), puts pressure on the computer staff to perform at high efficiency. The key to successful performance is to hold to a minimum the processing time between the input to the system and the production of picking labels and packing slips. Once these vital stock and shipping documents are printed, other features of the order-filling application can be completed at a more leisurely pace.

In an order-filling application, two massive processing runs must be made prior to the printing of picking labels and packing slips. These are the posting of order transactions both against a customer master file and against an inventory parts file. The first posting operation compares input by customer account; the second, by part or product number. Because both of these files are large, a sequential magnetic tape file lengthens processing. Accordingly, these two posting operations are the major justification for indexed-sequential file disk storage, which allows direct access to file storage locations.

10-1   AN INVENTORY-LOCATION MODEL

Inventory records simulate the actual contents of a warehouse. In effect, an inventory-location model, based on arithmetic counts and totals, is designed as though it were a miniature warehouse. Logically, if this model, or inventory parts file, shows enough material on hand to fill an order, enough material should be actually in the warehouse to send to a customer. The principle is sound, but real life may not be logical. For example, order pickers (those who fill orders from stock) sometimes select incorrect stock. This error causes too little stock to be where the incorrect material was obtained.

Because of problems such as this, the modeled representation of the contents of the warehouse is not always exact for all part numbers. However, differences between what is predicted and what exists can be resolved in two ways: by adjustment slips and by periodic physical inventory of all stock. Suppose that the computer assigns 100 items of part number 003 to a customer order; the computer inventory file shows an on-hand balance of 120 items, but the order picker finds only 95 items in the warehouse bin for part number 003. It is then necessary to adjust not only the customer's record to show the reduction in material actually sent but also the inventory record to reflect the actual count of parts in the bin. An *adjustment slip* can be used to correct both the amount sent to the customer and the on-hand field of the inventory record that corresponds to part 003. Clearly, the greater the validity of the inventory-location model, the better the performance of the order-filling system. Through the use of adjustment slips, the model is brought closer to reality.

Periodic physical inventory is an accounting of all items in an inventory. This manual procedure is discussed in the next chapter.

10-2 INPUT DESCRIPTION

There are several types of input, other than adjustment slips, to the order-filling system. The most familiar—the *customer order*—supplies two types of input: information for filling an order and information for updating the customer file. In the latter case, provisions must be made for adding new customers to the customer master file or for changing billing and shipping instructions for existing customers.

Actual receipt of an order can take a variety of forms. Order clerks initially prepare handwritten order forms. A typical order form is shown in Figure 10-1. (In this example, the section for special instructions gives space to enter special shipping instructions or the name and address of a new customer.) Sometimes orders are obtained from branch sales offices if salespersons are assigned to branch offices rather than to a central office. In this case, when orders are received from customers, the orders are completed at

COMPUTER ORDER FORM

HUDSON HOUSE, INC.
PORTLAND, OREGON

C	MO	DAY	YR	DPT	ORDER NUMBER	CUST #	BO	SUB	UPCH	SP	PRI
	5	17	2	6	039957	8787					

SPECIAL INSTRUCTIONS

CODE	QTY	CODE	QTY	CODE	QTY	CODE	QTY
04168	1						
00148	2						
28608	1						
00616	1						
22217	1						

FIG. 10-1 Handwritten order form

the branch and sent as a batch to the order-filling warehouse. Generally, batch orders are received just prior to the deadline for processing orders for the day. The data entry staff must convert orders to computer input in time to meet the processing schedule. Telephone orders and teletyped requests are also received during the day. These enter data entry and are converted following a more flexible schedule.

Unless the customer master file is very stable, as it would be for exclusive sales to franchised dealers, order forms must provide space for recording customer address changes and for entering information about new customers. Customer change information should be accepted with order information to permit the most current customer data to be used in preparing picking labels and packing slips. Customer change information alters the name and address records of the customer file just prior to the posting of order transactions themselves. This is an extremely important procedure, as will be explained later. Customer order forms also provide space for special shipping or routing instructions. These data should be keyed with the order information, since they will be printed on the packing slip.

While the latest customer data must be used in processing to permit shipment of merchandise to the correct address, the same necessity does not govern changes in the inventory parts file. Because the company has control over what is or is not in the file, the inventory file is more stable than the customer file. In addition, changes to the inventory file are made on the basis of either new shipments from manufacturing or suppliers, or physical inventory adjustments. The inventory file should be changed with considerable caution, since it represents the contents of the inventory-location model for the warehouse and also represents the direct dollar investment for inventory by a company.

Another input to an order-filling system is the *credit memo,* which adjusts a customer's file for items being returned. Generally, credits are given so long as merchandise can be resold. Still another input is the *adjustment for overstated items in stock.* In the previous example of insufficient material, computer records showed 120 items on hand, and yet the warehouse crew found only 95 items in stock. If the crew later finds the missing stock in some other bin and moves it to the correct bin, the on-hand quantity must be further adjusted to show the withdrawal and replacement of the missing material.

The last two types of input to the order-filling system are orders that have been suspended and those placed on back order. *Suspended orders* result from errors detected in customer order data, such as an invalid part number or incorrect customer number. Because picking labels cannot be delayed while records in error are corrected and reprocessed, these records are flagged and segregated into a suspense file. Suspense relief procedures are followed daily (see Fig. 7-10) to allow suspended orders to be processed with the next order-filling run. *Back orders* are orders than cannot be filled because of insufficient stock. New stock must arrive before back orders can be filled. Hence any unfilled balance of a customer order is placed in a special file, the back-order file. Normally, completing back orders is a high priority, but they may not be processed daily. The attempt to fill them is usually made after new stock has been received from warehouse suppliers and inventory records have been updated to show the increase. Back orders are processed against this enlarged file during the next order-filling operation.

Input to the order-filling system consists of keyed data for new orders, credit memos, and adjustments. It also includes two input files: one for back orders and one for items released from suspense. Each input is controlled by priorities associated with how processing should be sequenced—which orders should be filled first from available stock. Every record used by the system is assigned a priority code.

10-3 THE ORDER-FILLING SYSTEM

Figures 10-2 and 10-3 illustrate the processing stages of the order-filling system. The systems flowcharts—one for order-filling preparation, the other for order-filling processing—identify four main files that support the processing of order transactions:

1. back-order files
2. suspense files
3. customer master file
4. inventory parts file

The *back-order files* store orders taken but not filled; the *suspense files* store orders found in error. The *customer master file* contains up-to-date listings of customers for whom orders are placed. This file is the same as that required in invoice, cash receipts, and accounts receivable computer applications. However, for this application, the ship-to as well as the bill-to address must be contained in each customer record. The *inventory parts file* represents an accurate accounting of on-hand materials carried in stock. This file is made up, in part, of the data elements contained in the inventory pricing file, as required in customer invoicing. Inputs to the order-filling application consist of:

1. customer orders
2. batch controls
3. credit memos
4. adjustments

These are in addition to inputs from the four basic files. Outputs from the system include:

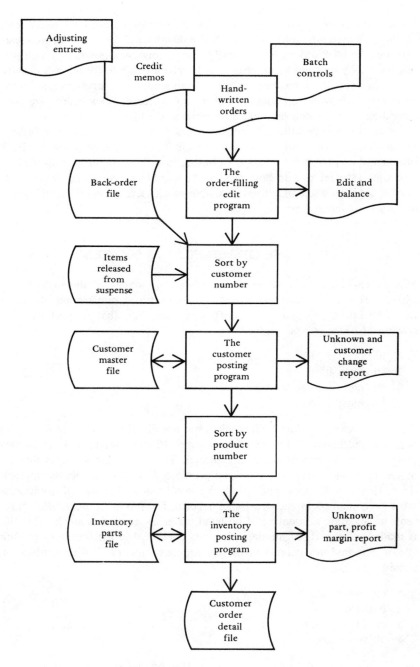

FIG. 10-2 Order-filling preparation flowchart

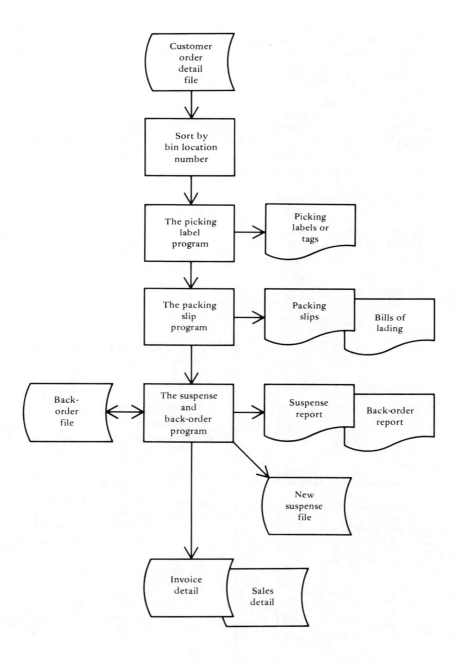

FIG. 10-3 Order-filling processing flowchart

1. updated back-order and suspense files
2. updated customer file
3. updated inventory parts file
4. invoice detail file
5. sales detail file

The *invoice detail file* stores data for use in preparing customer invoices and monthly statements. The *sales detail file* is used to analyze sales of stock, by customer, and thus helps predict inventory requirements. Outputs other than updated files consist of the following reports or printed materials:

1. edit and balance report
2. unknown and customer change report
3. unknown parts report
4. picking labels or tags
5. packing slips and bills of lading
6. suspense report
7. back-order report

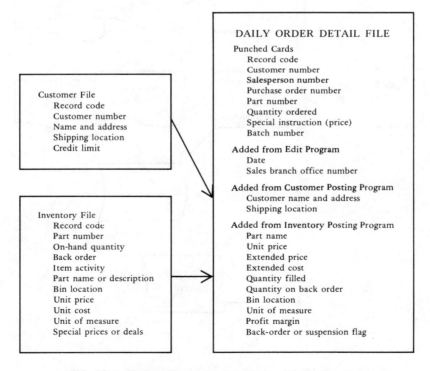

FIG. 10-4 Typical file contents of the order-filling system

Typical contents of the customer, inventory, and daily customer order detail files are shown in Figure 10-4. The customer file is arranged by record code and customer number. The inventory file is arranged by record code and part number. The daily customer order detail file can be shown at several stages of processing. Keyed input is initially arranged by record code, customer number, purchase order number, part number, and quantity ordered. The edit program adds the processing date and the sales branch office number, if desired. The customer posting program adds the customer's name and address, used in preparing the packing slips. Finally, the inventory posting program adds inventory file detail, such as the unit price and cost of the merchandise ordered; the quantity to be filled; the bin location of the merchandise; and whether or not the order is to be suspended or placed on back order.

The order-filling application is complex because it involves several processing stages and massive files. The customer file requires the name and address of every customer who orders merchandise from the company. The inventory file contains an accurate accounting of all inventory, by bin location, within a warehouse. Processing must be done quickly to allow prompt filling of customer orders. All orders must be filled accurately to ensure that customer service consistently meets industry standards as well as the customer's needs. This is a difficult data processing task, and computer programs for this application must be carefully designed.

The Order-Filling Edit Program

The edit program for the order-filling computer application identifies and prints errors resulting from faulty input data. These errors should be corrected immediately and the edit program rerun, even though this procedure consumes valuable processing time. Failure to correct faulty input at the beginning results in an overly large suspense file—and many dissatisfied customers. A few of the possible errors that may be detected are invalid record code, missing salesperson number, and incomplete numeric fields (for example, incomplete part numbers). A common error is the quantity ordered by a customer. Since there is really no way to check the quantity ordered, the running total of each order line is compared to an external batch control total.

The edit report can be programmed either to list all order entries or simply to print diagnostic and error messages (see Fig. 10-5). It is generally preferable to list the complete detail, even though this listing requires additional print time. If there are errors in the input, as there almost always are, the complete listing is invaluable in locating and correcting them. The diagnostic message lists the number of the invalid entry to facilitate locating the error; it should also report the type of error to aid correction.

```
                              ERROR
        PART #           BIN #  CONDITION                 P.O.  INVOICE #

      C-8769, I-Y0885  Q- 001 N.I.F.                        P31828
      C-8797, I-Y0912  Q- 001 N.I.F.                        P31864
      C-8733, I-Y1868  Q- 003 N.I.F.                        P31862
      C-3541, I-55756  Q- 001 N.I.F.                        M32090
      C-7492, I-55756  Q- 001 N.I.F.                        M32079
      C-3541, I-56437  Q- 001 N.I.F.                        M32090
      C-6534, I-56437  Q- 001 N.I.F.                        M32016
      C-0096, I-56437  Q- 001 N.I.F.                        M32175
      C-0841, I-00211  BAD BID COST    6.75 BID   6.54   1  I32154
      C-3136, I-01575  Q- 001 N.I.F.                        I32036
      C-1072, I-44260  Q- 001 N.I.F.                        F32135
      C-7878, I-45638  BAD BID COST    5.55 BID   3.85   3  F32060
      C-7396, I-45952  Q- 001 N.I.F.                        F32112
      C-7396, I-45953  Q- 001 N.I.F.                        F32112
      C-3679, I-91153  BAD BID COST    3.05 BID   3.00   3  I31984
      C-6072, I-H2629  Q- 001 N.I.F.                        I32044
      C-8536, I-H5663  Q- 004 N.I.F.                        I31995
      C-4349, I-H6334  Q- 001 N.I.F.                        I32039
      C-0449, I-H6440  Q- 001 N.I.F.                        I32031
      C-8862, I-H7139  Q- 001 N.I.F.                        I31996
      C-6279, I-H8789  Q- 002 N.I.F.                        I31988
```

FIG. 10-5 Order-filling edit report

One optional feature that may further speed editing is the suppression of the detail print lines during any repeat of the edit program. If detected errors are corrected, it is necessary to print only control totals and any diagnostics that occur. Errors should have been resolved during the first pass through the program. Hence suppressing the detail printing will significantly increase the speed of rerunning the edit.

Recycled orders from the suspense or back-order files can also be processed by the edit program. However, since they have already successfully cleared the edit, another edit will do little good. To save time, these files are put into the sort program, which follows the edit of new orders.

The Customer Posting Program

As mentioned, an order-filling system can utilize a direct access disk file to facilitate rapid access to file storage locations. Even so, a sort of the edited daily order detail is necessary to sequence transactions by customer number for posting against the customer name and address file. After this sort, actual posting begins by checking the validity of all customer numbers in the order detail. Customer data are then added to the customer order detail file. The customer posting program also verifies the acceptability of new orders by using customer credit information included in the customer record. Furthermore, if the order-filling system incorporates multiple sales office data, branch office data retained in the customer record are copied to the enlarged order detail file.

The unknown and customer change report printed by the customer posting program shows customers not on file and changes made in the customer file. Customers appearing on the unknown section of the report cannot be processed further. These orders must be suspended. Stated differently, *the entire order must be suspended even if it can be filled*. Without an accurate customer record, there is no way to address the invoice or shipping papers or to determine whom to bill for the material ordered.

Deleting the customer order (that is, dropping the records for an unknown customer) is dangerous even if the deletion is printed on the unknown customer report. The chances are too great that follow-up action will not be taken, since resubmission requires a manual operation. This customer problem may never be solved, and an irate customer will undoubtedly protest. In addition, deleting orders disrupts any batch controls being maintained, thereby confusing the audit trail and making it difficult to satisfy company auditors that all processing steps are as exacting as they should be. Accordingly, each record associated with an unknown customer should be flagged. Once the picking labels and packing slips are completed, the flagged records can be written to the suspense file. Moreover, the suspense file can be printed, with diagnostic messages to explain the problem.

The unknown and customer change report also indicates any modifications in the records on current customers as well as deletions of old customers or additions of new ones. To minimize confusion resulting from a missing or incorrect record for a customer, provisions should be made during the customer posting program to record changes in customer records and add new customers. Obviously, customer sort keys should be associated with each change to the customer file so that these changes are sorted before order detail is processed. Changes to the customer name and address must be made before the program enlarges the order detail, or the detail will be in error.

The customer change section of the unknown and customer change report is a register of actual changes made to the file (see Fig. 10-6). An is/was reporting format shows the contents of a record before and after a change. Considerable care must be taken in reviewing this portion of the report because changes to customer records are not subject to programmed error detection, nor can they be batch controlled. Therefore it is not uncommon to find names and addresses changed incorrectly. Any errors discovered can be manually corrected by changing incorrect shipping papers after they are printed. At this point in processing, it is too late to stop the program to correct errors. Instead, the file must be corrected during the next order-filling run.

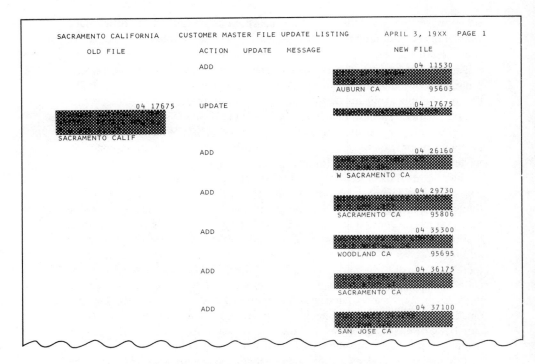

FIG. 10-6 Unknown and customer change report

It is quite possible that the customer posting program will be too large and complex both to enlarge the daily order detail and to alter the customer file in one processing step. Both operations require several diagnostic tests. Rather than continually fight this problem, it is possible to design a separate customer file update routine to run while the edit report is being reviewed and errors corrected. Regardless of which method is used, however, the customer file must be as correct as possible to minimize the number of orders placed in the suspense file.

The Inventory Posting Program

The enlarged order detail file that results from customer posting contains both the original input and customer names and addresses. If a customer places more than one order, the detail file will contain a separate set of customer records, one for each order, since this is the easiest way to print picking labels and shipping documents. Since customer records are not affected by the inventory posting program, they can be sorted and placed at the end of the detail file. This procedure shortens the processing time required for the actual posting of inventory to customer orders.

The inventory posting program follows naturally after the customer posting program. For example, if a customer's order is flagged for suspension,
no attempt is made to fill the order; thus on-hand inventory cannot be posted
to orders that will later be suspended. An order that passes all diagnostic
tests but cannot be filled because of a stock shortage is also flagged. This
shortage is also flagged and later written to a back-order file.

Prior to inventory posting, the order detail file is sorted by part number
sequence. Then, within each part number sequence, records should be sorted
by record code, which controls the order in which records are processed by
the inventory posting program. The first coded records processed for a part
number are items being returned to stock, as shown by credit and adjustment
records. These inventory adjustments must be processed with great care.
They should record a change in count, not the total physical count of stock in
a warehouse bin. If a bin count is made and submitted and a receiving report
is also processed, there is some question as to whether the adjustment accounts for newly received material. Because of these difficulties with adjustments, one practice is to handle adjustments at a separate time and to
require the signature of the warehouse supervisor to verify the accuracy of
adjustments to inventory records.

After the processing of records that add to or adjust available inventory,
customer orders are posted against available inventory. The first type of customer order posted is preshipped orders—orders where stock items have
been picked from warehouse bins and shipped to the customer prior to processing the order against the computer inventory file. In this case, inventory
posting does not mean filling an order, since the customer already has received items from stock. Rather, posting acknowledges that the order has
been filled from stock. For this reason, preshipped orders must precede other
customer orders. Moreover, a preshipped order must be posted even if the
computer file shows that an inadequate amount of stock is available to fill
the order. Unless there was adequate stock, the preshipment could not have
been sent. This contradiction usually indicates that the items used for preshipment had been designated for another order, but the picker preparing the
preshipment had simply gotten to the warehouse bin first. Therefore, credit
for an inadequate amount of stock will be forthcoming to adjust for the sales
overage.

The next records to be processed are customer back orders. Back orders
are only submitted when additional stock has been received from company
vendors. Since they are older orders, they are filled before current requests
are processed. Finally, current orders for stock are posted against the inventory file by part number. On occasion, current requests may be processed
using a priority code. For example, orders released from the suspense file or
franchised dealer orders may be processed before other customer orders. In
sum, a system of record priorities—returns, adjustments, preshipments,
back orders, and current requests—necessitates the sort prior to inventory

posting. Otherwise, the posting of inventory to customer orders would proceed randomly.

The daily order detail file used during inventory posting is updated and, at times, copied to another file. If a disk file is used for order filling, the order detail is simply updated. This saves time needed to copy previously processed records to another file. Besides adding the quantity of material released from stock for each order in the order detail file, the posting program adds other data from the inventory master file, such as the normal cost and price of ordered material; warehouse bin location of the material; and special flags for back orders or suspended orders.

The inventory posting program should list all order entries that are unacceptable and therefore suspended, as well as entries placed on back order. In addition, the unknown parts report serves to identify part numbers not contained in the inventory file (see Fig. 10-7). In an expanded form, this report can show other types of information. It can be used:

1. to summarize batch control balances
2. to summarize actual transactions and record the new on-hand balances for all items in stock
3. to print price exceptions

Price exceptions occur when company policy permits quoting special prices to favored or large customers. Also, in competitive situations, sales personnel may need to quote a lower price than the established one. If this practice is allowed, the quoted price must override the standard price stored in the inventory master file. Price exceptions show the cases in which the price has been reduced. Reporting these situations aids in controlling excessive discounting. For example, a company may allow price overrides but require an average profit of 25 percent for every item sold. Sometimes the quoted prices may give less than the average profit. These situations must be controlled to keep price concessions in line with overall company objectives.

```
                                        UNKNOWN PARTS REPORT
                                        DECEMBER 21, 19XX

THE FOLLOWING PART NUMBERS WERE NOT FOUND IN THE INVENTORY FILE

PART NUMBER      ORDER NUMBER      CUSTOMER NUMBER
62151            35107                  121
62189             9725                 3400
80302            14110                15020
94921             3532                  762
```

FIG. 10-7 Unknown parts report

Besides the update of the daily order details, the inventory master file itself must be updated. On hand, back-order, and item activity fields are altered within the active inventory master records. Usually a tally is maintained of the quantity sold during a fixed period of time, such as one month. This item activity is then used to forecast future stock requirements, as well as to evaluate the profitability of each item in inventory.

Fields other than on-hand, back order, and item activity are not changed by the inventory posting program. The altering of fields such as unit price and bin location can be completed with a special update, as was the payroll master file. If fields such as these were updated as part of daily order processing, there would be a high probability that errors in the inventory file would be tolerated because of the pressure to fill and ship customer orders.

The Picking Label Program

The daily order detail file now contains the necessary data for printing picking labels. Once again, the file is not in the proper sequence. Before picking labels are printed, the file must be sorted into sequence by bin or warehouse location numbers within order number within customer number. This sequence is important. Warehouses are organized to facilitate the picking and filling of orders. Picking labels should be in a sequence that allows line items of a customer's order to be picked efficiently, so that the picker does not have to organize picked items at a shipping table prior to packing. Grouping items at a shipping table causes too many items to be sent to the wrong customers through order mix-ups. Also, there are considerable freight savings if several orders for one customer can be gathered for packaging. Hence, to expedite picking of items for orders, each member of a warehouse crew receives a portion of the printed picking labels, representing one or more customers. He or she then organizes filled orders for shipment, consolidating orders for each customer to allow single shipments.

Figure 10-8 shows that a picking label contains the part name and number, the quantity to be picked, the customer's name and number, the customer's order number, and the bin (slot) location number. The bin location number directs the picker to the location of the part in the warehouse.

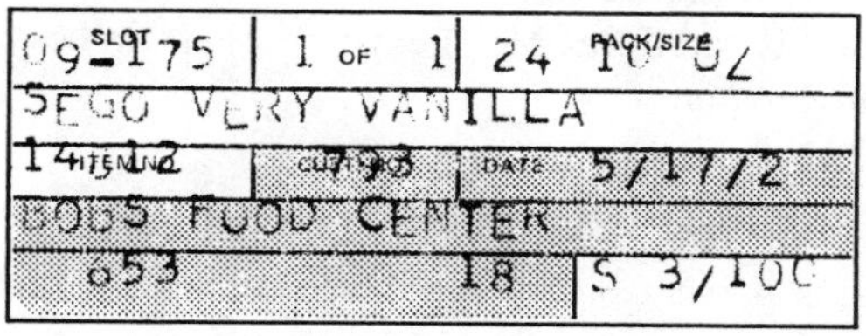

FIG. 10-8 Picking label

The picking label print program will inevitably result in the computer's being print-bound, since considerable time is spent in printing, and there is little need for other components of the computer. Therefore the picking label program may be used for extending and totaling line items for each customer. Since the daily order detail file is sorted by order number within customer number, a summary record for each complete order can be prepared, reflecting the total amount due from the customer following shipment. This summary is used later to prepare invoices and monthly statements.

If the warehouse crew is unable to locate assigned stock, it becomes necessary to credit customer billing records. These credits are difficult to document on the packing slip and even more difficult for the customer to understand. Credit memos are used to provide customers with an accurate and clear statement of what was purchased and to advise them of any changes.

Invoices can be prepared for every order and shipment to a customer (see Chapter 7). Alternatively, many organizations produce a weekly invoice to summarize all filled orders and to print the detail recorded on prepared packing slips. If credits have been made, they appear on the invoice to underscore the difference between the original order and the merchandise shipped. Quite often, this invoice is used by the customer to pay for merchandise received.

The picking label print program can also be designed to separate back orders and suspended orders for later processing. If, however, there are processing limitations, this separating can be performed by the next program.

The Packing Slip Program

Picking labels are sent directly to the warehouse to permit the filling of orders from stock immediately. While this work progresses, packing slips are printed, such as the one shown in Figure 10-9. The packing slips printed by the computer provide all the shipping directions needed except in the case of unusual transportation such as freighter to a foreign port. For such an exception, shipping documents are apt to be lengthy and complex, and are manually prepared.

Completed packing slips are sent immediately to the warehouse crew to speed the shipment of customer orders. Once they have been printed by the computer, most of the pressure associated with order filling is past, and the computer schedule is more flexible. Less important processing jobs can be scheduled for processing.

The Suspense and Back-Order Programs

The final programs process orders flagged for either suspension or back order. In addition, the programs produce suspended and back-order reports. As previously stated, one reason for failing to complete an order is that some

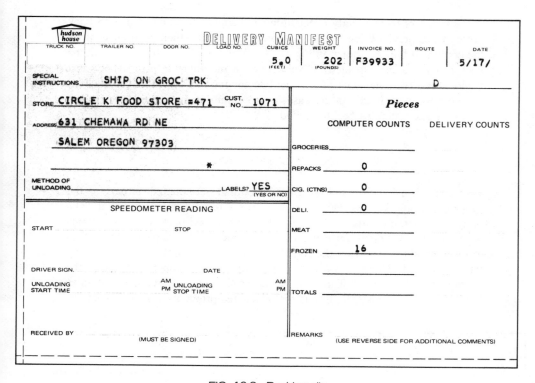

FIG. 10-9 Packing slip

mistake led to its being suspended. The suspense report explains why an order was not acceptable. The procedures for creating and later relieving a suspense file are described in Chapter 7. The same procedures are followed in the order-filling application.

Another reason for not completing an order is that items are not in stock. If more than one item appears on an acceptable customer order, items that can be filled from inventory should be shipped immediately. *Only those items that cannot be filled should be transferred to the back-order file.* In this way, orders held for back order represent only unfilled items from inventory.

The back-order file is usually only processed when the warehouse receives new merchandise from company vendors. While it is possible to compare part numbers listed on receiving reports with those in the back-order file, this process is time-consuming. It is more practical to sort the entire back-order file together with the daily order detail file. Even though most back orders are generally returned to the back-order file, this approach avoids a separate processing run, at no great loss in efficiency to the overall order-filling process.

Back orders from a daily order-filling run should be combined with back orders from previous runs. The back-order report can then be used to print the combined file. As shown in Figure 10-10, the stock number placed on the back order and the expected delivery time (in months) are printed. In most business transactions, back orders that become too old are no longer honored by the customer. If this is the case, a programming procedure allows out-of-date back orders to be eliminated.

10-4 BIN LOCATION ANALYSIS

Warehouse bin location studies are not routinely conducted as part of the order-filling application. However, they are a natural extension of it. The daily order detail file that produced picking labels and packing slips contains a record of every order for every part. This record allows part activity files to be maintained, showing the *sales frequency*—the number of times every part is ordered. These files are used to compute the number of parts on the average customer order. If the average order size and the frequency of sales are known, it is possible, given the space requirements for each part, to

| | | | | EXPEDITING REVIEW REPORT | | | | | PAGE 0038 | | |
| | | | NONUNIVERSAL ITEMS WITH ZERO ON HAND AND/OR QTY ON BACK ORDER | | | | | | DATE 11 17 | | |
STOCK NUMBER	DESCRIPTION	CONTRACT NUMBER	LAST PO/PR	AVG MO DEN USAGE CD	ON-HAND QTY MO	REORD LVL	DELIV MONTHS	CONF CODE	ON-HAND RATIO	QTY ON ORDER	QTY ON BACKORDER
69343200	ENVELOPE	000100	3704	14.1 BX	.0	28	2.00	2	.0 %	200	10
...											
69346200	BAG, PAPER	000100	3704	2,605.8 EA	.0	2,606	1.00	2	.0 %	62,000	125
...											
69357700	RIBBON, TYPEWRITER	000183	3928	30.5 EA	.0	44	1.00	1	.0 %	180	33
...											
69410000	POST	000100	3512	16.5 BX	.0	31	1.00	2	.0 %	122	43
...											
69425200	CARD, TABULATING	39428A	3535	4.8 CS	.0	9	1.00	1	.0 %	18	
...											
69506300	PAPER, INDEX BLUE	000180	3115	27.7 PG	.0	98	2.50	1	.0 %	127	24
...											
69506400	PAPER, INDEX BUFF	000180	3345	9.5 PG	.0	25	1.25	1	.0 %	49	3
...											
69508600	FILM	048730	9847	140.3 RL	192 1.4	617	1.50	2	31.1 %	1,888	1,008
...											
69527500	PAPER, MASTER	000177	1428	1,750.0 EA	.0	4,779	1.50	1	.0 %		500
...											
69545500	DRUM HYDROQUINNONE	000100	3901	2.0 DM	.0	7	2.00	1	.0 %	14	1
...											

FIG. 10-10 Back-order report

calculate how much space to devote to each part and where to locate parts in the warehouse to increase order picking efficiency. This, in essence, is bin location analysis.

Figure 10-11 shows a computer-assisted system for changing bin locations in an order-filling operation. Following a sort by part number, a report of the order frequency and average order size for inventoried parts is prepared from the daily order detail file. This report shows which parts are the most popular. The review and change of bin location is then handled manually. In some systems, changes are controlled by a programmed algorithm, which includes order frequency and average customer order as well as such information as dollar value of the part and seasonal buying patterns.

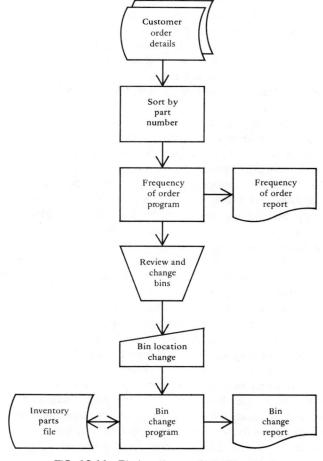

FIG. 10-11   Bin location analysis flowchart

Following the review and change of bin locations, these changes must be entered immediately on the inventory parts file. The next printing of picking labels must reflect any bin changes. Failure to update the master inventory file would confuse the picking of orders, and cause large numbers of improperly filled orders.

10-5 MANAGEMENT IMPLICATIONS

Management can expect immediate results from the implementation of a computer-based order-filling system. A computer order-filling system can achieve faster turnaround between the time a customer order is received and the time it leaves a warehouse. The system can reduce not only the time needed to prepare the initial order-filling documents, the picking labels, but also the time required to pick orders from stock. The latter savings is due to printing picking labels in an orderly sequence for the warehouse crew.

Because of improved turnaround, management is better able to respond to customer needs and yet achieve excellent utilization of the warehouse crew. For example, cutoff of new orders is likely to occur when order clerks go to lunch—say, at 11:30 A.M. Data entry staff leave for lunch when they have completed the last batch of orders—perhaps at noon. The order-filling computer schedule should facilitate the printing of picking labels by 1:00 P.M., when the warehouse crew returns from lunch. If this schedule is followed, orders received before 11:30 A.M. will be filled and shipped by 5:00 P.M.

If the warehouse crew spends the afternoon picking and shipping, they are free in the morning to restock bins and conduct inventories. The computer can be used to print inventory forms for a block of the parts file or to update the inventory file, adding new stock to the on-hand fields. This activity, combined with other normal warehouse activities or computer operations, leads to a balanced work load throughout the day.

Computer order filling can also improve control over inventory. No manual system using bin tags, cardex, or whatever can provide the control over inventory offered by a reliable computer inventory file. This file, accurately maintained, contains dollar sales, returns, number received, number on hand, and number on order for every part in the warehouse. Once accurate, any shorts (which indicate an absence of stock) can be identified. Shorts, in turn, must be caused by incorrect picking of stock (leading to an improper shipment); incorrect storage of new stock or returns; or loss of stock due to pilferage. It is often necessary to place special controls on the items in inventory that have exceptional appeal to the pilferer, such as radios, liquor, cigarettes, and nylon stockings. A log should be maintained of all shorts, and an occasional analysis made of the resulting distribution. Any incidence of missing items greater than expected from a normal distribution should trigger immediate investigation.

The order-filling process can create a computer inventory history file of immense value to a company. The next two chapters deal with uses of this important file. Just as the accounts receivable file served several purposes, the inventory file can be used for purposes other than to post inventory to customer orders. It can provide billing detail for customers; evaluate the location of parts within a warehouse; help detect pilferage or errors in picking orders; forecast future inventory needs; and create purchase orders for vendors.

Besides these important uses, information acquired in order filling can be used to evaluate the stock activity of individual parts, product lines, product strategies, or even the performance of a warehouse as a whole. Inventory turnover—or shelf life—of a part directly affects its profitability. The longer an item remains in stock, the fewer number of times stock investment can be turned during a year. Low turnover means less profit since company funds are tied up for a longer period of time. This argument will be extended in the next chapter dealing with inventory.

REVIEW OF IMPORTANT IDEAS

The order-filling system produces three main products: the documents necessary to pick stock from inventory and ship it to the customer; the updated inventory file after the filling of customer orders; and the records by which to bill the customer for stock shipped.

The computer center usually experiences a tight operating schedule from the time the last customer order enters data entry until picking labels are printed for use in filling orders. Consequently, the order-filling portion of the system receives priority until picking labels are printed. This portion of the system must be designed efficiently in order to minimize processing time.

Types of input to the order-filling system range from parts returned to inventory to customer orders of various priorities. In addition, there may be changes and additions to the master customer name and address file. Additions to inventory should be processed before filling customer orders from inventory. This updating allows the maximum amount of inventory to be shipped to customers, avoiding as many back orders as possible. Changes in the customer name and address must also precede inventory posting to avoid numerous suspended orders.

If errors are detected during the inventory posting program, the order should be flagged for later transfer to a suspense file. If the error is in the customer number, the entire order must be suspended. If the error is in the part number, only that single line item is suspended. Other line items are filled and shipped to the customer.

Picking labels are printed in a sequence that facilitates efficient order picking by the warehouse crew. Bin locations are sequenced within order number within customer number.

If not enough stock is available to fill an entire order, shipments are made as complete as possible and the unfilled balance is placed on back order. When additional stock is received by the warehouse, the back-order file should be passed through the daily order-filling run. The entire file is passed to fill as many orders as possible prior to current daily orders.

The details maintained by the daily order-filling runs are used to prepare bin location studies. Factors considered in bin location analysis include number of customer orders for a part, average quantity ordered, and space requirements of the part. Bin location changes are completed either manually or by use of a manually checked computer algorithm.

REVIEW QUESTIONS

1. What are the three primary functions of the order-filling computer application?

2. Two major file posting computer programs are required in an order-filling computer application. What are they? What does each posting program accomplish?

3. The inventory parts file should show the exact count of inventory on hand, but at times does not. What conditions lead to an inaccurate accounting? What must be done to adjust the file and keep it accurate?

4. Customer change information is processed along with customer order detail in an order-filling computer application, but price changes to the inventory file are processed separately from customer orders. Why? What are the dangers in changing inventory prices during the processing of customer order detail?

5. What is the difference between a suspended customer order and a customer back order? How is each treated in processing?

6. Why is the entire input printed during the initial edit of customer order detail? Why is the listing suppressed during a rerun of the edit program?

7. Three separate sort operations are required in an order-filling operation. What does each sort accomplish?

8. In what sequence are customer orders posted against the inventory file?

9. How is excessive discounting by sales personnel uncovered during the processing of order detail in the order-filling computer application?

10. When the warehouse crew is unable to locate stock printed on the picking label, what must be done to adjust the customer's records? What documents are then sent to the customer?

EXERCISES

1. A company must process three types of orders for sales: orders received from sales warehouse outlets, orders that result from standing purchase agreements, and regular customer orders taken by sales personnel. How must order filling be designed to process all three types? (A standing purchase agreement involves shipping a regular quantity of merchandise at a scheduled interval.)

2. A common business practice is for a customer to request an alternative part from inventory when an ordered part is not in stock. How would this type of request be incorporated into an order-filling system?

3. Another common business practice is to contract with a customer to make a split shipment over, for example, a three-month period. One example of a split shipment is where one-half of the order is shipped immediately and the other half is shipped in three months. How would this type of contract be fitted into the order-filling computer application?

4. Another business practice is to write future orders, where the customer specifies an order in advance of actual shipment (weeks or even months). Explain how an order-filling application must be modified to handle future orders. Why would a business strive to obtain a large number of future orders?

5. Explain and flowchart a system which decentralizes its order-filling procedures and centralizes its customer billing procedures.

11

INVENTORY FORECAST AND CONTROL

Traditionally, the inventory carried by a firm serves as a buffer for stages of production or channels of product distribution. In keeping with this view, inventory management may seek to retain only enough inventory to meet the demand for stock, to never run out of stock, and to allow economic lots of stock to be purchased as well as carried in inventory. The term *economic order quantity* became popular in business literature primarily because of this last goal.

With the advent of the computer, the management of inventory has taken on a new dimension based on viewing inventory as an investment. In the case of an independent middleman (someone who buys from manufacturers and sells to other manufacturers, retailers, or customers), an emerging goal in the management of inventory is to stock only items whose product or stock turnover is consistent with expected return on investment. This return is the profit resulting from rapid turnover of stock divided by the investment in the stock. An example illustrates the importance of this concept. A firm with $20 million in sales operates with a net capital worth of less than $5 million and receives a gross profit in excess of $2 million. In order for this firm to operate at such a high leverage, funds invested in inventory must be obtained through interest-bearing short-term notes. The major source of revenue to the company is sales to customers, and invoices must be processed soon after sales are made. Moreover, items carried in inventory must sell quickly to permit short-term notes to be paid. The company in this example uses a computer inventory system to coordinate all three activities: securing

185

of capital, purchase and sale of items carried in inventory, and recovery of cash from customers. A 40 percent return on investment ($2 million in profit and a $5 million investment) is the result of this method of operating.

This chapter describes a computer inventory application where the decision to carry inventory is independent of the decision to manufacture for inventory. (Chapter 13 discusses the case where the decision to stock is dependent on manufacturing.) It is assumed that supplies to stock are from several manufacturers; demands for stock are from many customers; and the size of the firm is large enough to support a computer inventory system.

11-1 CREATING AN UPDATED MASTER INVENTORY FILE

Three alternative inventory management systems are possible. The first design follows from an extension of the order-filling computer application. A firm can base its inventory management on extended use of the updated inventory file. The second design is based on a modified accounts payable and customer invoicing computer system. Accounts payable are used to predict the supply of inventory; customer invoices represent the demand on inventory (as detailed by the quantity and part number of every item shipped to customers). The third design is a combined point-of-sale and accounts payable system. The quantity sold is recorded by part number at the cash register. The recording is either placed on paper punch tape, which is collected and stored, or read directly by the computer.

The primary input to the computer inventory application is the updated inventory parts or inventory master file, regardless of the design favored. If the computer is used in order filling, the inventory file will contain most of the necessary detail, although it may have to be expanded to include past stock activity (for example, sales by month over a one-year period). Thus the first prerequisite for an inventory computer application is the historical record of stock activity together with the current record of stock on hand, or available for sale. The second requirement is a method of determining when and the amount of stock to order, based on the calculation of stock reorder points and of economic order quantities. The final prerequisite is a record of stock on order, so that on-order and on-hand totals balance to the expected demand for stock.

Figure 11-1 flowcharts a computer inventory system where the inventory master file is created from accounts payable and customer invoice file detail. Invoice detail supplies information on the quantity shipped and billed to customers, by part number. Accounts payable detail supplies information on the quantity received into inventory, again by part number. In many instances, information must be keyed, as the payables application does not lend itself to the creation of a file that can also be used in an inventory system.

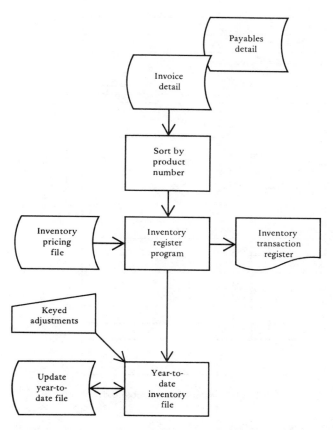

FIG. 11-1 Flowchart of an inventory system requiring the creation of a master inventory file

Figure 11-2 shows that an accounts payable extract slip records both inventory and vendor information. Inventory parts detail includes the quantity received, the part number, the cost of the part, and the date parts were received into inventory. Vendor detail consists of the vendor number. Batch control information is entered into processing by accumulating the total quantity added to inventory. It is used to prepare a balanced edit file.

Point-of-sale detail can be substituted for customer invoice detail as input to the inventory system. Cash register transactions enter as input the quantity sold, by part number. This information is typically collected daily and processed after the closing of the store. The point-of-sale approach is used for collection inventory data when invoices do not accompany sales to customers.

The sort/merge processing routine that follows submission of input data is complex because data are entered into the system at irregular intervals. In-

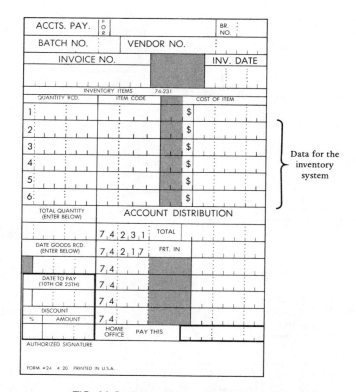

FIG. 11-2 Accounts payable extract slip

voice and point-of-sale detail is usually entered every day; payables detail generally once or twice a week. The inventory system is run at most once a week, or at least once a month. It is advisable to merge and sort input data as they are made available instead of collecting them and then processing the sort/merge routine in line with the reorder-to-stock and the preparation of inventory reports. Updating the inventory file requires considerable processing time, and the new data must be carefully edited and balanced.

Balance control can be best maintained if input data are processed as they become available. Batch control is needed on the total quantity of stock entering inventory and the quantity leaving inventory. If an inventory pricing file is available during this stage of processing, it becomes possible to compare the value of assigned parts priced both by the payables detail and by detail stored in the pricing file. Batch control procedures also help maintain accuracy in the master inventory file.

Figure 11-3 illustrates the *inventory transaction register* produced after the sort of input. It shows each transaction total and any difference between computer quantity totals and batch control totals. Receipt of stock from

DATE 12/10/						INVENTORY TRANSACTION REGISTER			
PART NO	PRODUCT CLASS	UNIT MEASURE	RECORD CODE	DATE	RECEIPT	ACTUAL RETURNS	TRANSACTION ISSUE	ADJUST	BATCH ERROR
01406	520	AA	1	12 9	5000				
14324	429	AAA	2	12 9		500			
.	.	.	.	.					
43210	523	B	1	12 9	4000				
BATCH TOTAL									
01406	520	AA	3	12 9				4000	
.	.	.	.	.					
.	.	.	.	.					
.	.	.	.	.					
BATCH TOTAL									
GRAND TOTAL									

FIG. 11-3 Inventory transaction register

vendors and issuance of stock to customers are listed by transaction. Return of stock to vendors and adjustment to inventory following returns are also listed. The transaction register serves as a working document in inventory management. It aids in the preparation of stock adjustments during the update of the inventory master file.

Accounting or inventory personnel submit adjustment instructions to the inventory system after carefully reviewing the transaction register. Most often, adjustment is needed because the register is not in balance, although physical inventory adjustments are also entered at this time. The importance of physical inventory adjustment is discussed later in this chapter. The *inventory update program* then proceeds to update the year-to-date inventory file. This program combines current demand with the historical demand for each part in inventory. It also updates the current supply of inventory. The updated year-to-date inventory file is now ready to begin inventory forecasting and order-quantity determination.

The process described so far leads to the creation of a computer file that is equivalent to the inventory parts file (see Chapter 10) by using invoice and payables data rather than operating the complete order-filling system. However, building an inventory file apart from an order-filling computer application is hazardous. Not only is additional preliminary work required to create the file, but also it is likely that the file will not be as reliable. The order-filling computer application uses better audit controls to ensure the accuracy of the inventory file. The file is also more current than one based on post-shipment data and dated payables. For example, several days may elapse from the time invoices and payables are processed until they become input to the inventory system. Since the data stored in the file are not as current as in an order-filling system, considerable judgment must be used in deciding whether to accept inventory forecasts based on this file.

The size of the updated inventory master file is determined by the computer processing that led to its creation. If built exclusively for inventory forecasting and order-quantity determination, it contains relatively small records. If built in conjunction with order filling, it contains additional detail necessary to process customer orders. If it is combined with a purchasing and receiving computer application, it contains vendor and back-order information.

Figure 11-4 illustrates the four major types of file detail that a master inventory file is likely to contain:

1. descriptive and price detail
2. reorder and inventory forecasting detail
3. current part activity detail
4. historical part activity detail

Inventory performance measurements by part number can also be computed.

Descriptive and price detail identifies each part carried in inventory by part number, part description, unit price, unit cost, and unit of measure.

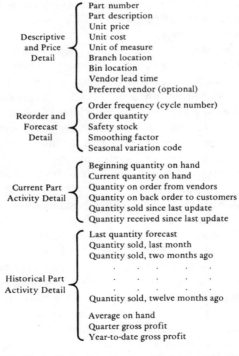

Descriptive
and Price
Detail
- Part number
- Part description
- Unit price
- Unit cost
- Unit of measure
- Branch location
- Bin location
- Vendor lead time
- Preferred vendor (optional)

Reorder and
Forecast
Detail
- Order frequency (cycle number)
- Order quantity
- Safety stock
- Smoothing factor
- Seasonal variation code

Current Part
Activity Detail
- Beginning quantity on hand
- Current quantity on hand
- Quantity on order from vendors
- Quantity on back order to customers
- Quantity sold since last update
- Quantity received since last update

Historical Part
Activity Detail
- Last quantity forecast
- Quantity sold, last month
- Quantity sold, two months ago
- Quantity sold, twelve months ago
- Average on hand
- Quarter gross profit
- Year-to-date gross profit

FIG. 11-4 Typical contents of the inventory file

Price and cost detail permits calculating profit per part. Branch and bin location numbers specify where parts are stored. Branch codes become essential when a business operates from several warehouse locations. Vendor number and vendor lead times are placed in the file when a part is always supplied by the same vendor or when the purchasing and receiving computer applications are integrated into the inventory application. This will become clear in the next chapter.

Reorder and forecast file detail establishes the conditions under which additional stock is added to inventory. The amount to be ordered (order quantity) and the cycle or time of placement of orders (order frequency) are stored. The safety stock is also stored. (Safety stock is the stock reserve to guard against unusually long vendor lead times or rapid increase in the demand for a part.) The smoothing factor and the seasonal variation code are used in preparing the inventory forecast. The concept of smoothing follows a weighted average approach to forecasting. This topic is discussed later as one of several possible forecasting techniques. Either, neither, or both of these codes may be necessary in forecasting, depending on the method of forecasting incorporated into the inventory system.

Current part activity detail includes the record of the current quantity on hand in inventory, the quantity sold, and the quantity received into inventory. The quantity on order from vendors and the quantity on back order to customers show what material is to be received and how much of it is already committed to customers. These figures are used to determine whether to reorder stock. If the quantity on hand plus the quantity already on order from vendors is not enough to (1) fill existing customer back orders, (2) satisfy forecasted sales for the coming period, and (3) provide adequate safety stock to cover emergency demands, then additional stock must be ordered.

Historical part activity detail consists of the previous inventory forecast and the quantity sold during the past 12 months. This detail is used to compute moving averages. It also allows the inventory manager or buyer to review the historical trends of a part contained in inventory and to calculate inventory performance as a whole or part performance in particular. Average inventory on hand, quarterly gross profit, and year-to-date gross profit are common performance measures used to evaluate the management of inventory.

11-2 THE INVENTORY FORECAST AND ORDER-DETERMINATION SYSTEM

Inventory forecasts and determination of inventory order quantities are prepared after the year-to-date inventory master file has been updated to contain the latest stock status information based on entry and adjustment of current input details. The balance of this chapter assumes that the inventory file being used either is created according to the steps just described or is available as a result of order filling (see Chapter 10). Figure 11-5 flowcharts the rest of the inventory computer application. The primary input to the system is the updated year-to-date inventory file. Other input consists of cycle call and buyer change instructions. *Cycle call instructions* control processing of different sections of the inventory file. Reorder cycles permit the buyer to review on a scheduled basis (for example, every week) the products to be ordered. The practice makes it unnecessary to review the entire file during every processing run. *Buyer change instructions* permit the purchasing agent or buyer to overrule reorder cycles and order quantities set by the computer. If the buyer finds that a computer-determined computation is unrealistic because of rapid or unexpected changes in market demand, he or she can substitute the quantity to be ordered and set the next review period. Otherwise, computer-based calculations become the final decisions on what and when to order to stock.

Outputs from processing include the initial stock status report and the adjusted stock status report. The *initial stock status* prints computed stock requirements for inventory items that should be ordered at this time (cycle). The *adjusted stock status* shows instances where the reorder cycle and the order quantity have been altered by the purchasing agent or buyer.

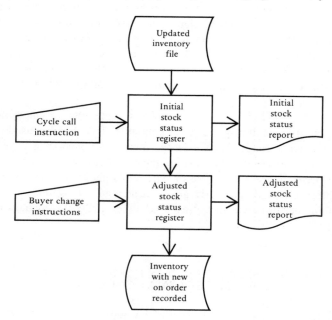

FIG. 11-5 Inventory system flowchart

Computation of the inventory sales forecast begins the initial stock status computer program. The forecast may be prepared using one of several forecasting methods. But, no matter what method is selected, the sales forecast will be incomplete. For example, it does not consider the quantity of stock on order, the quantity on hand, nor the vendor lead time required to order and receive stock. Without this information, the forecast predicts what will be sold, but not what is needed in stock to meet actual sales. The amount to order during the coming inventory period is the true inventory stocking forecast. The second part of the initial stock status computer program prepares this forecast.

Inventory Forecasting

The inventory sales forecast is prepared after the inventory file has been updated to contain the current and the yearly sales totals broken down by month and by part number. Thirteen sales totals are retained instead of twelve, so current monthly sales can be compared to monthly sales a year ago. The current and historical sales totals are shifted monthly, and the oldest data are dropped from the file.

There are several ways in which historical sales data can be used in the preparation of an inventory forecast. One way—which was used by many companies long before the advent of the computer—is to compute a running average of the monthly demand, by part number. This average then becomes the probable monthly demand for the next month.

As one might imagine, the calculation of a running average is, at best, simplistic. This approach does not take into account recent changes in product demand. For example, suppose that one part carried in inventory has been selling at the rate of 100 parts per month and that over the past two months demand has suddenly doubled. Computed over one year, the running average would forecast an expected demand of 117 parts per month [$(10 \times 100 + 2 \times 200)/12$], even though it is more likely that sales will remain at a level of 200 or more. As this example shows, the running average approach is not responsive to rapid shifts in product demand.

To refine this technique, a second sales forecasting approach has been used, called a *weighted moving average*. Current sales are given more weight than those of previous months by the assigning of weights to past sales. One weighting scheme (there are several) is to assign a weight of 24 to the sales history. The most recent three months are assigned a weight of 3, the next six months a weight of 2, and the last three months a weight of 1. The forecast then becomes:

$$F_n = \frac{3(D_{n-1} + D_{n-2} + D_{n-3}) + 2(D_{n-4} + \ldots + D_{n-9}) + (D_{n-10} + D_{n-11} + D_{n-12})}{24}$$

where

F_n = forecast for period n, where $n = 12$

D_{n-i} = demand in period $n - i$, where i varies from 1 to 12

Using our previous example, the weighted average provides a forecast of 126 parts per month, or

$$F_{12} = \frac{3(500) + 2(600) + 1(300)}{24} = 126$$

Although this forecast does not predict a continuation of sales of 200 per month, it is some improvement over the running average of 117 per month.

Both the running average and the weighted average require retention of historical part activity file detail. One might question whether the cost of retaining these data compares favorably to the forecast that results from their use. Because of the high file storage cost and the rather cumbersome method of forecasting that uses a simple or weighted moving average, most forecasting systems advocated by computer vendors use the forecasting method known as *exponential smoothing.*

Exponential smoothing is also a weighted average approach to forecasting. Its theoretical advantage, compared to the weighted average just described, is that it requires minimal file storage. The analytic expression for first-order exponential smoothing is (there is a second- and third-order expression as well):

$$F_n = \alpha D_{n-1} + (1 - \alpha)F_{n-1}$$

where

F_n = forecast in period n

D_{n-1} = demand in period $n-1$

F_{n-1} = old forecast

α = smoothing factor

The new forecast (F_n) is equal to the smoothing factor (α) times the latest demand or actual sales (D_{n-1}) plus 1 minus the smoothing factor $(1-\alpha)$ times the latest forecast (F_{n-1}). The smoothing factor can take any value from 0 to 1. Where α equals 0, the new forecast is equal to the old forecast:

$$F_n = F_{n-1}$$

Where α equals 1, the new forecast is equal to the latest actual sales:

$$F_n = D_{n-1}$$

Suppose in our example that α is set at .9 and that the exponentially smoothed forecast is equal to actual sales before demand doubled. During the first month following the doubling of sales, actual demand would be 200; the old forecast would predict 100. However, the forecast of demand for the second month becomes:

$$F_{n-1} = \alpha D_{n-2} + (1 - \alpha)F_{n-2}$$

$$= .9(200) + .1(100) = 190 \text{ parts per month}$$

During the second month in which demand has doubled, the forecast becomes:

$$F_n = D_{n-1} + (1 - \alpha)F_{n-1}$$

$$= .9(200) + .1(180) = 198 \text{ parts per month}$$

Clearly, the forecast based on exponential smoothing is more responsive to changes in product demand than either of the other two forecasting approaches. However, it is necessary to set the smoothing factor correctly. Note that if α equals .1 rather than .9, F_{n-1} would equal 110 parts per month and F_n would equal 119 parts per month. Exponential smoothing, in this instance, offers no better response than either of the other two forecasting approaches.

Exponential smoothing, then, offers two advantages. As referred to previously, it requires less computer file space. Only one period of historical information—the last forecast—needs to be retained, compared to twelve periods of past sales. Second, it is responsive to shifts in product demand. Moreover, the purchasing agent or the buyer (or the computer) can alter the value of the smoothing factor. Each part in inventory can be given its own smoothing factor.

One disadvantage, however, is that past sales activity cannot be printed by previous months, quarters, or years, unless the relevant historical data are stored in addition to the last forecast. Furthermore, many managers, buyers, or stock clerks find exponential smoothing difficult to accept. They may calculate their own forecasts, using some pet forecasting scheme. This practice undermines the goal of replacing manual calculations. A person should only need to review the forecast and change projections that do not reflect rapid change. If massive manual calculations continue, the potential dollar savings and other benefits expected from the computer application are lost. The moral is clear: Exponential smoothing as a forecasting approach must be understood and accepted, or it will not have the impact desired—the removal of manual inventory forecasting from the management of inventory.

A major problem with all approaches to forecasting considered thus far is that they do not adjust for seasonal variations. It is obvious that the sales of products such as ice cream or snow tires follow seasonal patterns. The final forecasting alternative to be reviewed requires the use of seasonal variation charts to forecast expected sales. A *seasonal variation chart* modifies the demand forecast, based on expected seasonal shifts in demand for a class of inventory. Suppose that Figure 11-6 graphs the seasonal variation in the demand for ice cream. Demand is shown as greater in summer than in winter. In fact, sales in June, July, and August are twice as great as sales in De-

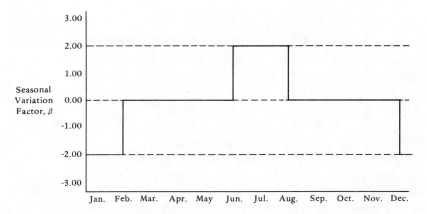

FIG. 11-6   Fictitious seasonal variation chart of the demand
for ice cream

cember, January, and February. The other six months show a constant sales
level halfway between the summer and winter months.

Expressed in analytic terms, the seasonally adjusted forecast is based on a
seasonal coefficient (β) times the *deseasonalized average demand*.

$$F_n = \beta D_{average}$$

The deseasonalized average demand is then modified by use of a smoothing coefficient (α). The seasonal coefficient is adjusted in a similar manner.

Suppose that the deseasonalized average demand for ice cream is 100 and
that the seasonal coefficient is 2.00 in June. The June sales forecast then
becomes:

$$F_{June} = \beta D_{average} = 2.00 \, (100) = 200$$

Suppose further that actual demand in June is 250. With a smoothing coefficient α of .2, the new deseasonalized average demand becomes:

$$D_{June \, (deseasonalized)} = 250/2.00 = 125$$

$$D_{average} = \alpha \, (D_{June}) + (1 - \alpha) \, D_{average}$$
$$= .2 \, (125) + .8 \, (100) = 105$$

The seasonal coefficient is also adjusted. The June coefficient becomes:

$$\beta_{current} = 250/100 = 2.50$$

$$\beta_{June} = \alpha(\beta_{current}) + (1 - \alpha)\beta_{June}$$
$$= .2 \, (2.50) + .8 \, (2.00) = 2.10$$

If the forecast for July with a seasonal coefficient of 2.00 is modified by the new deseasonalized average, the forecast becomes:

$$F_{July} = \beta D_{average} = 2.00 \,(105) = 210$$

If actual demand is less than or greater than 210, another adjustment of the deseasonalized average demand is made and the July value of β is changed.

As this example shows, the seasonally adjusted forecast is an excellent method of predicting sharp swings in demand. The fit of the seasonal coefficient factor β is the major problem in the use of seasonal variation charts. It becomes necessary to adjust two forecast coefficients: α and β. Nonetheless, given fairly uniform swings in demand, this approach to forecasting has been very successful. The improved accuracy of prediction far outweighs the additional file storage cost and the manual expense required to implement and maintain seasonal variation sales activity.

The Order Quantity, the Order Frequency, and the Safety Stock

The quantity expected to be sold (the demand forecast), the customer back order, the quantity on hand, the quantity on order, the quantity set aside as safety stock, and the vendor lead time are variables used to determine the quantity of material to order and the order frequency. Analytically, the quantity to order is expressed as:

Quantity to order = (quantity to be sold + safety stock

+ customer back order)

− (quantity on hand + quantity on order)

This equation assumes that material will be ordered without due regard for purchase order costs and inventory carrying costs. It also assumes that the order frequency is known and that the safety stock is specified.

Realistically, the order frequency and the safety stock must be calculated by using an analytic expression that attempts to minimize inventory costs. One method of calculation uses an economic lot size formula. The simplest expression of the economic order quantity (E.O.Q.) is:

$$\text{E.O.Q.} = \sqrt{\frac{2\ (\text{annual demand})(\text{purchase order cost})}{(\text{cost per unit})\ (\text{inventory carrying cost})}}$$

This square root expression weighs the cost of purchasing materials against the cost of holding material (carrying cost) in inventory until it is sold. With a known E.O.Q., order frequency is determined. The number of orders to be placed during the year is calculated by dividing annual demand by the E.O.Q.

$$\text{Number of orders} = \frac{\text{annual demand}}{\text{E.O.Q.}}$$

The order frequency (in days) is found by dividing the number of working days (250) by the number of orders to be placed during the year.

$$\text{Order frequency} = \frac{\text{annual working days}}{\text{number of orders}}$$

Finally, the safety stock is computed. Safety stock is equated to the difference between the maximum and the normal demand expected during the vendor lead time and the order frequency time.

$$\text{Safety stock} = (\text{maximum less normal demand for material})$$
$$\times (\text{vendor lead time} + \text{order frequency})$$

Figure 11-7 shows the interrelationships among the four variables. Ideally, the last item on hand should be sold when the stock level reaches the safety stock, at which time a new shipment of material is received. The safety stock protects against customer demand greater than normal and is kept high enough to avoid a significant number of customer back orders.

The analytic approach to inventory management, even though based on reasoned formulations, is not without its problems. When both vendor lead time and product demand vary considerably, the computation of safety stock is subject to question. Some people have also questioned the value given to the inventory carrying cost, which can directly affect the size of the E.O.Q. The determination of annual demand is another concern. Annual demand is

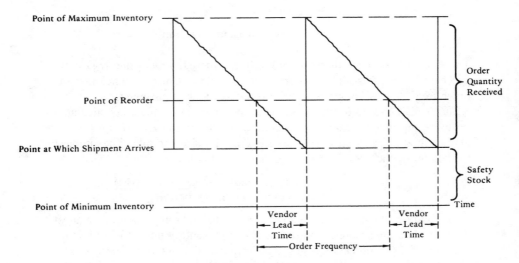

FIG. 11-7 Simplified inventory model

influenced not only by past sales, but also by expected annual sales. No sales forecasting approach predicts annual sales, having more than enough difficulty predicting next month's sales; and yet annual sales directly affect the E.O.Q. and the order frequency. Finally, the focus of the E.O.Q. model is to minimize inventory costs, which may or may not maximize return on capital invested in inventory. Because of this last condition, many companies have turned to factor buying to evaluate the return on invested capital.

11-3 FACTOR BUYING

Factor buying is the practice of following consistent cycles in the order of stock to inventory. Generally, each item is reordered every two weeks or so, in an attempt to maximize the turnover of inventory and to derive a satisfactory return on capital invested in it. Suppose that annual demand for a given part in stock is 480 units. Suppose further that stock is ordered 12 times a year, and that 40 units of stock arrive each month. The average stock on hand becomes 20 units (40 units ÷ 2), and the dollar turnover rate becomes 24 times a year (480 units ÷ average stock on hand)—twice the usual 12 because sales dollars from the first half of the month result in reinvested capital.

The return on invested capital in the above example is computed using the gross margin and the inventory carrying cost (if significant) of each item in stock. The formula is shown below.

$$\text{R.O.I.} = \frac{(\text{G.M.})(\text{T.R.}) - (\text{C.C.})}{C} \times 100$$

where

  R.O.I. = return on investment
  G.M. = per unit gross margin
  T.R. = dollar turnover rate
  C.C. = per unit yearly carrying cost
  C = per unit cost

A product that costs $1.00, sells for $1.25, and has an annual carrying cost of $.50 per unit and a turnover rate of 24 would yield a return on investment of 550 percent.

$$\text{R.O.I.} = \frac{(.25)(24) - (.50)}{1.00} = 5.50 \times 100 = 550\%$$

This example suggests that operating at high leverage can be successful if the inventory is managed with a view to maximizing return on investment.

In this example, by ordering twice a month, return might be increased even more. If, for instance, the turnover rate is 48, the return on investment equals 1,150 percent, assuming a constant carrying cost. In many cases, it is realistic to order weekly by establishing a standing purchase order with a vendor. The vendor then ships merchandise each week and does not need additional purchase order documents. In many cases, however, a standing purchase order cannot be written. Customer demand or vendor lead time (or reliability) may make reorder to inventory on a standing order basis impractical. Safety stock, which must be carried to avoid running out of inventory (called "stockouts" or "shorts"), increases the average inventory on hand, thus reducing the turnover.

To illustrate the effect of safety stock, we return to the example where 40 units of inventory were purchased each month, resulting in a dollar turnover rate of 24. In this situation, consider that a half month's supply is retained in stock to protect against a stockout. This extra supply reduces the actual turnover rate from 24 to 12, since the average inventory now carried equals 40 units rather than 20. The equation is as follows:

$$\text{Turnover} = \frac{480 \text{ (annual usage)}}{40/2 \text{ (average monthly)} + \text{safety stock}}$$

$$= \frac{480}{20 + 20} = 12 \text{ times per year}$$

Similarly, the return on investment is reduced from 550 percent to 250 percent. Safety stock, in other words, drastically affects return on capital invested in inventory.

There is a final factor that must be considered in factor buying: vendor lead time—the length of time from when goods are initially ordered to when goods are delivered and placed in the warehouse. The longer the time required by the vendor, the more units there will be in an order status. However, what is important is that a longer lead time does not necessarily mean that each order placed with a vendor will be larger. Instead, more than one order to a vendor will probably be outstanding, each with a different delivery date.

The computer application performs its role in factor buying by computing and storing the order frequency by part number. Suppose that the weighted and seasonally adjusted weekly sales for a product come to 10 parts. In addition, it is known that 60 parts are on hand, that an additional 80 are on order, that the vendor lead time is 3 months, and that the safety stock requirement is 70 parts. Provided this detail, the computer would suggest that an additional 50 parts be ordered, making the total inventory 190 parts (3 months of forecast sales plus 70 units of safety stock) either on hand or on order.

The important advantage of factor buying is its flexibility. Knowing the vendor lead time, the current on-hand and on-order stock level, the computer-determined average weekly sales, and the necessary safety stock, the purchasing agent or buyer can review the quantity to reorder and change that quantity if it is believed sales, lead time, or safety stock are incorrect. Simplicity in understanding is another important advantage. Finally, the emphasis on return on investment, as opposed to inventory carrying cost, is a strong reason for the implementation of factor buying. The decision to overrule a programmed result is often due as much to turnover rates, changes in gross margin, and cost of material purchased as to increased inventory cost. This realization has permitted many companies to seek and to secure a more than satisfactory return on their investment in inventory.

The Stock Status Report

Figure 11-8 shows a possible report format resulting from the use of factor buying. The report is entitled the *initial stock status report,* since it records the inventory forecast before adjustment by purchasing. The price and cost information for each part are printed, together with current sales and profit information. Current sales can then be compared with historical sales. Current stock status is also recorded. The suggested new stock, the stock on hand and on order, and the safety stock level provide the manager with information needed to make decisions about inventory. Finally, stock performance detail is printed. The stock turnover and return on investment can be shown on a monthly and year-to-date basis.

| DATE 1/28/ | | | | | | | STOCK STATUS REPORT | | | | | | |

PART NO	PRICE	COST	LAST MONTH BOUGHT SOLD		YEAR TO DATE BOUGHT SOLD		CURRENT SALES $	PROFIT $	YTD PROFIT $	TURNOVER MO	YTD	ROI MO	YTD
62014	4.20	3.90	12000	12100	12000	12100	50820	3630	3630	16	16	105	105

SUGGESTED NEW DEMAND	SUGGESTED NEW STOCK	ON HAND	ON ORDER	SAFETY STOCK	DAYS LEAD TIME	DAYS CYCLE TIME
12050	9051	5999	0	3000	5	20

¤¤¤¤¤¤¤¤¤¤¤¤¤¤¤¤¤¤¤¤¤¤¤

TOTAL $ VALUE NOW	ITEMS BY MONTH AND YTD		GROSS PROFIT		TURNOVER		EXTENDED $ VALUE	
BOUGHT—MONTH—SOLD	BOUGHT—YTD—SOLD		MONTH	YTD	MONTH	YTD	ON HAND	ON ORDER
4,387,600	3,980,865		55000	55000	22	22	2,674,450	3,294,660

FIG. 11-8 Initial stock status report (fictitious)

An abbreviated performance summary is included in most stock status reports. Figure 11-8 shows that the total dollar value of stock bought and sold is summarized for all parts carried in stock. Gross profit, stock turnover, and the extended dollar value of current stock are also summarized. To be complete, the stock summary must take into account the needs of the manager. The report illustrated is an example of the information that can be reported as part of the inventory computer application.

Figure 11-9 shows an actual stock status report. It gives the item number, pack and size, the part description, and the last four weeks' sales detail. It also shows the number of lowest sales totals (lows) and the number of stockouts (outs) experienced during the week. Finally, it shows current price and cost detail and the current status of stock both on hand and on order.

After reviewing the initial stock status report, purchasing agents or buyers indicate changes to be made in the computer-calculated decisions to order stock. Buyer change instructions are prepared, following which the inventory file is updated a second time. The *adjusted stock status* report is produced following the second update. This report is similar to the initial report, with the exception that buyer decisions are flagged to allow them to be verified. If buyer decisions are few, it may not be necessary to print the entire stock status report again. Instead, only exceptions to the initial status report are printed to permit decision verification.

11-4 DANGERS ASSOCIATED WITH A COMPUTER INVENTORY APPLICATION

It would not be fair to leave the topic of a computer inventory application without discussing the dangers associated with its use. Experience has shown that a computer inventory system can have unexpected consequences. For example, during the 1960s when American business enjoyed an unparalleled boom period, many companies began using a computer forecasting system to assist in inventory management. All, or nearly all, of the computer systems followed a design similar to the one described. Largely because of computer forecasting techniques, a business upswing was predicted for May through September 1969. This same unfortunate phenomenom recurred in the early 1970s, but to a lessor degree. In both instances, these were periods in which business was actually beginning a substantial downswing. However, the computer forecasting programs reacted slowly to the change in business trends.

Slow response time in forecasting systems, as should be obvious, leads to a variety of business problems. Companies find that too much stock is on hand and on order, and that there is not enough cash to meet business com-

ITEM	PACK & SIZE	DESCRIPTION OF ITEM	LAST WEEK REC.	4 WEEKS PREV. SALES	4TH WEEK	3RD WEEK	2ND WEEK	THIS WEEK	OUTS	ADJ. + OR -	ON HAND	ON ORDER	FTR.	SLOT	P.O. FREQ.	REG. COST	REG. SELL	INST. SELL	COMMENTS	PALL. QTY.	CUBICS
	90PE	BUYER OPTION	CARROTS																		
12503	24 303S	HUDSON HSE DICED CARROTS		23	6	7	6	2			24	10	10	06395	10	3.80	4.09	4.49			.6
12515	24 303S	HUDSON HOUSE SLI CARROTS	::	41	11	13	8	3	LOWS		11	20 10		06420	10 OUTS	4.70	5.05	5.49	MINUS		.6
			:: ::	:: ::	TOTAL		2				DISC						T.O.				
	90QE	BUYER OPTION	BEETS																		
12406	24 303S	HUDSON HOUSE SLI BEETS		35	13	5	7	2			15	20	10	06395	10	4.20	4.49	4.95			.6
12415	24 303S	DUNDEE SALAD BEETS		271	44	31	23	9			72	10		06395	10	3.20	3.40				.6
12424	24 303S	HUDSON HOUSE DICED BEETS		30	8	4	7	2			23	10		06395	10	3.15	3.37				.6
12428	24 303S	H H CRLY CUT BITS		4	2			1			25	10		06410	10	3.65	3.89				.6
12438	24 303S	H H SHOESTRING BEETS		15	4	2	3				33	10		06410	10	3.65	3.89	.00			.6
12445	24 303S	H H BABY WHOLE BEETS		20	6	5	4	2			8	20		06410	10	4.55	4.88				.6
12447	24 303S	DUNDEE MED WHOLE BEETS		22	5	7	5	2				10		06410	10	3.60	3.98				.6
12487	24 303S	H H SLI PICKLED BEETS		30	13	16	11	4		1	OUT	30 10		06410	10	4.95	5.28	.00	MINUS		.6
			:: ::	:: ::	TOTAL		8	LOWS			DISC.				OUTS	1	T.O.				
	90IE	BUYER OPTION	ASPARAGUS																		
10903	24 300S	H H ASPAR AG BLEND SPEAR		38	3	4	1	1		1	33	10		06340	10	12.37	13.29	14.59	MINUS		.6
10912	24 300S	DUNDEE ASPARAGUS SPEARS	:: ::	60	16	9	12	3	LOWS		OUT	100 10		06340	10 OUTS	10.52	11.35				.6
			:: ::	:: ::	TOTAL		2				DISC.					1	T.O.				
	90UE	BUYERS OPTION	H H PEARS					3 STAR IRREG PEARS													
07411	24 303S	DUNDEE PEARS		76	42	20	9	3			104	10		06225	10	4.82	5.24				.6
07413	24 2 1/2S	DUNDEE PEAR HALVES		40	7	7	6	6			6	30 6		07465	10	7.07	7.75			1.1	1.1
07423	24 8 OZ	HUDSON HOUSE PEAR HALVES		38	7	13	7	4	D D PEARS		25	35 7		07540	10	3.32	3.62	3.95			1.4
07425	24 303S	HUDSON HOUSE PEAR HALVES		95	15	13	4	4			46	10		06235	10	5.17	5.64			1.1	.6
07427	24 2 1/2	HUDSON HOUSE PEAR HALVES		49	14	12	6	4			37	6		07470	10	7.72	8.41			1.1	1.1
07432	24 2 1/2	YAMHILL IRREG PEAR HAVS		42	7	16	6	3			46	6		07470	10	6.57	7.11	9.19		1.1	1.1
			:: ::	:: ::	TOTAL		6	LOWS			DISC.				OUTS		T.O.				
	90VN	BUYER OPTION	IREG. FR. PEACHES																		
07308	24 2 1/2	NTR/SWT FS PEACHES IRREG		462	16 30	30	2	6	LOWS		903	10		07445	10 OUTS	6.00	6.49		MINUS		1.1
			:: ::	:: ::	TOTAL		1				DISC.						T.O.				
	90WA	BUYER OPTION	OLEO																		
70601	24 1 LB	MAYFAIR SOFT OLEO		215	46	75	47	13			170	10		56445	10	6.77	6.91				1.1
70603	30 1 LB	MAYFAIR 1/4 S OLEO	:: ::	812	136 164	169	36	36	LOWS		342	10		28085	10 OUTS	5.76	5.88		MINUS		1.0
			:: ::	:: ::	TOTAL	2					DISC.						T.O.				

FIG. 11-9 Initial stock status report (actual)

mitments. Their vendors become more insistent upon prompt payment, since they too suffer from optimistic forecast predictions. As a consequence, many companies were forced to accept the fact that a forecast technique based on historical sales does not react quickly to a change in economic trends. This hazard of a computer inventory system must be realized in advance.

The problem of sales forecasting cannot be easily solved. It would be desirable to correlate expected sales with predictions for the overall economy. The addition of such a correlation to sales forecasts might have avoided some of the mistakes of the late sixties and early seventies. However, government statistics did not show that a business downswing was pending. Moreover, even if correlation did prove successful, a business downswing must be recognized in advance of orders sent to vendors, especially those that require a long vendor lead time. It would not help to know today that the economy was beginning a change in trend if vendor orders were or should have been reduced six months ago. In sum, there is no one best solution to the problem of a computer inventory forecast.

11-5 PHYSICAL INVENTORY

The taking of a physical inventory is a manual check that verifies the accuracy of the contents of the master inventory file. The importance of this manual activity cannot be overstated. Many companies do not really know the current value of their inventory.

Figure 11-10 flowcharts the activities and the computer programs necessary to perform a physical inventory. The first step is the printing of *count*

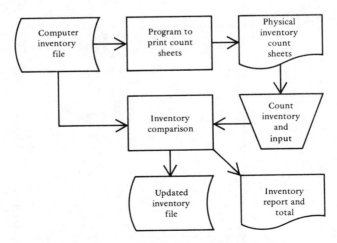

FIG. 11-10 Physical inventory flowchart

sheets. These sheets are used by the warehouse crew to record the amount of stock on hand. Printed information on the sheet includes the part number, the part location, the part description, and the unit of measure. There is some question as to whether the amount on hand should be printed on the actual count sheet. Some people argue that printing the amount helps in locating all materials on hand. Others argue that if the total is shown, people making a check will expect to find the amount shown. For instance, if a person thinks there are a dozen parts in stock, he or she will count a dozen, even though there are actually only eleven.

The second step in taking a physical inventory is the actual counting of stock on hand. Counting occurs at a time when no other activity in the warehouse is scheduled. It must occur when customer orders are not being filled or new material received. Such activity would be at cross-purposes with the effort to obtain an exact count of the contents of the warehouse.

The physical count is returned to data processing where it is keyed. The total amount stored on file and the total keyed count are then compared. The result of this comparison is printed to show the quantity and the dollar value of stock on hand. The report serves as a register of the total value of inventory. If there is a difference between the two counts, this should be scored in a distinctive manner. Normally, small differences are overlooked, but even these must be regulated by company policy. For instance, a policy might be to print any stock discrepancy that exceeds 5 percent of the quantity on hand or twenty-five dollars in sales value.

Whenever a significant discrepancy results, the physical count is repeated. If the physical count is the same the second time, it can be assumed that the computer file record is incorrect. The record is then altered to reflect the actual status of inventory. The extended value of the inventory file is also adjusted. Only then does it actually show the value of stock stored in inventory.

11-6 MANAGEMENT IMPLICATIONS

By now most of the management implications of a computer inventory application should be clear. There may be advantages as well as disadvantages associated with the implementation of this application. One significant aspect of this system is what it permits a company to do, in contrast to the limits placed on a company without a computer inventory system. First, it permits continued growth in a firm that carries a substantial inventory. Growth is supported because inventory is controlled by the computer record-keeping activity. A warehouse containing 100,000 or more different parts is not likely to be operated efficiently on a strictly manual basis. The sheer task of ordering to stock and maintaining accurate records of stock on hand or on order in a very large inventory is either impractical or impossible. Size has provided one important reason for adapting inventory procedures to fit a computer.

Liquidity is another important reason for the advance of computer inventory systems. A properly designed system should reduce the actual stock carried by a firm and lead to the rapid sale of any stock carried. Both change the liquidity position of a firm by requiring less investment in inventory. This reason alone has influenced the officers of many companies to decide to purchase a computer.

Measurement of inventory performance on the basis of each part or unit stocked is another reason for the decision to place inventory on the computer. Inventory turnover, return on investment, increase in annual sales, and gross profit are very difficult to determine without a computer system. It is not the sophistication of the analysis that makes manual measurement and evaluation difficult, but the large numbers of calculations.

These three aspects of a computer inventory system—the computer record-keeping activity, the ability to operate at a higher leverage, and the measurement of inventory performance—by no means exhaust the list of benefits of this application. The discussion of the inventory application in this chapter should not be considered complete. Treated thoroughly, the subject of inventory management would require an entire book. Although not necessarily difficult, many considerations are beyond the scope of this chapter. Among these are the procedures required to update the level of safety stock and to develop the seasonal variation charts, incorporation of probability to assist in determining the safety stock and the stockout cost, the design of a "tracking" signal to monitor the inventory forecast, and the development of an external market forecast that can be used in conjunction with the inventory sales forecast. These and other topics are covered in texts that deal with inventory management.

REVIEW OF IMPORTANT IDEAS

The inventory computer application is one of the more popular computer systems, since successful operation can lead to substantial improvements in cash flow and profit margins. The system focuses on the turnover of inventory that can be achieved by stocking the correct amount and by placing purchase orders with vendors to ensure that customer demand will be served. If this purpose is achieved, every dollar invested in inventory should bring about a satisfactory return.

The primary input to the inventory application is the inventory master file. This file can be created either as part of an order-filling application or using files from other computer applications. It can also be built especially for the inventory application. In any case, the inventory file contains a history of demand for every item in inventory. In the complete inventory system, the file contains current and historical part activity detail.

The history of sales is used in preparing the inventory forecast. The forecast predicts demand for every item in stock in the month or months ahead. A running average, a weighted moving average, exponential smoothing, and seasonal variation charts are some of the forecasting approaches in use. Each approach responds differently to shifts in product sales. For this reason, any forecast must be carefully reviewed by those preparing purchase orders.

Factor buying is one method of evaluating the requirements for inventory. Three factors—return on investment, safety stock, and vendor lead time—are involved in determining how often and in what quantity stock should be ordered. The order frequency established in factor buying is used by the computer in deciding whether to recommend ordering additional stock.

A computer inventory system can be dangerous. Most systems do not give adequate weight to the influence of external factors such as the expected condition of the economy. If the only basis for estimates of future sales is the record of past sales, the computer-prepared forecast will often be misleading.

Computer inventory records should be checked against the actual contents of the warehouse on a periodic basis. If the discrepancy between physical inventory counts and stored file content is significant, an attempt must be made to determine the cause. When the count is completed, the computer inventory file is altered to agree with the actual content stored in the warehouse. A total dollar value for inventory is then computed.

REVIEW QUESTIONS

1. What are the primary objectives of inventory management? Why are these goals difficult to achieve?

2. What is the primary input to the inventory computer application? How is this input created?

3. How is it possible to validate the accuracy of the contents of the inventory file?

4. What are the disadvantages in designing an inventory file separate from an order-filling computer application? How should these weaknesses be treated during the analysis of reports prepared as a result of a specially created inventory file?

5. What is the difference between cycle call and buyer change instructions? How does each affect the preparation of the inventory stock status report?

6. What major types of file detail are contained in the inventory file? How is each type used in processing?

7. Why is exponential smoothing advocated by computer vendors in the forecasting of product demand? What are the disadvantages of this forecasting technique?

8. Of what value are seasonal variation charts in forecasting inventory requirements? What is the main difficulty in using these charts?

9. How is the inventory forecast used in computing the quantity of inventory to be ordered to stock?

10. How are the following terms related: economic order quantity and order frequency; safety stock and vendor lead time? Why is a knowledge of these interrelationships important in the management of inventory?

11. What difficulties are associated with the use of economic order quantity computations?

12. What is meant by the term *factor buying*? How does the use of factor buying differ from the use of economic order quantity calculations in ordering stock to inventory?

13. What is the effect of safety stock on the overall return on capital invested in inventory? What can be done to minimize this effect?

14. What dangers are associated with the use of the computer to forecast inventory requirements?

15. Why is the taking of physical inventory especially important when inventory requirements are determined by computer?

16. What reasons can you give for the rapid development of computer inventory systems in business?

EXERCISES

1. Product sales for part number 43015 were forecast at 12,000, while actual sales were 12,500 during the month of March. Using first-order exponential smoothing with an assigned α of .2, compute the sales forecast for April.

2. The deseasonalized average demand for part number 16,000 is 200 and the seasonal coefficient is 1.50 for June. Given this information, compute the June sales forecast.

   Suppose that actual demand in June is 250. Given an α value of .2, compute the revised deseasonalized average demand and the revised June seasonal coefficient.

3. A product carried in inventory has an estimated annual demand of 60,000 units, maximum weekly demand of 1,500 units, and average weekly demand of 1,250 units. Each unit is purchased for $2.00 and sells for $2.20. The purchase order cost is $53.33 per order and the inventory carrying cost percentage is 20 percent. The vendor lead time is 10 days, and there are 250 working days in a year. Assume that safety stock is on hand, no customer back orders exist, and there is no quantity on order.

   Using economic order quantity formulations, calculate (a) the economic order quantity, (b) the order frequency, (c) the safety stock, and (d) the return on investment, assuming a carrying cost of $.20 per unit.

   Using an order frequency of every 10 days, calculate (a) the order quantity, (b) the safety stock, and (c) the return on investment, assuming a carrying cost of $.25 per unit.

4. A production supervisor claims that a computer-based method of planning and controlling inventory will not work because of the newness of most product offerings. In comparing new to established products, it is found that 20 percent of all products carried in inventory are new—that is, they were not carried in inventory 12 months ago. Equipped with this information, how would you respond to the supervisor's claim? Then, explain how new versus established product records would be processed by the computer inventory application.

12

PURCHASING
AND
RECEIVING

The last chapter focused on a computer application for forecasting future inventory requirements and for determining stock reorder points and order quantities. It did not discuss the preparation of purchase orders by the computer, although this is an obvious possibility. However, there are both technical and behavioral reasons why a computer-printed purchase order may not be feasible. One technical reason is that inventory records may not include complete or accurate statements of what stock is on hand or on order. Without these data, it is impractical to prepare purchase orders by computer. Another technical obstacle is that the source of stock may vary or there may be several sources, depending on when and where stock should be delivered. Finally, not all price concessions can be stored in the inventory file. These are factors that cannot be evaluated by the computer.

There are also behavioral reasons for not preparing purchase orders by computer. Purchasing agents, or buyers, often find computer forecasts for sales and computed order quantities questionable. Before any computed purchase order is prepared, each forecast is reviewed to determine whether the computer predictions are misleading. For example, if variable lead time and variable demand for stock are major considerations in placing purchase orders, buyers may insist on adjusting computer-formulated order quantities before the purchase order is prepared. Another reason is simply one of human beings controlling the decisions made by computer. Since the purchasing agent is ultimately responsible for purchase order decisions, he or she reviews formulated order quantities before allowing company funds to be used.

In spite of these technical and behavioral obstacles, preparing purchase orders by computer can frequently be more efficient and reduce costs more than preparing them by hand. If the on-hand and on-order fields of the master inventory records are accurate and if vendors can be selected by computer, the virtues of using the computer to write purchase orders are indeed great. Records that result from order writing by computer can be incorporated into the inventory file and used to verify the accuracy of receiving reports and billing invoices sent by vendors. Purchase order information also completes the cycle by providing full cost accounting data for the planning and control of inventory.

12-1   EDIT AND REVIEW BY PURCHASING AGENTS

Purchase order writing, in most instances, is controlled by an edit and review process after stock requirements have been forecasted and before purchase orders have been written. The purchasing agent is advised, by the *stock report,* of the immediate requirements for stock. As shown in Figure 12-1, this report enables the purchasing agent to compare the stock on hand with the historical sale of stock. For example, if 120 stock items are on hand and sales average 40 items per month, there are 3 months of stock on hand. With a stock lead time of two weeks, the purchasing agent must decide whether to order additional stock.

This approach to order writing does not use the computer to decide order quantities. A more sophisticated approach computes the difference between forecasted sales and stock on hand and on order to compute the amount to be ordered, which is then printed for review by the purchasing agent. This approach adjusts the quantity to be ordered to take advantage of quantity discounts, shipping and freight savings, and vendor location and reliability. Since this computation requires considerable manipulation of files by the computer, the separate steps used during processing are usually summarized, so that the purchasing agent can comprehend how the quantity order figure is derived. If the agent understands, he or she is less likely to alter the computer order quantity.

The stock report serves as a working document. It is reviewed by the purchasing agent in order to obtain better use of company funds. This manual review allows buyers to adjust purchase orders to cover special sales or deals for customers. *Not all demand conditions or price concessions can be included in the inventory master file.* Moreover, the computer cannot be programmed to predict these factors, since they are usually not based on historical trends. Unless the purchasing agent is allowed to override computer order quantities, regular inventory will be stripped by special pur-

13 MONTHS SALES REPORT   DATE 01/31/   PAGE 111

ITEM	DESCRIPTION	PACK/SIZE	JAN	FEB	MAR	APR	MAY	JUN	JUL	AUG	SEP	OCT	NOV	DEC	JAN	TOTAL	MOH
03782	FNY FCE LOUD MOUTH PUNCH	72S			3	15	35	37	26	16	6	0	1	3	10	152	17
03785	FNY FCE JOLLY OLLY ORNGE	72S	0	0	2	22	45	38	29	22	7	2	3	3	8	186	13
03789	FNY FCE ROOTIN RASPBERRY	72S	0	0	3	24	48	51	23	20	1	7	4	0	5	185	9
03792	FNY FCE FRKLE FCE STRAW	72S	0	0	2	20	15	37	18	12	0	1	5	1	6	117	18
03793	FNY FCE PRSWT CHERRY	96S					76	34	31	18	6	8	5	1	1	181	19
03794	FNY FCE PRSWT GRAPE	96S					82	35	31	9	9	9	4	3	3	197	17
03795	FNY FCE PRSWT LEMONADE	96S					72	36	29	9	6	8	3	2	1	168	12
03796	FNY FCE PRSWT ORANGE	96S					74	37	30	16	6	0	3	3	2	168	15
03797	FNY FCE PRSWT PUNCH	96S					72	31	50	10	5	9	3	3	7	167	17
03852	KOOL POPS	36 8S	8	18	25	93	46	87	59	32	17	9	8	6	3	414	59
	DISCONTINUED	12 24 S			34	54	75	88	58	53	7	10	2	1	3	281	6
03855	WYLERS LEMONADE	48S	52	77	119	152	168	397	336	188	98	55	37	43	56	1778	20
03858	WYLERS ORANGE	48S	29	31	54	74	38	116	99	59	26	16	17	17	15	571	6
03860	TWIST DIET LEMONADE	48S	0	0	0	145	43	96	53	16	12	4	9	12	5	389	20
03873	TWIST NATURAL LEMONADE	72S	26	62	39	127	39	179	128	55	51	15	17	20	20	770	32
03875	TWIST NATURAL ORANGE	48S	14	32	17	11	97	110	80	32	16	8	20	7	17	461	46
04081	CHEVY CHASE TOM JERRY	12 9 1/2 OZ											113	98	5	216	74
04083	CHEVY CHASE BUTTERED RUM	12 11 OZ											121	123	4	248	60
08284	TANG BREAKFAST DRINK	12 9 OZ	157	145	167	147	113	97	111	144	143	138	154	101	184	1801	33
08286	TANG BREAKFAST DRINK	24 18 OZ	138	142	158	151	106	99	104	120	134	126	158	138	120	1674	50
08288	TANG BREAKFAST DRINK	12 27 OZ	194	336	422	179	0	330	265	65	126	50	121	714	323	3125	269
08288A	TANG BRK DRNK PREM PK	12 27 OZ													305	305	125
08293	START INSTANT ORANGE	48 4 5/8	119	32	2	81	30	0	130	0	28	213	92	76	31	834	124
08293A	START ORANGE W/PITCHER	48 4 5/8													522	522	54
08299	START INST P/APPLE ORANG	24 4 2/3	43	40	36	27	38	48	32	32	21	26	19	22	13	397	19
11345	O/C FRIED ONIONS	24 300S	53	57	71	44	47	66	11	0	0	0	22	40	72	483	18
11345A	DISCONTINUED	24 300S													1	1	0
12204	BETTY CROCKR POTATO BUDS	12 5 OZ	90	72	76	71	70	82	64	41	2	0	44	68	60	740	26

FIG. 12-1 Stock report

chases and normal customer orders will go unfilled. This is one main objection to computer-based systems for inventory control.

12-2 PURCHASE ORDER INPUT

The main input to the purchase order application is the stock report. This report is used by a purchasing agent to decide what to order from vendors. If the agent disagrees with computer-based order quantities, the printed order-quantity calculation is altered. It is also possible to change the recommended vendor, since the vendor number appears on the report. Finally, stock not listed as requiring a reorder may be ordered. All changes override the reorder information stored in the master inventory file.

After the purchasing agent has completed making changes in the stock report, it is sent to data entry. The keyed data include stock number, order quantity, and selected vendor number. Since the stock report is printed in the same sequence as the inventory file, the purchase order change instructions can be read in order by the computer. In other words, no sort is needed before posting purchase order changes to the inventory file.

12-3 THE PURCHASE ORDER SYSTEM

Figure 12-2 illustrates the flow and processing stages for a purchase order application. Two main files support the processing of purchase order transactions. The *inventory master file* contains stock items to be reordered subject to approval by the purchasing agent. (The updated inventory master file contains stock items to be ordered following any change by the purchasing agent.) The *vendor master file* stores vendor numbers, names and addresses, and freight rates. This file is used to complete the vendor purchase order.

Inputs to and outputs from the system are minimal. As previously stated, the only input to the system is the stock report. The outputs, other than the updated inventory file, consist of the following:

1. purchase order change report
2. vendor purchase orders
3. general ledger summary

The contents of the inventory master file and the vendor master file were shown in Chapters 11 and 5, respectively. Figure 12-3 shows the *purchase order record detail,* which consolidates information from both files. The purchase order number, added during the purchase order print program, is

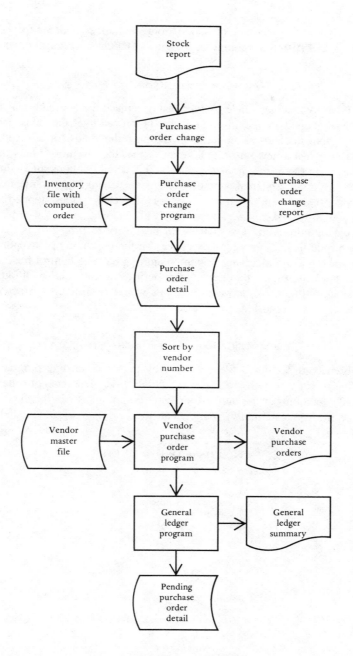

FIG. 12-2 Purchase order writing flowchart

either assigned by computer or added from prenumbered order forms. The general rule is to let the computer assign the purchase order number.

The Purchase Order Change Program

Order quantity changes made by purchasing replace the computer-calculated quantities retained in the inventory file. In processing, the revised order-quantity input updates the contents of the on-order fields for affected stock records to reflect a new on-order amount. Then, the inventory file is directly used to create the *purchase order detail*. This detail contains all stock to be ordered from an assigned vendor. The order change program, in other words, continues from where the inventory forecast system stopped.

The *purchase order change report* lists all changes to the on-order fields made by the purchasing agent. It is not necessary to print orders that have not been modified, as they already appear on the purchase order report. The reason for reporting all changes is to compute a balance control for comparing the total of vendor purchase orders written to the total additional on-order stock. Differences between the totals would be difficult to trace unless all changes were reported.

The Vendor Purchase Order Program

The purchase order detail file produced by the order change program contains one record for each stock number being ordered. Parts not ordered by either the computer or the purchasing agent do not appear in this file. Therefore the file is substantially smaller than the inventory file. Nonetheless, it

PURCHASE ORDER DETAIL

From Keyed Purchase Order Changes
   Stock number
   Quantity ordered
   Vendor number (if different)
   Unit cost (if special)
   Freight rate (if special)

Added from Inventory Master File
   Stock description
   Unit cost
   Unit of measure
   Vendor number

Added from Vendor Master File
   Vendor name and address
   Freight rate (if known)

Added from Order Print Program
   Purchase order number
   Date of purchase order

FIG. 12-3 Typical file contents of purchase order detail

probably is fairly large, and the sort that follows the order change program will require a fair amount of time, since the sequence must be the same as in the vendor master file.

After the sort program, the purchase order detail can be combined with data from the vendor master file (see Chapter 5) to produce printed purchase orders. A typical vendor purchase order records vendor number, vendor name and address, stock number ordered, quantity ordered, stock description, unit cost, and unit of measure. Freight and shipping specifications are also noted, if stored in the vendor file. Some error diagnostics may be required to identify problems such as an invalid vendor number. However, with suitable safeguards, this should happen rarely, if ever. It might appear that the vendor master file should be updated by the purchase order detail. That is, purchase order activity for each vendor could be retained and summarized. Since this information is now available in the purchase order detail, which is also retained, any change to the vendor file at this point is unnecessary.

Actual printing of purchase orders can be done using prenumbered forms or programming the computer to assign a purchase order number. Manual procedures for preparing purchase orders generally use prenumbered purchase orders supplied by a forms manufacturer. Forms tablets use consecutive numbers starting with 1 and running through, say, 99,999. However, it is advantageous to let the computer assign the purchase order number. The arguments against prenumbered checks (see Chapter 6) also hold here. If computer purchase order forms are prenumbered, it is more difficult to prepare the printer for the computer. Any mistake in setup or any subsequent failure of the printer results in a substantial rerunning of the vendor purchase order program.

The General Ledger Program

If the costs of purchasing are known at least reasonably well, a *general ledger summary report* is used in encumbering budgeted expenses. The ability to encumber (that is, to set aside) purchasing costs in advance allows a company's financial officers to prevent unauthorized expenditures or expenditures that exceed acceptable limits. If accounting waits until stock is received to determine whether too much cash is being spent, it is too late to rectify overextended budget expenditures. By encumbering expenses before the vendor receives a purchase order, excesses can be identified and avoided.

The cost of purchasing may be made explicit if costs are fixed in advance. However, if they vary, the encumbrance of funds will be only an estimate of actual stock expenditures. Estimates are based on an average of previous prices. If freight and handling charges can be predicted and posted to separate accounts in a budget, they should also be segregated on the general ledger to allow the cost of stock to be clearly identified. Unfortunately, freight and handling, as well as the forthcoming vendor discount, may not be known with any accuracy when the purchase order is written. Consequently, the actual cost of stock may be difficult to predict accurately in advance.

After the general ledger report has been printed, the purchase order file should be either set aside or combined with other pending files to be used in processing reports on stock received from vendors.

12-4   INPUT TO RECEIVING

After stock has been received from a vendor, a company must have a systematic procedure for comparing received stock to that ordered. One possibility is initially to match the corresponding purchase order stored in a manual file to determine whether the order is complete. Stock from vendors is accompanied by a packing slip, which should be checked against the contents as they are unpacked. A copy of the purchase order should also be compared to the receiving document. If the order is complete, it is possible to reduce the time to input data. In this instance, the receiving document can be coded as filled. If the purchase order and the packing slip do not agree, it becomes necessary to input the entire detail for each part received. In any event, details on quantities received must be entered into the computer and batch-controlled to permit on-hand fields of the inventory file to be updated accurately.

12-5   THE RECEIVING SYSTEM

Figure 12-4 illustrates the flow and processing stages for the receiving application. As with the purchase order system, two main files support the processing of receiving transactions. The *inventory master file* contains the records of stock items to be updated on account of additions to stock. The *pending purchase order detail file* stores the records for ordered stock, which are to be matched to the records for received stock.

The input to receiving consists of keyed packing slip information. If the packing slip is exactly the same as the purchase order, only the vendor packing slip number, the purchase order number, and the date of receipt need to be entered as input. If it differs from the original purchase order, the entire packing slip must be keyed. An incoming stock quality index may also be keyed, after a sampling of a shipment has been inspected to determine whether it should be accepted. This practice is becoming more common with many companies as they seek to identify defective parts before acknowledging receipt and payment for ordered merchandise.

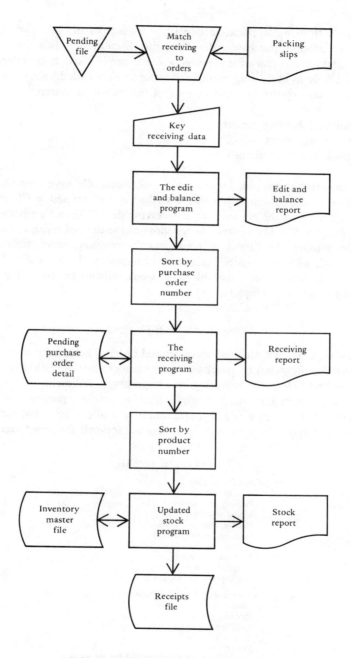

FIG. 12-4 Receiving stock flowchart

Outputs from the application consist of a receipts file and two updated files—the pending purchase order detail file (from the purchase order application) and the inventory file. The *receipts file* can be used in an order-filling application or in evaluating company vendors, often called vendor analysis. The following reports are also outputs of the receiving system:

1. edit and balance report
2. receiving report
3. stock report (optional)

The contents of the pending purchase order detail file have been shown in Figure 12-3. The inventory file was described and illustrated in Chapter 11. Figure 12-5 shows the content of the receiving detail file, which is the same as the receipts file. Data entry always supplies the date of receipt, the packing slip number, the vendor number, and the purchase order number. All other detail, with the possible exception of a quality check, is stored in the pending purchase order detail file and needs only to be entered as input when an order is incomplete.

The Receiving Program

Packing slips are not received in sequential order. Therefore it is necessary to sort receiving detail by purchase order number after the edit and balance program and before the receiving report program. Following the sort, the receiving program removes the detail from the pending purchase order file for purchase orders received in their entirety and alters the detail for orders partially received. Changes to the purchase order detail are transferred to the

RECEIVING DETAIL

From Packing Slips
   Date of receipt
   Packing slip number
   Purchase order number
   Vendor number
   Stock number (optional)
   Quantity received (optional)
   Unit cost (if special)
   Freight rate (if special)
   Stock quality (if practiced)

Added from Pending Purchase Order Detail
   Stock number
   Quantity received
   Vendor name and address
   Unit cost
   Freight rate
   Vendor lead time (determined by program)

FIG. 12-5 Typical file contents of receiving detail

receipts file, from which the receiving report is printed. One other function of this program is to capture vendor lead time, or turnaround. First, the date of stock is compared to the date stock was ordered. Second, this information is used to update vendor lead time for a stock item. Vendor lead time is vital in computing the safety stock for a stock item, as discussed in the inventory forecasting application. It is also useful for evaluating a vendor's ability to supply stock.

Figure 12-6 shows an audit of a receiving report. This report prints the purchase order number, date of receipt, packing slip (or invoice) number, vendor number, stock number, pack and size, description of item, pack cost, quantity ordered, quantity received, and extended cost. Any discrepancy between the original purchase order and the receipt of goods should be indicated on the receiving report. Normally, vendors advise a company if there are any changes in ordered quantities. Unfilled portions of orders are usually put on back order by a vendor and sent later. If so, items received are transferred from the purchase order detail and printed on the receiving report. The purchase order detail, while altered, is not removed for the purchase order in question. The unfilled items are retained in the purchase order detail file to permit back-order shipments to be reconciled.

Purchasing may also deem it necessary to delete unfilled or partially filled orders rather than have them filled at a later date. If this is desired, the receiving report program should accept delete instructions to remove unfilled orders. These deletions are recorded on the receiving report to provide a

```
AUDIT OF RECEIVINGS  DATE 02/23/     PAGE 1

P.O.     DATE    B/L    VDR.    ITEM    PACK-SIZE    DESCRIPTION OF ITEM        COST   Q-ORD   Q-RECD   EXT-COST
18113   02-22-   07734   26NS   10016   24 303      HOOD RIVER C S CORN        3.90    20      20       78.00
18113   02-22-   07734   26NS   10061   24 303      HOOD RIVER WK CORN         3.90    30      30      117.00
18113   02-22-   07734   26NS   10238   24 303      HOOD RIVER PEAS            4.15    20      20       83.00
18113   02-22-   07734   26NS   10427   24 303      HOOD RIVER GREEN BEANS     3.85    30      30      115.50
18200   02-15-   51023   47XR   Y1929   6 15 CT     CHEESE POPCORN              .54    80      80       43.20
18200   02-15-   51023   47XR   Y1931   6 10 CT     CARMEL CORN 1 3/4 OZ        .30    80     200*      60.00
18200   02-15-   51023   47XR   Y1933   6 15 CT     BUTTER POPCORN              .54    80      80       43.20
18200   02-15-   51023   47XR   Y0372   3 59 CT     PEANUT BRITTLE              .93    80     160*     148.80
18200   02-15-   51023   47XR   Y1911   6 49 CT     CARAMEL CORN 8 OZ          1.76    80      80      140.80
18200   02-15-   51023   47XR   Y1920   6 39 CT     POPCORN KING SIZE          1.35    80      80      108.00
18200   02-15-   51023   47XR   Y1921   6 49 CT     CHEESE POPCORN             1.65    80      80      132.00
18174   02-17-   52012   18LN   06407   24 1/2S     BUMBLE BEE RED SALMON     14.37    16      *          .00
18174   02-17-   52012   18LN   06409   24 1S       BUMBLE BEE RED SALMON     23.51    20      *          .00
18174   02-17-   52012   18LN   06430   24 1/2S     BUMBLE BEE PINK SALMON    11.12    16      16       177.92
18174   02-17-   52012   18LN   06431   24 1S       BUMBLE BEE PINK SALMON    18.51    30      *          .00
18174   02-17-   52012   18LN   06516   24 1/2 SP   BB ALBCR WHT/LB TUNA0122  12.02    40      40       480.80
```

FIG. 12-6 Receiving report

clear audit trail. In these cases, the vendor should be notified that an order is being cancelled.

The Updated Stock Program

The receipts file, produced by the receiving program, can be used to update the inventory file and produce a revised stock report. Another alternative is to use the receipts file in an order-filling system prior to posting customer orders to inventory. Updating the inventory file during the receiving application is advantageous because there is more time to check the completeness of items added to stock. The inventory file should be changed with considerable caution, as it models the quantity of stock in inventory and represents the direct dollar investment of the company. The disadvantage of updating at this time is that it requires an additional, separate processing of the inventory file. The chance for error in processing increases in proportion to the number of times a file is updated. Hence, by combining the receipts to stock with customer demands against stock, as in the order-filling application, processing time is saved and the chance for human error is reduced. Whether time allows for an update during order filling, however, is the critical factor. An update during the receiving application might be necessary because of the critical time limitations imposed on order filling.

12-6   VENDOR EVALUATION

The receipts file serves an additional purpose—to evaluate vendor performance. Factors to be considered in evaluating vendors are the price of merchandise, vendor turnaround or lead time, frequency of back orders, and freight charges attached to the average order. There are other considerations that may or may not be stored in receiving details. These include such factors as the condition and quality of received merchandise.

Figure 12-7 illustrates one type of vendor evaluation. It shows, by vendor number and name, the current and year-to-date receipts for all vendors who sell to a company. Moreover, year-to-date purchases are compared to those for last year in order to record increased or decreased activity.

Figure 12-8 flowcharts the system used to prepare vendor analysis and evaluation reports. The receipts file is first sorted by vendor number. After the sort routine, receipts are posted to a year-to-date receipts file. This file, an accumulation of vendor receipts, is the basis for vendor analysis and evaluation. Two types of reports are commonly prepared. The first is an activity and performance review of each vendor in the file. It includes evaluation criteria processed by the computer as the basis for further evaluation of the vendor by purchasing. The second type of report, which requires another

PURCHASE ANALYSIS BY VENDOR						
VENDOR'S NO.	VENDOR'S NAME	AMOUNT THIS MONTH	RETURNS YEAR TO DATE	NET AMOUNT YEAR TO DATE	NET AMOUNT LAST YEAR TO DATE	INCREASE OR DECREASE
27	ABBOT MACHINE CO	1286 44		3194 26	3010 42	133 84
53	ACE TOOL CO			1975 15	1259 75	115 39
66	ACME ABRASIVE CO	342 36		1505 93	1452 50	23 43
324	ALLAN ALLOYS CO		95 10	4675 22	4410 15	265 07
367	AMERICAN TOOL CO			936 74	1293 34	307 10 CR
425	ANGUS METAL WORKS			342 39	795 22	47 67
475	APEX CORPORATION	2316 84	245 73	10478 79	9473 65	1003 14
502	ARCO STATIONERY CO			319 42	445 93	126 51 CR

FIG. 12-7 Purchase analysis by vendor

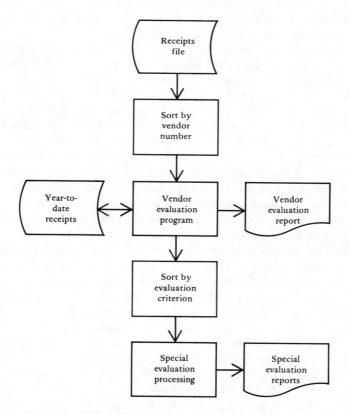

FIG. 12-8 Vendor analysis and evaluation flowchart

sort of the year-to-date receipts file, is a ranking of vendors by one of several factors. A common listing shows the dollar value of purchases during the year. It is also possible to list vendors who fail to perform within established criteria, such as stated delivery times. The type of secondary sort and the content of special evaluation reports must be determined by purchasing agents, since they are responsible for evaluating company vendors.

12-7 MANAGEMENT IMPLICATIONS

The purchasing and receiving computer system differs from other computer systems discussed thus far, as use of previously processed file detail is required. The purchase order application requires the inventory file and can be viewed as an extension of the inventory control computer application. The receiving application requires pending purchase order detail. This application, on the one hand, is also an extension of inventory control. On the other hand, the way in which the inventory file is used makes receivables an adjunct to the computer order-filling system.

The purchasing and receiving computer applications offer considerable assistance in making decisions concerning a company's purchasing procedures and policies. Computer-determined order quantities remove much of the daily routine from purchasing, and yet purchasing agents retain necessary flexibility in ordering stock. Override provisions allow them to concentrate on stock items that they expect to experience rapid or unusual shifts in demand and to coordinate special sales or deals offered by company vendors. On the other hand, use of a fully automated purchase order application without override provisions has led many companies to experience continuous and unnecessary problems. Limits must be placed on a computer-based inventory control system—*limits that are controlled by the manager*.

The receiving application offers managerial assistance by providing an accurate, current receiving report. The report is of great value for production planning and scheduling and also permits vendor analysis and evaluation to be undertaken. It is sometimes thought that the accounts payable system is well suited for vendor analysis. In truth, the average payables system can tell little about the vendor other than comparing quantity ordered to quantity delivered. The receiving application, in contrast, is able to evaluate vendors on a more realistic basis. Quantity ordered, quantity received, quantity on back order, quality of received merchandise, vendor turnaround time, and freight charges as a percentage of total purchase price can all be determined and used in the evaluation process. Hence, vendor analysis is a natural by-product of the purchasing-receiving computer system, while the payables system, even when modified to evaluate vendors, is not as comprehensive nor is analysis a typical by-product of it.

As a final consideration, the purchasing and receiving system is not only an extension of the order entry and inventory control systems, but is also the initial stage in a computer work-in-process and production control system. A wholesaler can immediately use newly received inventory for sales to customers. A manufacturer wants to have stock available for the production of products or for the acceptance of a customer order. Material requirements are matched with available inventory to determine when and if products can be produced.

REVIEW OF IMPORTANT IDEAS

Data supplied by the system can be used to prepare purchase orders for vendors. However, suggested order quantities must first be reviewed by purchasing to ensure that the forecast and the resulting order quantity are reasonable, for at this point computed order quantities can be altered to better reflect the business environment. If a computed order quantity is changed, the inventory file must also be changed to update the on-order field.

The purchase order detail file is used to print purchase orders. It is then retained to form a pending purchase order file, which is used in posting stock received from vendors.

When a warehouse receives stock from vendors, shipping papers are checked against actual stock. They are then compared to the original purchase order. After this second check, receiving information is extracted from the shipping papers. A receiving file is created and posted against the pending purchase order file.

The receiving report indicates the stock received, as well as the items ordered but not yet received. It may also list purchase orders that have not been received.

The receipts file can also be used to prepare vendor evaluation reports, which aid in selecting vendors. Evaluations showing performance totals and rankings of vendors are used by purchasing to determine which vendors to use.

REVIEW QUESTIONS

1. For what reasons are purchase orders not prepared as an integral part of the inventory computer application?

2. What generally occurs if a purchasing agent is not able to understand how an order quantity is determined by the computer? What should be done in this instance?

3. What should happen to the inventory file when a purchasing agent decides to change an entry listed on the stock report?

4. Why is it usually better to let the computer assign the purchase order number, rather than use prenumbered order forms?

5. Why is the purchase order detail file smaller than the inventory file? How must the order file be sequenced prior to the printing of vendor purchase orders?

6. Why is it suggested that purchase order costs be encumbered after a purchase order is printed and before the vendor receives and fills the order?

7. What is the first step in the preparation of input to the receiving application? Why is this step extremely important?

8. In the receiving application, what changes are made to the pending purchase order file when an order is received in its entirety? When an order is only partially received?

9. How does the receiving application capture vendor lead time? Of what value is this information in the management of inventory and in the selection of company vendors?

10. The receipts file produced by receiving can be used in several ways. Explain the various options open to a firm.

11. What is the purpose of vendor analysis? Why is the purchase order and receiving system better suited to the analysis of vendor performance than the accounts payable computer application?

EXERCISES

1. A purchase order is deleted from the pending purchase order detail because of slowness on the part of the vendor to ship ordered merchandise. It is then discovered that ordered material was received but mislaid in the receiving department. Explain the data processing procedures necessary to rectify this situation.

2. Discuss processing procedures to be followed when incorrect parts are shipped form vendors.

3. A major consideration in vendor purchases is the cost of transportation. Suppose you operate a business in Hawaii and must order the majority of your supplies from the continental United States. How would you modify inventory forecasting and purchase order systems to aid in controlling excessive shipping costs?

4. Purchasing and receiving file detail should be used to verify the accuracy of billing invoices sent by vendors. Design a modified accounts payable computer application to support this feature.

13

WORK-IN-PROCESS AND SCHEDULING

Not all sales to customers are from parts held in inventory and then reordered from vendors. Many companies manufacture to fill customer orders (manufacture-to-order). Others add to their supply of finished goods and later sell them to customers (manufacture-to-stock). This chapter looks at a computer application that assists in processing work orders through a manufacturing operation.

A manufacturing work-in-process computer application translates actual or expected customer orders into estimates of raw material and subassembly requirements, and projects work load schedules for the various manufacturing assembly operations. Work loads are defined by loads for machines or tasks for work stations in a manufacturing shop. Customer orders are scheduled through the shop by the type of job as recorded on a manufacturing work order.

Since there will normally be several jobs in progress within a manufacturing shop at a time, different jobs compete for use of machines and work stations. The computer application balances the overall work load, thereby permitting shop resources to be properly utilized. Extra expenses of overtime or penalties for late shipments are avoided when balancing is successful. The application must also expedite a particular order so that parts are finished on time for sale and delivery to customers.

A manufacturing operation's profitability is directly affected by proper utilization of shop resources and timely completion of manufacturing work orders. Scheduling is crucial, and this chapter considers the ways in which computers can be used to improve scheduling of plant operations. Computers can also be used to integrate sales forecasts from branch sales offices with production schedules developed within the manufacturing shop. High shop efficiency and effectiveness can thus be maintained in relation to customer requirements.

13-1 INPUT DATA

The manufacture-to-order or custom manufacturing shop produces finished goods for customer orders. The order starts the production cycle. Data recorded on the purchase order are used to procure raw material and to translate customer product requirements into shop requirements. The details of the stock or goods required; the method of customer payment; the date when finished goods are promised; and other miscellaneous data serve as input to the computer system. The sum of all orders in a shop constitutes the total work load, which must be converted into the master shop schedule.

It is more difficult to create a master shop schedule for the manufacture-to-stock shops, because manufacture is completed without firm customer orders. In this case, invoice detail or detail from the master inventory file may be used to predict demand for sales. This prediction is then used to prepare or to modify the schedule of shop activity. Another possibility is to require branch sales offices to forecast customer sales. Many companies are composed of branch sales offices or sales outlets. Each maintains an inventory of manufactured stock. Similarly, each is capable of forecasting stock requirements. When a branch or an outlet needs additional stock, it orders the stock from the company factory or factories.

Various demands by sales outlets affect the length of scheduled production runs and the mix of products to be manufactured. These considerations in turn affect plant efficiency and overall product profitability. The longer the run, the more efficient the operation. Also, manufacturing every possible variation of a product lowers overall profits.

Rather than manufacture to meet one sales branch order at a time, it is far better to schedule production so that one production run fills several sales orders. To accomplish this difficult task, it is necessary to forecast *aggregate demand*. This forecast can be prepared by accumulating individual sales branch and outlet forecasts of projected sales by product line. Although one branch office may not accurately forecast its demand for an individual product, the accumulated total from all branch offices is most often a good measure of expected demand.

If the aggregate demand forecast is relatively stable over time, it becomes the basis for scheduling the use of shop resources. Setup costs (the costs to prepare employees and equipment to produce a product) can be kept low, since longer production runs are scheduled. Preventive maintenance can be scheduled and followed, further reducing the cost of machine downtime. Work schedules for hourly employees can be maintained, thereby reducing the expense of hiring more employees than necessary, adding work shifts, or paying overtime.

Another advantage of a relatively stable aggregate demand forecast is that it can be used to schedule the manufacture of products in a desired sequence. The mixing of sizes, shapes, colors, and other properties can be sequenced to minimize setup times and production waste or scrap, which results from product changeovers.

In-plant inventory levels for finished goods are also lowered by a schedule based on an accurate aggregate demand forecast. In this instance, the expense of having finished goods on factory shelves for long periods is eliminated. This, in turn, releases working capital that can be used for productive purposes. A smooth flow of goods to inventory also reduces the number of rush orders, with their associated high cost of manufacture.

As a final advantage, an accurate aggregate demand forecast can reduce the number of purchase orders to replenish the supply of raw material, thus lowering unit costs of manufacturing. In theory, the supply of raw material should arrive as it is needed in the shop. Ordering material in large enough lots and yet not tying up excessive cash in raw material supplies is a problem that must be considered in the design of a work-in-process computer application. Clearly, there are many more problems in the development of a computer work-in-process computer application when manufacturing is done on a manufacture-to-stock basis than when it is done on a manufacture-to-order basis.

Input data for the manufacture-to-stock application consist of sales forecast detail prepared by branch sales offices or outlets. This detail is placed in a computer file, where it is combined by part or product number. In this form, it is similar to the customer order file (Chapter 10). The requirements for manufacture are stored by part number and by sales branch or outlet. From this file, the aggregate demand forecast is prepared and the breakdown, or "explosion," of inventory parts into product components is accomplished.

13-2 THE WORK-IN-PROCESS SYSTEM

Figures 13-1 and 13-6 flowchart the major stages of a work-in-process computer application. The first half of the application converts customer orders (manufacture-to-order) or branch sales forecast detail (manufacture-to-stock) into the master shop schedule. The second half of the application compares completed work with the schedule, amending the schedule as the need

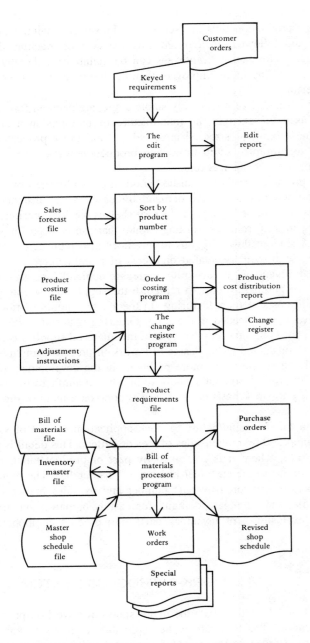

FIG. 13-1 Work-in-process flowchart: preparation of the master shop schedule

arises, removing orders from the schedule as they are completed, and preparing the final cost report and customer invoices. The more complex series of processing activities are those necessary to produce the master shop schedule.

Four or more main files support the processing stages in the preparation of the master shop schedule.

- The *sales forecast file* supplies forecast detail by product number from sales branches or outlets. This detail is used to predict product requirements.

- The *product requirements file* is then produced.

- The *product costing file* adds standard price and cost information to the product requirements file. When a quoted price must be reviewed, it is compared with the standard on file. The product costing file is also used to verify the correctness of the product number.

- The *bill of materials file* is used to break down, or "explode," product requirements into subassembly and part requirements. This is the key file in the work-in-process application. Product requirements are transformed into manufacturing requirements by translating demand for finished goods into demand for raw materials, the manufacture of parts, and the assemblage of work-in-process inventory.

- The *inventory master file* stores raw materials available, the level of work-in-process inventory by completed manufactured parts or subassemblies, and the level of finished goods inventory. This file, combined with detail contained in the product requirements file and the bill of materials file, is then used to prepare the master schedule.

- The *master shop schedule file* stores the detail from the previous processing of the master shop schedule. The new detail is merged with the old to produce the master shop schedule and other reports needed to manufacture.

Inputs other than these primary files consist of keyed customer order requirements and adjustment details, which are used to correct or to adjust the product requirements file. Adjustments are necessary in the work-in-process application, as they were in the inventory and the order-filling applications. Production control, in this instance, modifies the contents of the file to bring customer orders or sales predictions in line with conditions within the manufacturing environment.

The following reports are prepared in the processing of the work-in-process application:

1. edit report
2. product costing report
3. change register
4. purchase orders
5. master shop schedule
6. work orders

Besides these main reports, other reports are often produced. Some of these are individual machine and work station schedules, work reporting tickets, extended parts lists for each job (bill of materials), and route sheets for each scheduled job.

Figure 13-2 illustrates the typical file contents of the master shop schedule as well as the contents of the product requirements file, the product costing file, the bill of materials file, and the inventory file. The master shop schedule contains a job number (assigned during processing); product information; standard time and cost information; work requirements; and scheduled work completion dates. Product information is obtained from the product costing file and the bill of materials file. The latter file identifies the product by subassembly and component (part) numbers. Standard time and cost information are also obtained from the product costing and the bill of materials files. Work requirements are determined by comparing the inventory available, at various stages in manufacture, to the quantity of material required. If there is a shortage of required material, it becomes a manufacturing requirement. The work sequence (routing), the standard work times, and the work stations assigned to complete a job require the master shop schedule file. The latter assigns work sequences and stations. Finally, work completion dates are determined during processing by the assignment of a beginning work date and the summation of standard work times that follow the work sequence.

The file contents in the illustration approximate a typical work-in-process computer application. By no means, however, should this listing be inferred to apply to all applications. The contents of files used in support of a work-in-process application will be determined by the systems design prepared for a specific plant or shop. Moreover, if the bill of materials processor program is purchased from a computer vendor, the specifications of the vendor's design will largely determine the requirements for file design and conversion.

The Edit Program

The edit program in a work-in-process computer application checks all detectable errors that might result from keyed input. After the customer order is received, input data consist of the customer account number, the branch or

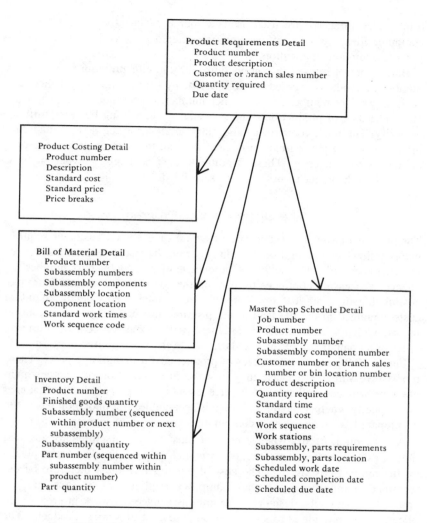

FIG. 13-2 Typical file contents of the work-in-process computer application

sales office, the product number, the number of items desired for each product ordered, the price the customer is willing to pay, the date of product delivery, and the date of the customer order. When a customer inquiry is processed rather than an order, the input data represent a request for price and delivery information. The computer application is also used to provide this information. Edit of incoming data may not be necessary if branch office sales forecasts are used as data sources. These data are placed on computer files, by sales office, and are entered directly into the work-in-process computer application.

Batch control is used in conjunction with the edit program to verify the number of products ordered, or forecasted, by product number. Other data such as product number and customer number are verified later in processing. The date of product delivery is crucial in scheduling but very difficult to verify. The most common invalid entry is an incorrect year of manufacture. Products requested close to or earlier than the date of processing may or may not be in error. These conditions must be flagged to permit back orders or rush orders to be properly scheduled.

The Order Costing Program

The sort of the newly created file of actual or expected customer requirements follows completion of the edit program. The sort program sequences the customer order file detail by product number and by part number sequence. Processing continues by passing the sorted detail against a product costing file or a product inventory file that contains cost detail. Standard costs contained in the file lead to the printing of a product cost distribution report, which will be either a statement of the expected cost of filling an order or a comparison of the standard cost to the price quoted the customer.

Figure 13-3 gives two examples of product cost distribution reports. These reports are valuable because they give the first indication of whether manufacture will be profitable. If a price quotation is prepared, the customer must specify whether the quoted price is acceptable. If a quotation has yet to be prepared, a standard cost computation can be used in preparing a bid.

An exception occurs when a product must be manufactured for the first time. In this situation, no standard costs and no price breaks can be placed on the product costing file. The cost of manufacture must therefore be determined manually, or another computer application—a cost analysis application—must be designed. The only assistance the work-in-process application can provide is to show the standard cost of similar products. The cost of similar products can then be compared to the manually prepared cost details. Overhead, administrative expenses, and profit margins can be appropriated accordingly.

The Change Register Program

The change register is printed after the product cost distribution report has been reviewed. The register is a listing of product requirements, including adjustments by product schedulers. Adjustments are entered by punched

MATERIAL COST DISTRIBUTION

Date _____

☐ E.P. CUSTOMER ☐ E.P. STOCK ☐ CLOSED ORDERS
☑ I.P. CUSTOMER ☐ I.P. STOCK ☑ WORK IN PROCESS

ORDER NO.	RAW MATERIAL		OUTSIDE PURCHASES			MANUFACTURED COMPONENTS	TOTAL	REMARKS
	BAR STOCK	CON-O-CLAD	PARTS	SERVICES	FREIGHT			
300380		6 33					6 33	
300590		59 45					59 45	
301190		132 97					132 97	
302191						8 59	8 59	
303220		10 00	1 12			11 45	22 57	
303610		24 71					24 71	
303900	2 30	1 49	127 84			9 63	141 26	
304420						2 53	2 53	
304790		2 25					2 25	
304880		19 24					19 24	
							419 90	

JOB COST DISTRIBUTION

Date _____

☐ E.P. CUSTOMER ☐ E.P. STOCK ☐ CLOSED ORDER
☑ I.P. CUSTOMER ☐ I.P. STOCK ☑ WORK IN PROCESS

ORDER NO.	SALES AMOUNT	INVOICE AMOUNT	LABOR HOURS	LABOR AMOUNT	BURDEN AMOUNT	MATERIAL AMOUNT	TOTAL COST	REMARKS
300380	46 20		1 0	2 50	4 20	6 33	13 03	
300590	1617 65	176 95	2 5	6 24	10 52	59 45	76 21	
301190	379 10	347 60	4 8	11 96	20 21	132 97	165 14	
302190	213 00		4 0	13 16	13 16		26 32	
302191			2 3	6 25	13 28	8 59	28 12	
302390	483 27							
303220	196 20	98 10	4 7	11 69	19 80	22 57	54 06	
303610	334 69		16 6	51 12	51 42	4 29	106 83	
303620	166 80		6 3	17 31	24 68	20 42	62 41	
303780	331 20		1 2	2 99	5 05		8 04	
303790	60 57							
303900	672 32		11 6	28 92	48 83	141 26	219 01	
304040	22 14							
304420	97 15	62 20	1 3	3 24	5 47	2 53	11 24	
304530	430 15							
304740	36 75							
304790	1215 00		6 6	20 44	23 18	2 25	45 87	
304880	142 60		1 6	3 99	6 74	19 24	29 97	
304910	175 65		2 0	5 79	7 49		13 28	
305010			1 7	4 24	7 16		11 40	
			68 2	189 84	261 19	419 90	870 93	

FIG. 13-3 Product cost distribution reports

card (or computer terminal) to increase or decrease production runs. Total product requirements might be 890, for example, when it is advantageous to produce 1,000 and carry the additional 110 in finished goods inventory. Then, too, the profit margin might be low on product requirements, or the number of any one product required might be impractical to produce. All these conditions merit adjustment, perhaps by informing sales personnel that the product requested will not be produced until demand is greater or by insisting on a higher selling price in order to meet the cost of manufacture.

Product requests that cannot be produced should not be allowed to enter the work-in-process computer application. That is, customer orders should not be permitted to enter into processing when a single feature of the product cannot be produced. Tolerance limits, nonstandard raw materials, and the like need to be carefully screened by product schedulers before they are allowed to enter the computer application. In a large manufacture-to-order setting that must process at least 2,000 orders at any one time, computer processing will be delayed if careful screening has not preceded data entry. Even then, some orders that cannot be produced will enter the application. The product costing program should identify these. Adjustment instructions should then remove unacceptable orders from the product requirements file.

The Bill of Materials Processor Programs

After adjustment, the product requirements file contains an accurate representation of what needs to be supplied by manufacturing. It is possible, for example, to establish the raw materials necessary to complete several jobs that are to enter the shop. It is also possible to smooth actual production by removing parts from raw material inventory, from work-in-process inventory, and from finished goods inventory to satisfy, in part or in total, demands for finished goods.

Three conditions must be properly regulated in the decision of the quantity of material to manufacture. One is what products, or parts of products, should be purchased. Part procurement is an essential component of most manufacturing activity. The second condition is what products, parts of products, or subassemblies should be withdrawn from inventory. Inventory control is most often charged with this responsibility. The third condition is what products or subassemblies should be manufactured. Production is charged with this responsibility.

Coordinating procurement, inventory, and production activity is not easy. This task is supported by the bill of materials processor program, or set of programs. This program determines what should be purchased, what should be withdrawn from inventory, and what should be placed in the master shop schedule and manufactured. Thus the bill of materials processor program accomplishes a wide variety of activities. It permits work orders to be written, inventory release slips to be prepared, and product procurement to be initiated.

The program begins by passing the products requirements file against the bill of materials file and the inventory file. The bill of materials file explodes product requirements into part and subassembly requirements. Figure 13-4 illustrates the procedure followed in processing. Suppose that 100 units of product A are defined in the product requirements file. The bill of materials file shows that one unit of product A requires three subassemblies (B, C, and D) and five part numbers (1, 2, 3, 4, and 5). The total quantity of subassemblies and parts in one unit of product A is 13. To produce 100 units of product A, subassembly requirements are 100 of B; 200 of C; and 100 of D. Part requirements are 200 of 1; 300 of 2; 200 of 3; 100 of 4; and 100 of 5.

After determining subassembly and part requirements, the next step in processing is to determine the extent to which subassemblies can be taken from the work-in-process inventory to satisfy product requirements. The work-in-process inventory file is surveyed (either as a separate file or incorporated into the inventory master file), and completed subassemblies are assigned. A shortage of stock represents demand for production. This process is repeated for all product requirements stored on file. The net effect is to reduce the level of finished goods, work-in-process, and raw material inventory to best satisfy product demand. Any shortage must then be filled by manufacture, using existing shop capacity to replenish inventory levels.

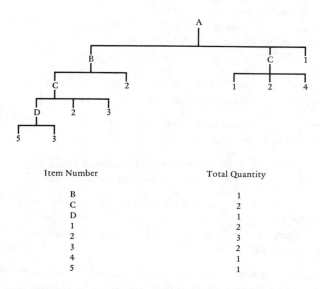

Item Number	Total Quantity
B	1
C	2
D	1
1	2
2	3
3	2
4	1
5	1

FIG. 13-4 Part and subassembly requirements to produce one unit of product A

One important result of the bill of materials processor program is determining what parts must be purchased or produced by the shop. Deciding whether to "make or buy" can be based on the overall shop work load and promised delivery deadlines.

Another result is the construction of a master shop schedule that shows what orders are due (by day or week) to pass through assigned work stations. This schedule may also indicate what materials are necessary at each station. It must account for work-in-process that is currently being routed through the shop. Usually when a revised schedule is prepared, new orders are placed in a queue, to be processed after scheduled assignments. However, some violation of this rule is allowed. Since some previously scheduled work is to replenish inventory, it may be of a lesser priority than a new order. A priority code is thus used to preempt scheduled assignments in order to produce rush items—those with high priority. It is also possible to reallocate raw material assigned to low-priority items. However, constant adjustments and reallocations can lead to confusion and greatly reduce production efficiency. Schedule alteration must be administered with great care to avoid these unpleasant consequences.

Figure 13-5 shows a master shop schedule. Jobs are scheduled by product number and indicate the quantity to be produced. The scheduling program makes assignments by following one of several basic scheduling rules such as first job received, first scheduled; jobs with shortest processing time scheduled first; jobs with the smallest number of operations scheduled first; or jobs scheduled randomly.

In addition to the master schedule, several other reports are often produced. Some of these are:

- *Machine and work center schedules,* which are reports of activities to be performed by type of operation and by scheduled work order.

- *Work orders or authorizations,* which are forms used to release stock from inventory for machine processing or assembly, by work stations.

- *Work reporting tickets,* which are prepunched cards used by work stations to report their progress on scheduled activities.

- *Extended parts list,* which is a report of item numbers for subassemblies and parts and the quantity of each required to assemble a work order. It is also the individual bill of materials for a single manufacturing order.

- *Manufacturing route sheets,* which are sheets showing the path the order will take through the shop from start to completion.

PRODUCTION SCHEDULE REPORT # 312-05 WEEK 24 JUNE 19, 19XX

PL PRODUCT	24	25	26	27	28	29	30	31	32	33	34	35	36	37	38	39	40	41	42	43	44	45	46	47	48	49	50	51	52
7 2021	30	30	30	30	30	40	30	30	30	30																			
7 2022	80			70	80	70	80	70																					
7 2042	10	20	10	20	10	20	10																						
7 2051			10	10			10																						
7 2051901C			100																										
7 2052	10	10	10	10	10	10	10																						
7 2053			10	10			10																						
PLANT TOTAL	280	221	310	280	270	250	310	230	170	150	25		10	20	55	45													

FIG. 13-5 Master shop schedule

These reports represent the major kinds of documents produced by the bill of materials processor program. Other reports such as the cash flow schedule; the dollar commitment schedule; the direct labor requirements; the overtime schedule; and the on-hand inventory dollar evaluation schedule might also be produced. However, the process is highly complex without these additional processing requirements.

One might question whether the bill of materials processor program is too complex for the typical firm to administer. Fortunately, many computer vendors are able to supply partial or complete assistance in its development. Even then, however, one must remember that, to be fully utilized, the system must be understood. Explosion of the product requirement file and the construction of the master schedule are a large part of a very complex process.

13-3 WORK-IN-PROCESS REPORTING

The second half of the work-in-process computer application is the reporting of work completed, as compared to the master shop schedule. Figure 13-6 flowcharts this processing arrangement. Work reporting tickets, which have been processed partially by the bill of materials processor program, and material receiving reports are inputs to processing. These data are edited and balanced by an edit program and then sorted by job number. The sorted file detail is then passed against the master shop schedule file to produce an amended shop schedule. Finally, completed jobs are removed from the schedule, passed against the inventory file, and moved to a finished goods file. From the latter file, cost reports and, in some cases, customer invoices can be prepared as a supplement to the work-in-process application.

Work-in-process reporting serves many necessary functions. If a job becomes significantly ahead or behind schedule, the master schedule is revised and the change is reported on the amended job schedule. The update of the master schedule changes the placement of jobs in a queue by extending their time there (the waiting time) or by permitting the start of manufacturing earlier than expected (the arrival time). In a similar manner, the presence or absence or raw materials scheduled for delivery by vendors affects the status of the schedule. If materials are unavailable, jobs cannot be started. If materials arrive earlier than expected, it is often possible to begin a job earlier than was planned.

Movement of completed jobs from the master schedule produces an up-to-date accounting of products, subassemblies, and parts that can be entered into the bill of materials processor program from the inventory file. It is essential to hold work-in-process inventory to a reasonable level. Being able to combine subassemblies soon after they have been completed meets this important objective.

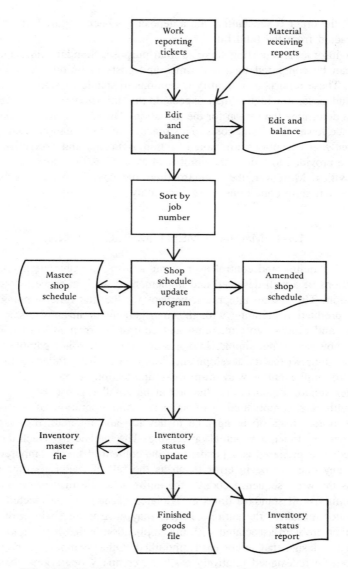

FIG. 13-6 Work-in-process reporting and summary flowchart

Placement of completed jobs in a separate finished goods file can speed customer billing. The customer master file can be passed against the file to prepare the customer invoice soon after manufacture is completed. The invoice, similar to those discussed in Chapter 7, informs the customer of the quantity shipped, the amount to be paid, and the appropriate date of payment. If the order is substantial and a deposit has been required, the deposit is subtracted from the total bill.

Work-in-process reporting serves a final purpose. Standard time and cost totals can be compared to actual times and costs to produce cost control reports. These reports can identify exceptions to standards stored on file. If times and costs are higher than expected, this information can be investigated to determine the reason for the deviation. The same is true of jobs that experience lower times and costs. This practice of investigation is *exception management*—exceptions are noted, action is taken, and corrective measures are provided to reduce the number of exceptions in future manufacturing activities. Moreover, the standard time and cost figures are revised to reflect actual shop conditions more accurately.

13-4 MANAGEMENT IMPLICATIONS

Improved planning and control over manufacturing are obvious managerial implications of a well-designed and implemented work-in-process computer application. The system integrates, perhaps for the first time in many companies, production planning with the management of inventory, sales projections, and product cost planning and control. Correct utilization of the system, however, is not simple. In one sense, the system is a gamble for the firm that underwrites its development. Many firms have failed in their attempts to implement a work-in-process application, even though outside computer vendor support was obtained at no small expense.

As with less complicated systems, successful operation of a work-in-process system rests on being able to develop and maintain the computer files necessary to support actual processing. The method by which the master schedule is prepared is dependent on the content of these computer files. Should any one file be in error (such as the bill of materials file, which contains the work sequence codes), the entire schedule may prove unworkable. Similarly, if standard times are violated because of unexpected delays or operator mistakes, the entire schedule may once more be in error.

Another problem associated with this application is that it tends to lock a firm into a design that is not easily modified. Other computer applications can often be redesigned relatively easily as company operations change or evolve. Since the work-in-process application is highly integrative, modification can be difficult. A change of one component alters other processing procedures, sometimes unknown to the systems analyst or programmer making the change. Without highly qualified personnel, the work-in-process application has been observed to deteriorate, leading to its eventual discard.

Some firms have chosen to avoid the complexity of the design presented in this chapter. One firm, for example, maintains only a shop status file. This file, updated by work tickets, shows the location and status of each scheduled job. Scheduling is a manual operation done with computer time-shared assistance. It is not an integral part of a work-in-process computer application. Other firms have elected to maintain a bill of materials file and an inventory file separately from each other. The job of scheduling is performed manually, using the bill of materials file for reference.

Several variations on the application described may be designed. This computer application does have a certain amount of inherent flexibility. Effective management of work-in-process requires either an integrated computer application or single-purpose computer applications supported by manual effort. Far too often, however, the manual support is not enough, so that work-in-process inventory and hectic production scheduling result in overly large expenses. While the risks in the design of an integrative computer application must be appreciated, the risks of not using an integrated system must also be understood. A reasonable outlay of cash to finance work-in-process, a balanced shop schedule, adequate production runs, and accurate shop standards are but some of the benefits of an integrative work-in-process computer application.

REVIEW OF IMPORTANT IDEAS

Both manufacture-to-order and manufacture-to-stock involve the need to adjust shop facilities to fit actual or expected sales to customers. The fitting process is permitted by the master shop schedule, a document that shows what, when, and in what order to manufacture. The work-in-process computer application replaces the complex task of preparing the master schedule. It translates product requirements into job requirements. It then sequences job requirements through the shop, recording the planned sequence on the master schedule. It also adjusts the schedule as jobs are completed and as new jobs are required.

Shop efficiency should be improved as a result of the work-in-process computer application. Productive time compared to machine setup time or delay should be increased. This is made possible by being able to schedule longer production runs and by avoiding excessive product changeovers. Higher efficiency leads to lower cost of manufacture, a benefit enjoyed by manufacturing, sales, and customers.

The work-in-process computer application consists of two parts: the preparation of the master shop schedule and work-in-process reporting and summation. The former is the more complex of the two. The files that support this processing are extensive and vary by the results expected from the system. The bill of materials files and programs are so complex as to require purchase from the computer vendor. Even then, problems can be encountered.

Standard times, costs, work sequences, and product explosion detail are required in an integrated work-in-process application. Because of their importance to the system, production standards must be constantly reviewed to verify their accuracy.

As jobs progress through a shop, personnel at work stations use work tickets to report their progress. The tickets show the stage of manufacture for a given job. Actual time is then compared to scheduled time to allow adjustment of the master schedule. Standard times may also require adjustment if jobs consistently fall either ahead or behind the expected times.

Because of the risks involved in the design of a work-in-process application, some firms have chosen to use only portions of the application. Although this usage avoids some problems, it does not permit production planning and control to be totally integrated within manufacturing.

REVIEW QUESTIONS

1. What is the basic function of a work-in-process computer application?

2. What is the difference between manufacture-to-order and manufacture-to-stock?

3. How is an aggregate sales forecast prepared? Of what importance is such a forecast to a work-in-process computer application?

4. Describe the bill of materials file, the inventory master file, and the master shop schedule file.

5. Why is the product distribution report prepared? The change register report?

6. Why does the bill of materials computer program initially explode product requirements into part and subassembly requirements?

7. What information is generally contained on the computer-prepared master shop schedule?

8. What main functions are served by the work-in-process reporting computer application?

9. How is exception management, or management by exception, practiced as a result of the work-in-process computer application?

10. Why is the work-in-process computer application, in one sense, a gamble for the firm that underwrites its development? What payoffs accrue to management as a result of successful implementation?

EXERCISES

1. The parts list for each unit of product A is shown below,

Part Number	Quantity Required
1	1
2	3
3	1
4	3
5	2

The subassembly requirements for each unit are as follows:

Subassembly	Quantity Required	Subassembly Composition
B	1	C,E,2
C	2	2,4
D	1	C,3,5
E	1	4,1,5

a. Diagram the subassembly and part requirements that, when combined, form one unit of product A.

b. Flowchart the computer processing necessary to create bill of materials records and thus to explode demand for product A. (Use the product requirements file and the master inventory file as inputs to processing.)

2. Describe how the computer translates the original customer order into the final shop schedule. What are the major steps? (Assume that the bill of materials file has been updated.)

3. If a single inventory master file is used to store raw materials (parts), subassemblies, and finished goods inventory, what problems might result? What alternatives would you recommend? Design an inventory file or files to be used in support of the work-in-process application. Compare the contents of file records to those of the inventory file used in inventory forecast and control (Fig. 11-4).

14

LABOR
DISTRIBUTION
AND
JOB COSTING

In the last chapter, product and job costing was mentioned as a possible processing by-product. Work reporting tickets were used to update the master shop schedule and thus could be used to determine job costs. This chapter examines job costing when data are entered from employee time cards. The time card, as used in the payroll computer application (see Chapter 4), can serve a variety of purposes other than supplying data to be converted to dollars earned. It can be used to analyze the cost of various stages of work, such as picking and packing orders in an order-filling operation. It can be used to associate employee time with vehicle use to obtain a good measure of vehicle costs or the cost of running company equipment; these costs can then be prorated to the overall cost of a product, job, or project. Time cards can also be used to record idle or delay times during the manufacture of a product.

14-1   THE EMPLOYEE TIME CARD

Figure 14-1 shows an employee time card with space for recording job numbers, or codes, and hours worked. Each employee uses job numbers to record the amount of time spent on each job. Since employees often have to complete time cards daily, it is important that this task requires little additional clerical work. If data are recorded when work is done and extracted as part of the payroll input operation, the handling of data is kept to a

CLACKAMAS COUNTY DEPT. OF PUBLIC WORKS						DAILY TIME CARD	

Employee Name___*Knee*_____

Employee No. __*49935*_____ Date __*3 - 1*__19 *72*

FOREMANS SIGNATURE
Smith

HOURS		JOB CODE	EQUIPMENT		PROJECT NO.	WORK COMPLETED	REMARKS
REGULAR	OVERTIME		NUMBER	HOURS			
1		26	208	1	PL02472		
½		26			PL11871		
1		26	208	1	PL08369		
2½		26	208	1½	PA 3		
3		26	208	½	AA 3		

GLOBE 219209-0

FIG. 14-1 Employee time card with job reporting provisions

minimum. Confusion and clerical error are reduced both within the data entry department and in job control activities. In addition, the details of time spent on each job assignment can be balanced against the total time recorded when computing the employee's wage.

One hazard must be recognized when asking employees to apportion their time. If employees are told that the sum of hours assigned to each job must equal the total time worked, some individuals will adjust the time distribution to make sure the two totals match. However, if idle time is missing, the record of time distributed by job is likely to be in error. Moreover, employees frequently view time reporting as a threat. They suspect that management will penalize them if they submit time reports showing that they are not always productive—and frequently this view is correct. Too often management equates hours worked with productive hours, although the two are usually not the same.

There are at least two ways to avoid the problem of overstated time recording. The first is to assign jobs to employees with work completion times estimated in advance. Time reporting can then be compared to time estimates and if reported time appears high (or low), follow-up investigations can be made. The second is to provide an idle time code to be used by employees to record time when "not working on a job." This code should not be designated as "idle time," since this term connotes wasteful effort. A term such as "nonbillable" or "self-improvement" is more likely to help employees properly assign time to this special designation. If such time becomes excessive, remedial action may be needed. Normally, every employee should record some nonbillable time. The presence of a small amount of such time indicates that the employee is conscientiously allocating work time to assigned projects.

The time card can also be used to report material, machine, or vehicle usage. Extraction of these data leads to their appearance on the payroll edit report, where they may be reviewed. This review is necessary as there is almost no way to machine-edit the accuracy and completeness of material or equipment usage data.

The time card serves a variety of purposes, depending upon the needs of a company. Some companies prepare reports of employee activity on a job or project basis. This procedure is typical of public works, construction, aerospace, and other industries that charge for their service on a cost-plus basis. The cost-plus approach to pricing is the first type of job costing system discussed in this chapter. The fixed price alternative, where profit is or is not realized in the everyday working relationships between a company and its customers, is then discussed. In this case, products or projects are costed to determine whether they are profitable. Manufacturing, service, retail, and wholesale operations are typical of companies that use this type of job costing system.

14-2 PRELIMINARY PROCESSING

Data recorded on time cards used in job costing can also be utilized by the labor distribution computer application. In either case, preliminary processing by the payroll computer application is required to extract employee-recorded data. This creates an input file suitable for both applications. Moreover, this procedure saves machine processing and clerical time since both the payroll and the labor distribution applications use data from time cards. Figure 14-2 illustrates the modified payroll application. After data entry, an enlarged edit report is prepared.

The edit report prints employee times, and material and equipment usage by job number. This information is reviewed and corrected by payroll personnel before it is allowed to pass to the labor distribution application. Since payroll detail does not require the same corrective procedures, it is allowed to pass directly to the next payroll processing stage, which leads to the posting of the employee's name to the input data. Labor distribution detail is placed in a separate file for later use.

The distribution correction report that accompanies the labor distribution file lists the detail totals plus submitted corrections or additions to the file. After the edit and the distribution correction reports have been reviewed, the distribution file is in its final form. Meanwhile, the normal payroll operations will have been completed and employee checks distributed.

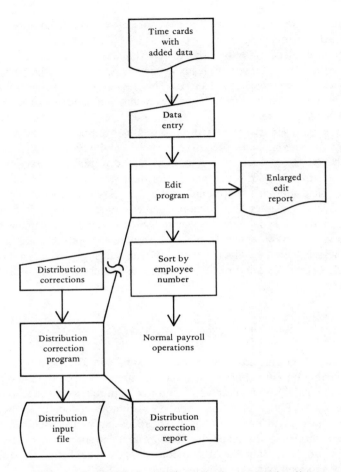

FIG. 14-2 Modified payroll application: preparing the
labor distribution file

14-3 THE JOB COSTING SYSTEM

Figure 14-3 shows that the job costing computer application is similar in
design to the order-filling and invoicing applications. The file of input detail
is sorted and passed against a *materials reference file* and an *equipment
costing file*. Both files partially validate information in the distribution input
file and increase the amount of detail by adding reference file information.
The *job ledger file* is the third file maintained by the application. This master
file stores the updated charges assigned to all jobs or projects. It represents
the final product of computer processing.

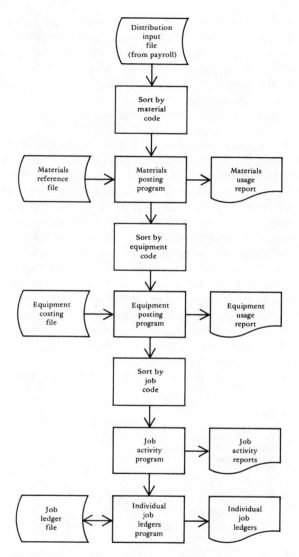

FIG. 14-3   Flowchart of the job costing computer application

Three sort and four processing programs are shown as representative of the job costing application. The first sort program places file detail in material code sequence; the second, in equipment code sequence; and the third, in job or project number sequence. The processing programs are primarily print routines designed to produce a specific report. The materials posting program leads to the printing of the *materials usage report*. The equipment posting program prints the *equipment usage report*. The *job activity report* and *individual job ledgers* are also printed. The job activity report summarizes work station or project status and serves to determine how well personnel are performing. Individual job ledgers show all charges posted against each job or project. These are used in the pricing of jobs or projects when pricing is on a cost-plus basis, or in indicating whether a project is profitable on a fixed-price basis.

Typical file contents used in printing individual job ledgers are shown in Figure 14-4. From the preliminary processing of payroll the following data are extracted: the department number, the employee number, work classification, the date, the job number, the hours worked and their extended cost, the quantity of materials or parts used, and the length of time equipment was used. Unit costs for material and hourly rates for equipment are then added from the material and equipment reference files. All additional file detail is added from the master job ledger file, updated each time by computer processing. Data contained in this file include the start and the deadline dates for each job, the budgeted dollars for each job, the budgeted labor hours required to complete each job, the labor expenditures to date, the material expenditures to date, and the equipment expenditures to date.

These file contents correlate with the reports prepared during processing. Because of the importance of the job costing reports, the next section enlarges on the content of each. The primary purpose of each computer program in this computer application is to prepare one of the job costing reports.

Original Labor Distribution File – from Payroll
    Department number
    Employee number
    Work classification
    Date(s)
    Job number(s)
    Hours worked and extended cost
    Materials used and part numbers, quantity
    Equipment used, numbers and length of time

Additional Detail from Material and Equipment Reference Files
    Material description and unit cost
    Equipment description and hourly rate

Additional Data Contained in the Job Ledger File
    Start and deadline dates for each job
    Budgeted dollars for jobs
    Budgeted or estimated labor hours to complete entire project
    Labor expenditures to date, segregated by work classification
      within job
    Material expenditures to date
    Equipment expenditures to date

FIG. 14-4 Typical file contents retained to prepare
individual job ledgers

Job Costing Reports

Each computer-prepared report in the job costing computer application serves a special purpose besides balancing and editing input detail. For example, the *materials usage report* (see Fig. 14-5) reviews supplies used during employee activity. This report is not exactly the same as an inventory usage report or a materials requirement report, as used in purchasing. It is assumed that the materials consumed or utilized are of a limited variety and that the quantity is not excessive. The materials depend upon the type of operation being performed. Road crews require asphalt, gravel, curb sections, and drainage tile. Building crews check out construction hardware, which is noted on their time cards, as well as lumber and reinforcing rods, which are recorded on another form. The use of standard unit costs permits the employee to record only the material code number and the quantity used. These data are recorded on an employee time card (not shown) and keyed as input to processing. It is then possible to extend the quantity used into the total cost of materials.

Figure 14-6 shows an example of an *equipment usage report*. Such a report records the cost of using major tools and equipment such as computers, bulldozers, trucks, and milling lathes. It shows the gainful use of equipment, as well as apparent idle or nonproductive time by machine. Hours of machine use are converted into equipment costs by averaging purchasing and operating costs (fuel, power, maintenance) by the hourly life expectancy of the equipment. The average or standard cost is stored in the equipment costing file and assigned to the project or projects that required use of the equipment.

The *job activity report* is prepared following the sort of the file detail by job, project, or work station number. Figure 14-7 shows the number of jobs worked on during the current pay period, and the number of productive hours compared to the number of nonbillable hours. This report aids project

```
                              ANYBODY COMPANY
                              MATERIALS CONSUMED
                              JULY, 19XX

EMPLOYEE  MACHINE   JOB      MATERIAL                    UNIT     QUANTITY   EXTENDED  DATE
NUMBER    NUMBER    NUMBER   NUMBER    DESCRIPTION        COST     USED       VALUE     USED

    321     516                103     776X15 TIRE       75.000    2          150.00    7/21/
    321     516                 12     REGULAR GAS        0.250   40           10.00    7/21/
  10923             23931     62000    8 ¢ NAILS-PND       .900   10            9.00    7/25/
  10996             21735       788    2X6 LUMBER-FT       .180  150           27.00    7/25/

                                       MATERIALS TOTAL                        193.00***
```

FIG. 14-5   Materials usage report

```
                                    ANYBODY COMPANY
                                    EQUIPMENT USAGE
                                    JULY, 19XX
        EMPLOYEE   MACHINE                  JOB      HOURLY    DATE     HOURS    DOLLAR    MACHINE
         NUMBER    NUMBER   DESCRIPTION    NUMBER     RATE     USED     USED     AMOUNT    TOTAL

            321      516    BACKHOE        21735     25.500    7/21/     3.0      76.50
            321      516                   23921     25.500    7/21/     1.0      25.50
            588      516                   23921     25.500    7/21/     2.0      51.00
            588      516                   23921     25.500    7/22/     6.0     153.00
                     516                                                                   306.00*

           7321     1293    3 YARD TRUCK   21735     22.000    7/21/     8.0     176.00
           7321     1293                   23921     22.000    7/22/     8.0     176.00
           7321     1293                   23921     33.000    7/22/     3.0      99.00
                    1293    3 YARD TRUCK                                                    451.00*

                           EQUIPMENT TOTAL                                                  757.00***
```

FIG. 14-6　Equipment usage report

managers in determining how well their staff is producing. It is distributed to appropriate managers who can then compare expected plans and forecasts to actual conditions.

In addition to the job activity report, *individual job ledgers* are printed for each job or project. These show all accumulated charges and activities that have been assigned to the projects. That is, new information is added to previously stored information from prior processing of the job costing computer application. The entire ledger is printed each pay period for review by

```
  WORK    ACT.HRS.   STD.HRS.    IDLE      OFF STD.   REWORK   DIRECT HRS.   TOTAL     ACCT.
 STATION   OPER.      OPER.     TIME HRS.    HRS.      HRS.      TO IND.    ACT.HRS.    NO.
 NUMBER

   100     14.20      11.73                                                  14.20     2000
   103      5.83      10.83                                                   5.83     2000
   104     17.04      10.72                                                  17.04     2000
   110                                                            3.23        3.23     1821
   110                            .38                                          .38     2202
   110                            .75                                          .75     2203
   110                           8.40                                         8.40     2208
   110                           1.94                                         1.94     2209
   110                                        2.52                            2.52     3003
   110                                        4.33                            4.33     3004
   113      7.55       4.70                                                   7.55     2000
   117     23.51      18.34                                                  23.51     2000
   118     14.20      15.67                                                  14.20     2000
   119      4.78       8.51                                                   4.78     2000
   123      7.52       6.40                                                   7.52     2000
   124     17.15      13.62                                                  17.15     2000
   126     20.53      25.01                                                  20.53     2000
   131      4.08       2.58                                                   4.08     2000
   132      7.56       7.11                                                   7.56     2000
   151      1.04        .92                                                   1.04     2000
   153      1.38       8.48                                                   1.38     2000
   154                  .80                                                            2000
   155      6.68       2.74                                                   6.68     2000

          153.05     148.16     11.47        6.85                 3.23      174.60 *
```

FIG. 14-7　Job activity report

job or production control staff. In order to control a project properly, it is vital to have all pertinent facts registered and summarized in one report.

Figure 14-8 shows a typical individual job ledger. It divides all charges pertaining to a particular project and totals all expenditures by invoice number. Given this report, it is possible to predict the likelihood of a cost overrun. This prediction can be made visually or with assistance from the computer. A simple method of highlighting the chance of an overrun is to compute a percentage of completion based on estimated labor hours required. Actual labor hours are divided by estimated labor hours to determine the percentage of completion. This estimate is then used as a reference in determining whether a project is likely to exceed allowable costs, based upon extending the present charges against work to be done. The difficulty with this method is that it does not account for project stages that require greater direct labor support. As a result, the percentage of completion estimate is subject to considerable interpretation.

JOB COST DETAIL LEDGER

CUSTOMER NAME	INVOICE NUMBER	ITEM NO	PART NUMBER	OPERATION NUMBER	QUANTITY PRODUCED	MATERIAL COST ALLOWED	MATERIAL COST ACTUAL	LABOR & BURDEN COST PER OPERATION ALLOWED	LABOR & BURDEN COST PER OPERATION ACTUAL	
HARRISON RADIATOR	3240	01	3002399	1	5000	2400	4950			
								22500	1060	
						2400	4950	22500	1060	::
HARRISON RADIATOR	3240	01	3002399	1	5000	2400	4950			
								22500	2120	
				20				1250	2160	
				80				1499	1520	
						2400	4950	25249	5800	::

FIG. 14-8 Typical individual job ledger

14-4 THE LABOR DISTRIBUTION COMPUTER APPLICATION

Many companies do not plan and control their operations on a project basis. They sell a product or perform a service and assign operating costs by department rather than by billable job. Figure 14-9 flowcharts the procedures required in preparing a labor distribution report, when material and equipment costs need not be considered. This application is much simpler than the job costing application. The input from the payroll edit program consists of the employee number, department number, hours worked, and labor costs.

The labor distribution report is printed after the master labor distribution file has been updated. Before the update, the file of input records is sorted and sequenced by department number. If there are multiple offices or divisions in the company, the division number must also appear in the sorted detail. This permits the distribution report to be totaled by division office.

Figure 14-10 shows the labor distribution report. A breakdown of labor costs by department within a branch office is printed (if there are several branch offices). The distribution detail from month to month allows comparisons between current and past operations or between current and budgeted expenditures. Past detail most often is a single summary record for each department. While it is possible to save all detail from month to month, retention is expensive. It is more important to summarize past operations, showing total costs so far during the year, and to project expected costs based on past trends. In this way, the labor distribution report is valuable in assessing costs for various activities in the company and in controlling those areas where cost is, or is expected to become, excessive.

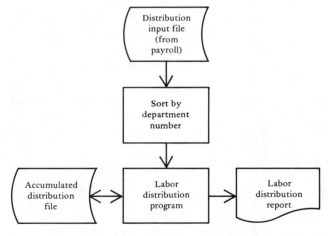

FIG. 14-9 Labor distribution report flowchart

SAMPLE CORPORATION
DECEMBER 31, 19XX
LABOR DISTRIBUTION REPORT

DEPARTMENT NUMBER	TYPE OF LABOR ACTIVITY – HOURS											
	ORDER FILLING		RE-STOCKING		INVENTORY		SHIPPING		MAINTENANCE		OTHER	
	THIS MO.	LAST MO.	THIS MO.	LAST MO.	THIS MO.	LAST MO.	THIS MO.	LAST MO.	THIS MO.	LAST MO.	THIS MO.	LAST MO.
1100	128	140	96	100	96	90	40	45	10	9	30	20
2100	155	172	120	125	125	110	50	62	15	11	5	0
4000	70	72	50	55	40	45	25	25	15	22	40	21
4100	120	100	78	70	70	75	35	38	12	10	5	7
4500	84	80	58	55	60	66	20	20	8	11	10	8
TOTAL	557	564	402	405	391	386	170	190	60	63	90	56

FIG. 14-10 Labor distribution report

14-5 MANAGEMENT IMPLICATIONS

The job costing and labor distribution computer applications identify project and labor costs and thus make it easier to control them. As direct labor is becoming a high cost of many projects, products, or services, its control leads to many changes in operations: marginal products or unprofitable products, projects, or services are cancelled; product lines are regularly checked for profitability; projects previously accepted are refused. The need to know period-by-period complete project cost detail within a company is becoming imperative. Increased competition both at the national and international levels has forced many companies to evaluate carefully product and project costs, and to streamline work station performance in order to provide products and services at a marketable cost.

The job costing and labor distribution computer applications are not difficult in design, nor do they require extensive computer processing time. Why more firms have not capitalized on this application, giving it a high design priority, is not at all clear. More than ever before, employees also realize the need to operate on a competitive basis. Most are willing to participate in a job costing program once they understand its importance. Unfortunately, many managers ask employees to apportion their time without explaining why it is necessary. Moreover, too fine a coding procedure, such as reporting times to complete individual job steps, reduces the application to meaningless clerical activity in the view of employees. The job costing application is not a replacement for preparing standard times or costs. Job and cost analysis must continue to be a manual activity outside the job costing and labor distribution computer applications. The manually prepared standards are then placed in the reference files that support these computer applications.

REVIEW OF IMPORTANT IDEAS

The job costing and labor distribution computer applications can be produced as an extension of the payroll computer application. Additional data are placed on the employee time card, such as labor distribution by project or department code, material consumed by project code, and equipment or vehicle charges by project code.

The job costing computer application requires the use of reference files to extend the data submitted by the employee. One example of how data are extended is labor-hours converted into dollar charges. The posting of direct labor, material, and equipment costs—summarized by job—leads to better assessment of the cost of an ongoing project.

The main reports produced by the job costing computer application are a materials usage summary, an equipment usage report, job activity reports, and individual job ledgers. The job ledgers show all charges against a project since its inception.

Labor distribution reporting is accomplished differently. The labor distribution computer application does not measure performance project by project. Instead, labor charges are distributed by department within the company or branch offices. The labor distribution report is used in the analysis of departmental performance.

The results of job costing and labor distribution studies include better control over company costs. Why more firms have not designed costing systems is not clear. The design is simple; the results produced by the applications lead to better understanding of overall company costs and permit faster response to cost-related company problems.

REVIEW QUESTIONS

1. What hazard must be recognized when employees are asked to apportion their time on an employee time card? How might this hazard be avoided?

2. Why is preliminary processing by the payroll computer application required in preparing the labor distribution file?

3. What purpose is served by each of the three sort routines in the job costing computer application?

4. Of what value is the individual job ledger? How does it relate to the job activity report?

5. Of what value to a company is the labor distribution report?

EXERCISES

1. List the possible file contents of the accumulated distribution file in the labor distribution computer application.

2. Many companies keep cost and usage records on their transportation fleet. To allow comparisons between different types of vehicles and to reflect current and to-date total expenditures for each vehicle, data on

certain items must be readily available: amount of gas used and its cost (company fueled or placed on charge account); maintenance labor and replacement equipment charges; miles driven; miles per gallon; and the cost per mile or per hour.

a. Using these items as critical variables, design a computer application that analyzes and reports cost and usage rates for company cars.

b. On the basis of your computer application design, design a current and to-date cost and usage printed statement for a single vehicle in the fleet.

3. Compare and contrast the job costing and labor distribution flowcharts to the work-in-process reporting and summary flowchart in Chapter 13. Is it possible to combine applications, so that job costing information is a product of work-in-process reporting? So that labor distribution information is a product of work-in-process reporting? Explain the design implications in each case. Also discuss the advantages and disadvantages of any combined approach.

IV

COMPREHENSIVE ACCOUNTING APPLICATIONS

Few companies can justify a data processing operation as long as its activities are limited to the daily processing of single-purpose computer applications such as payroll or accounts payable. These tasks can be done manually at generally less cost. However, when files created specifically for these single-purpose applications are integrated, as in the applications discussed in this part of the text, the computer system performs a service not available by manual efforts. The computer system, in its own right, becomes a company profit center.

15

FIXED ASSETS
AND
DEPRECIATION

A company invests or expends its financial resources in many things. Cash must be reserved to meet the expenses of the company payroll and other current payables such as vendor invoices. A set amount of cash may be held temporarily to defer future expenses. A considerable amount of company resources is invested in plant and equipment, which include buildings, machines, furniture, and facilities. These latter, long-term investments are *fixed assets*. They remain in the possession of a company and are not normally sold or transferred to customers. The length of such investments is determined by the time in which an asset becomes obsolete or is worn to the extent that it must be replaced.

The two subjects covered in this chapter are the recording and maintenance of fixed asset information and the processing of tax write-off information (for example, reporting of depreciation). The fixed asset and depreciation computer application prepares a file of data that is used in both operations. This is one example of an integrated computer application. Usage of stored information common to more than one operation reduces the amount of effort that would be required if the fixed asset system were kept separate from the processing of tax write-off information.

15-1 FIXED ASSETS, TAX WRITE-OFFS, AND DEPRECIATION

It is important that a company retain reasonable control over its fixed assets. The major reason is that a company may depreciate and write off a fixed asset investment (excluding the purchase of land) over the investment's useful life. The amount of the write-off is deducted from gross income before taxes are computed. Most companies tend to write off as much of an investment as possible during its early years—normally within five to seven years. At the end of this period, the item is considered to have no residual (book) value at least for taxation purposes. It may retain a scrap or replacement value for purposes of insurance evaluation.

A company is permitted to select its method of depreciation for the fixed asset write-off period. The various methods are established and controlled by the federal Internal Revenue Service. For our purposes, two methods of depreciation are considered: straight-line and double-declining balance. With a straight-line method of depreciation, the same amount of the fixed investment is deducted from taxable income during the useful life of an investment. For example, allowable depreciation for a $1,000 investment with a useful life of 10 years would be $100, and this amount would be deducted every year for 10 years.

The double-declining method is more complex. Double-declining balance is computed as 200 percent times the straight-line depreciation during the first year; 200 percent times the adjusted straight-line depreciation the second year; and so forth. Using the example of the $1,000 investment, the allowable depreciation in year one is $200, or 200 percent of $100. Depreciation during year two is $160, which can be calculated in two ways:

1. as 200 percent of the adjusted straight-line balance:

$$\frac{\$1,000 - \$200}{10 \text{ years}} \times 200\% = \$160$$

2. as 20 percent of the remaining book value:

$$(\$1,000 - \$200) \times 20\% = \$160$$

The virtue of the double-declining method of depreciation is that it allows a larger amount to be deducted from taxable income when an investment is new. It thus encourages a company to invest more heavily in fixed assets by allowing a more immediate reduction of federal tax. The intention of the government is to encourage company and economic growth, by increased capital expenditures as an alternative to the payment of federal tax.

A fixed assets accounting system provides information that may be used for other purposes besides reducing taxes—for example, determining the capital worth of a company and establishing fire and other insurance rates. (That is, a decline in the value of plant and equipment should be reflected in lower insurance premiums.) A final purpose of a fixed assets system is to provide information useful in deciding whether to purchase new equipment or to replace existing equipment. While this decision is not actually discussed in this chapter, the means of analysis should be evident in the treatment of a fixed assets computer application.

15-2 INPUT DATA

Information on new additions to fixed assets can be derived simply by modifying the accounts payable system so that invoices from vendors are coded to indicate which purchases represent new property rather than materials and supplies used in manufacture or in resale to customers. This coding allows the extraction of the date of purchase, purchase cost data, the quantity purchased, and the vendor number. These data become a part of the fixed asset record.

Other information is required besides data obtained from the accounts payable system. A fixed asset number must be assigned; the name or description of the asset must be recorded; and the location of the assets must be identified—generally by another code. The location code is usually limited to a department number or a room number. There is little value in attempting to designate the exact location of an asset such as a piece of furniture or equipment, since it may be moved occasionally. The final information needed is the particulars to be used in the depreciation of the fixed asset. Some of these data include the method of depreciation, the number of years of tax write-off, and the estimated scrap or salvage value. All of these types of data must be collected manually as inputs to the fixed assets computer application.

15-3 THE FIXED ASSETS AND DEPRECIATION SYSTEM

Figure 15-1 flowcharts the computer application used in the retention of fixed assets information and the calculation of tax write-offs. As presented, the application is both simple and straightforward. Other activities or reports may be incorporated into the system after its implementation.

The first stage in processing is the preparation of the *fixed assets new purchase report*, which is extracted from the payables computer application. It is combined with other information supplied manually by purchasing, accounting, and department heads. Then the next processing step creates the *new property file*.

The new property file is used to prepare a *new property report* and special *identification labels*, which are printed by the computer. Labels are placed on new pieces of property to allow their identification and control. Following this stage in processing, the new property file is merged with the *master property file*, which contains the records of all fixed assets (other than land and, in some cases, buildings). It stores both the original and the current (book) value of all assets. The *property and value report* is printed as a by-product of the merge of the two files. This report may list only new records added to the property file, or it may list all fixed asset detail stored on file.

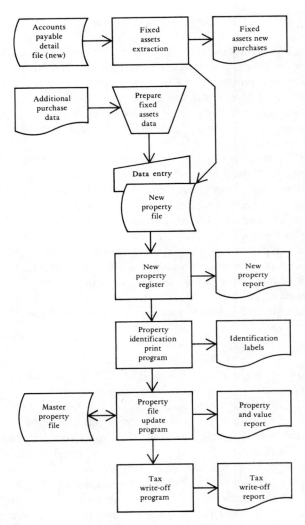

FIG. 15-1   Fixed assets and depreciation flowchart

The *tax write-off report* is prepared from the property file. The tax deduction obtained from the depreciation of fixed assets is detailed by item. The total write-off is summarized to show the dollar amount of tax shelter provided by all fixed assets. While this report is being printed, the property file is updated.

Figure 15-2 illustrates typical file contents of the master property file. The accounts payable file supplies the original purchase price of the asset, the

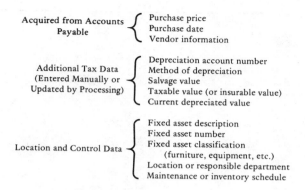

FIG. 15-2 Typical contents of the master property file

date of purchase, and the original vendor information. Further purchase data (entered manually) add tax, location, and control detail to the file. Tax detail includes the depreciation account number, the method of depreciation (type and frequency), and the salvage value. The net taxable value and the current depreciated value of the asset are computed during processing. Location and control information consists of the asset's description, number, classification, and location. A maintenance or inventory schedule may also be retained in the master file. This ensures that control is properly maintained and guards against loss or misuse of the asset.

New Property Reporting and Identification

The use of accounts payable detail greatly assists in creating fixed asset records. However, as stated earlier, it does not provide all the information needed to describe new property. The *fixed assets new purchase report,* printed from accounts payable, serves as a reminder of most new depreciable purchases. The report itself shows what information is available and what is still needed and thus aids in data acquisition.

Figure 15-3 shows one possible fixed assets new purchase report format. Entries that must be appended manually are indicated by this report. The column headings shown and their meanings are as follows:

- The *vendor number and invoice,* which permits tracing the purchase back to the original vendor.

- The *purchase date,* which is the starting date for depreciation.

- The *purchase cost,* which is the amount to be depreciated, which includes freight and installation charges.

VENDOR #	VENDOR INVOICE	PURCHASE DATE	PURCHASE COST	QUANTITY RECEIVED	ITEM NUMBER	ITEM DESCRIPTION	LOCATION CODE	FIXED ASSET CLASSIFICATION	DEPRECIATION TYPE	DEPRECIATION PERIOD	SALVAGE VALUE
33705	6A216X3	2-5-	$1,575.00	1							

Information obtained from the accounts payable detail file

Information to be placed in the fixed assets detail file, which must be recorded manually

FIG. 15-3 Fixed assets new purchase report

- The *quantity received,* which is the actual quantity depreciated, since the original invoice may contain several items.

- The *item number and description,* which are the number and name or phrase used to identify the property.

- The *location code,* which is the physical location of the item, in code.

- The *fixed asset classification,* which is special code used to organize property classification reports.

- The *type of depreciation,* which is the method of depreciation used.

- The *period of depreciation,* which is the number of years over which the property will be depreciated.

- The *salvage value,* which is the estimated value of the property following its total depreciation.

Considerable space should be left between successive lines of the fixed assets new purchase report, since the vendor invoice may contain more than one piece of property. As additional information is available, it can then be entered in the spaces on the right-hand side. Additional lines for multiple-item invoices are printed in the space between vendor numbers. The purchase price is distributed, showing the approximate value of each item of property received from a vendor. Once completed, the report moves to data entry for input to the computer. However, if a report such as the one shown is not used, a comparable input form must be devised.

The fixed assets new purchase report completes one phase of data acquisition, since not all data on fixed assets pass through the payables system and some payables detail may not be suitable for preparing fixed asset records. For example, some vendors submit summary invoices, which do not detail items purchased. However, the most common type of fixed asset data that escapes the payables system results from interoffice transfer of equipment and property. Some companies handle transfers as purchases by the recipient and as sales by the former owner. Obviously, such interoffice sales must be kept separate from normal sales to customers.

Interoffice or interdepartmental transfers can be processed by the payables system as special sales/purchase transfers. However, it is more common to simply transfer property records of the prior user to records of the office or department receiving the property. In this case, a *fixed asset coding sheet* (see Fig. 15-4) is required to record the transfer. This coding sheet has space for considerably more detail than does the fixed assets new purchase report shown in Figure 15-3. It is part of a more comprehensive and complex fixed asset computer application than the example discussed in this chapter. The

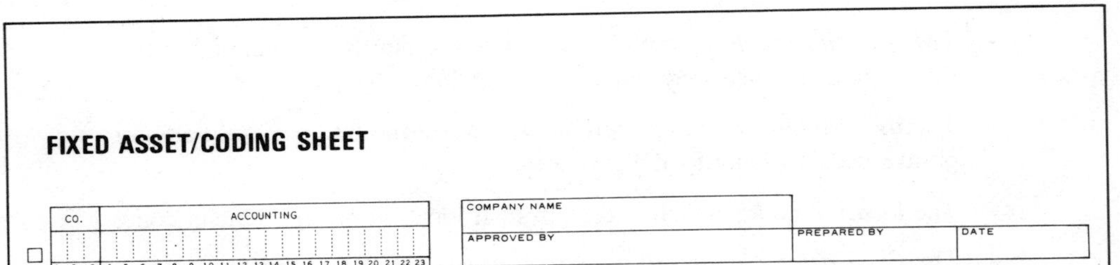

FIG. 15-4 Fixed asset coding sheet

two forms, however, do contain similar information: property description, cost, location, and salvage value plus space to specify how the item is to be depreciated. The additional data requested by this more complete coding sheet are used in preparing comprehensive fixed asset reports. Obviously, every company should tailor its data acquisition requirements to best suit its internal needs.

All keyed input must be edited by computer and by personnel to verify the completeness of the data acquisition process. That is, in a fixed asset computer application, there is no easy way to test the validity of the information, as there is in other applications such as payroll or accounts receivable. Consequently, a careful manual review is required. This review must be completed before the printing of identification labels is allowed to begin.

Figure 15-5, the *new property report*, lists all data acquired on newly added pieces of property and interoffice transfers. This report is subject to a visual edit. The report format resembles the fixed assets new purchase report, making it easy to compare the initial input to the records now placed

ABC CORPORATION   FIXED ASSETS

DEPT NO	DESCRIPTION	CLASS CODE	VENDOR CODE	DATE OF ACQUISITION	COST	LIFE	SALVAGE VALUE
3	CHAIR	TK	BFC	05/	50	5	30
3	DESK			05/	250	8	50
3	TABLE	TK		01/	80	8	20
1				00/	0	0	0
1	CHAIR	TK		03/	0	5	4
1	DESK	DK	PEM	06/	280	8	50
1	CHAIR	TK	PEM	06/	50	0	0
8	COUCH		INT	11/	350	8	50
8	LAMP		INT	11/	50	3	3
8	TABLE	TK	INT	11/	80	8	20
8	CHAIR	TK	INT	11/	50	5	10
8	CHAIR	TK	PEM	11/	60	5	10
4	FILE			08/	60	8	5
4	FILE	BP	BOS	08/	60	8	5
4	FILE	BP	BOS	08/	60	8	5
8	CARPET		HOC	12/	2,000	10	0
2	TERMINAL	11	DAT	09/	85	8	50
2	TERMINAL	11	DAT	09/	85	8	50

TOTAL ITEMS   18

FIG. 15-5 New property report

on computer file. Notice that at this time there is no controlling number assigned to new property. This number is generated and assigned by the next computer program. It is a continuation from a set of consecutive numbers retained in the master property file.

Items transferred from one department to another are listed on the new property report as transferred or used. Any computation of the increased value of fixed assets should *exclude* this type of entry, since its value is already stored in the master property file. During the update of this file, the prior user department's fixed asset records are changed to reflect the current, depreciated worth of the item transferred. The recipient department's records are increased by a like amount. The net value of the company is thus unchanged by the transfer.

Permanent labels are printed after property records have been reviewed and approved. These labels can be ordinary gummed labels or special-purpose metallic labels, which last a considerable time. In either case, they should be affixed to the items in the master property file. Figure 15-6 displays a sample label printed by the computer. While computer-prepared labels are not as strong as those prepared by embossing machines, they are durable and meet the needs of most companies. Finally, it is important to distribute and affix labels to new property as quickly as possible, before new property becomes mixed with existing property. The label print program can also be modified to permit replacement labels to be printed, should the original label wear out or be destroyed.

Master Property File Update and Depreciation Reporting

Printing identification labels is one result of the fixed assets identification computer program. The storage of the assigned identification numbers in the new purchase file is another. After processing, the entire newly created file must be added to the master property file. This is accomplished by a merge of the two files, which in turn updates the master file. Once completed, the updated master property file represents all fixed assets of the company, excluding real estate and other nondepreciable investments. It is from this updated file that depreciation and other fixed asset reports are prepared.

A typical fixed asset depreciation report is the *property and value report* (see Fig. 15-7). This report may be prepared in one of several ways. It may be a listing of items newly added to the property file, or it may be a complete listing of all property stored on file and the value of the property. Another alternative is to list all fixed assets by department or location code. This method enables department managers to review physical assets for which they are accountable.

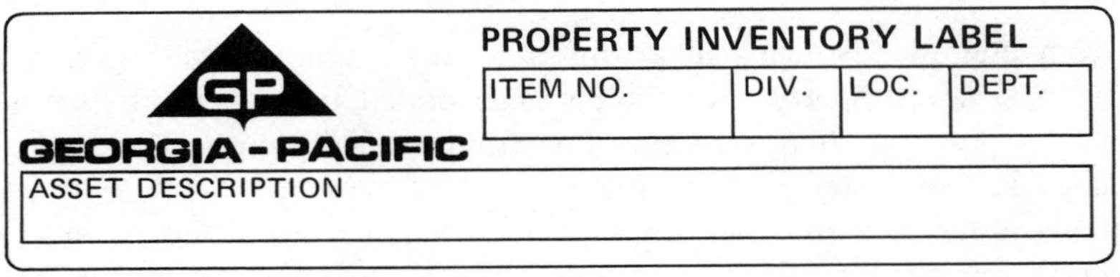

FIG. 15-6 Identification label

DATE OCTOBER 31, 19XX   F I X E D   A S S E T S   R E P O R T

DEPARTMENT SUBSIDIARY NO.	ASSET DESCRIPTION SERIAL NO. BLDG. ROOM	ACQ. DATE TIME IN SVCE	ESTIMATED LIFE	ASSET COST DEPREC. BASE	ACCUM. DEPREC. SALVAGE VALUE	BOOK VALUE 1ST YR ALLOW.	YTD DEPREC. MTD DEPREC.
82-561 3000000016	TYPEWRITER SELECTRIC IBM RE CMN	10/15/ 01 YR 00 MO	00 YR 60 MO	240.50 240.50	48.10 .00	192.40 .00	48.10 4.01
82-561 3000000017	CALCULATOR 22	10/15/ 01 YR 00 MO	00 YR 60 MO	250.00 250.00	50.00 .00	200.00 .00	50.00 4.17
82-561 3000000018	DICTATING MACHINE EDISON 22	10/15/ 01 YR 00 MO	00 YR 60 MO	55.50 55.50	11.10 .00	44.40 .00	11.10 .93
82-561 3000000019	DICTATING MACHINE EDISON 21	10/15/ 01 YR 00 MO	00 YR 60 MO	55.50 55.50	11.10 .00	44.40 .00	11.10 .93
82-561 3000000020	DICTATING MACHINE EDISON 16	10/15/ 01 YR 00 MO	00 YR 60 MO	55.50 55.50	11.10 .00	44.40 .00	11.10 .93
82-561 3000000022	DICTATING MACHINE EDISON 4	10/15/ 01 YR 00 MO	00 YR 60 MO	55.50 55.50	11.10 .00	44.40 .00	11.10 .93
82-561 3000000023	CALCULATOR UNDERWOOD-OLIV 07	10/15/ 09 YR 00 MO	00 YR 60 MO	185.00 185.00	185.00 .00	.00 .00	185.00 .00
82-561 3000000024	TYPEWRITER SELECTRIC IBM SE CNE	10/15/ 09 YR 00 MO	00 YR 60 MO	240.50 240.50	240.50 .00	.00 .00	240.50 .00

FIG. 15-7 Property and value report

The property and value report includes the original and current depreciated value for individual fixed assets and in total. The location code is also important since items are frequently moved from one department to another. The age of the asset is subject to continuous review. Age, rather than condition, often determines when to replace a physical asset.

The other occasional report frequently produced by processing of the property file is the *tax write-off* or *depreciation report*. This report lists the particulars of the property—original value, age, and so forth. It also shows the total depreciation taken to date and may also illustrate the amounts to be depreciated in future years. This latter information is totaled and used in planning future tax write-offs.

Figure 15-8 shows a typical tax write-off or depreciation report. Because this report is a major supporting document to the tax forms filed by a company, it should be prepared with care on custom forms. Copies should be retained over several years to provide evidence in the event of a tax audit.

The property file is updated any time changes are made in the balance to be depreciated. If taxes are paid quarterly, depreciation is calculated quarterly, and the file is updated accordingly. Once updated, the file is retained for use in adding new fixed assets or in preparing additional fixed asset reports. In any case, the master file is kept as up-to-date as possible to retain the entire fixed asset record of a company.

15-4 MANAGEMENT IMPLICATIONS

A manager is likely to react to a need for some tool or piece of equipment by immediately authorizing its purchase. Unfortunately, the inevitable result of this practice is that a company ends up owning an excessive amount of property, much of it inadequately utilized. In addition, far too much capital is invested in unproductive resources, drastically obstructing efforts to improve return on invested capital. An obvious way to minimize excessive investment in fixed assets is to transfer such things as equipment, furniture, and fixtures

```
                           TAX WRITE-OFF REPORT

DEPRECIATION FOR THE MONTH OF MARCH, 19XX

DEPARTMENT      ASSET      DATE OF      ORIGINAL      DEPRECIATION      TOTAL DEPRECIATION
NUMBER          NUMBER     PURCHASE     COST          THIS MONTH        TO DATE

101             259        12/31/         50.00          1.50              35.00
101             650        12/15/        300.00          4.00             120.00
300              16         5/23/       1000.00          1.00             957.65

TOTAL DEPRECIATION FOR MONTH                              6.50
```

FIG. 15-8 Tax write-off report

from one location without need for the items to another with an expressed need. This is relatively easy to accomplish in a small company, but the process becomes complex as a company expands. Fixed assets computer systems assist management by controlling the way in which assets are allocated within a company. This, in turn, permits the dollar amount invested in fixed assets to be better controlled.

Pilferage of fixed assets is usually a lesser problem than the theft of finished goods inventory. Perhaps the major reason why pilferage is less is that fixed assets are normally more visible. If a desk calculator is missing, for instance, someone is sure to notice. However, prudence dictates that an inventory be taken of all fixed assets to verify their presence and to determine their condition. If a piece of equipment is badly deteriorated or neglected, it is often possible to write off the equipment sooner than initially expected. The condition of equipment is also a major factor in the determination of whether it should be replaced, regardless of the balance remaining to be depreciated. The fixed assets computer file should be used to monitor this physical inventory. After the accounting, plans can be made for replacement of some items or the removal of others from the permanent file.

The tax shelter provided by fixed assets is another reason why this application must be properly managed. That is, fixed asset depreciation is treated as a business expense and is used to provide tax write-offs in future accounting periods. With accurate fixed asset information, it thus becomes possible to estimate how large a tax write-off will be available in future periods as well as the impact of fixed asset purchases on the expected profits of a business.

REVIEW OF IMPORTANT IDEAS

A large portion of the capital worth of a company is tied to its fixed assets—property not normally sold to customers or consumed in manufacturing. Depreciable fixed assets used for tax write-offs have a useful life greater than one year, and their cost can be charged against the running of a business. (This definition excludes the purchase of land.)

The fixed assets computer application is simple and straightforward. It prepares and retains the master property file and as a result generates three major products. The first is identification labels, which give the controlling number and location of an asset, the date of purchase, and other pertinent information. The second is the property and value report, a listing of the property file in part or in total. This listing details the type of fixed asset, its original cost, and its current depreciated value—information used in deciding whether to purchase additional equipment, in establishing insurance premiums, and in transferring equipment from one location in a company to another. The last major product is the tax write-off or depreciation report.

This lists the amount of tax shelter obtained through fixed asset depreciation and the balance to be depreciated in future years. This report serves as a supporting document in the filing of federal, state, and local income and personal property tax statements.

REVIEW QUESTIONS

1. For what purposes can a company use a fixed assets computer system?

2. How can accounts payable detail assist in the development of a fixed assets computer application?

3. What are the differences between the new property file and the master property file? Why is each file necessary?

4. What data must be collected manually as input to the fixed assets computer application?

5. When and how are interoffice transfers of equipment processed in a fixed assets computer application?

6. The property and value report and the tax write-off report are prepared as a result of the fixed assets computer application. Of what value to management is each report?

7. Why might proper management of fixed assets be viewed as one form of tax shelter for a company?

EXERCISES

1. Compute both the first year's and the second year's depreciation on a $70,000 investment using each of the following methods of depreciation and the number of years given. (Assume that the asset will have no salvage or residual value at the end of its investment life.)

   a. Straight-line depreciation over seven years
   b. Straight-line depreciation over five years
   c. Double-declining balance depreciation over seven years
   d. Double-declining balance depreciation over five years

2. The senior management of a company is interested in extending the fixed assets computer application so that a property and value forecast

report can be prepared. This report would show the expected value of company property both one year from now and five years from now, based on past, present, and future company fixed asset expenditures.

What modifications would have to be made in the fixed asset system in order to prepare this report? Develop a systems flowchart for your answer, and describe the typical contents of the computer files required in support of your design.

16

THE GENERAL LEDGER

The general ledger computer application is a truly integrative data processing activity. Several subsidiary accounting applications precede its development. As a document, the general ledger is the final consolidated record of all financial transactions within an organization. Transactions are summarized by account, as defined by the company chart of accounts. All accounts must balance both in debits and in credits in order to validate the general ledger document and thereby provide an exact accounting of the total financial activity of an organization.

The preparation of subsidiary general ledger files has been referred to several times throughout the description of various computer applications. Each subsidiary file summarizes the detail for a particular application, such as accounts payable, payroll deductions and accruals, and capital assets. These summary totals are posted to the current general ledger in much the same way as new stock is posted to the inventory file in a receiving application. Posting is cross-referenced, to permit tying back to each subsidiary ledger. That is, should a summary total be questioned, it must be possible to locate the figures that led to the questionable item. The cross-reference to a subsidiary ledger provides this audit trail. It is possible to isolate a particular transaction or a batch of transactions, such as a series of payroll checks. The different levels of data accumulation—general ledger, subsidiary ledger, and batched transactions—reflect the hierarchy followed in a financial reporting system. Upper levels of accounting and management depend upon reports that are created using these subsidiary ledgers, which are summaries of individual financial transactions.

281

A general ledger computer application may be almost completely designed as an extension of other computer applications. An examination of each computer application previously considered by this text shows that summary data can be extracted for direct input into the general ledger application. In an accounts payables computer application, for example, the original vendor invoices are recorded on the payables register report. This report shows detail such as the invoice number, the vendor number and name, the batch number, the date the batch is submitted to the computer, and the date when the invoice is to be paid. This payables information is then summarized into a payables journal suitable for posting directly to the general ledger (see "other payables reports" within Section 5-2). The payables journal links the payables register to the payables entry in the general ledger.

Journals from other computer applications supply other forms of input to the current general ledger. For every entry in the general ledger, at least three supporting documents will have been prepared. In the case of payables, these documents are the vendor invoice, the payables register, and the payables journal. Corrections and adjustments may be necessary at any one of these supporting levels. Balance controls have already been provided in the treatment of invoices and the payables register. Similar provisions must be made for correction of the payables journal input to the general ledger. These corrections and adjustments are normal accounting procedures and must be incorporated in the design of the general ledger application.

16-1 SOURCES OF INPUT TO THE GENERAL LEDGER

Figure 16-1 shows several sources of general ledger summary file input, which result from previous computer applications. For each source of input, a summary report is prepared showing the transaction totals for a particular processing activity. This set of totals is balanced against totals obtained from the input documents and files, to ensure that posting to the general ledger is accurate. The computer file content reflecting the activity of each computer application is controlled by account number as specified by a chart of accounts. These numbers are necessary to post properly to the general ledger. Several sources of input data are reviewed below, using Figure 16-1 as a guide.

1. The payroll computer application produces the payroll journal summary report (see Fig. 4-10). This report accumulates and totals, by department or budget number, such items as gross pay, federal withholding, state withholding, Social Security insurance, and voluntary deductions. The summary file used to create the report can be used as direct input to the general ledger system. Each item subtotal is entered into a general ledger account.

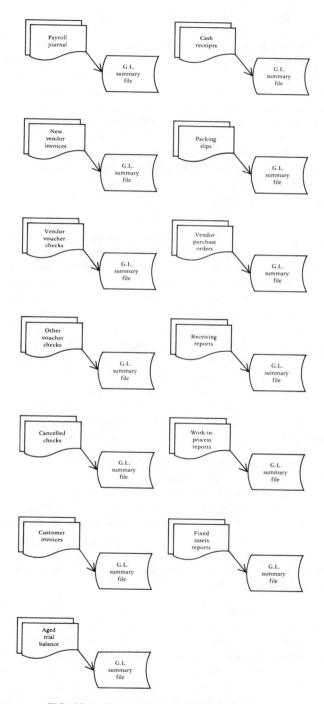

FIG. 16-1 File input to the general ledger

2. The accounts payable application provides two types of input to the general ledger system. In this application, new invoices from vendors are initially edited and then combined with the pending invoice file (see Fig. 5-2). Just before the two files are merged, it is possible to extract general ledger data. This newly created summary file contains new additions to payables, not all pending payables. Totals in the file must balance the batch totals used to validate the correctness of input data. The second source of input to the general ledger system results from the printing of voucher-checks. The payables summary program (see Fig. 5-3) prints the general ledger report, which is a listing of funds charged against each general ledger account. This file, which is used in processing, serves as a direct input to the general ledger system.

3. The check-writing and reconciliation computer application also provides two types of general ledger input. If special checks are written, their total is posted to the general ledger. Other check-printing files should already have been tied to a general ledger summary file. If not, the check-printing files should be used to create a general ledger input file. As indicated by Figure 6-1, this summary file is prepared after the printing of checks and vouchers. The amount of money disbursed is posted to an account number within the general ledger. Check reconciliation is used to provide additional general ledger information. It is necessary to post cancelled and returned checks, so that all outstanding claims against the company are known. The most likely source of this information is the file used to prepare the balance report (see Fig. 6-5). This file contains a current accounting of all cancelled checks and can be tied to general ledger account numbers.

4. The final program in preparing a customer invoice prints the invoice and creates an accounts receivable summary file (see Fig. 7-4). Although this summary file is not suitable as direct input to the general ledger system, the information in the file can be modified and used as source data. One good solution is to create, as part of the invoice print program, a secondary summary file that places data in a form that allows posting to the general ledger. This file is already balanced, since the invoice totals must agree with external controls obtained through batched input.

5. The accounts receivable computer application creates a file of data used to produce the aged trial balance report (see Fig. 8-5). This file is a source of general ledger information since the total amounts of receivables due appear in this consolidated report. Moreover, this report is intended to itemize input into the next month's accounts receivable processing. Although the summary file that creates the aged trial balance reports is balanced and has known controls (much like

the invoice summary file), it is not in a format suitable for direct input to the general ledger system. Once again a summary computer file can be prepared while the trial balance is being printed. This file then becomes input to the general ledger system.

6. The cash receipts computer application also creates a summary file—the total of cash receipts (see Fig. 9-3). This file is not suitable for general ledger purposes, for it does not contain the discount allowed the customer. However, it is possible to modify the computer records so that both the actual amount paid and the amount of discount allowed are retained and balanced. Then the summary file can be used as input to the general ledger system.

7. The order-filling computer application provides the next potential source of input to the general ledger system. The second part of this system (see Fig. 10-3) prepares packing slips. Since this program represents the dollar sales to customers and the dollar reduction in inventory, these totals can be summarized as input to the general ledger system. A summary file created by either the picking label or the packing slip program is balanced to inventory control totals and is suitable to use in posting to the general ledger.

8. The purchasing and receiving computer application provides the next entries to the general ledger system. Following the printing of vendor purchase orders, a general ledger summary is prepared (see Fig. 12-2). This summary shows encumbrances on future funds arranged by chart of account codes. The entire summary serves as input to the general ledger system. Receiving detail used to print the receiving report is also summarized to provide input (see Fig. 12-5). In this instance, the chart of accounts must contain an entry for goods received but not yet billed. This information provides another view of encumbrances on future funds.

9. The work-in-process computer application (see Figs. 13-1 and 13-6) is a rich source of data for the general ledger system. Customer orders, purchase orders for raw materials, material receiving reports, inventory status reports, and final customer billing information are all possible inputs to the general ledger. As the production system is developed, there will be several points at which appropriate files can be prepared for these summary inputs.

10. Finally, the change in value of the fixed assets of a company (the update of the master property file) should be reflected in the general ledger accounts to show the book value of the company (see Fig. 15-1). The capital worth general ledger account results from this computer application.

Collectively, the data files indicated in Figure 16-1 represent a massive amount of information that has been summarized into a form suitable for posting to the general ledger. These files supply the bulk of all entries to the ledger. Posting in this way represents an obvious savings in human effort compared to the manual entry of summary totals.

Before the actual processing of the computer files, it is necessary to sort all data. Most files are not in a sequence that allows immediate posting by general ledger account number. It will also be necessary to introduce additional ledger entries or corrections transferred from manually prepared *journal entry coding sheets*. Figure 16-2 shows a typical coding sheet. It contains spaces for describing the nature of the manual entry and for properly assigning the entry to a general ledger account number.

Considerably more detail (and authorization) is expected for a manual entry than for data that are extracted from an existing computer application such as payroll. At first glance, this might appear to be an unnecessary

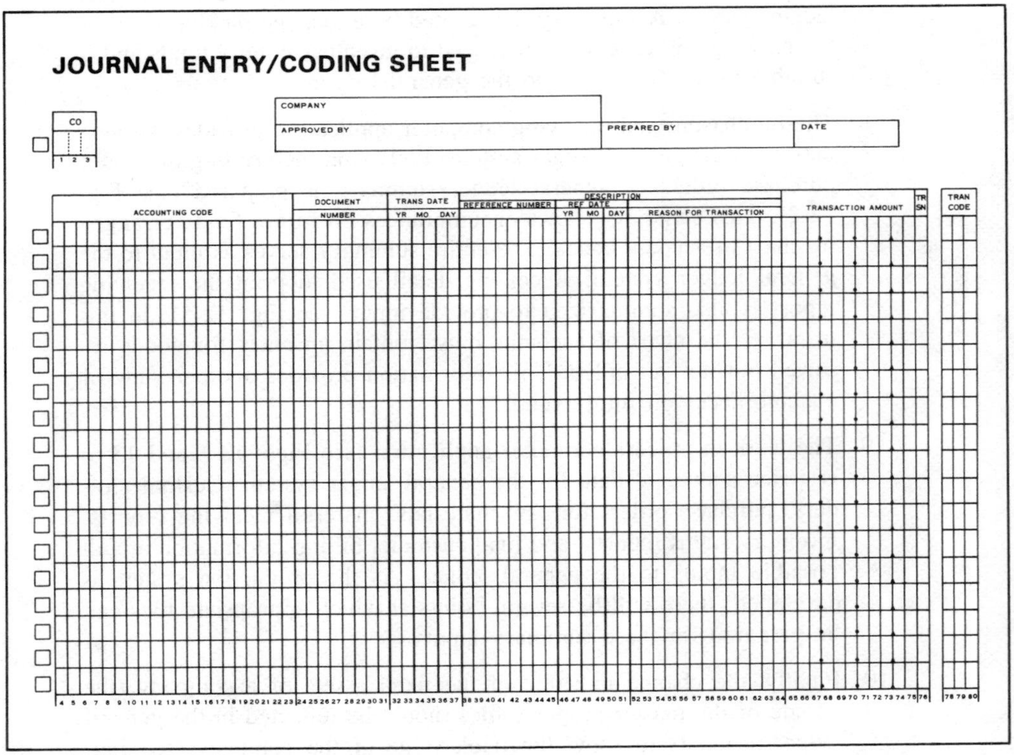
JOURNAL ENTRY/CODING SHEET

CO

1 2 3

COMPANY

APPROVED BY

PREPARED BY

DATE

ACCOUNTING CODE

DOCUMENT NUMBER

TRANS DATE YR MO DAY

DESCRIPTION

REFERENCE NUMBER

REF DATE YR MO DAY

REASON FOR TRANSACTION

TRANSACTION AMOUNT

TR SN

TRAN CODE

FIG. 16-2 Journal entry coding sheet

restriction; but consider that the data acquired from a lower level computer application such as payroll have already received considerable review, justification, and authorization. The same is not true of a manual entry. Therefore, the coding sheet has several provisions for justifying each one.

16-2 THE GENERAL LEDGER SYSTEM

Figure 16-3 flowcharts the general ledger computer application. The manually prepared journal entries and the summary files from other computer applications are the initial inputs to the system. Processing begins after journal entry coding sheets have been keyed and verified. A balanced *journal entry report* is then printed, showing all manual entries to the general ledger file. Next, the many files of summary data are combined with the journal entry file. The printing of the *general ledger trial balance report* is one result of the merge of the two files. This report is returned to accounting where it is reviewed and, if necessary, corrected. Corrections are coded, keyed, and listed by another journal entry report. Adjusted entries are then included in the overall general ledger file.

The *current general ledger report* and the *consolidated general ledger report* are printed to show the current (generally monthly) and the year-to-date summary totals, formatted to match the company chart of accounts. The printing of *detail ledgers* completes the application. These ledgers show all file detail for a given account.

Figure 16-4 shows the typical contents of the *consolidated general ledger file*. The date of the summary, the general ledger account number, the transaction code (debit, credit, or for information only), the description of the transaction, the dollar amount of the transaction, and the source or batch control number are acquired directly from previously processed file detail. As the general ledger files are prepared, this information is added.

Journal Entries and the General Ledger Trial Balance

The files illustrated in Figure 16-1 provide the bulk of the data used to produce the general ledger reports. As we have seen, however, additional input must be supplied by journal entries. Reports on petty cash, handwritten checks to corporate officers, and other sources of debit and credit transactions must be processed by the computer, even though these data do not originate in any of the subsidiary computer applications. In addition, there will be some errors in the input data, particularly in the areas of payroll, cash receipts, and accounts payable. Corrections to the general ledger system will have to be made to alter the general ledger records once errors are detected. Posting corrections is also done by means of journal entries.

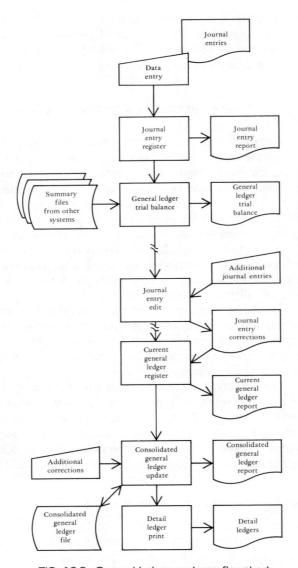

FIG. 16-3 General ledger systems flowchart

Journal entries must be carefully verified, since a high degree of accuracy must exist in each data field. Following this, the journal entry computer program edits all input to establish a batch balance. The journal entry report, which is printed during processing, provides a further check against the original input to ensure that no errors have been overlooked.

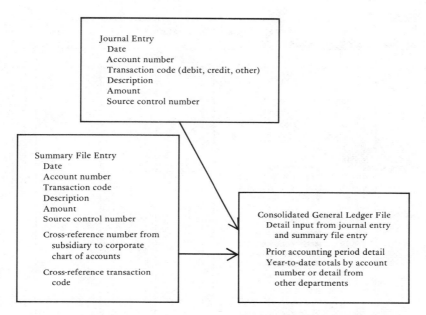

FIG. 16-4 Typical contents of the consolidated general ledger file

The output file that results from the journal entry program is combined with the general ledger summary files from the dozen or so computer systems that support this application. This stage requires a major computer sort, as made apparent by Figure 16-1. The resulting computer file is sequenced by date of transaction within account numbers specified by the chart of accounts. For instance, the data acquired from the payables system may represent several batch dates and will probably be posted to more than one general ledger account number. Therefore, these data, together with other input data, should be sorted before they are posted to general ledger accounts.

After all input files have been sorted, the *general ledger trial balance report* (Fig. 16-5) can be printed. By now this report should be in balance. However, it frequently requires additional adjustment. For example, a payroll check that has been cancelled because of an error on a time card often means the manual preparation of a new paycheck. A general ledger adjustment must be made to correct the now altered payroll input and to incorporate this manual financial transaction into the payroll summary totals. Adjustments such as these justify the trial balance at this stage in processing. Processing is stopped while accounting reviews this report. If some entries are in error, the journal entry computer program is rerun to build an error-free computer file for inclusion in the current and the consolidated general ledger reports.

GENERAL LEDGER TRIAL BALANCE

FOR PERIOD ENDED	PAGE
8/31/	12

MO.	DAY	ADJ	CODE	DEPT	SOURCE	DESCRIPTION	DEBIT	CREDIT	CURRENT PERIOD	YEAR TO DATE
07	31		541	15		MISCELLANEOUS				
						ACCT TOTAL				::
07	31		551	15		DESIGN & DRAWINGS				
						ACCT TOTAL				::
07	31		553	15						
						ACCT TOTAL				::
07	31		554	15		FIELD WORK				238 50
08	15		554	15	1	03492	130 00			
08	15		554	15	1	03492	36 00			
08	31		554	15	1	03498	136 50			
08	31		554	15	1	03501	45 00			
						ACCT TOTAL	347 50		347 50	586 00 ::
07	31		555	15		OTHER				151 50
08	15		555	15	1	03492	26 00			
08	15		555	15	1	03494	45 00			
08	31		555	15	1	03498	58 50			
08	31		555	15	1	03501	27 00			
						ACCT TOTAL	156 50		156 50	308 00 ::
07	31		560	15		INTERIOR DESIGN				
						ACCT TOTAL				::
07	31		570	15		LANDSCAPE DESIGN				
						ACCT TOTAL				::
07	31		581	15		STRUCTURAL				146 90
08	31		581	15	4	JE309	146 90			
						ACCT TOTAL	146 90		146 90	293 80 ::
07	31		582	15		MECHANICAL				266 29
08	31		582	15	4	JE309	266 29			
						ACCT TOTAL	266 29		266 29	532 58 ::
07	31		583	15		ELECTRICAL				127 74
08	31		583	15	4	JE309 RECH BLDG	127 74			
						ACCT TOTAL	127 74		127 74	255 48 ::
07	31		584	15		LANDSCAPE				
						ACCT TOTAL				::
07	31		585	15		INTERIOR DESIGN				
						ACCT TOTAL				::
07	31		586	15		OTHER				
						ACCT TOTAL				::
07	31		590	15		PRINTING				
						ACCT TOTAL				::
07	31		595	15		OVERHEAD APPLIED				390 00
08	31		595	15	4	JE310 UT TECH COLLEGE	774 00			
						ACCT TOTAL	774 00		774 00	1 164 00 ::
						DEPT TOTAL	1 818 93	1 932 84	113 91-	725 82-::

FIG. 16-5 General ledger trial balance report

The Current and the Consolidated General Ledger Reports

Figure 16-6 illustrates the final, balanced *current general ledger report,* which lists all active ledger accounts and summarizes the total activity for the month. Debit and credit amounts and the net change in the amounts are recorded by date of summary. The account total is also shown to represent the account balance at the end of the current period. This report is distributed to all interested corporate officers and should therefore be clean in appearance and easy to read.

The *consolidated ledger* (Fig. 16-7) is printed immediately after the current ledger. This ledger reports both current and year-to-date account activity. The layout is similar to that of the current general ledger, with the exception that account totals are on a year-to-date basis. Both this report and the current statement of account activity permit company officers to identify weaknesses in the financial position of the company. This feature is especially important when officers are held responsible for the management of specific account totals.

```
DATE 01-31-                          GENERAL LEDGER                                    PAGE 0001

   ACCT                          SRC  DATE      DEBIT        CREDIT        NET
    NO        DESCRIPTION        CODE MO-DAY    AMOUNT        AMOUNT      CHANGE       BALANCE

101000000 CASH IN BANK-CHECKING        12-31                                        2,500.31
101000000 1-01 CASH IN BANK          J 01-31                 2,121.17
101000000 REC. TOTAL OFFSET          O 01-31   7,746.85
101000000 TAPE TOTAL OFFSET          O 01-31                 4,123.23
          ACCOUNT TOTALS                       7,746.85      6,244.40   1,502.45     4,002.76 *

110000000 ACCOUNTS RECEIVABLE          12-31                                        9,712.19
110000000 ACC. REC. OFFSET 01-31     O 01-31   3,733.31
          ACCOUNT TOTALS                       3,733.31          .00   3,733.31     13,445.50 *

201000000 ACCOUNTS PAYABLE             12-31                                        3,317.95-
201000000 ACC. PAY. OFFSET 01-31     O 01-31                   154.10
          ACCOUNT TOTALS                            .00        154.10    154.10-     3,472.05-*

202000000 FICA PAYABLE                 12-31                                          314.12-
202000000 1-01 FICA PAYABLE          J 01-31                   245.19
202000000 725  LARSON BANK           C 01-01     300.00
          ACCOUNT TOTALS                         300.00        245.19     54.81        259.31-*

203000000 FEDERAL W/H PAYABLE          12-31                                        1,417.19-
203000000 1-01 FED W/H PAYABLE       J 01-31                   727.50
          ACCOUNT TOTALS                            .00        727.50    727.50-     2,144.69-*

204000000 GROSS SALARIES               12-31                                        9,927.74
204000000 1-01 GROSS WAGES 01/72     J 01-31   3,093.86
          ACCOUNT TOTALS                       3,093.86          .00   3,093.86     13,021.60 *

301000000 RETAINED EARNINGS            01-01                                        8,463.31-
          ACCOUNT TOTALS                            .00          .00       .00      8,463.31-*

401000000 GROSS SALES                  12-31                                       12,605.00-
401000000 GROSS SALES FOR CURR. MTH. O 01-31                11,480.16
          ACCOUNT TOTALS                            .00     11,480.16  11,480.16-   24,085.16-*

501000000 MANUFACTURING SUPPLIES       12-31                                        3,977.33
501000000 MAN. MATERIALS COST        O 01-31   3,977.33
          ACCOUNT TOTALS                       3,977.33          .00   3,977.33      7,954.66 *
```

Fig. 16-6 Current general ledger report

ACCOUNTANT	CLIENT				FOR PERIOD ENDED	PAGE
▓▓▓	▓▓▓	▓▓▓▓▓▓▓▓▓▓▓▓▓▓▓▓▓▓▓▓▓▓			8/31/	1
POSTING REFERENCE		DESCRIPTION	CURRENT PERIOD		YEAR TO DATE	
CODE	DEPT		PERCENT OF TOTAL INCOME	AMOUNT	PERCENT OF TOTAL INCOME	AMOUNT
		▓▓▓▓▓▓▓▓▓▓▓▓▓▓▓▓▓▓▓▓				
		INCOME				
401 01		ARCHITECTURAL FEES	100.00	860.75-	100.00	971.75-
410 01		MISCELLANEOUS				
		TOTAL INCOME	100.00	860.75-	100.00	971.75-××××
		DIRECT COSTS				
		SALARIES & WAGES				
		EXPANDED SERVICES				
503 01		RESEARCH & PROGRAMMING				
504 01		OTHER EXPANDED SERVICES				×
		TOTAL EXPANDED SERVICE				
		SCHEMATICS				
511 01		DESIGN & DRAWINGS	1.57	13.50	1.39	13.50
512 01		SPECIFICATIONS				
513 01		ESTIMATE OF COSTS				
514 01		FIELD WORK				
515 01		OTHER				
		TOTAL SCHEMATICS	1.57	13.50	1.39	13.50 ×
		DESIGN DEVELOPMENT				
521 01		DESIGN & DRAWINGS				
522 01		SPECIFICATIONS				
523 01		ESTIMATE OF COSTS				
524 01		FIELD WORK				
525 01		OTHER				
		TOTAL DESIGN DEVELOP				×
		CONTRACT DOCUMENTS				
531 01		DESIGN & DRAWINGS				
532 01		SPECIFICATIONS				
533 01		ESTIMATE OF COSTS			2.78	27.00
534 01		FIELD WORK				
535 01		OTHER				
		TOTAL CONTRACT DOC			2.78	27.00 ×
		BIDDING				
541 01		MISCELLANEOUS				
		TOTAL BIDDING				×
		CONSTRUCTION				
551 01		DESIGN & DRAWINGS				
554 01		FIELD WORK			2.78	27.00
555 01		OTHER			2.78	27.00
		TOTAL CONSTRUCTION			2.78	27.00 ×
560 01		INTERIOR DESIGN				
570 01		LANDSCAPE DESIGN				
		TOT SALARIES & WAGES	1.57	13.50	6.95	67.50 ××
		CONSULTANTS & SUB CONT				
581 01		STRUCTURAL	96.78	833.00	85.72	833.00
582 01		MECHANICAL				
583 01		ELECTRICAL				
584 01		LANDSCAPE				

FIG. 16-7   Consolidated general ledger report

Careful analysis by company officers may, on occasion, lead to the discovery of errors in back issues of the general ledger report. Most often, errors occur from the posting of an item to an incorrect account number. Interaccount transfers are required to correct this problem. The incorrect entry is transferred from one account number to the correct account number. Corrections submitted as input to the consolidated general ledger computer program permit this additional posting to take place. The *master consolidated general ledger file,* updated during each period of processing, is the second type of input to this computer program. During the printing of the consolidated general ledger report, the master file is updated so that it can (1) serve as the input file to the printing of detail ledgers and (2) be retained as the master file and be used during the next processing cycle.

General ledger reports can be prepared by department or division, as an alternative to a company-wide general ledger consolidated statement. The ledger may then represent more than one statement of financial conditions. Because of this alternative, the term *consolidated general ledger* is ambiguous. When this method of processing is practiced, general ledger account numbers are kept separate for every branch office or division in a company. The records must then be merged to produce a company-wide consolidated general ledger. This activity (discussed in more detail in a later section) is not as simple to accomplish as one might imagine, because of the lack of cross-reference codes.

Processing of the general ledger file is frequently delayed by many companies until late in the ensuing accounting cycle or period. It is not uncommon for a consolidated ledger to be printed two or three months after the end of the fiscal year. This practice is difficult to accept from an operational standpoint. Almost all data required in processing result from other computer applications, although some must enter as journal entry input. If high priority is given to the completion of miscellaneous journal entries, it is reasonable to produce the general ledger statements shortly after the close of an accounting cycle. A timely printout is much more valuable than one that is delayed. Because of the importance of the general ledger as a management tool, every effort should be made to expedite its production.

General Ledger Detail Reports

The printing of *detail ledgers,* or itemized account number listings, follows the printing of the consolidated general ledger. Figure 16-8 shows a typical detail report. All information for a given account is printed to show the transaction source document numbers, the transaction amounts, and the department or branch charged or credited the amount. Examples of a detail ledger include union dues withheld from payroll, sales tax withheld, and a listing of flooring payments (payments against long-term loans or merchandise for resale to customers). Some accountants view the check register as a subsidiary general ledger report.

				JRL REG	8/31/	1
0831	61400	JE305	DEPREC EXPENSE			125.00
0831	12200	JE305	ACCUM DEPR AUTOS			125.00-
0831	10200	JE306	CASH IN BANK			31,468.78
0831	10600	JE306	PHARMACY BASEMENT			841.85-
0831	10600	JE306	TECH BUILDING			1,932.84-
0831	10600	JE306	SKYLINE HI SCH			1,350.00-
0831	10600	JE306	PARIS PARK			1,804.81-
0831	10600	JE306	NEWHOUSE BLDG			111.00-
0831	10600	JE306	WAK CONSTRUCTION			1,035.18-
0831	10600	JE306	MEA CREDIT UNION			302.18-
0831	20800	JE306	MEI-PROFIT SHARNG			1,800.00-
0831	20700	JE306	MEI-PENSION SHARG			5,819.09-
0831	10600	JE306	NEWHOUSE BLDG			103.60-
0831	10600	JE306	MIDWAY 2ND WARD			441.20-
0831	21000	JE306	WALKER BANK			15,000.00-
0831	10200	JE307	CASH IN BANK			35,662.17-
0831	10600	JE308	ACCTS RECEIVABLE			11,808.75
0831	40121	JE308	PHARMACY BASEMENT			841.86-
0831	40127	JE308	SKYLINE HIGH SCH			675.00-
0831	40115	JE308	TECH BUILDING			1,932.84-

FIG. 16-8 Typical detail ledger

16-3   THE COMPANY CHART OF ACCOUNTS

Other special reports can be readily prepared if a company carefully plans its corporate *chart of accounts*. Figure 16-9 shows a meaningful chart of accounts. The first three digits of the account number classification indicate the ledger entry function or purpose (for example, 503XX for research and programming). The last two digits subdivide the account number structure. Account XXX08, for example, might designate entries that apply to job or project eight. The first three digits make it possible to establish the total charge throughout all jobs for a particular type of expense, or the total income throughout all areas of revenue. The same source of detail can be used to produce a balanced general ledger report and, as importantly, a cross-listing of revenue and expense classifications.

The chart of accounts must be carefully designed and rigorously followed to permit the restructure of accounts during processing. Unfortunately, too many companies are unable to carry through on this important processing requirement. Many charts of accounts are designed when a company is small and there is little need to prepare detailed reports by separate account. As the firm grows, the chart of accounts evolves without a carefully considered system of classification. Consequently, more recent account numbers do not tie to older numbers in a meaningful way. It also frequently happens that an original chart of accounts was designed for a small business, and no provisions were made for additional company divisions. As the company expands, perhaps by adding new product lines and sales territories, the original chart

ASSETS

Current Assets
- 102-00 Cash in bank
- 103-00 Savings
- 104-00 Investments in savings certificates
- 105-00 Investment in WAK stock
- 106-00 Accounts receivable
- 115-00 Prepaid expenses
  - Total Current Assets

Fixed Assets
- 121-00 Automotive equipment
- 122-00 Accumulated depreciation (automotive equipment)
- 123-00 Office furniture and fixtures
- 124-00 Accumulated depreciation (office furniture and fixtures)

Other Assets
- 132-00 Good will
  - TOTAL ASSETS

LIABILITIES

Current Liabilities
- 202-00 Accounts payable
- 203-00 FICA payable
- 204-00 Federal income tax withheld
- 205-00 State income tax withheld
- 206-00 Medical insurance premiums withheld
- 207-00 Pension trust
- 208-00 Profit sharing trust
- 210-00 Notes payable
  - Total Current Liabilities
  - TOTAL LIABILITIES

NET WORTH
- 301-00 Capital stock
- 302-00 Retained earnings
- 395-00 Ending profit or loss

INCOME
- 401-00 Architectural fees
- 410-00 Miscellaneous
  - Total Income

DIRECT COSTS

Salaries and Wages
Expanded Services
- 503-00 Research and programming
- 504-00 Other expanded services
  - Total Expanded Services

Schematics
- 511-00 Design and drawings
- 512-00 Specifications
- 513-00 Estimate of cost
- 514-00 Field work
- 515-00 Other
  - Total Schematics

Design Development
- 521-00 Design and drawings
- 522-00 Specifications
- 523-00 Estimate of cost
- 524-00 Field work
- 525-00 Other
  - Total Design Development

Contract Documents
- 531-00 Design and drawings
- 532-00 Specifications
- 533-00 Estimate of cost
- 534-00 Field work
- 535-00 Other
  - Total Contract Documents

Bidding
- 541-00 Miscellaneous
  - Total Bidding

Construction
- 551-00 Design and drawings
- 554-00 Field work
- 555-00 Other
  - Total Construction

- 560-00 Interior design
- 570-00 Landscape design
  - TOTAL SALARIES AND WAGES

Consultants and Subcontracts
- 581-00 Structural
- 582-00 Mechanical
- 583-00 Electrical
- 584-00 Landscape
- 585-00 Interior design
- 586-00 Others
  - Total Consultants and Subcontracts
- 590-00 Printing
- 595-00 Overhead applied
  - TOTAL DIRECT COSTS

INDIRECT COSTS
- 601-00 Administrative and office salaries
- 602-00 Office supplies and expense
- 603-00 Payroll taxes and insurance
- 604-00 Rent
- 605-00 Telephone and telegraph
- 606-00 Taxes and licenses
- 607-00 Legal and accounting
- 608-00 Dues and subscriptions
- 609-00 Advertising and promotion
- 610-00 Travel and subsistence
- 611-00 Gas, grease, oil, parking, and tires
- 612-00 Mileage allowed
- 613-00 Insurance (property, liability)
- 614-00 Depreciation
- 616-00 Interest expense
- 617-00 Medical insurance
- 618-00 Donations
- 620-00 Bonuses
- 621-00 Pension trust
- 622-00 Profit sharing
- 624-00 Overhead applied
- 625-00 Miscellaneous
- 627-00 Federal income tax
- 628-00 State income tax
  - TOTAL COSTS

FIG. 16-9 Chart of accounts

is not systematically altered. Account numbers are allowed to take on different meanings, depending on which division is using them. Still another case results from conglomeration, where the merging of companies does not entail the development of standard accounting practices. The merged organizations frequently retrain their own charts of accounts, which not only carry different numbers, but also are used in different ways. All of these examples illustrate severe obstacles to the implementation of a consolidated company-wide ledger system.

Once a company begins to allow several charts of accounts to exist, several accounting systems must exist in parallel, at least to some degree. Otherwise, the thread of a company's financial activity will be broken, leaving company officers and auditors thoroughly confused. However, drastic measures are not required, if a common consensus among divisions of a company can be reached concerning the use of account numbers. This agreement must include such basic considerations as what items constitute an expense and what components add to revenue. Divisional charts of accounts can then be related to a master chart. For example, account number 51A34X, used by one division, can be tied to account number 813-554 in the master chart of accounts. Another divisional account number, such as IMPST-99, can be tied to the same master number, thereby allowing different numbering systems to be integrated and consolidated. Even though this cross-referencing can be confusing, it does allow different charts to be combined. The result is a company-wide consolidated general ledger, which permits ledger detail reports to be produced.

16-4 MANAGEMENT IMPLICATIONS

The general ledger is often viewed as just an accounting and audit document. However, it can serve a much broader function because of the computer's ability to produce general ledger information. A timely, properly summarized general ledger report is invaluable for top-management financial advice and control. The ideal general ledger system clearly presents financial facts, with little or no obscuring detail and no omission of unflattering data. It presents meaningful summary figures prepared in such a way that repetitive detail is deleted. At the same time, the method of summarizing should not cover potential or present financial weaknesses. Careful presentation of key entries within the general ledger reports should make it possible to detect excessive leakage of funds or unauthorized financial activity.

Because a summary review is of little value if reports are not readily available at the end of an accounting cycle, every effort should be made to expedite the processing of this important computer system. Consolidated ledgers that are delayed weeks or months have little impact when used to improve financial areas of a firm. This computer application has the distinction of being a managerial tool as well as a means of processing large quantities of data. Management action reports can be prepared that probe financial accounts, making the general ledger computer application extremely valuable to a well-managed company.

REVIEW OF IMPORTANT IDEAS

The general ledger system can be operated using summary computer files from many of the other computer applications. In fact, these systems can be designed to supply the bulk of the detail information going into the final ledger reports. Even then, there will be a fair amount of manual entries that must be included in the file of data used to prepare the final reports. Provisions for corrections and adjustments must be made as well. The resulting massive computer file is then used to prepare the general ledger report for the current accounting period.

Once the current ledger is produced and balanced, the consolidated general ledger can be prepared. This report may be a combination of current and year-to-date details for the entire company. Alternatively, it may be a compendium of the general ledger reports for many company divisions that combine to form the consolidated company-wide general ledger statement.

The many diverse activities of separate company divisions can be successfully related through a company chart of accounts. The chart should use a classification that divides source input data into precise accounts, so that different expenses and revenues can be extracted and examined. If company divisions are accustomed to using different and incompatible account numbers, the problem of company-wide consolidation becomes immense. To correct this situation, a cross-reference scheme must be adopted. Division accounts can then be related to a master chart of accounts, and a consolidated general ledger statement can be prepared.

It is desirable to devise a system of accounts whereby the general ledger detail can be organized by function as well as by sequential account number. If this is done, the computer can produce cross-reference ledger detail reports that summarize items such as expenses of a given type, or all revenues that stem from particular company dealings. These reports are of great value to managers in their attempts to understand the details and the trends of financial transactions within the various departments of a company.

REVIEW QUESTIONS

1. What is the general ledger?

2. How is it possible to design a general ledger computer application almost completely as an extension of other computer applications?

3. What is the difference between the current and the consolidated general ledger files?

4. Prior to the processing of the massive general ledger input files, all data must be sorted. Why is this sort operation necessary? In what sequence are file records placed after the sort operations?

5. Why do manual entries to the general ledger system require more review than do file entries?

6. If a firm uses several charts of accounts, by what means are file records consolidated?

7. Why can the term *consolidated general ledger* be ambiguous?

8. What typical detail is generally printed on a detail ledger, which is prepared after the printing of the consolidated general ledger?

9. Why must the chart of accounts be carefully designed?

10. What advantages are there in preparing general ledger statements by computer?

11. How does the general ledger computer application assist in the design of better financial controls in a company?

EXERCISES

1. Design a chart of accounts that you might use to summarize your personal financial transactions. Design a system that would permit you to capture summary data and create a general ledger file.

2. Which computer application should a company design first: an accounts payable system or a consolidated general ledger system? Explain the benefits of your suggested approach and the problems of the alternative.

3. Large companies and tax-supported public agencies add two entries to each general ledger account number: the amount of money budgeted to the account and the amount of money encumbered but not expended. For example, $5,000 has been budgeted for auto tire purchases, $4,000 has been expended to date, and $500 has been encumbered as a result of ordering more tires. Devise a general ledger system that screens entries to ensure that the total amount expended and encumbered does not exceed the budgeted amount.

17

FINANCIAL
STATEMENTS

The implementation of the general ledger computer application does more than consolidate financial transactions and print transaction summaries and cross-listings. It also encourages further development of a financial management reporting system. Financial statements can be printed directly (subject only to manual additions or corrections) as an extended use of the consolidated general ledger file. The most common financial statements are the company balance sheet and the statement of corporate income. Other statements as important, if not more important, to modern management track the performance of a corporate profit planning system and of a budget planning system.

This chapter examines the extended use of the general ledger file to produce financial statements. Traditional financial statements, as well as statements prepared in conjunction with financial planning and control, are considered. Together, these financial statements measure the income and expense patterns of a firm and indicate both past and future deviations from financial plans.

17-1 INPUT TO THE FINANCIAL REPORTING
COMPUTER APPLICATION

The financial statement computer application requires as initial input the consolidated general ledger file. If financial statements such as the income statement are printed weekly, the source files of the general ledger must be summarized weekly. Actually, the financial statement reports are apt to be a consolidated summary of only those items deemed important for frequent measure—they are not complete recapitulations of the entire accounting transaction activity. This effort is too costly and its value is questionable.

After the general ledger has been balanced, corrected, and printed, it is practical to prepare financial statements immediately. As we will soon show, additional manual entries and corrections are required to support this print operation. However, the number of entries is far smaller than when the general ledger file is initially prepared. The major file input has already been corrected and balanced. In addition, supporting files to the application, such as the consolidated profit plan master file or the year-to-date budget file, can be prepared in advance of processing. Computer file input then becomes routine, with no delay because of separate in-line preparation or special auditing activities. As with the general ledger, financial statements should be prepared and released as soon as possible after the close of an accounting cycle. Report contents can then be reviewed in time to permit management to correct apparent financial imbalances.

17-2   THE FINANCIAL SYSTEM

Figure 17-1 flowcharts the financial reporting computer application examined in this chapter. The financial statements prepared result primarily from the two general ledger computer files discussed in the last chapter: the current general ledger file (used to prepare the current month's general ledger) and the consolidated general ledger file (used in year-to-date reporting). If the consolidated file is a company-wide consolidation of several departments rather than an abbreviated year-to-date file, it serves as the major input to the system. Otherwise, several general ledger consolidated files, one for each division, must serve as input.

Two supporting master files are illustrated in addition to the consolidated general ledger file. These files are both updated during processing. The *consolidated profit plan file* stores forecasted profit, income, revenue, and expense data, which are compared to actual figures. The *year-to-date budget file* stores uncumbered funds, which are compared to actual expenses. Both files are updated and carried forward to the next accounting period until the end of a fiscal year. At this time, a new set of files is started to allow carry-forward processing. Each computer file update program permits insertion of keyed adjustments to add or to alter records in the master files.

Four types of reports are produced by the computer application.

- The *profit and loss statement* (the statement of corporate income) shows the increase or decrease in net income realized by a firm. Interdepartmental comparative income statements and other types of in-

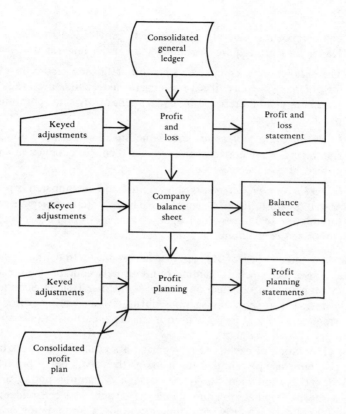

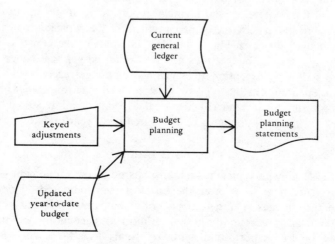

FIG. 17-1 Financial reporting system flowchart

come reporting can also be printed, provided that several general ledger files are required as input and can be integrated.

- The *balance sheet* compares assets to liabilities to record the change in the company's equity. If several general ledger files are available, this statement can be prepared by department or division, permitting comparative analysis.

- *Profit planning statements* are a modification of the profit and loss statements. They emphasize the expected cost of conducting a business instead of the income received.

- *Budget planning statements* show actual and encumbered expenditures posted against planned expenses. These statements represent a recapitulation of the general ledger, comparing actual expenditures with authorized expenditures for the year.

The first three types of reports can be produced from the consolidated general ledger file, since this summary file usually contains the detail necessary to prepare consolidated financial statements. Budget statements are usually designed to show transactions during an accounting period, and so the current general ledger file is used to ensure precision in posting by general ledger account number.

The preparation of each type of report is associated with a separate computer program, usually entitled the same as the report being printed. If the detail in the consolidated file is excessive and requires undue processing time, a short computer program should be designed to consolidate the file further by collapsing entries into summary totals. Consolidation prior to the printing of financial statements preserves the account balances and permits faster preparation of printed financial statements.

Typical file contents of the financial reporting computer application have been shown, in part, by the contents typical of the consolidated and current general ledger files (see Fig. 16-4). File contents of the consolidated profit and the year-to-date budget files are similar to the general ledger files with the two following exceptions: (1) planned or budget account estimates are stored (depending on the type of master file) to permit comparisons with actual account totals; and (2) historical account detail is stored to permit planned or budgeted totals to be compared on a year-to-date basis.

Income Statements

Figure 17-2 shows a typical computer-prepared income statement—the *profit and loss statement*. It is often the first statement prepared, since it briefly reviews the changes in earned income of a company division or of the entire company over an accounting period. Almost all accounting activity is summarized on this report, and summary totals usually balance to general

```
                           A. B. C. CORPORATION

                      STATEMENT OF INCOME AND EXPENCE

                     FOR THE YEAR ENDED AUGUST 31, 19XX
  ACCOUNT
    NO.
    999    SALES
    999        MANUFACTURING                      $120,493.41
    999        FINISH PRODUCTION                    72,839.27
    999        RENTAL INCOME                         1,907.87
    999        OTHER                                   119.03
                                                                    $195,359.58

    999    DIRECT COSTS
    999        CONSULTING                         $  9,286.92
    999        EQUIPMENT RENTAL                     81,153.46
    999        OUTSIDE SERVICES                      2,017.23
    999        SALARIES AND WAGES                   45,885.62
    999        SUPPLIES                              1,587.30
                                                                     139,930.53
                                                                    $ 55,429.05

    999    GENERAL AND ADMINISTRATIVE EXPENSES
    999        ACCOUNTING                         $  1,307.50
    999        ADVERTISING                           3,034.88
    999        AUTO EXPENSE                            702.06
    999        BUSINESS PROMOTION                      925.51
    999        BAD DEBTS                               552.23
    999        DEPRECIATION                          6,299.00
    999        DUES AND SUBSCRIPTIONS                  162.90
    999        INSURANCE                             4,354.55
    999        INTEREST AND BANK CHARGES               67.79
    999        OFFICE EXPENSE                        1,073.58
    999        ORGANIZATION EXPENSE                    72.00
    999        RENT                                  2,990.00
    999        REPAIRS AND MAINTENANCE                 237.66
    999        TAXES - PAYROLL                       2,847.87
    999        TAXES AND LICENSES - OTHER             300.93
    999        TELEPHONE                             2,156.64
    999        TRAVEL                                2,920.19
    999        UTILITIES                               573.98
    999        SUNDRY                                   25.02
                                                                    $ 30,604.29
    999        NET INCOME BEFORE FEDERAL INCOME TAX                 $ 24,824.76
               FEDERAL INCOME TAX                                      5,507.09

    999        NET INCOME AFTER FEDERAL INCOME TAX                  $ 19,317.67
```

FIG. 17-2 Profit and loss statement

ledger totals. However, the report categories shown on the profit and loss statement may not, in many cases, resemble general ledger totals. Data are rearranged to emphasize major financial categories. For example, interest expense and costs of obtaining credit are often combined, although they are separate on the general ledger report. This additional consolidation is done to facilitate review and to highlight the most important income and expense categories such as sales and cost of sales, direct costs of operations, and administrative overhead costs. The report is intended to summarize the current status of major company activity. It therefore must be designed so that it isolates revenue and expenses incurred by the main company operations.

The degree to which the general ledger can be consolidated to best fit income reporting requirements is determined by the flexibility of the chart of accounts. If account number consolidation is relatively easy, preparation of the income statement presents no real processing problems. If the opposite is true, the computer program designed to prepare the income statement be-comes complex, requiring additional cross-reference numbers to allow the integration of account numbers.

The preparation of different types of income statements depends on the file structure of the general ledger system. If separate general ledger files are maintained by the divisions of a company, interdivisional statements can be prepared so that revenues and expenses can be compared across divisions. Similarly, if both current and year-to-date general ledger totals are used as input to the system, current and year-to-date income totals can easily be printed. Figure 17-3 illustrates the latter type of income statement. Current revenue and costs expressed in dollars and in percent are compared to year-to-date totals over an accounting period. This method of reporting facilitates review because it shows the accounts that appear in any given month to deviate from past reporting periods.

The Balance Sheet

Figure 17-4 shows a typical *balance sheet* that can be prepared from the general ledger file. This financial statement recapitulates the detail found in the general ledger report. It is a complete, balanced company reporting of

```
        APLDATA SYSTEMS
        DEPARTMENT 1
        INCOME STATEMENT
        FOR PERIOD ENDING AUGUST 31, 19XX

                           CURRENT    PRCNT      TO DATE    PRCNT

        REV FROM OPERATIONS
4000    INCOME FROM OPER   2,560.00   98.65     2,560.00   98.65
4070    OTHER INCOME          35.00    1.35        35.00    1.35
                           ---------  ------     ---------  ------
TOTAL REV FROM OPERATIONS  2,595.00  100.00     2,595.00  100.00
        COST OF OPERATIONS
5010    SALARIES             800.00   30.83       800.00   30.83
5200    SUPPLIES              48.00    1.85        48.00    1.85
5220    OFFICE RENT          525.00   20.23       525.00   20.23
5250    TELEPHONE             18.50    0.71        18.50    0.71
5400    TAXES AND LICENSES    26.75    1.03        26.75    1.03
5900    MISCELLANOUS         100.00    3.85       100.00    3.85
                           ---------  ------     ---------  ------
TOTAL COST OF OPERATIONS   1,518.25   58.51     1,518.25   58.51
                           ---------  ------     ---------  ------
TOTAL NET INCOME           1,076.75   41.49     1,076.75   41.49
                           ---------  ------     ---------  ------
                           ---------  ------     ---------  ------
```

FIG. 17-3 Current and year-to-date comparative income statement

ASSETS

CURRENT ASSETS
```
102   CASH IN BANK            $     1,279.14
103   SAVINGS ACCOUNT         $       231.98
104   INVESTMENTS-SVNGS CERTS
105   INVESTMENTS-W A K STOCK $     1,200.00
106   ACCOUNTS RECEIVABLE     $    41,426.27
115   PREPAID EXPENSES        $       655.99
         TOTAL CURRENT ASSETS         $    44,793.38
```

FIXED ASSETS
```
121   AUTOMOTIVE EQUIP        $     8,559.00
122   ACC DEPN-AUTO EQUIP     $     6,526.59-
123   OFFICE FURN & FIXTURES  $    10,055.92
124   ACC DEPR-OFFICE F & F   $     6,996.79-
         TOTAL FIXED ASSETS           $     5,091.54
```

OTHER ASSETS
```
132   GOOD WILL               $     3,000.00
         TOTAL OTHER ASSETS           $     3,000.00

      TOTAL ASSETS                            $    52,884.92
```

LIABILITIES

CURRENT LIABILITIES
```
202   ACCOUNTS PAYABLE        $    24,179.34-
203   FICA PAYABLE            $       269.21-
204   FED INC TAX W/H         $       931.70-
205   UT INCOME TAX W/H       $       192.54-
206   MEDICAL INS PREMIUMS    $        63.95-
207   PENSION TRUST           $
208   PROFIT SHARING TRUST    $
210   NOTES PAYABLE           $    15,874.50-
         TOTAL CURRENT LIAB           $    41,511.24-

      TOTAL LIABILITIES               $    41,511.24-*
```

NET WORTH
```
301   CAPITAL STOCK           $    14,000.00-
302   RETAINED EARNINGS       $        16.23
395   ENDING PROFIT OR LOSS   $          .10-
      PROFIT OR LOSS          $     2,610.19

      TOTAL NET WORTH                 $    11,373.68-

      TOT LIAB & NET WORTH                    $    52,884.92-
```

FIG. 17-4 Balance sheet

assets and liabilities over an accounting period. Updated on a monthly basis, this statement contains the permanent recording of company assets and outstanding liabilities.

The general ledger file should contain more than enough account entries to produce the company balance sheet. Even then, a provision should be made to allow keyed adjustments as part of computer processing in the event that additional data are needed. If several divisions within a company prepare separate general ledger files, it is also possible to produce separate balance statements. In this case, the computer program will consist of two phases: the preparation of divisional financial balance statements and the printing of the company or consolidated balance statement.

Another type of balance sheet report is the *trend report,* prepared monthly to reflect changes in assets and liabilities. Figure 17-5 illustrates this type of financial statement. Total dollars and percent of total dollars are printed to assist in reading the report. In addition, financial ratios are often computed during processing and placed on this report. These ratios indicate the financial strengths and weaknesses of the company and any change in trend. A variety of ratios exist; the purpose of the analysis will suggest which ratios should be computed. In any event, liquidity, leverage, activity, and profitability ratios can all be incorporated into the trend report to show changes in the financial position of a company.

Profit Planning

Profit planning is most often a modified method of analyzing a business income statement, with special emphasis on expected rather than actual costs of operating a business. This analysis begins with the development of yearly goals and objectives for an operating division, which are then translated into revenue, expense, and income projections. These are entered into the yearly profit plan for the division. Data from several divisions are collected to form the consolidated yearly profit plan.

Typical information in a yearly profit plan includes expected sales dollar volumes by month and by major product line; anticipated direct costs for material and labor in support of projected sales; and estimated overhead costs allocated by overhead accounts. Other measures deviate somewhat from standard income statement determinants by including projected inventory turnover rates; the expected return on invested capital in machinery or inventory; the planned increase in factory capacity; and the planned reduction in unit costs of production.

After profit plan measures have been selected, the yearly profit plan is adopted and categorized by account number. This plan includes monthly projections that enable actual revenues, expenditures, income, and other items to be compared periodically with planned totals. Moreover, since most

MONTH OF: MAY

SOUTHERN CALIFORNIA FIRST NATIONAL BANK

JUNE 10, 19XX

ASSETS (MILLIONS)

| | LOANS | | | | | | | | | | SECURITIES | | | | | | | | | |
| | COMMERCIAL | | REAL ESTATE | | INSTALLMENT | | LOSS ALLOW | | TOTAL | | U.S. GOVNMT | | MUNICIPALS | | OTHER | | LOSS ALLOW | | TOTAL | |
MONTH	AMT.	%LOAN	AMT.	%LOAN	AMT.	%LOAN	AMT.	%LOAN	AMOUNT	%E.A.	AMT.	%SEC	AMT.	%SEC	AMT.	%SEC	AMT.	%SEC	AMOUNT	%E.A.
JAN	167.2	46.6	140.6	39.2	51.1	14.4	4.9	1.4-	358.9	74.1	43.5	34.6	69.6	55.4	13.6	10.8	.9	.7-	125.7	25.9
FEB	162.7	45.6	140.9	39.5	52.8	14.8	4.9	1.4-	356.4	74.7	38.2	31.6	69.8	57.8	13.4	11.1	.7	.6-	120.8	25.3
MAR	159.8	44.7	142.0	39.7	55.8	15.6	5.0	1.4-	357.6	75.4	35.3	30.3	70.0	60.1	11.7	10.1	.6	.5-	116.4	24.6
APR	161.7	44.3	143.4	39.3	59.6	16.3	6.0	1.6-	364.8	76.1	35.9	31.2	70.6	61.5	8.8	7.6	.5	.4-	114.8	23.9
MAY	158.5	43.4	143.3	39.2	63.3	17.4	5.9	1.6-	365.1	76.1	34.2	29.9	72.7	63.5	8.1	7.1	.5	.4-	114.6	23.9
JUN ::	170.1	44.2	153.6	40.0	60.8	15.8	4.8	1.2-	384.4	73.6	52.4	37.9	76.2	55.1	10.7	7.8	1.1	.8-	138.2	26.4
JUL ::	172.9	44.2	155.6	39.8	62.6	16.0	4.8	1.2-	391.1	73.9	52.0	37.7	76.4	55.4	10.8	7.8	1.0	.8-	138.0	26.1
AUG ::	174.8	44.1	157.3	39.7	64.3	16.2	4.9	1.2-	396.4	74.2	51.6	37.5	76.6	55.6	10.8	7.8	1.2	.9-	137.8	25.8
SEP ::	178.0	44.3	158.8	39.4	66.1	16.6	4.8	1.2-	402.9	74.6	51.2	37.2	76.6	55.9	10.8	7.8	1.2	.9-	137.5	25.4
OCT ::	181.8	44.3	160.4	39.1	68.0	16.6	4.8	1.2-	410.2	74.9	50.8	37.0	77.0	56.1	10.8	7.9	1.3	.9-	137.3	25.1
NOV ::	184.9	44.4	162.1	38.9	69.7	16.7	4.9	1.2-	416.8	75.2	50.5	36.8	77.2	56.3	10.8	7.9	1.4	1.0-	137.1	24.8
DEC ::	188.4	44.5	163.5	38.6	71.7	16.9	4.9	1.1-	423.5	75.2	50.6	36.9	76.0	54.9	10.8	7.9	1.4	1.0-	138.4	26.8
PLN	167.0	44.2	151.9	40.2	58.9	15.6	4.9	1.3-	377.9	73.2	52.8	38.1	76.3	56.3	10.7	7.7	1.1	.8-	137.2	26.8
VAR	8.5	.8-	8.6	1.0-	4.4	1.8	1.0	.3	12.8	2.9	18.6	8.2-	3.3	8.6	2.6	.6-	.6	.4	23.8	2.9-

LIABILITIES (MILLIONS)

| | DEPOSITS | | | | | | | | | | CAPITAL | | EARNING ASSETS | | LOANS | TOTAL |
| | DEMAND | | SAVINGS | | TIME | | TOTAL TIME | | TOTAL | | | ASSETS | | % OF | TO | RESOURCES |
MONTH	AMOUNT	%DEP	AMOUNT	%DEP	AMOUNT	%DEP	AMOUNT	%DEP	AMOUNT	LQ RATIO	AMOUNT	TO S/E	AMOUNT	TOTAL ASSETS	DEP	
JAN	227.5	44.6	166.7	32.7	115.6	22.7	282.3	55.4	509.8	19.7	41.7	5.4	484.5	73.0	70.4	664.0
FEB	218.3	44.1	163.7	33.1	113.2	22.9	277.1	55.9	495.4	18.0	42.2	5.6	477.1	73.7	71.9	647.0
MAR	221.5	44.3	165.8	33.2	112.3	22.5	278.1	55.7	499.6	18.8	42.2	5.6	474.0	72.1	71.6	657.2
APR	236.1	46.2	161.2	31.5	114.1	22.3	275.4	53.8	511.4	20.5	42.4	5.6	479.6	73.3	71.3	672.9
MAY	223.5	44.7	160.5	32.1	116.2	23.2	276.7	55.3	500.2	19.9	42.7	5.6	479.6	73.3	73.0	654.4
JUN ::	244.0	46.1	174.0	32.9	111.6	21.1	285.5	53.9	529.6	16.7	41.0	5.4	522.7	80.5	72.6	649.2
JUL ::	250.6	46.6	175.6	32.6	111.7	20.8	287.4	53.4	538.0	16.8	41.5	5.4	529.1	80.4	72.7	657.8
AUG ::	252.0	46.6	177.1	32.7	111.8	20.7	289.0	53.4	540.9	16.3	41.9	5.4	534.1	80.6	73.3	662.9
SEP ::	256.0	46.8	178.7	32.7	112.6	20.6	291.2	53.2	547.2	16.2	41.8	5.3	540.3	80.6	73.6	670.6
OCT ::	261.7	47.1	180.7	32.5	113.3	20.4	293.6	52.9	555.4	16.0	42.3	5.3	547.5	80.6	73.9	678.9
NOV ::	265.9	47.5	179.7	32.1	114.1	20.4	293.9	52.5	559.8	15.6	42.8	5.4	553.8	80.8	74.4	685.3
DEC ::	269.6	47.7	180.8	32.0	114.8	20.3	295.6	52.3	565.2	15.3	42.8	5.3	560.7	80.8	74.9	694.2
PLN	240.7	45.8	173.2	33.0	111.3	21.2	284.4	54.2	525.2	17.1	41.2	5.5	516.3	80.4	72.0	641.9
VAR	17.2	1.1-	12.7	.9-	4.9	1.1	7.7	1.1	25.0	2.8	1.5	.1	36.7	7.1-	1.0	12.4

FIG. 17-5 Balance sheet trend report

planning measures follow the general ledger account sequence, the comparison between planned and actual company activity in relatively simple to compute and to prepare. Difficulty arises when activity measures are not retained in the general ledger file. In these cases, input of actual totals (or additional file input) is required during processing. Increases in plant capacity, for example, are one item that must be entered manually.

Figure 17-6 illustrates a typical, though simplified, profit planning financial statement. Actual performance, planned performance, and the variance

```
                              YOUNG CORPORATION
                          PROFIT PLANNING ANALYSIS
                              FOR MARCH 19XX


            CURRENT  CURRENT   CURRENT    CURRENT      YTD      YTD        YTD        YTD
            PROFIT    MONTH     MONTH      MONTH       PLAN    ACTUAL   $VARIANCE  %VARIANCE
             PLAN     ACTUAL  $ VARIANCE % VARIANCE

GROUP 1
 PRODUCT 1   3,000    3,069       69        102%     9,400    9,167      (233)       98%
 PRODUCT 2  11,500   14,645    3,145        127%    39,000   38,090      (910)       98%
 PRODUCT 3     800      800                 100%     2,400    2,392        (8)       100%
 PRODUCT 4   3,900    1,424   (2,476)        37%     8,800    8,462      (338)       96%
 PRODUCT 5     500      168     (332)        34%       820    1,108       288        135%

  TOTAL     19,700   20,106      406        102%    60,420   59,219    (1,201)       98%

GROUP 2
 PRODUCT 1  17,600    2,304  (15,296)        13%    22,400   35,744    13,344       160%
 PRODUCT 2     650      617      (33)        95%     1,950    2,336       386        120%

  TOTAL     18,250    2,921  (15,329)        16%    24,350   38,080    13,730       156%

GROUP 3
 PRODUCT 1  41,100   37,595   (3,505)        91%   139,400  113,297   (26,103)       81%
 PRODUCT 2  63,600   41,552  (22,048)        65%   148,400  160,484    12,084       108%
 PRODUCT 3  18,500   18,315     (185)        99%    55,500   53,650    (1,850)       97%
 PRODUCT 4  24,500   21,805   (2,695)        89%    73,500   71,295    (2,205)       97%
 PRODUCT 5   7,200    4,465   (2,735)        62%    18,400   18,128      (272)       99%

  TOTAL    154,900  123,732  (31,166)        80%   435,200  416,854   (18,346)       96%

GROUP 4
 PRODUCT 1   3,300    2,400     (900)        73%     8,700    8,579      (121)       99%
 PRODUCT 2  24,500   24,990      490        102%    73,500   49,612   (23,888)       67%
 PRODUCT 3            3,772    3,772          0%     8,200    7,626      (574)       93%
 PRODUCT 4     300      161     (139)        54%       626      611       (15)       98%

  TOTAL     28,100   31,323    3,223        111%    91,026   66,428   (24,598)       73%

GROUP 5
 PRODUCT 1     650      300     (350)        46%     1,250    1,200       (50)       96%
 PRODUCT 2   5,700    5,757       57        101%    17,100   17,100                 100%
 PRODUCT 3                        0%                 5,700    5,358      (342)       94%
 PRODUCT 4     250      156      (94)        62%       613      596       (17)       97%

  TOTAL      6,600    6,213     (387)        94%    24,663   24,254      (409)       98%

 TOTAL
 PROFIT    227,550  184,295  (43,255)        81%   635,659  604,835   (30,824)       95%
```

FIG. 17-6 Profit planning financial statement

(the difference between actual and planned) are printed by account number. Current and year-to-date totals permit monthly averaging of deviations, which helps to identify significant changes in planned company performance. Other types of profit planning statements are similar to the one shown. Actual versus planned company activity is compared to show deviations, thereby permitting corrective action to be taken by company officers.

Budget Planning

The preparation of company budgets naturally follows the design of the yearly profit plan. In this instance, the primary purpose of the budget is to limit expenditures of each division, department, or cost center within a company. Although some cost overruns are permitted, the funds allocated by the budget usually limit disbursements and expenses during the budgeted period.

The form of the budget itself is sequenced by account number, following the chart of accounts used in preparing the general ledger. Constructed on a monthly basis, the budget becomes an estimated recapitulation of the general ledger. Budgeted expenditures are compared to actual and encumbered expenditures stored in the general ledger file, thereby allowing some control over the monthly budget.

Because of the closeness of the company budget to the general ledger, some organizations (particularly county and city governments) do not prepare a general ledger. Rather, the budget serves a dual purpose. Actual expenditures are posted against budgeted accounts on a monthly basis. Processing in this way produces a consolidated financial report and, in addition, updates the yearly budget.

Figure 17-7 illustrates a budget format that is tied to the general ledger chart of accounts. Total budget dollars are compared to actual dollars to show the variance in dollars and in percent. The budget is also flexible and shows the changes in company performance (standard hours minus actual hours times the standard rate). By permitting budgeted dollars to vary according to actual business volumes, budgeted versus actual costs of operations can be measured on a meaningful basis. The proper use of standard times and costs provides the means by which this measurement is accomplished.

Normally, budgets such as the one illustrated are prepared and distributed by department or division in a company. This procedure allows the responsible company officer to review his or her portion of the budget. The budget report should indicate which accounts are in danger of exceeding the amount specified—the upper limit during the fiscal year. In many instances, no provision is made to allow a stated budget amount to be exceeded. In other

03060 LA MESA BR   03/31/   PERFORMANCE REPORT – DETAIL   STD070   PAGE NO. 2

G/L NO.	JOB CLASS	MIS PLAN	VARIABLE BUDGET	PROGRAMMED BUDGET	STANDBY BUDGET	TOTAL BUDGET	ACTUAL	VARIANCE DOLLARS	VAR %	VOLUME VARIANCE	RATE VARIANCE	PERFORMANCE VARIANCE
460100		350			350	350	417	67	19			67
460200		370			370	370	206	164-	44-			164-
460300		80			80	80	71	9-	11-			9-
460400		5			5	5	5					
460500							146	146	100			146
460600		25			25	25		25-	100-			25-
460900		5			5	5	2	7-	140-			7-
480100		40			40	40	149	109	272			109
OTHER FEES		5,330			5,330	5,330	3,974	1,356-	25-			1,356-
* TOT FEE INC		10,020			10,020	10,020	8,810	1,210-	12-			1,210-
** TOT INCOME		146,547	119,561		10,020	129,581	130,383	802		16,966	2,012	1,210-
511110	011113		849			849		849	100			
511110	011115						1,525	1,525-	100-			
511110	011310		1,929			1,929		1,929	100			
511110	011312						1,001	1,001-	100-			
511110	011508						725	725-	100-			
511110	TOTAL	3,300	2,778			2,778	3,251	473-	17-	522	153-	320-
511130	011312						49	49-	100-			
511130	TOTAL						49	49-	100-			49-
511210	031007						598	598-	100-			
511210	031009		1,435			1,435		1,435	100			
511210	031209		723			723		723	100			
511210	TOTAL	1,355	2,158			2,158	598	1,560	72	803-	257	1,303
511230	031007						7	7-	100-			
511230	TOTAL						7	7-	100-			7-
511410	051003		2,960			2,960	2,181	779	26			
511410	051004						494	494-	100-			
511410	051005		1,138			1,138	479	659	57			
511410	051103						440	440-	100-			
511410	051104		2,498			2,498	1,484	1,014	40			
511410	051105						438	438-	100-			
511410	051203						223	223-	100-			
511410	051204		179			179		179	100			
511410	051304		359			359		359	100			
511410	051506						593	593-	100-			
511410	051603		122			122		122	100			
511410	051703		389			389	470	81-	20-			
511410	051804		519			519	439	80	15			
511410	051903		547			547		547	100			
511410	059008						717	717-	100-			
511410	TOTAL	8,512	8,711			8,711	7,958	763	8	199-		753
511420	051003						2	2-	100-			
511420	051804						1	1-	100-			
511420	TOTAL	50			50	50	3	47	94			47
511430	051003						74	74-	100-			
511430	051004						6	6-	100-			

FIG. 17-7 Financial budget statement

circumstances, funds may be transferred from one budget line to another, or standby funds may be used. However, the approval of a top administrative officer is required before the transfer of funds may take place.

The budget information collected during a fiscal year can be used to prepare the budget for the next fiscal year—another reason for using a computer application to produce financial statements. The data acquired and stored on computer files serve as a reasonable history in predicting future budget requirements. Usually, predictions are straight-line extensions of the trends in expenditures. Suppose, for example, that the expenditures for supplies have increased at the rate of 10 percent a year over the last three years. A straight-line extension of the supply trend would estimate that 10 percent more than actually spent during the current year should be budgeted over the next fiscal year. Accounts such as payroll can be predicted even more closely. Since current payroll costs are known and the amount of pay increases during the next year can be specified, the payroll budget line accounts can be estimated almost exactly. The final predictions, which are similar to the examples given, result in the computer printing of budget forecast worksheets directly from maintained files. The worksheets are then used for budget conferences where operating managers and financial officers review and modify the details of the yearly budget. Afterward, budget changes are added to the computer budget master file. The new budget for the coming year can then be printed. All in all, this budgeting process represents a great savings in the time of corporate managers. Moreover, the final budget is based on rational consensus rather than on intuition and group persuasion.

17-3 MANAGEMENT IMPLICATIONS

Far too many companies use a computer to process financial transactions such as receivables, and then fail to use it to assist in preparing financial statements. Instead, financial statements are prepared manually. This has two obvious disadvantages: (1) financial reporting is needlessly delayed, and (2) there is no assured correlation between the summaries shown by the manually prepared financial statements and the summaries generated by computer-processing activities.

It makes sense to use the computer to develop financial management reports, even if the computer-printed results must undergo manual revision before they are submitted to management. If the administrative financial reports are generated from the same computer files used in daily operations, errors in these daily applications are more likely to be detected. Moreover, data processing will be partially controlled by senior company officers. When financial reporting is kept separate from daily processing of transactions, there is the danger that computer applications will wander from an acceptable path. This danger can be avoided if major planning reports are compared to actual processed transaction detail.

Decision making should improve as a result of using financial control reports. For example, a profit planning and control report allows managers to forecast their profit expectations and to have the computer compare these projections to actual profit totals. This exercise should help managers understand the activities that lead to improved profits. Similarly, with up-to-date budget information, managers should be better able to control internal expenditures. They can track expenditures by department to find out which departments are well within budget (suggesting a possible surplus) and which will exceed their budget (indicating a shortage). Department-by-department analysis should enable management to quickly reconcile budget variance. Finally, accurate and timely financial statements are of great importance in evaluating the financial soundness of a business. For example, a dip in sales revenue can be analyzed in terms of its effect on total net income; or, higher than expected accounts payable can be studied in terms of their impact on the assets, liabilities, and net worth of a business. Numerous other examples featuring the extended use of financial information might be given. However, all would point to the use of financial information to improve the profit and cost performance of business.

REVIEW OF IMPORTANT IDEAS

In this chapter a financial planning and control computer application was related to four types of financial statements. These statements should be completed soon after the closing of the monthly books, since much of their value is tied to the reporting of current financial information. They are of considerable interest to senior management, such as the heads of major departments or operating divisions of a company.

The company income statement, the first type of financial statement, indicates current changes in earned income. It compares revenues to expenses and permits cost overruns to be identified and corrected. Current totals are compared to year-to-date totals to reflect any change in the trend of earned income resulting from company operations.

The balance sheet recapitulates the financial status of the company by comparing assets and liabilities. It serves as an analysis document, especially if tied to key financial ratios. It then becomes important to company officers as well as to company investors and stockholders. A year-end financial statement can be prepared showing the change in status over 12 months. Quarterly statements are also prepared and released to outside investors.

Profit planning involves using the computer to store expected revenues and costs of operations. Projected by account number, actual versus projected totals are compared during the year. Significant deviations from plan are identified to permit corrective action to be taken. In a dynamic company, this action may well determine its profitability.

Budget reports are tied to the general ledger accounts and to company profit planning. Budgets are prepared to encumber funds against planned expenditures. By computer update, the planned budget is compared to actual expenditures. This review of all account balances shows which are well within budget and which are not. Again, action is taken to correct problems before they become more serious. This procedure allows serious shortcomings in company financial expenditures to be identified quickly.

REVIEW QUESTIONS

1. The general ledger computer application gives impetus to the development of a financial reporting computer application. Why?

2. Four types of reports are prepared as a result of the financial reporting computer application. What are they? How is each utilized by management?

3. What is the difference between the consolidated profit plan file and the year-to-date budget file?

4. What factors determine whether desired income and budget statements can be produced from the financial reporting computer application?

5. In what way does the balance sheet trend report differ from the more traditional balance sheet?

6. How does the financial reporting computer application assist in the preparation of yearly budgets, by department, in a company?

EXERCISES

1. Most large companies use the computer not only to process financial transactions such as receivables, but also to implement a general ledger computer application. Financial statements, however, continue to be prepared manually. Given several reasons that explain why systems development has evolved in this way. Is this condition likely to exist in the future? Explain.

2. A manager discovers that actual expenditures during the first 11½ months of the year represent 85 percent of budgeted expenditures. What can be done in this situation? If a computer system is used to report actual versus budgeted expenditures on a monthly basis, what possible actions are open? Which situation is better for the manager? For the company?

3. A company president wants a one-page financial review for her desk every Monday morning. The report should recapitulate the assets and liabilities of the company and specifically detail last week's sales, credits, collection, and inventory purchases. Modify the application described in this chapter in order to accommodate the president's request.

18

SALES ANALYSIS AND MARKET PENETRATION

This final chapter provides another extension of computer files created and maintained by lower level computer applications. In this instance, the focus of the discussion shifts from financial management to marketing management. Two separate computer applications are introduced: *sales analysis* and *market penetration*. The second requires input from the first, but both applications help relate current company sales to expected sales as well as to historical sales. Sales managers and other company officers are vitally interested in better understanding the conditions under which products can be successfully marketed. These two computer applications can greatly assist the development of sound market product strategy by identifying which types of customers and products are profitable to the firm and which market areas are likely to yield satisfactory sales volumes relative to market size.

Sales analysis studies use internal invoice data. Market penetration studies use these data, and also data external to normal company data processing and reporting systems. A sales analysis serves to analyze the performance of (1) company sales personnel and their contribution to profits, (2) customers and their contribution to profits, and (3) parts carried in inventory and their contribution to profits. A market penetration investigation, which assists in making future sales predictions, makes predictions based on historical data matched against (1) company performance expectations, (2) possible actions by competitors, (3) anticipated growth in product markets, (4) and estimated growth in the general economy.

315

The sales analysis computer application will be discussed in more detail than the market penetration application. It is important to develop a comprehensive sales analysis computer application to permit later ties with expected sales performance. Combining sales analysis with market penetration then gives an overview of potential weaknesses in marketing strategy, especially in regard to the assignment of sales personnel to market territories and the alignment of products to market areas.

18-1 SALES ANALYSIS INPUT REQUIREMENTS

The invoice detail files are the primary source of current sales data. Besides being used to print the customer invoice, these files become input to the sales analysis computer application. File details contain items sold, their original cost, and the gross profit realized on each transaction. Other data in the files may also be of interest, such as the dollar amount of cash sales or the dollar amount of collected freight charges. These additional factors affect profitability and are often included in a comprehensive analysis of actual sales. However, invoice detail alone is not sufficient in the preparation of a meaningful investigation of sales. Data describing customer buying habits should also enter into the analysis. It is possible to sell large quantities of merchandise to customers and yet not realize a profit. Consequently, accounts receivable records of customer payments serve as additional input in the determination of actual compared to potential gross profit, as shown by the customer invoice. The aged trial balance is especially useful in identifying with customers reduce gross profit below acceptable levels.

Other factors that affect profits resulting from sales are related to parts carried in inventory. The accounts payable files and the inventory files maintained by the computer can be utilized to isolate customer and product line sales patterns that are not profitable. For example, the frequency of returned orders from customers is an indicator of reduced profits. Frequently, a customer does not wait for a back order to be filled but instead buys merchandise elsewhere. When items on back order are received, they are returned with a request for credit. While the computer cannot effectively relate activities such as this to profits, some indication of returned items from back orders can be obtained.

The work-in-process computer files may also provide data of interest to sales analysis studies. For example, cost overruns seriously affect the profitability of a company, and their causes should be diagnosed. Similarly, scheduled jobs that fall behind in production not only are in danger of being cancelled by a customer, but also back up other scheduled jobs and often lead to high overtime expenses.

A final form of input to the sales analysis computer application consists of manual adjustments. Even though files from other computer applications should be in balance, it is necessary to make occasional adjustments. For instance, an adjustment must be made to the accounts receivable input when one has been made to an outstanding invoice. All adjustments should be entered into processing as separate file records. Each record must contain the fields of other records on file. It is also necessary to add or to subtract the adjusting value, based on a controlling code entered on the record.

18-2 THE SALES ANALYSIS SYSTEM

Figure 18-1 flowcharts the sales analysis computer application. The inputs to the system are:

- monthly invoice details
- file adjustments
- accounts receivable payment schedules
- accounts payable or parts inventory detail

Two year-to-date master files are also shown:

- The *customer-to-date analysis file* contains summary data showing the profitability of each customer to the firm.

- The *parts year-to-date analysis file* stores summary data showing the profitability of each product or of each product line carried in inventory.

Before these two files are created, however, three files are created in conjunction with the analysis of sales performance:

- The abbreviated *customer summary file* stores, by customer, total dollar sales and gross profits resulting from sales.

- The *sales force summary file* holds summary data showing the total sales, returns, and net profit of each member of the sales force.

- The *parts summary file* stores the quantity sold by part number, the selling price of the part, the initial cost of the part, and other expenses such as overhead charges.

A wide variety of reports can be prepared as a result of sales analysis processing. The three following reports provide different types of data analysis to illustrate specific company activities:

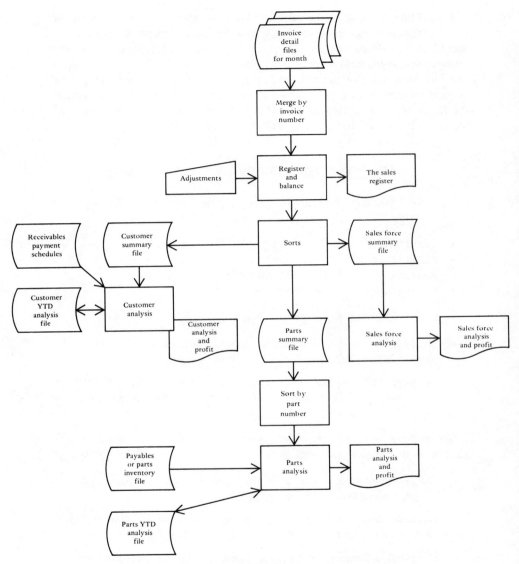

FIG. 18-1   Sales analysis systems flowchart

- The *sales force analysis and profit report* breaks down total sales by salesperson.

- The *customer sales and profit report* shows total sales and profits by customer account number.

- The *part analysis and profit report* illustrates the quantity sold and profits by inventory part number.

Separate computer programs are required to prepare each of the above reports. Besides these processing programs, a large merge routine and several sort programs are required to place data into files in proper sequence. The merge routine places all invoice details into one large file, sequenced in the same order as the invoice print computer program—document number, within document code, within customer number, within salesperson number. This sequence permits the grouping of all customers assigned to each member of the sales force. Within each customer grouping, all invoices for a given customer are filed, followed by the customer's credit memos. This same sequence is used for the next customer and so on, until all customers within a salesperson's account are filed.

Some programs are required to split the large invoice detail file into the customer summary file, the parts summary file, and the sales force summary file. These programs are advised to reduce the overall computer processing time in the three analysis programs that follow. Without them, the large file of invoice details would require several lengthy sort operations of several hours each to provide the required data for each analysis.

The Analysis of the Sales Force

Figure 18-2 illustrates a *consolidated sales force analysis and profit report*. It provides a summary of total sales generated by each member of the sales force. Current total sales, returns, net sales, and net profits are printed together with year-to-date summary totals. This report is printed after the merge of all monthly invoice details and the input of adjustment records. In order to verify the accuracy of the analysis and permit further use of the

CONSOLIDATED DISTRIBUTORS, INC.
SALES BY SALESPERSON

DATE   JULY 31

SALES-PERSON NO.	SALESPERSON	THIS MONTH				YEAR-TO-DATE			
		SALES	RETURNS	NET SALES	NET PROFIT	SALES	RETURNS	NET SALES	NET PROFIT
93	ADAMS G K	1621.43	10.07	1611.36	128.90	9823.40	63.60	9759.80	731.98
127	BELLOWS J I	5002.37	52.95	4949.42	445.45	27425.60	296.52	27128.78	2983.94
282	CAYCE F A	2537.92	43.02	2494.90	299.39	13296.00	43.02	13252.98	1391.56
362	DEAN P E	2941.45	127.35	2814.10	267.35	15137.20	629.40	14507.80	1291.19
367	DENNEY F T	3795.01	268.19	3526.82	458.48	22277.36	1403.90	20873.46	2296.08

FIG. 18-2   Sales force analysis and profit report

invoice file, all summary totals must balance external accounting controls before processing is continued.

When invoice details are not sequenced by a salesperson account number, it is usually not practical to print sales force summary totals immediately. It is best to merge the invoice details, make necessary adjustments, and balance the files. Control totals are printed on a *sales register* (see Fig. 18-3), which lists all sales by invoice number. After the balancing of the file, sales force summary detail will then either be appended to the customer analysis program or, as shown, be placed in a separate file.

Customer Analysis and Reporting

The processing of the customer file follows immediately, unless the original file of merged invoice details can be used directly in preparing the customer sales and profit report. Whether to use the larger invoice file or to produce first a smaller summary file must be decided on the basis of the number of storage devices available and the efficiency of computer processing. Creating an extra summary file shortens the time required to process the customer analysis program but it also lengthens the time to produce the sales force analysis and profit report. To resolve this dilemma, the following decision rule is often practiced: if the customer file requires additional sorting before it is used, customer analysis should take place after the initial sort of the larger invoice detail file; otherwise, customer analysis should take place following the summary of the merged invoice file. Following this rule will shorten overall computer sort time and more than offset any increases in the

					SALES REGISTER							
INVOICE NUMBER	ACCOUNT NUMBER	ACCOUNT NAME	TRANS TYPE	DATING MO DAY	REFERENCE NUMBER	INVOICE DT MO DAY YR	MDSE TERMS	ACCOUNTS RECEIVABLE	PARCEL POST	MERCHANDISE AMOUNT	SL #
16783	11885	FINES FASHIONS INC	INV		3051	4 18 --	2	86 40		86 40	16
16784	12093	FINNEGANS INC	INV		3025	4 18 --	2	403 10		404 10	41
16785	12128	FISHER BROS INC	INV		3046	4 18 --	2	345 05		345 05	43
16786	12206	FLOR DELIOS INC	INV		3017 · 4	18 --	2	700 60		700 60	16
16787	12720	FORDHAM FABRICS CO	INV		3022	4 18 --	2	1 253 40		1 253 40	18
16788	12803	FRANKELS & SMITH	INV		3029	4 18 --	N	48 52	3 02	45 50	17
16789	12815	FREEMANS & FOSTER	INV		3049	4 18 --	2	107 05		107 05	23
16790	12900	GADSONS INC	INV		3012	4 18 --	2	345 10		345 10	41
16791	13260	GIBNEY & SONS	INV		3066	4 18 --	2	165 35		165 35	22
16792	13265	GLOBAL DISTR INC	INV		3028	4 18 --	2	316 05		316 05	16
16793	12390	HAYES DROBNEY INC	INV		3011	4 18 --	N	43 60	2 95	40 65	43
16794	14619	HIGH BRIDGE	INV		3053	4 18 --	2	1 129 02		1 129 02	13

FIG. 18-3 Sales register

processing time of the sales force analysis and profit report. However, this trade-off in operating procedures will have to be evaluated during the design phase of this computer application.

Figure 18-4 illustrates the *customer analysis and profit report*. The summary information printed for each customer includes monthly sales in dollars, gross profit resulting from sales, and perhaps other factors such as quantity discounts. These summary data—one record per customer—and the customer's name should be enough information to extract from the invoice details. The same data can be accumulated in a customer year-to-date file to permit comparisons with previous monthly activity. This year-to-date file is updated by the customer analysis program or is replaced by an updated year-to-date file. (The data in Figure 18-4 are not factual and are intended only to illustrate possible processing results.)

As mentioned earlier, it may be desirable to use other computer files as additional references in the analysis of customer buying habits. The accounts receivable file is one such possible input file. The information obtained from the receivables file consists of an evaluation of the payment patterns followed by customers. Questions such as whether a customer pays outstanding bills in time to justify expected profit margins can be investigated. The method of analysis requires the assignment of a payment rating to customer balances in the accounts receivable file. If a customer pays all bills promptly, keeping delinquent invoices to a minimum, this information can be used to assign the customer a high payment rating. However, if a customer is consistently delinquent and builds up a large past-due receivables balance, it may be necessary to reduce a payment rating. A low rating often leads to placing the customer on a cash-only basis.

The delay between the time merchandise is shipped and the time payment is made by customers can be expensive, especially for a highly leveraged firm. Moreover, the longer receivables are outstanding, the more apt they are to be forfeited, increasing the company's dependence on other sources of income and its need to establish open lines of credit. These factors account for the use of accounts receivable data as an additional reference in the study of customer sales patterns.

Parts Analysis and Reporting

Because of the potential value of customer analysis reporting, it is generally scheduled as soon as possible after month-end closing. Processing then proceeds to the last type of sales analysis reporting—the profitability of inventory. This study requires the parts summary file, as sorted by the initial file balance computer program. It represents a collection of records for every sale of every part. Because the file is large and is not sequenced by part number, another sort program is required. This second sort may take several hours to complete.

CUSTOMER NUMBER AND NAME	NET SALES	RENTALS OWNED EQUIP.	RENTALS NON-OWNED,	SALES SHORING	RENTAL SHORING	TOTAL VOLUME	GROSS PROFIT $	SALES %	SALES GR. PR. %
00000 SAN FRANCISCO BRANCH									
07440	50					50	33	66.0	66.0
YEAR TO DATE	50					50	33	66.0	66.0
07800	35					35	16	44.8	44.8
YEAR TO DATE	35					35	16	44.8	44.8
08380	29-	16				13-	10-	33.5	46.9-
YEAR TO DATE	29-	58				29	10-	33.5	165.7
10170		9				9		0.0	100.0
YEAR TO DATE		34				34		0.0	100.0
14297	334					334	152	45.4	45.4
YEAR TO DATE	334					334	152	45.4	45.4
15001		7-				7-		0.0	100.0
YEAR TO DATE	14					14	5	34.2	34.2
16290	14					14	5	34.2	34.2
YEAR TO DATE								0.0	0.0
17250	18					18	7	39.4	39.4
YEAR TO DATE								0.0	0.0
23330	90					90	54	60.0	60.0
YEAR TO DATE								0.0	0.0
23970	1	15				17	13	36.7	95.4
YEAR TO DATE	39	9				48	63	33.5	45.8
24330	309	30-				279		20.4	12.0
YEAR TO DATE								0.0	0.0
26300		1				1		0.0	100.0
YEAR TO DATE								0.0	0.0
27758	103					103	47	46.1	46.1
YEAR TO DATE	155					155	47	30.0	30.0
29690	324					324	104	32.0	32.0
YEAR TO DATE		10				10		0.0	100.0
32003		19				19		0.0	100.0
YEAR TO DATE								0.0	0.0
32005	1,141	400				1,141	392	34.3	34.3
YEAR TO DATE	1,141-	1,492				741-	392-	34.3	1.2-
32340	155	45-				110	35		102.3
YEAR TO DATE	155	23-				133	70	44.8	22.3
							70	44.8	35.5

FIG. 18-4 Customer analysis and profit report

The *parts analysis and profit report* (Fig. 18-5) is printed after the sequencing of the parts summary file. A year-to-date parts history file is entered as input in processing to permit current and year-to-date part summary totals to be printed. These two sets of summaries provide the basis for evaluation of part performance. The parts analysis report should take into account the cost of the goods compared to the final selling price. It is also advantageous to find out how long merchandise has been held in stock. The storage and handling costs of the part should be added to the landed cost (the initial cost of the item). Obviously, the longer a part is held in inventory, the less real profit is received from its sale, no matter what the gross profit figures are. Turnover rates can also be determined during processing, in a manner similar to that discussed in Chapter 11. These rates are used in adjusting gross profit totals in an attempt to better evaluate the profitability of every part in inventory.

The immediate result of parts analysis reporting is a better understanding of what items in stock contribute most to company sales and profits (which may not be related). With this information, the adjustment of product lines is simplified. Of course, decisions to alter the product line should also be based on the study of market demand, which we turn to next.

18-3 MARKET PENETRATION

Both sales and financial statement analyses attempt to reduce the uncertainty associated with top management decisions. However, they share the same limitation: neither type of investigation considers external conditions. To predict company performance, each relies, in most instances, on extensions of past company activities. These predictions, however, are valid only so long as past trends reflect similar trends in the immediate future. Unfortunately, the future does not always adhere to the evidence of the past. The recession in the 1970s, for example, was a sharp diversion from the previous pattern of continuous growth. Studies based on past performance gave no indication of a business downturn until too late. By and large, these studies did not consider external economic factors that directly and indirectly influence business activities.

To improve prediction, some firms are attempting to relate their present level of sales performance to future expectations by using external information that predicts economic conditions. This type of analysis is called *market penetration*. It compares the anticipated market share to the actual market share realized by a company. In one sense, market penetration is an extension of sales analysis. It incorporates external market prediction data that are compatible with the sales analysis data stored on file.

COUNT	ITEM NUMBER	UNIT COST	ANNUAL USAGE	YRLY DOLLAR INVESTMENT	TOTAL RETURN	NET RETURN	RUNNING TOT. N/RET	E.O.Q.	ORD/ YR	RUNNING TOT. ORD/	%PRO
1	WEC05168	8.950	4,680	41,886.00	60,699.60	18,813.60	41,886	646	7.2	7	44
2	WEC05108	13.443	780	10,485.54	15,724.80	5,239.26	52,371	345	2.3	9	49
3	WPC05260	13.721	780	10,702.38	14,976.00	4,273.62	63,073	340	2.3	11	39
4	WEC05143	6.660	1,560	10,389.60	12,979.20	2,589.60	73,462	432	3.6	15	24
5	WJC05626	8.230	780	6,419.40	8,985.60	2,566.20	79,881	374	2.1	17	39
6	WNC05177	3.820	1,560	5,959.20	8,330.40	2,371.20	85,840	588	2.7	20	39
7	WKC05619	6.642	780	5,180.76	7,511.40	2,330.64	91,020	324	2.4	22	44
8	WIC05864	.913	10,140	9,257.82	11,559.60	2,301.78	104,277	2,980	3.4	26	24
9	WEC05107	5.772	780	4,502.16	6,520.80	2,018.64	104,779	429	1.8	27	44
10	WJC05741	6.020	780	4,695.60	6,567.60	1,872.00	109,474	321	2.4	30	39
11	WDC05479	1.177	3,120	3,672.24	5,491.20	1,818.96	113,146	1,571	2.0	32	49

FIG. 18-5 Parts analysis and profit report

One external data source is the Dodge Construction Report (see Fig. 18-6). This report is published regularly for nearly every major sector of the country. The information in the report covers a wide range of economic estimates, such as when and in what dollar amounts funds are to be released for construction activity over the coming months. These estimates are based upon completed contracts, approved and funded government projects, and other sources of construction activity data.

Because the data in the Dodge report can be divided into many categories, it has a wide range of uses in measuring the future growth potential of a company. Suppose a company markets construction materials such as nails and reinforcing bars. A study of the Dodge report may help correlate sales activity of the firm's product lines to the available potential. Another use of the report is to forecast market conditions in the immediate future. The normal inventory forecasting system predicts increased sales for the next month, if sales have increased in the recent past. However, the Dodge report figures may not tie to predictions based on inventory processing. If the inventory forecasts predict increased sales, while the Dodge report forecasts a reduction in sales, this fact should be used to reduce the optimism associated with inventory forecasting. Inventory should be replenished at a more modest level, thereby smoothing the effects of a sudden business downturn.

There are several sources of external market indicators besides the Dodge report. Valuable data might include cost of living indices prepared by the federal government. Data are often supplied by trade associations or chambers of commerce doing business in an area. The sales force may also be valuable in obtaining future sales requirements. The problem, especially with the last two sources, is that the data they collect may be either too optimistic or too pessimistic. In an apparent growth market, for instance, all members of a trade association may predict higher sales and a larger market than can be attained. A far safer source of data is one that is not based on collective opinion or on internal estimates, but on external measures that are kept independent of possible bias.

The correlation of external data to internal company file records is not a simple task, even if a quality source of external data is available. External data are often in different formats from existing internal file coding sequences, or require extensive input preparation time. However, the producers of the Dodge Construction Report provide input in machine-readable form, thereby reducing data entry time. Besides format and data preparation problems, though, the time base of external data may pose processing difficulties. For example, there may be a lag between the letting of contracts summarized in the Dodge report and their effects on a business. A company that specializes in the sale of office furniture may discover a lag of several months between the funding of a contract and the actual purchase of furniture. Thus, even if a quality source has been found, the use of external data must be compatible with and comparable to existing company records.

ST CTY	USE NAA	O W N	DODGE REPORT NUMBER OFC NUMBER	STY	NUMBER OF PROJECTS/ BUILDINGS	NUMBER OF UNITS DWELLING	FLOOR AREA SQ.FT. (000)	VALUE $ (000)	VALUE % OF REPORT TOTAL	QRT	MO/Y	I/P TYPE
54 30	48 AL	CO	WES 348101		1			32	.0006	1	7	1
54 30	43 AD	MU	WES 331273	1	1		22.0	545	.0098	1	7	1
54 30	42 AL	MU	WES 358072		1		.0	29	.0005	1	7	1
54 30	42 NW	MU	WES 029736	1	1		102.9	2,499	.0450	1	7	1
54 30	41 AD	MU	WES 183371	1	1		11.2	255	.0046	1	7	1
54 15	43 NW	MU	WES 335642		1		4.3	94	.0017	1	7	1
PROJECT GROUP......... 23 TOTAL				12	17		349.5	8,344	.1502			
54 30	140 NW	PR	WES 351347	1	1		12.0	173	.0031	1	7	1
54 37	142 AL	MU	WES 354456		1		.0	171	.0031	1	7	1
54 37	141 NW	MU	WES 128302	2	1		46.0	1,629	.0293	1	7	1
54 37	140 NW	FD	WES 306924	6	1		150.0	6,098	.1098	1	7	1
54 36	140 AD	CO	WES 353868		1		2.7	78	.0014	1	7	1
PROJECT GROUP......... 26 TOTAL				9	5		210.7	8,149	.1467			
SALES TERRITORY........ 904 TOTAL				623	5,137	10,737	16,477.4	295,817	5.3254			
54 19	93 AL	CO	WES 358464	1	1		.0	40	.0007	1	7	1
54 19	93 AL	PR	WES 358122	1	1		.0	18	.0003	1	7	1
54 19	93 AL	FD	WES 354629	1	1		.0	11	.0002	1	7	1
54 19	93 AL	FD	WES 354628	1	1		.0	13	.0002	1	7	1
54 19	93 AL	FD	WES 352151	1	1		.0	60	.0011	1	7	1
54 19	93 AL	FD	WES 351996	1	1		.0	19	.0003	1	7	1
54 19	93 AL	FD	WES 350430	1	1		.0	226	.0041	1	7	1
54 19	93 AL	PR	WES 350416	1	1			15	.0003	1	7	1
54 19	93 AD	PR	WES 357409	1	1		.4	10	.0002	1	7	1
54 19	93 AD	FD	WES 354800	1	1		45.0	750	.0135	1	7	1
54 19	93 AD	PR	WES 354243	1	1		.7	17	.0003	1	7	1
54 19	93 AD	PR	WES 344158	5	1		100.0	5,400	.0972	1	7	1
54 19	93 AD	PR	WES 315999	1	1		29.3	1,750	.0315	1	7	1
54 19	93 AD	PR	WES 028769	10	1		347.8	14,000	.2520	1	7	1
54 19	93 NW	PR	WES 318871	1	1		20.0	380	.0068	1	7	1
54 19	93 NW	PR	WES 318501	1	1		80.4	2,144	.0386	1	7	1
54 19	93 NW	PR	WES 031803	5	1		130.0	5,140	.0925	1	7	1
PROJECT GROUP......... 04 TOTAL				26	17		753.6	29,993	.5399			
54 19	94 AL	MU	WES 337344	1	1		.0	38	.0007	1	7	1
54 19	94 NW	FD	WES 347887	1	1		6.0	129	.0023	1	7	1

FIG. 18-6 Dodge Construction Report

18-4 THE MARKET PENETRATION COMPUTER APPLICATION

Figure 18-7 flowcharts the processing stages required in correlating external market data to existing internal computer file records. The external data are presented in report form and must be keyed to a record format suitable for

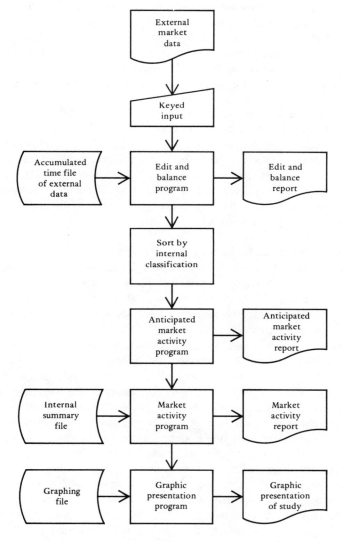

FIG. 18-7 Market penetration systems flowchart

computer input. (In the case of Dodge report data, this step would be eliminated.)

The initial processing step, which is characteristic of most applications, is the edit of the input data. Data are then posted to a composite file that stores data from previous months. It is necessary to acquire external data over several months, if the predictive computer programs are to have measurable value. It is also necessary to group data in a time-dependent series. Current data are placed on one record, followed by historical records in a descending sequence for each external indicator being filed. Since a lag is highly likely between external predictions and their correlation to company activities, this sequencing procedure permits a number of tests to be conducted to best fit estimated market conditions to actual product sales.

A sort program generally follows the edit program to sequence external data in the same order as the order within internal company files. This processing may not be easy. A major obstacle is that external measurements rarely tie to company records by product line. For example, company records classify inventory by product lines such as nails, bolts, and power tools. External measurements may be grouped in such categories as private dwellings, public buildings, and new housing. The problem is to relate planned increases in a category such as new housing to the increase in sales of an internal category such as six- and twelve-penny nails. This problem can be partly resolved by assigning sort keys to help relate external to internal product line classifications.

The *anticipated market activity report* can be printed after the sort program has been completed. In its simplest form, this report is similar to inventory forecasting reports. Data from previous months can be smoothed or averaged to predict company activity several months in advance. However, they share the same defect as inventory forecasts—they are based on historical evidence, which can be misleading.

The *market activity report* (see Fig. 18-8) represents a more practical use of external market data. It is prepared by comparing the accumulated time file of external data with an existing internal summary file, such as the sales analysis file. External and internal market patterns are then compared to measure actual sales performance against external market predictions.

The comparisons on the market activity report can be devastating or enlightening, depending upon one's point of view. On the one hand, total sales look exceedingly good in a growing market. On the other hand, when sales performance is measured against the potential of the existing market, sales records may not be as impressive. Conversely, sales that fall below expectations may be isolated and tied to a business downturn in a market territory. While market penetration studies and reports are not apt to uncover new methods of marketing products, they do provide management with an additional tool to use in evaluating and in predicting sales performance.

Report No.: 135

**Dodge Product Potentials
Executive Summary**

Report Date: 4/28/   Page: 4

Client: ABC BUILDING MATERIALS COMPANY   Quarter Covered: 1/

Product: EXFOLIATED VERMICULITE   This Report Covers (X) Elapsed Period
                                                                      ( ) A Forecast
                                                         Product Potential in Units of M DOLLARS

Dodge Number	Marketing Area	Projects Causing Demand			Product Potential	Product Sales	Penet. Ratio
		M Dollars	M Sq. Ft.	#DU			
020501	BIRMINGHAM	65,317	4,017	1,015	105	31	29.5
020502	MOBILE	69,029	2,857	1,378	95	34	35.8
020503	CHATTANOOGA	76,009	5,115	918	123	28	22.8
020504	JACKSON	41,318	3,079	375	74	20	27.0
020505	NEW ORLEANS	123,507	10,917	2,134	185	42	22.7
020506	SHREVEPORT	31,019	2,053	318	58	18	31.0
020599	*GULF DISTRICT	206,199	28,038	6,318	640	173	27.0

FIG. 18-8 Market activity report

Columnar formats can sometimes be avoided in the reporting of market conditions. While it is convenient to display all enumerated data, the true meaning of market trends may be obscured. Consequently, a final processing step in the market penetration application is the conversion of data to a format suitable for graphing (see Fig. 18-9). Most computer printers can be programmed to produce reasonably good graphs. Computer graphics terminals also can be used to prepare nonlinear graphs. In any case, the drawings should summarize market predictions and compare them to actual sales. This visual means of presenting market penetration findings greatly assists top management in comprehending overall sales and market activity.

18-5 MANAGEMENT IMPLICATIONS

By preparing product/market forecasts and sales and market analysis reports, a computer system can begin to realize its potential: to provide management reports that would be very difficult to obtain manually. Manage-

SIZE2   FPLOT   CURVE2

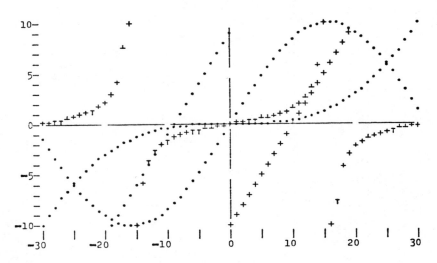

FIG. 18-9   Computer-printed graph

ment can benefit from these reports in several ways. Analyses of the sales force, of customers, and of parts carried in inventory permit managers to study existing business policies and practices. Customers, parts, or sales persons who may have appeared to contribute most to a company's profit are often shown to have less value. For example, a firm may find that high-volume customer accounts are not as profitable as lower volume accounts, that certain popular parts carried in inventory contribute little to company profits, or that high-volume salespersons add little to profits because they sell products with low gross margins.

Market penetration investigation is also revealing. Periods of supposedly excellent sales might be judged differently when total market sales are reported. Similarly, low sales might be outstanding when compared to existing market potential. Managerial benefits such as these bear directly on ways in which data processing activities can be justified.

More data processing staff time should be spent in the design of integrative systems such as the sales analysis and market penetration applications. These particular applications can be developed after the installation of two lower level applications—the invoice and the accounts receivable applications. Their development makes it possible to justify the extended use of the computer system.

REVIEW OF IMPORTANT IDEAS

Sales analysis reports are commonly broken down by salesperson, customer, and product line. In most cases, the reports summarize the detail used in preparing current customer invoices, combined with year-to-date summary totals. A better sales analysis can be produced by comparing dollar sales totals to the cost of sales and the cost of receiving customer payments. Such comparisons provide a more accurate measure of the profitability of salespersons, of customers, and of products. It can be determined, for example, that a customer who does considerable business with a company may not contribute much to overall company profits, because of low gross margins and poor payment habits. The parts carried in inventory that are in greatest demand may also be found to return inadequate profits to a company.

Although sales analysis reports are a good measure of company performance, they often do not correlate with external factors that affect company sales. To better evaluate these factors and their relationships to company and employee performance, it is necessary to conduct market penetration investigations. These investigations correlate internal company performance and external economic indicators, and are used to predict the sales and profits a company can expect. They also aid in measuring the performance of the sales force, of customers, or of product lines in achieving these expectations.

REVIEW QUESTIONS

1. How do the input data requirements of the market penetration computer application differ from those of the sales analysis computer application?

2. Sales analysis is conducted to serve at least three functions. What are they?

3. What file detail from other computer applications is required in the sales analysis computer application? How is it used in processing?

4. Why is invoice detail split into smaller files in the sales analysis computer application?

5. What purpose is served by the printing of the sales register?

6. What are the main differences between analyses of the sales force, customers, and parts carried in inventory?

7. For what reasons are computer-based market penetration studies conducted in conjunction with sales analyses?

8. What major systems design problems are encountered in the development of a market penetration computer application?

EXERCISES

1. Use Figure 18-1 as a guide to describe the typical file contents of the following files: customer summary, parts summary, updated year-to-date customer analysis, and updated year-to-date parts analysis.

2. One major advantage of buying a franchised business is that prior to purchase, a market investigation is made to determine the projected profitability of the business in its proposed location. The investigation projects the costs of operating the business (for example, building lease costs, wages, utilities) and usually also includes such factors as traffic volumes, general wealth of the area, customer buying habits, and the performance of similar businesses in the area.

    Design a computer application that would permit the printing of the market investigation report. Explain how appropriate data would be acquired in support of the design.

3. Suppose your firm manufactures carpeting used in commercial buildings. Having access to the Dodge Construction Reports (which summarize dollar volumes of construction contracts by geographical areas), you are asked to use these data to measure market performance and to improve control over inventory of carpeting materials. Design both a sales analysis reporting system and an inventory analysis reporting system. What problems must be resolved before either system will function correctly?

SUPPLEMENTARY READINGS

PART ONE

Awad, Elias M. *Introduction to Computers in Business*. Englewood Cliffs, N.J.: Prentice-Hall, 1977.

An introduction to data processing, computers, and information systems.

Bohl, Marilyn. *Information Processing*. Chicago: Science Research Associates, 1976.

A concise introduction to data processing and to hardware and software systems.

Bohl, Marilyn. *Flowcharting Techniques*. Chicago: Science Research Associates, 1971.

Emphasizes problem solving and exercises.

Boutell, Wayne, S. *Computer-Oriented Business Systems*. Englewood Cliffs, N.J.: Prentice-Hall, 1973.

A revision of a text that emphasizes techniques for the novice.

Brabb, George. *Computers and Information Systems in Business*. Boston: Houghton Mifflin, 1976.

Part II emphasizes the analysis and design of information systems.

Chapin, Ned. *Flowcharts*. Chicago: Auerback Publishers, 1971.

A good reference on flowcharting but with few exercises.

Clark, Frank, J.; Gale, Ronald; and Gray, Robert. *Business Systems and Data Processing Procedures*. Englewood Cliffs, N.J.: Prentice-Hall, 1972.

An elementary but comprehensive survey of the analysis and design techniques used by a systems analyst.

Davis, Gordon B. *Management Information Systems: Conceptual Foundations, Structure, and Development*. New York: McGraw-Hill, 1974.

Section two deals with the structure of a management information system.

Johnson, Richard A.; Kast, Fremont E.; and Rosenzweig, James E. *Theory and Management of Systems*. New York: McGraw-Hill, 1973 (Chapter 15).

Kindred, Alton R. *Data Systems and Management*. Englewood Cliffs, N.J.: Prentice-Hall, 1973.

An elementary introduction and survey.

Kroenke, David. *Database Processing: Fundamentals, Modeling, and Applications*. Chicago: Science Research Associates, 1977.

Contains an excellent discussion of input/output processing and file organization.

Mader, Chris, and Hagin, Robert. *Information Systems: Technology, Economics, and Application*. Chicago: Science Research Associates, 1974.

An introduction to data processing for the business student.

Murach, Mike. *Business Data Processing*. Chicago: Science Research Associates, 1977.

A comprehensive introduction to business data processing.

Moore, D. W. "Management's Problems in the 1970's—Systems Analysts." *Design and Management of Information Systems*. Compiled by David H. Li. Chicago: Science Research Associates, 1972 (pp. 288–97).

Orilia, Lawrence S.; Stern, Nancy; and Stern, Robert A. *Business Data Processing Systems*. New York: Wiley, 1972.

Includes four elementary case studies on accounts receivable, inventory, payroll, and personnel.

Sanders, Donald H. *Computers in Business*. New York: McGraw-Hill, 1972.

A very readable introduction to business data processing.

Shelly, Gary B., and Cashman, Thomas J. *Business Systems Analysis and Design*. Fullerton, Calif.: Anaheim Publishing Company, 1975.

An introduction to systems analysis with numerous case studies; emphasis on applications.

Semprevivo, Philip C. *Systems Analysis: Definition, Process, and Design*. Chicago: Science Research Associates, 1976.

A very readable introduction to systems analysis.

Vazsonyi, Andrew. *Introduction to Electronic Data Processing*. Homewood, Ill.: Irwin, 1977.

Appendix 2 contains a supplement on data processing applications and flowcharting.

PART TWO

Accounts Payable Processing (UNIVAC Publication UX-5312).

Accounts Receivable Processing (UNIVAC Publication UP-7711).

Boutell, Wayne S. *Computer-Oriented Business Systems*. Englewood Cliffs, N.J.: Prentice-Hall, 1973 (pp. 354–84).

Kanter, Jerome. *Management-Oriented Management Information Systems*. Englewood Cliffs, N.J.: Prentice-Hall, 1972 (case studies on pp. 110–34).

O'Brien, James A. *Computers in Business Management*. Homewood, Ill.: Irwin, 1975.

Chapters 10 and 11 discuss computer applications in business.

Orilia, Lawrence; Stern, Nancy; and Stern, Robert A. *Business Data Processing Systems*. New York: Wiley, 1972 (case studies on pp. 197–222, 244–91).

Thierauf, Robert J. *Systems Analysis and Design of Real-Time Management Information Systems*. Englewood Cliffs, N.J.: Prentice-Hall, 1975.

Examines management information systems as required by the main functional areas of a business.

Watson, Hugh J., and Carroll, Archie, B. *Computers for Business: A Managerial Emphasis*. Dallas: Business Publications, 1976.

Chapters 2 and 8 review applications in accounting and finance.

PART THREE

Basic Principles of Wholesale IMPACT—Inventory Management Program and Control Techniques (IBM Publication E20-8105-1).

Boutell, Wayne S. *Computer-Oriented Business Systems*. Englewood Cliffs, N.J.: Prentice-Hall, 1973 (pp. 404–10).

Carlson, John G. H. "Item Identification and Classification in Management Operating Systems." *Production and Inventory Management* 12, no. 2 (1971): 23–32.

Case Study in Business Systems Design. Chicago: Science Research Associates, 1970.

A very detailed case study; a comprehensive instructor's guide available.

Dawson, Peter P., and Gallegos, Frederick. *Case Study II: Medco, Inc.* Chicago: Science Research Associates, 1973.

Similar in format to 1970 *Case Study* but more polished.

Hoffmann, Thomas R. *Production: Management and Manufacturing Systems*. Belmont, Calif.: Wadsworth, 1971 (pp. 305–66).

Moore, Franklin G. *Manufacturing Management*. Homewood, Ill.: Irwin, 1965 (pp. 710–41).

Orilia, Lawrence; Stern, Nancy; and Stern, Robert A. *Business Data Processing Systems*. New York: Wiley, 1972 (case studies on pp. 223–43).

Reiter, Stanley. "A System for Managing Job-Shop Production." *Journal of Business* 39 (1966): 371–93.

Voich, Dan, Jr.; Mottice, Homer J.; and Shrode, William A. *Information Systems for Operations and Management*. Cincinnati: Southwestern Publishing, 1975.

Includes materials on information for operational and managerial/ financial control.

PART FOUR

Davidson, Sidney, and Drake, David F. "Capital Budgeting and the Best Tax Depreciation Method." *Journal of Business* 34 (1961).

General Ledger Processing (UNIVAC Publication UP-7702).

Mockler, Robert J. *Information Systems for Management*. Columbus, Ohio: Charles E. Merrill, 1974.

Contains numerous case study exercises.

Optner, Stanford L. *Systems Analysis for Business Management*. Englewood Cliffs, N.J.: Prentice-Hall, 1975.

Contains numerous case study exercises.

Prince, Thomas R. *Information Systems for Management Planning and Control*. Homewood, Ill.: Irwin, 1970 (case studies on pp. 111–56).

Senn, James A. *Information Systems in Management*. Belmont, Calif.: Wadsworth, 1978.

Contains several good case studies which are placed in a case study module.

Stanton, William J., and Buskirk, Richard H. *Management of the Sales Force*. Homewood, Ill.: Irwin, 1965 (pp. 643–702).

INDEX

account inquiry. *See* accounts
    receivable system and application.
account numbers, 37. *See also* chart of
    accounts; customer number.
  customer, 234, 319
  ledger, 86, 94, 286, 294–96, 308
accounts payable system and
    application, 77-81
  batch control, 77, 81
  edit program, 81–82
  general ledger report, 86, 284
  input to, 76–77
  management implications, 88–89
  merge program, 83–84
  register program, 84–85
  vendor file update program, 82–84
  voucher-checks, 79, 80, 85, 86
    (fig.), 88
accounts payable detail slip, 77, 78
  (fig.), 87
accounts payable extract slip, 187, 188
  (fig.)
accounts payable register listing, 85
  (fig.)
accounts receivable file, 129, 130, 132
  (fig.)

accounts receivable statement, 136,
  137 (fig.)
accounts receivable summary file, 113,
  114 (fig.), 120
accounts receivable system and
    application, 129–32
  aged trial balance (aging schedule),
    28, 127, 138–40, 284
  batch control, 134, 136
  deleted invoice program, 134–36
  input to, 129–30, 140–41
  inquiry program, 132–35
  management implications, 141–42
  remittance stub, 138
  restart, 136
  statement program, 136–38
accounts, types of, 127–29
accumulated pending invoice file, 79,
  80 (fig.), 81
action-document program, 23
adjusted stock status report, 192
adjustments
  in accounts receivable, 130, 135
  in cash receipts, 150
  in general ledger, 282, 289
  in inventory, 189

adjustments *(continued)*
  in order filling, 162, 164, 165, 173
  in work-in-process, 233, 236, 240
aged trial balance. *See* accounts
    receivable system and application.
aggregate demand forecast, 230–31
algorithm, 179
alignment, in printing checks, 95–96
anticipated market activity report. *See*
    market penetration system and
    application.
assemblers, 10
audit trail,
  definition of, 26
  in accounts receivable, 135
  in check processing, 102
  in invoicing, 120
  in order filling, 171
  in receiving, 222
automatic cash application, 129,
    152–54

back order. *See the following systems
    and applications:* order filling;
    receiving.
back order file, 165, 173, 177
balance-due records, 134
balance-forward accounts, 127, 128,
    146
balance-only accounts, 127, 128, 146
balance report (check reconciliation),
    98, 284
balance sheet. *See* financial statements
    system and application.
batch control, 22, 26, 29. *See also the
    following systems and
    applications:* accounts payable;
    accounts receivable; cash receipts;
    check reconciliation; inventory
    control; invoicing; order filling;
    payroll; receiving;
    work-in-process.
batch number
  in accounts payable, 81, 87
  in cash receipts, 150
  in general ledger, 282
  in invoicing, 113, 115

billing statement
  as action document, 23
  in accounts payable, 76
  in accounts receivable, 132, 138
  in invoicing, 108
bill of lading
  in accounts payable, 76
  in invoicing, 109, 110 (fig.)
bill of lading number, in invoicing, 109
bill of materials file, 233, 234, 239,
    244, 245. *See also*
    work-in-process system and
    application.
bin location analysis, 169, 175,
    178–80
block diagram, 18, 26
blocking factor, definition of, 39
book value, 266, 285
breakdown of inventory parts, 231,
    233, 239
budget planning. *See* financial
    statements system and
    application.
business computer application, 4
business system, stages in, 18–20, 19
    (fig.)
buyer change, 192, 202
byte, 39

cancelled checks, 98, 102, 284
capital worth, 285
carrying cost, 197, 199, 201
cash discount. *See* discount.
cash flow, 88–89, 145, 147, 154–55
cash receipts file, 130, 150
cash receipts register, 151 (fig.)
cash receipts system and application,
    149–50
  batch control, 147, 150
  cash register program, 151
  edit program, 150
  input to, 147–48
  management implications, 155
  posting program, 150
  register program, 151–52
  remittance stub, 146, 148 (fig.)
central processing unit, 8

change or addition record, 44
chart of accounts
in accounts payable, 86
in budget planning, 309
in general ledger, 282, 294,
295 (fig.), 296
in income reporting, 303
check reconciliation reports, 98–101,
99 (fig.)
check reconciliation system and
application, 98–101
batch control, 98–99
balance program, 98–99
check register, 95, 96 (fig.)
check requisition, 93, 94 (fig.)
checks. *See also the following systems
and applications:* accounts
payable, check reconciliation;
check writing; payroll.
design of, 95, 100–101
kiting of, 88, 155
manual processing of, 101–103
signing of, 95, 101
check writing system and application
check register program, 95–97
edit program, 93–95
management implications, 103
printer alignment, 95–97, 101
summary report, 97–98
voucher-check program, 95–97
voucher-checks, 95, 97 (fig.), 100–101
closed account, 147
code. *See* location code; record code;
termination code.
collection of bad debts, 127, 139, 142
comparative income statement, 304
(fig.). *See also* financial
statements system and
application.
compilers, 10
computer graphics, 329, 330 (fig.)
computer programs, common types of,
20–23. *See also individual system
and application.*
computer system, 8–9
consolidated general ledger file, 287,
289 (fig.), 302

consolidated general ledger report. *See*
general ledger system and
application.
consolidated profit plan file, 300, 302
count sheets, 204–205
credit limits, 88, 142
credit memo
in accounts receivable, 135
in cash receipts, 146
in invoicing, 109, 110, 119
in order filling, 164, 165, 176
current general ledger file, 302
current general ledger report. *See*
general ledger system and
application.
customer change report, 116, 117
(fig.). *See also* unknown and
customer change report.
customer changes, 171
customer master file
in accounts receivable, 130
in invoicing, 113
in order filling, 162, 163, 164, 165
in sales analysis, 320–21
customer name and address file
in cash receipts, 149
in check writing, 93
customer number
in accounts receivable, 130
in cash receipts, 148, 150
in invoicing, 113, 116, 117
in order filling, 169, 170, 175
in work-in-process, 234
customer orders, 163, 165
customer sales and profit report, 318,
320–21, 322 (fig.)
customers, evaluation of, 142. *See also*
sales analysis system and
application.
cutoff date (accounts payable), 79, 84
cutoff point (accounts receivable), 134
cycle call cards, 192

daily order detail file, 168 (fig.), 169,
174, 175, 177
data entry, 25
data entry terminal, 5, 6 (fig.)

data extraction, 42

data field arrangement, 42

deferred payments, 84

delinquent accounts, 139

delivery manifest. *See* packing slip.

demand forecast. *See* aggregate demand forecast.

deposit slip, 147

depreciation
methods of, 266
reporting of, 274–76

deseasonalized average demand, 196

detail ledgers, 287, 293, 294 (fig.)

discount, 75, 76

documentation. *See* systems documentation; program documentation.

Dodge Construction Report, 325–26 (fig.)

double-declining depreciation, 266

economic order quantity (E.O.Q.), 185, 197

edit by purchasing agents, 212

edit program, 20–21. *See also the following systems and applications:* accounts payable, cash receipts, check writing, invoicing, order filling, payroll, work-in-process.

embezzling, 147

employee change procedure, 54–58

employee change report, 55, 57 (fig.)

employee master file, 54–55, 62 (fig.)

employee number, 54

employee time card. *See* time record.

encumbering of funds, 217, 309

equipment costing file, 252

equipment utilization report, 255, 256 (fig.)

evaluation. *See* customers, evaluation of; parts, evaluation of; salesmen, evaluation of; vendors, evaluation of.

exception management, 244

explosion. *See* breakdown of inventory parts.

exponential smoothing, 194–95

factor buying, 199–201

feedback, 19

field, 41

files. *See also* master files; pending files; summary files; year-to-date files.
coding, 25
design of, 41–42
justification of, 38–40
layout and identification, 25
reliability of, 40–41
types of, 22, 23
updating of, 44–46
verification of, 40–44. *See also* batch control; physical inventory.

financial ratios, 306, 307 (fig.)

financial statements system and application
balance sheet, 299, 302, 304–306, 305 (fig.), 307 (fig.)
budget planning, 299, 302, 308 (fig.), 309–11
management implications, 311–12
profit and loss (statement of corporate income), 299, 300, 302–303 (fig.), 304 (fig.)
profit planning, 299, 302, 306–309 (fig.)

fixed assets, definition of, 265

fixed assets new purchase report, 267, 269–71, 270 (fig.), 272

fixed assets system and application
file update, 274
identification label, 267, 274 (fig.)
input to, 267
management implications, 276–77
reporting, 269–74

flowcharting (systems), 17, 26–31

forecasting. *See* inventory system and application; aggregate demand forecast.

general ledger, definition of, 281

general ledger system and application

adjustments, 282, 289
balance controls, 282
consolidated general ledger report,
    287, 291–93, 292 (fig.), 302
current general ledger report, 287,
    291–93 (fig.)
detail ledgers, 293
input to, 282–87
journal entries, 286, 287–89
management implications, 296–97
trial balance report, 287, 289,
    290 (fig.)
gross margin, 199, 201

header information, 113

idle time code, 250
identification labels. *See* fixed assets
    system and application.
imprest account, 93
income statement, 302–304 (fig.). *See
    also* financial statements system
    and application.
initial stock status computer program,
    193
initial stock status report, 192, 201
    (fig.), 203 (fig.) *See also* stock
    report.
input. *See the following systems and
    applications:* accounts payable;
    accounts receivable; general
    ledger; invoicing; order filling;
    receiving.
inquiry report, 133 (fig.)
inquiry request instructions (accounts
    receivable), 130, 133
integrative computer applications, 265,
    281, 330
interaccount transfers, 293
interoffice transfers, 271, 273–74
inventory-location model, 162
inventory master file
    in invoicing, 186–91
    in order filling, 174, 175
    in purchasing, 214, 218
    in receiving, 218
    in work-in-process, 233

inventory model, 198 (fig.)
inventory system and application. *See
    also* physical inventory.
    adjustments, 189
    batch control, 187, 188
    dangers in, 202–204
    factor buying, 199–201
    file update, 186–91
    forecasting, 193–97
    management implications, 205–206
    order frequency, 191, 197–99
    order quantity, 191, 197–99
    safety stock, 191, 197–99
inventory transaction register, 188, 189
    (fig.)
inventory update program, 189
invoice detail file, 113, 114 (fig.),
    168
invoice edit report, 115, 116 (fig.)
invoice number
    in accounts payable, 87
    in accounts receivable, 130, 133,
        137
    in cash receipts, 150
    in general ledger, 282
    in invoicing, 108
    in job costing, 257
invoices
    as action documents, 23
    as input to fixed assets, 267
    as input to payables, 76
    description of, 108 (fig.)
    manual processing of, 87–88
invoice summary file, 129
invoicing system and application
    batch control, 109, 120
    customer posting program, 116–17
    edit program, 113–16
    input to, 109–11
    management implications, 123–24
    pricing program, 117–19
    restart, 120
    separation of suspended invoices,
        119
    statements, 107–108, 119–20
    summary detail, 120
is/was report, 171

job activity report, 254, 255, 256 (fig.)
job costing system and application, 252–54
  job costing reports, 255–57
  management implications, 260
  time card in, 249–51
job ledger detail file, 252
job ledgers, 254, 256, 257 (fig.)
job number
  in labor distribution, 249, 251, 254
  in work-in-process, 234
journal entries. *See* general ledger system and application.
journal entry coding sheet, 286 (fig.)
journal entry report, 287
journal report (payroll), 66 (fig.), 282
Julian date, 39

keypunch machine, 5 (fig.)
kiting. *See* checks.

labor distribution report, 258, 259 (fig.)
labor distribution system and application, 258
landed cost, 323
lead time. *See* vendor lead time.
lead record, definition of, 59
line item records, 116, 117
location code
  in fixed assets, 267, 271, 274
  in invoicing, 117
lock box, 155

management, role of, in systems activity, 13–15. *See also individual systems and applications.*
manual processing. *See* checks; invoices.
manufacture-to-order, definition of, 229. *See also* work-in-process system and application.
manufacture-to-stock, definition of, 229. *See also* work-in-process system and application.
market activity report. *See* market

penetration system and application.
market penetration system and application, 323, 325–29
  anticipated market activity report, 328
  management implications, 329–30
  market activity report, 328–29 (fig.)
master file, 22, 54. *See also the following types of master files:* customer; employee; inventory; payroll; property; vendor.
master shop schedule, 238, 240, 241 (fig.)
master shop schedule file, 233. *See also* work-in-process system and application.
materials reference file, 252
materials usage report, 254, 255 (fig.)
merge program, 10. *See also* accounts payable system and application.
MICR encoding, 103
multiple-page statements (accounts receivable, 135
multiple-page vouchers, 101–102

new property file, 267
new property report, 267, 272, 273 (fig.)
number. *See also* account number; batch number; bill of lading number; customer number; invoice number; job number; part number; purchase order number; salesman number; vendor number.
  bin location, 175, 191
  check, 95, 100–101
  control, 95
  department, 258, 267
  document, 137, 319
  employee, 54–55, 254, 258
  fixed asset, 267
  item, 271
  product, 235, 236
  project, 253, 255
  stock, 214, 216, 217, 221
  subassembly, 234

open-item account, 127, 128–29, 146
operating procedures, 26
operating systems. *See* supervisor
    programs.
optical reader, 6, 7 (fig.)
order detail file, 173
order-filling edit report, 169, 170 (fig.)
order-filling system and application,
    161–62, 165–69
    back order, 164–65, 173
    back order program, 176–78
    batch control, 165, 171, 174
    customer posting program, 170–72
    edit program, 169–70
    input to, 163–65
    inventory posting program, 172–75
    management implications, 180–81
    packing slip program, 161, 162,
        164, 176
    picking label program, 161, 162,
        164, 175–76
    suspense program, 176–78
order form, 163 (fig.)
order frequency, 191, 197–99
order quantity, 191, 197–99
override
    to due date cutoff, 84
    to computer order quantities, 212,
        224

packing slip
    in accounts payable, 76
    in order filling, 161, 162, 164, 177
        (fig.)
    in receiving, 218, 220
part number
    in invoicing, 113, 114, 117, 118
    in inventory, 186, 187, 190, 193,
        200, 205
    in order filling, 169, 173, 175, 179
    in sales analysis, 319, 321
    in work-in-process, 234, 236
part requirements, 233, 239 (fig.)
parts analysis and profit report, 319,
        323, 324 (fig.)
payables edit report, 82 (fig.)
paycheck

as action document, 23, 28
    in payroll, 65, 66 (fig.)
payment cycle, 83
payment drop. *See* lock box.
payment on account, 129, 152
payroll change input form, 55, 56 (fig.)
payroll edit report, 61, 63 (fig.), 251
payroll journal, 66, 67 (fig.)
payroll master file
    contents of, 61, 62 (fig.)
    update of, 54–59
payroll register, 62–65
payroll system and application
    batch control, 59, 61, 64
    edit program, 61
    input to, 58–59
    journal program, 66
    management implications, 71–72
    payroll check program, 65
    register program, 62–65
pending check detail file, 97–98
pending invoice file, 78, 80, 284
pending purchase order detail file, 216
        (fig.), 218, 220
petty cash account, 93
physical inventory, 162, 204–205
picking label
    as action document, 23
    in order filling, 161, 162, 164, 175
        (fig.)
pilferage, 180, 277
point-of-sale, 187
posting, definition of, 63
predicting sales, 193, 315, 323. *See
    also the following systems and
    applications:* market penetration;
    sales analysis.
prenumbered forms (purchase order),
        217
preshipped order, 173
price concessions, 174, 212
price exception report
    in invoicing, 118 (fig.), 124
    in order filling, 174
pricing file, 113, 122
pricing program. *See* invoicing system
    and application.

procedures audit, 13
product cost distribution report, 236, 237 (fig.)
product costing file, 233, 234
production control procedures, 26
product requirement file, 233, 238
profitability of inventory, 321. *See also* sales analysis system and application.
profit and loss statements. *See* financial statements system and application.
profit planning statements. *See* financial statements system and application.
program documentation, 17, 26
programs. *See* computer programs.
property and value report, 267, 274, 275 (fig.)
property master file, 267, 269 (fig.), 274, 276
purchase order, 76, 216–17, 218
purchase order change report, 216
purchase order detail file, 214, 216 (fig.)
purchase order number
  in invoicing, 108
  in order filling, 169
  in purchasing, 214, 217
  in receiving, 218, 220
purchasing system and application
  general ledger program, 217–18
  input to, 214
  management implications, 224–25
  order change program, 216
  vendor purchase order program, 216

941-quarterly report, 67–68 (fig.)

receipts (receiving detail) file, 220, 222
receiving report, 221 (fig.)
receiving system and application
  batch control, 218,
  input to, 218
  management implications, 224–25
  receiving program, 220–22
  updated stock report, 222
record, in data hierarchy, 42. *See also*

balance-due records; change or addition records; transaction record.
record codes
  definition of, 37
  in accounts receivable, 130
  in cash receipts, 150
  in invoicing, 113
  in order filling, 169, 173
register program, 22. *See also the following systems and applications:* accounts payable; cash receipts; payroll; work-in-process.
remittance stub. *See the following systems and applications:* accounts receivable; cash receipts.
report layout, 25
reports, preparation of, 46–47
residual value. *See* book value.
restart capability, 47. *See also the following systems and applications:* accounts receivable; invoicing.
return on investment, 104, 185, 186, 199, 201, 276
revolving account, 93
running average, 193

safety stock, 191, 197–99
sales analysis system and application, 317–19
  customer analysis, 320–21
  input to, 317–19
  management implications, 329–30
  parts analysis, 321–23
  sales force analysis, 319–20
sales detail file, 168
sales force analysis and profit report, 319 (fig.)
sales forecast file, 233
salesperson number
  in invoicing, 113, 115
  in sales analysis, 317, 320
sales register, 320 (fig.)
salvage value, 267, 271
seasonal coefficient, 196, 197